"One of the most compassionate, comprehensive and supportive books I have read for parents... truly outstanding."

> —GERALDINE DAWSON, PH.D., chief science officer, Autism Speaks

"This is the doctor who believes in your child! With *Autism Solutions* in hand you will not have to worry about the questions you forgot to ask. **Dr. Ricki's door is always open and this book will be turned to again and again as she embraces you with her wisdom and knowledge.**"

> —SERENA WIEDER, PH.D., coauthor of *Engaging Autism;* founder and associate chair, The Interdisciplinary Council on Developmental and Learning Disorders (ICDL)

"If having your child diagnosed with autism is like being cast out to sea, *Autism Solutions* is like a giant life raft filled with survival supplies. **If you have a child with special needs, plant yourself in a chair and read this book before you do another thing.**"

> —ERIK LINTHORST, director of *Autistic-Like: Graham's Story*

"Dr. Robinson brings a new perspective to Autism Spectrum Disorders based on her years of experience as a pediatrician and autism advocate and her theoretical grounding in DIR/Floortime. She offers **kind, honest advice about how a child with autism experiences the world and what this means to families... a unique resource for families and professionals.**"

> —CATHERINE LORD, PH.D., A.B.P.P., director, University of Michigan Autism and Communication Disorders Center

"Dr. Robinson brings remarkable heart, energy and depth of experience to a resource that promises to save countless children. This book is filled with the refreshing voice of a doctor who seems to be sitting on the floor with your child on her lap and the most forward-thinking knowledge at her fingertips."

> —PATRICIA STACEY, author of *The Boy Who Loved Windows: Opening the Heart of a Child Threatened by Autism*

"Drawing upon years of experience as a pediatrician who specializes in treating children with autism, Dr. Ricki infuses her passion, knowledge, wisdom and optimism in ways that empower parents to make more informed decisions about their child's care. Especially helpful is her skill in conveying complex medical knowledge so that it is understandable and helpful to parents. **Whether a parent or grandparent of a newly-diagnosed child, or one entering adulthood,** *Autism Solutions* **is the guide for you.**"

> —SUZANNE AND BOB WRIGHT, grandparents of a child on the autism spectrum and co-founders of Autism Speaks

"Dr. Ricki Robinson is that rare combination of brilliant scientific medical mind, and tremendous compassion and sensitive heart. She is an angel of autism. *Autism Solutions* will become **the 'go to' reference for understanding and working with special children and their families.**"

> —ELAINE HALL, founder of The Miracle Project and author of *Now I See the Moon: A Mother, a Son, a Miracle*

"**Indispensible to families who have children with autism.** Dr. Ricki's words will help parents be equipped with the insights and information they need to pursue the best solutions to guide their child's progress."

> —DEBORAH FLASCHEN, M.B.A., cofounder and president, The Floortime Foundation, founder and president, 3LPlace, Inc.

"Dr. Robinson is the pediatrician every parent wishes they had. **A must-read for any parent of a child with autism as well as any clinician or educator working with children on the autism spectrum.**"

> —NANCY D. WISEMAN, founder and president of First Signs and author of *The First Year®: Autism Spectrum Disorders: An Essential Guide for the Newly Diagnosed Child*

"**If you buy just one book about autism, this should be it.** Dr. Robinson gives parents hope and practical advice. Nowhere else can such a comprehensive collection of useful, up-to-date information about autism be found between two book covers."

> —PORTIA IVERSEN, author of *Strange Son* and cofounder, the Cure Autism Now (CAN) Foundation

Autism Solutions

How to Create a Healthy and Meaningful Life for Your Child

Ricki G. Robinson, M.D., M.P.H.

Foreword by Stanley I. Greenspan, M.D.,
author of *Engaging Autism*

⟨H⟩ HARLEQUIN®

AUTISM SOLUTIONS
ISBN-13: 978-0-373-89209-9

Illustrations by Post Positive Design, Andrew Robinson (www.postpositive.com)
Interior Design by Monica Baziuk

The health advice presented in this book is intended only as an informative resource guide to help you make informed decisions; it is not meant to replace the advice of a physician or other health care professional. Always seek competent medical help for any health condition or if there is any question about the appropriateness of a procedure or health recommendation.

The names and identifying details of some people in this book have been changed.

Library of Congress Cataloging-in-Publication Data
Robinson, Ricki G.
 Autism solutions : how to create a healthy and meaningful life for your child / Ricki G. Robinson ; foreword by Stanley I. Greenspan.
  p. cm.
 Includes bibliographical references.
 ISBN 978-0-373-89209-9 (trade pbk.)
 1. Autism in children—Popular works. 2. Parents of autistic children—Popular works.
  I. Title.
RJ506.A9R62 2011
618.92′85882—dc22   2010044200

www.eHarlequin.com

Printed in U.S.A.

=

To my parents, Jordan and Betty,
who taught me to believe that all things are possible.

To the families and children who trusted me with their stories
and showed me that all things are possible.

To my beloved husband, Joel,
and amazing children, Brett and Chad,
without whose love, encouragement and inspiration
none of this would have been possible.

=

Contents

Acknowledgments

I LOVE WHAT I do—talking with children and families and helping them navigate the maze of ASD. I especially enjoy my volunteer work with the Interdisciplinary Council on Developmental and Learning Disorders (ICDL), Cure Autism Now (CAN) and Autism Speaks (AS), where my specialty is networking with researchers and talking to parent groups. I couldn't imagine actually writing a book—although many parents had encouraged me to do so! Then I received a call in early 2008 that I had been selected as a recipient of the Harlequin More Than Words award for my contributions to the autism community, especially through CAN and AS, having been nominated by a dear friend and author, Meryl Sawyer. This seminal event introduced me to the world of publishing, eventually resulting in this book. So the first person I thank and for whom I have deep respect (writing isn't easy!) is Meryl.

Once the decision was made, I quickly discovered how much effort goes into producing a book. Just as it takes teamwork to support a child with ASD, it took a team of dedicated professionals, devoted friends and families from my practice, as well as my supportive, loving family, to bring this book to fruition. I am blessed with the support of so many. My thanks and gratitude abound.

Though I am a novice author, Harlequin treated me as if I were a known, successful member of their publishing house. My editor, Deb Brody, not only convinced me that my words would translate to the page, but gently and expertly guided me through the process so that medical information could be accessible to parents and families. I can't imagine a more patient, understanding and wise professional to help me through this project.

Sheila Curry Oakes helped me hone the words and stories into a cohesive manuscript, providing structure, organization and invaluable feedback. Carole Swemline literally sat by my side while I dictated the majority of the book, always cheering me on to tell her one more story or capture another thought, keeping me supplied with ever-present diet drinks. Jenny Bent, my agent, led me through the intricacies of the publishing world, encouraging me all the way. Andrew Robinson put his amazing pen to paper to sketch the diagrams and figures from my crude images (www.postpositive.com). My thanks to all of you for your passion, generosity and expertise. No doubt without all your support and care this manuscript would not have taken flight.

Stanley I. Greenspan and Serena Wieder, my mentors and colleagues, graciously taught and encouraged me to expand my medical practice to care for children with ASD. Their support has been phenomenal and a cornerstone allowing me to help so many. Everyone should be afforded such guidance as they continue to give me. Combining the DIR approach with my medical knowledge taught me new ways to practice medicine and change children's lives. Their friendship and collaboration have been a powerful force in my life and underscore the theme of this book. I am eternally grateful.

A very long list of friends read the manuscript in various stages and gave me invaluable advice: Drs. Eli Chesen, Joshua Feder, Clara LaJonchere and Carole Samango-Sprouse and parents Elana Artson, Liz Bell, Megan Brown, Judith Farrar, Deborah Flaschen and Laura Shumaker lent their time and expertise as professionals and parents to help bring focus and clarity to the text. I appreciate their insight and help.

There are several groups of people whose love and support were essential— allowing me to write while continuing to care for children and families. The first are Drs. Leonard "Skip" Baker, Tom Hartman and Marilyn Lange; Nurse Karen Hall and staff Jennie Hanks; Bonnie Delaney; Lorena Bunting; and our practice administrator Carole Swemline of Descanso Medical Center for Development and Learning. Some of us have worked together for more than thirty years. All are the best that medicine has to offer—totally devoted to children and families and doing all they can to make their lives better. I can't imagine working with more dedicated and loving people.

We all need a cheering section. The support of my friends has been invaluable, not just for this project but throughout the years. Martha Unickel, Pamela Nolan, Phyllis Kochavi, Bernard Bushell, Natalie Russo, Gretchen Willison, Judy Durff, Judith and Stan Farrar, Annsley Strong, Nancy Fredkin, John Wilson and my warm, supportive friends of the class of 2004 book club (guess what our next book's going to be!) have particularly sustained me through this process. Additionally, the amazing faculty of ICDL (you are far too many to name individually), I continue to learn from all of you. The board members of CAN and AS have been incredibly helpful by keeping me on the cutting edge of ASD research and treatment. In particular, I'd like to thank Jon Shestack, Portia Iverson, Peter Bell and Suzanne and Bob Wright, whose vision and leadership is a model for all.

I am forever indebted to the heroic children with ASD and their devoted families who entrusted me with their stories and their medical care. Thank you so much for also letting me share your experiences with others. I have learned so much from your resilience, courage and sheer will to do whatever it takes. We have laughed and cried together each step of our journey. The best moments of my clinical practice are when a child and his parents catch the mutual gleam in each other's eyes. In these moments of shared love, hope reigns, and we know that everything is possible.

Finally, I really can do what I do because of the love and devotion of my own family. I owe them so much. My parents, Jordan and Betty Ginsburg, my brothers, Mark and Scott Ginsburg, and their families, as well as the entire Robinson clan, have been there every step of the way. My husband, Joel, my daughter, Brett (who also spent countless hours critiquing the manuscript, each time making it better), and son, Chad, are the lights of my life. They give me inspiration moment to moment, love, honesty and patience that I so depend on. The three of you are my heart and soul. I love you more than you may ever know.

My heartfelt thanks to you all. You are the best team I could have!

Foreword

by Stanley I. Greenspan, M.D.

ALMOST EVERY family knows someone, either in their immediate or extended family or in their community, who is trying to meet the challenges of children who are given a diagnosis of autism. For more than thirty years, I have been working on improving the clinical approaches that will best help children and families. The primary difficulties children with an Autism Spectrum Disorder (ASD) evidence are in their capacities to relate, communicate and think. Having had the opportunity to direct a research center at the National Institute of Mental Health, my colleagues and I were able to study human development. We were able to look at many variations, from even before a baby is born up through childhood. Subsequently, I've had the honor of working with children of all ages, as well as adults, with these challenges.

Over the years, we developed a comprehensive approach built on the insights gained from our studies and clinical work. We describe this model as the Developmental, Individual Difference, Relationship-based (DIR)/Floortime approach. The value of this approach is in its ability to enable us to understand the uniqueness of every child and create a profile of that child. We are then able to enter the child's world and bring the child into a shared world. In this shared world, the child is able to progress up the developmental ladder and learn in a meaningful way. In its comprehensiveness, the DIR/Floortime approach captures the critical components of human development and puts the family at the forefront of helping their child.

Specifically, the DIR/Floortime approach is a framework that helps clinicians, parents and educators conduct a comprehensive assessment and develop an intervention program tailored to the unique challenges and strengths of children with ASD and other developmental problems. The objective of the DIR/Floortime model is to build healthy foundations for social, emotional and intellectual capacities rather than focusing on skills and isolated behaviors.

- The **D** (developmental) part of the model describes the building blocks of this foundation. Understanding where the child is, developmentally, is critical to planning a treatment program. The six social-emotional developmental milestones (see Chapter 4) describe the developmental milestones that every child must master for healthy emotional and intellectual growth. This includes helping children develop capacities to attend and remain calm and regulated, engage and relate to others, initiate and respond to all types of communication beginning with emotional and social affect-based gestures, engage in shared social problem solving and intentional behavior involving a continuous flow of interactions in a row, use ideas to communicate needs and think and play creatively, and build bridges among ideas in logical ways that lead to higher-level capacities to think in multicausal, gray area and reflective ways. These developmental capacities are essential for spontaneous and empathic relationships, as well as for the mastery of academic skills.

- The **I** (individual difference) part of the model describes the unique biologically based ways each child takes in, regulates, responds to and comprehends sensations such as sound and touch, and the planning and sequencing of actions and ideas. Some children, for example, are very hyperresponsive to touch and sound, while others are underreactive and still others seek out these sensations. "Biological challenges" describes the various processing issues that make up a child's individual differences and that may be interfering with his ability to grow and learn.

- The **R** (relationship-based) part of the model describes the learning relationships with caregivers, educators, therapists, peers and others who tailor their emotionally based interactions to the child's individual differences and developmental capacities to enable progress in mastering the essential foundations.

Central to the DIR/Floortime model is the role of the child's natural emotions and interests, which has been shown to be essential for learning interactions that enable the different parts of the mind and brain to work together and to build successively higher levels of social, emotional and intellectual capacities. DIR/Floortime is a specific technique to follow the child's natural interests and at the same time challenge the child toward greater and greater mastery of the social, emotional and intellectual capacities. With young children these playful interactions may occur on the "floor" but go on to include conversations and interactions in other places. The DIR/Floortime model, however, is a comprehensive framework that enables clinicians, parents and educators to construct a program tailored to the child's unique challenges and strengths. It often includes, in addition to DIR/Floortime, various problem-solving exercises and typically involves a team approach with speech therapy, occupational therapy, educational programs, mental health (developmental-psychological) intervention and, where appropriate, augmentative and bio-medical intervention. The DIR/Floortime model emphasizes the critical role of parents and other family members because of the importance of their emotional relationships with the child.

Parents have a unique opportunity in this book to gain insight into the model as it was envisioned. Dr. Ricki Robinson is the embodiment of a clinical practice true to the DIR approach in the hands of a warm, caring and seasoned clinician. She has been a valued colleague of mine and a keen supporter of the Interdisciplinary Council on Developmental and Learning Disorders (ICDL) initiatives since the early 1990s. She is extremely well trained and considered an expert in the field of pediatrics as well as in the clinical practice for children with ASD. She is a sought-after worldwide lecturer on this topic and an untiring educator for parents and professionals devoted to these children. Her warmth and engaging personality come through these pages as she guides parents and professionals on their treatment team through the multistep evaluation that informs the correct treatment approaches for their child's individual sensory-motor profiles, as well as solution-oriented suggestions to solve the many challenges, both developmental and medical, facing children with ASD and their families, especially as their child grows and develops.

Dr. Ricki, as she is known by the children and their families, is one of those rare individuals that both in her practice and in this book provides the full package, including the often elusive medical component. With all the controversy surrounding potential medical treatments in a comprehensive program, Dr. Ricki helps us understand the potential medical contributions and when they need to be considered. The wonderful case studies and the beautiful description of the DIR/Floortime model, coupled with the extremely thoughtful and comprehensive discussion of medical concerns, makes this a must-read for all those interested in or struggling with a youngster with an Autism Spectrum Disorder.

STANLEY I. GREENSPAN, M.D.
November 2009

Stanley I. Greenspan, M.D. (1941–2010), *was the founder and chairman of the Interdisciplinary Council on Developmental and Learning Disorders (ICDL), founding member and past board president of Zero to Three: National Center for Infants, Toddlers, and Families and former director of the National Institute of Mental Health's Clinical Infant Development Program and Mental Health Study Center. Dr. Greenspan was internationally recognized for his innovative approach to helping children with emotional and developmental issues. His legacy lives on through his work, which continues to help countless numbers of children and their families worldwide.*

Preface

PEDIATRICIANS BRING hope and help to our patients. We have the expertise gained through education and training to lend help to those in need. We provide assistance and information, formulate plans and support parents and children to give them hope. For children with Autism Spectrum Disorders (ASD) and their families, however, help and hope are not always easy to find.

Although I considered myself a well-trained and experienced pediatrician, when I encountered my first child with an autism diagnosis twenty years ago, I had little knowledge of it. When I first met Ryan and his family, whom you will meet through these pages, autism was about to emerge in epidemic proportions far exceeding professional understanding and services. Those services that were available tended to be education based but not medically based. Most doctors, including myself, were woefully underprepared to help these families. However, the networks I had built over the years afforded me access to a wide range of contacts. Casting a wide net across the country, I eventually obtained information to help support not only Ryan but also, ultimately, many children with ASD.

My search led to Drs. Stanley I. Greenspan and Serena Wieder, who proved to be superb mentors. They introduced me to the DIR model, a unique developmental approach to assessing and interacting with children, especially those who have delays. As I observed this treatment approach for the first time in my journey, I saw children with autism who were joyful, relating and communicating with their families—each in their own ways. This inspired me to adopt this model into my existing medical practice.

By 1998, it seemed that the number of children diagnosed with ASD was increasing daily. This convinced me to devote my practice solely to this group of children. At that time, my pediatric colleagues questioned whether there would be enough work in this field to sustain a viable practice. Within months my new practice "wait list" had grown shockingly to over one thousand children and families in need!

In *Autism Solutions,* I share my medical and developmental evaluation and treatment paradigm. As I saw more and more children with autism, medical patterns became evident. These children had numerous symptoms, in addition to their significant developmental delays. It was not unusual to find a child with a history of chronic diarrhea or constipation, allergies, potential seizures, severe sleep problems and recurrent infections. Behavior symptoms such as tics, aggression, hyperactivity and impulsivity, as well as debilitating anxiety, were common. Most of these concerns were not addressed by the prevailing explanations for ASD, were largely unrecognized and were poorly treated. Somehow the diagnosis of autism had clouded the fact that these were children who could experience the same childhood illnesses as any other child. It was also possible that certain chronic symptoms might even be related to their autism. In my entire career I had never met a more medically underserved group of children.

This was unacceptable to me. It was time to look at these children through a new lens. Yes, they might have developmental delays but they also showed intelligence (some superior) and untapped capabilities. Often their medical issues derailed their progress. By looking at each child individually, each with his own strengths and challenges, a unique profile could be developed. From this profile, a targeted treatment plan emerged that was tailored to his needs. Working together with families to discover ways they could relate and communicate with their children gave them renewed energy and hope. With increased hope came increased expectations for each child.

Treating a child's medical problems allowed him to feel better. When he felt better, he was more available to interact, develop relationships, get the most from his therapies and, eventually, make great developmental gains. When addressing all of a child's challenges appropriately, I witnessed changes that were unheard of at that time. Once the parents understood how their child interpreted the world, the door was opened to deepening their relationship. To see the happiness they had when their child related and communicated was extremely moving to me. I was convinced then—and more so today—that this powerful approach can significantly impact children's lives.

Research over the past decade continues to confirm the presence of medical issues in children with ASD. Yet in the early 1990s, very little research had been funded in the field of autism. At that time, I was fortunate to meet Jon Shestack and Portia Iverson, parents searching for answers for their son Dov, who had been diagnosed with ASD. They invited me to join the initial group of five, who met around their kitchen table, thinking about ways to stimulate research into the cause of and treatments for ASD. From these meetings (and due in large part to the courage and persistence of Jon and Portia), Cure Autism Now (CAN) was born—now called Autism Speaks. I was fortunate as a CAN board member to be able to immerse myself in the science, meeting many dedicated researchers trying to discover answers to the mysteries of ASD. Also about that time, I joined the founding board of the Interdisciplinary Council on Developmental and Learning Disorders (ICDL), an organization dedicated to educating professionals who work with children with ASD in relationship-based approaches. Through the ICDL November Research Conference and the Summer Institute, I have met and learned from hundreds of devoted professionals. Being privy to the newest in research and learning how to better support these children gave me a unique opportunity to provide the most up-to-date help to the children and their families in my practice.

Doctors learn the art of medicine from their patients, and mine have taught me volumes. I have been so privileged to be a participant in the journey of children with ASD and their families—in some cases for nearly twenty years. Each and every child has taught me over and over again to look beyond their behaviors to their uniqueness. In these pages you will meet many of these children. By addressing their abilities and adjusting their treatment plan to fit their needs over time, I have watched them make astounding progress. I have seen them grow to become related, creative, interesting, empathetic young adults, each blazing his own unique trail—often one never imagined for individuals with ASD. I expect this for your child, too.

Autism Solutions includes information covering both the developmental and medical concerns that parents, families and friends so often seek.

- Part I introduces autism and its potential causes.
- Part II reviews the nature of our sensory-motor systems and how an infant's development unfolds, as well as the unique developmental model that allows you to better understand your child's strengths and challenges.
- Part III presents my approach to the evaluation and development of treatment plans. I hope you will feel as if you are sitting in the office with me as we explore all the potential concerns for your child and help you formulate the necessary elements for his treatment plan, tailored to his needs and the needs of your family.
- Part IV reviews communication issues—both learning how to interpret your child's behavior as a means to letting you know what he is thinking and feeling, as well as ways to support the most challenged children who have severe motor-planning delays.
- Part V addresses the medical issues that may affect your child. I have tried to demystify "doctorspeak" so that you will be armed with useful information to help you get appropriate medical care for your child. In addition, you should be able to ask your doctor the questions most important to solving issues as they come up.

- Part VI puts all of this into the big picture of why you are working to get your child all the support he needs—so he will be prepared to live a happy and meaningful life.

Most of the concepts are illustrated by stories of children I've seen in my practice. In general, names have been changed to protect their privacy. In most cases, unless a girl is featured in a story, you will notice I have used "he" in describing a child with ASD. This has been done for consistency and simplicity.

As you seek solutions for your child with autism, you should always be in the driver's seat—no one knows your child better than you; no one cares for your child more than you; no one can advocate better for your child than you. This book will give you information that empowers you to remain central to the process. Your journey may be an extended one, with peaks and valleys, but it is one worth taking. May *Autism Solutions* bring you help and hope as you continue your journey and find the path with the best outcome for your child.

PART I

Is It Autism?

CHAPTER 1

Ryan

I WAS THRILLED when Diana, a good friend from college, called to tell me that she and her young family were moving to Southern California from New York. My husband and I had settled there about ten years earlier, after I had completed my pediatric residency and I had joined a popular pediatric practice as their first and only female pediatrician.

Shortly after they settled in, Diana brought her fifteen-month-old son to see me. "I'm worried about Ryan," she told me. "Something isn't right, and I can't put my finger on it."

"Let me have a look at him," I said. Ryan let me lift him up to the examination table. He didn't cling to his mother at all, which was unusual at his age.

She teared up. "Everyone tells me I'm crazy, that he's just a boy and boys are different, but I have this feeling in my gut...."

I handed her a tissue, and studied Ryan's face. A mother's intuition was something I took seriously. A detective by nature, I combed through Ryan's history while Diana told me her concerns.

"He's always been a happy baby, crawling around and looking at everything, but he doesn't babble the way his big sister, Jeannie, did. And he doesn't seem as connected to me. He'll say 'ma ma ma ma ma,' but not consistently, and he doesn't attach the word to me. When I call him by name, he doesn't look at me. It's just...weird."

Diana became pregnant at forty and had Ryan at forty-one, after a healthy pregnancy. She'd had an amniocentesis and ultrasounds throughout, and Ryan was born by C-section at full term. He weighed a healthy eight pounds, seven ounces. All of his first year developmental milestones had been reached.

He was a beautiful boy—with big blue eyes and a crown of strawberry-blond hair—just like his mother. I looked for that spark I've seen between hundreds of mothers and their babies. It wasn't there. When I tried to get his attention myself, he averted his gaze.

"How long have you had this feeling?" I asked while watching Ryan's face.

Diane responded, "I'd say since he was ten or eleven months old. Our daughter was babbling so much more at this stage, and she was so engaging. She loved peekaboo and waved at everyone. You remember," she said, wiping her eyes. "I was going to call you for advice, but thought I should wait and see, that maybe it was a boy thing. It's so different than how it was with Jeannie."

I gave Ryan the biggest smile I could, hoping he would smile back. He didn't. "After his first birthday," Diana went on, "it seemed there was nothing I could do to get him to babble or talk. I'm worried about him. Should I be?"

I told her what I had learned in medical school, residency and all my years of practice. Every baby develops at his own pace and boys can sometimes talk later—it might just be a matter of giving him some more time. In most babies, language doesn't take off until they are around two.

By the time Ryan was twenty months old, Diana and I knew we had to do something. His language simply was not developing. He was still detached from her and everyone else. I referred him to a speech therapist, who determined that Ryan had an expressive language delay, but that it wasn't autism.

LANGUAGE AND COMMUNICATION

Expressive language is the ability to use spoken language to communicate with another. *Receptive language* is the ability to hear, process and comprehend the spoken word and make meaning out of sound.

The fact that the therapist used the word "autism" alarmed me. In all my years of practice, I had never seen a child with autism. But since Diana had first brought Ryan to see me, I was starting to see a number of patients who had similar developmental delays.

"Why don't we take another look at Ryan in six months or so?" the speech therapist said to Diana. "He might just be a late bloomer."

An Autism Lecture

Once the speech therapist planted the seed, I decided I needed to learn more about autism. There was only one paragraph in my pediatric medical literature about the disorder. Serendipitously, one of my pediatric colleagues who focused on learning issues gave me a flyer announcing a talk by a local psychologist known to be an autism expert.

The lecture hall filled up quickly with medical professionals. I was surprised by the turnout. Although I'd seen some patients with delays, I wasn't aware that autism was such a common concern.

When the psychologist began to list the questions to ask that uncover the early warning signs of autism, I felt a pit opening in my stomach.

- Does the child respond to his name when called by the caregiver?
- Does the child engage in joint attention (the ability to tune in to someone else either by seeing them or hearing them)?
- Does the child imitate others?
- Does the child respond emotionally to others?
- Does the child engage in pretend play?

Ryan was now almost two and a half years old. And the answer to all these questions was no.

Several weeks later, I drove Diana, her husband, Tom, and Ryan to that same psychologist's office for a developmental evaluation. Diana and Tom were grateful for my friendship and support. It was important for me to learn firsthand what they were going through and I was interested in learning more about autism.

The three of us sat in the testing room and watched as the psychologist struggled to engage a very uncooperative Ryan. It took her a little more than an hour to conclude that, yes, Ryan was autistic.

"So what do we do next?" asked Tom. "What can we do to make him come out of it?"

"You can take him home and love him," said the psychologist. "Unfortunately, once they are autistic, they are always autistic. This is a devastating diagnosis and very little progress can be made. Your son will never go to a regular school, he'll never graduate and he'll never develop relationships," she continued. "He'll never live on his own or have any kind of independence."

Tom and Diana both looked like they were about to jump out of their chairs and strangle this woman, and I couldn't blame them. I, too, didn't believe what I was hearing. "Wait a minute," I said. "I'm a pediatrician who has spent years treating the most critically ill children, and I would never talk to parents that way. You can't leave them without hope. There is always something that can be done. I tell my patients I will look under every rock possible and find something they can do."

The psychologist looked at me and shook her head. "By rejecting what I'm telling them," she said, "you are encouraging denial, and denial will only make things worse."

"But there has to be something," said Tom, "some treatment, something we can do."

The psychologist had one suggestion. "Put Ryan into the hospital for a six-week intensive evaluation," she said. "Perhaps we can design a program for him based on the results."

As Diana and Tom shook their heads, I said, "You want them to put him in the hospital for six weeks? And separate him from the strength and love of his family? Are you crazy?"

"That is what I have to offer," she said, looking at Ryan's distraught parents. "Think it over and let me know."

The walk back to the car was quiet. "I know there has got to be more out there," I told them as Ryan climbed into his car seat, "and we are going to find it." As we drove away, I caught a glimpse of Ryan's face in the rearview mirror and at that moment, I knew what I had to do. This precious boy had a purpose, and so did I.

"I have helped a lot of people," I said, feeling energized by newfound resolve. "Doors will open."

Dr. Stanley I. Greenspan

While searching for a hopeful treatment plan for Ryan, I received an invitation to a conference from Dr. Stanley I. Greenspan, a leading child psychiatrist with expertise in the social and emotional development of young children. The conference focused on identifying and treating social–emotional-based developmental and learning disorders.

I called Dr. Greenspan immediately, introduced myself and told him about Ryan. We talked over the telephone, and he encouraged me to attend the conference and to send him a videotape of Ryan for evaluation purposes. He told me that I was the only physician who had shown interest in the conference—the rest of the attendees were occupational and speech therapists, educators and psychologists.

A month later, I sat with Diana and Tom in the front row for the opening of the conference. Dr. Greenspan was a warm, wonderful individual and I immediately felt connected to him, as did Ryan's parents. I'd never met a psychiatrist quite like him. He began talking enthusiastically about children with developmental delays and then cued up a video.

It was the video of Ryan.

In the video, Ryan, by now nearly three years old, was sitting with Diana on the floor, next to a toy house. At first glance it looked like Ryan was playing with the toy. However, a closer look revealed that he was repetitively maneuvering the mechanical parts of the house—opening and closing the doors and windows and moving the elevator up and down, going from one to another again and again. Ryan uttered the same phrase over and over. It

sounded like a line from "Ring Around the Rosie." Every time Diana introduced a play figure, Ryan would not glance in her direction. Instead he would
turn his back and move farther away. He did not make eye contact or make
any appropriate response to Diana's attempts to engage him. It was painful to
watch. Ryan's rejection must have been an undercurrent during all of Diana's
time with him. Grabbing her hand, I gave it a gentle squeeze as tears dropped
silently from our eyes.

After Ryan's video, Dr. Greenspan showed videos of children similar to
Ryan who had improved dramatically after the method of treatment, known
as DIR/Floortime. Following the talk, we had lunch with Dr. Greenspan.
After more in-depth conversation about Ryan, Dr. Greenspan said he expected
Ryan would thrive with this treatment philosophy.

"Thank you so much for giving us hope," cried Diana. "If he ever goes
to college, you'll be the first to know!"

"It's not *if* he goes to college," said Dr. Greenspan. "It's *when* he goes to
college."

CHAPTER 2

What Is Autism?

OVER THE past two decades, I have had the privilege of caring for hundreds of children with Autism Spectrum Disorders (ASD). I continue to be struck by the fact that no two are exactly alike—as evidenced from a typical day in my office:

My first patient of the day is six-year-old Aaron. He has good receptive and expressive language skills but is having difficulty making friends and learning in school. Next is fourteen-year-old Jake. Because Jake has no verbal language, we had no clue how brilliant this young man really was—at least not until he was given a computer keyboard and was able to communicate his thoughts and feelings through his typing. He struggles with many of the same issues that most teenagers do, along with a few extra physical and social challenges, which we continue to work through. The fact that he is now able to communicate when he's not feeling well or is in pain has allowed us to treat some of the physical ailments that were impeding his developmental progress. Following Jake, I see a new patient, four-year-old Alisha. She has no language, is not potty trained, does not sleep through the night and flaps her hands and spins much of the day. Her parents are exhausted, confused and worried. Next is seventeen-year-old Randy. As soon as I ask him how he's doing, he begins to talk—and doesn't stop. He would expound for the full hour, providing me with the most minute details about his beloved reptiles and trains, if time permitted.

Once considered rare, ASD now affects about 1 out of 110 children in the United States. Autism is a medical disorder with a neurobiological basis, most likely due to unusual connections within a child's brain. The hope and expectation are that early detection and intense intervention offer great opportunity for improving a child's developmental delays if he has been diagnosed with autism.

Autism is essentially a disorder of relating and communicating. It is a developmental disorder—which means that the skills required for these interactions are not achieved when expected. In ASD the delays are usually recognized by the age of three, when a child should be able to talk, although the subtle roots of the symptoms are typically present much earlier. By twelve to eighteen months most children with ASD have already shown a rapid decline in eye contact, social smiling and responsiveness compared to typically developing children. At least two-thirds of children with ASD have this early onset of symptoms.

In regressive-onset autism, a child will seem to have normal developmental growth for his first eighteen to twenty-four months. This normal development may be followed by a clearly defined time when he loses his communication and interaction skills and develops symptoms in all the core areas of ASD.

A child with Asperger's disorder may not be diagnosed before the age of three, because he has some language skills. The diagnosis will usually be made once his delays in social communication, as well as sensory-motor abilities and learning issues, are recognized. If a child has Asperger's disorder, his ability to socialize and communicate effectively with others is impacted. He may also be socially awkward and exhibit an all-absorbing interest in specific topics.

Core Features of ASD

No two children are alike—including children with ASD. However, if your child has autism, he will have symptoms in all three areas that make up the core features of ASD. You may note that he has:

- Significant communication delays involving his understanding (receptive) and use (expressive) of language
- Resistance to change and repetitive behaviors
- Delay in the development of typical social interactions with you and others

These core features are precisely defined in the *Diagnostic and Statistical Manual of Mental Disorders* (*DSM*), version IV-R (see Appendix 1). This manual, published by the American Psychiatric Association, contains the criteria for diagnosing mental disorders. It is used by all health professionals to determine and communicate a mental health diagnosis following an evaluation.

The presence of all three of the core features of ASD will help you and your doctor confirm whether your child has an ASD (see Chapter 7).

Communication Delays

The language problems experienced by children with ASD are usually very serious and can differ in each child. A child with ASD has greater difficulty with language than, for example, a three-year-old who is not talking yet understands everything you tell him and easily follows your instructions. This nontalking child has an expressive language delay different than what is seen in ASD. A child with ASD doesn't accurately process or understand language. As a result, your child with ASD may be receiving inaccurate messages (if he is receiving any messages at all), and what he says or does is then not what you expect. He may be unable to respond to what you or others say to him. In fact, he may not speak at all. Or, he may have expressive language and be able to speak, but his response may not make sense. If he has language, he might reverse his pronouns and put together his sentences in different ways, or his voice may have a robotic quality. He may not successfully engage in the back and forth of conversation (known as discourse) using both verbal and nonverbal (gestural) language. Your child may have good auditory memory, resulting in the repetition of words or phrases (known as echolalia). He may be able to repeat phrases that he has heard in conversations or on TV, including whole segments from his favorite movies. However, this isn't useful language, because it doesn't help him engage with or respond to others or get his needs met. He may also lack the ability to spontaneously initiate conversation or connection, especially in "make-believe" play or social imitation play. Children with ASD will have at least one, and quite possibly many, of these characteristic language issues.

Resistant to Change and Engages in Repetitive Behaviors

If your child is diagnosed with ASD, he may have repetitive patterns and a need for sameness that can dictate many of his daily activities. His need for sameness may lead to restricted, repetitive and stereotypical patterns of behavior (words, sounds or actions he uses or repeats most often). You may find that he is inflexible or that he has a persistent preoccupation with certain toys (such as trains, trucks and books). He may express interest in parts of objects (such as wheels on trucks, water flowing from faucets and blades of fans) and repetitive motor movements (such as hand or finger flapping, twisting or complex whole-body movements). These behaviors are often described as "odd" but they may well be a coping mechanism for him. He may have developed his own patterns of responding to sensory input and rely on them as he interacts with the world. Children with ASD will have at least one of these characteristic behaviors.

Because it is not unusual for a toddler to focus his attention on a favorite toy or blanket, this core symptom of ASD is often difficult to readily recognize in a very young child but may become much more prominent as he gets older. As your child grows, watch for the variety of interests he develops and note whether he is interested in only one or two items rather than eagerly exploring his space as is generally seen in a child his age. Then look to see how he uses the items and whether or not he gets overly focused on certain parts of the toy (such as the wheels on the truck). This overfocus may be an early sign of future repetitive behavior.

Delays in Developing Typical Social Interactions

At an early age, children with ASD usually display a delay in developing the first step of social-emotional development, known as joint attention. Joint attention is the ability to become aware of and focus on the presence of someone through seeing or hearing them. You can see it in your infant when he turns to the sound of your voice or when his whole face lights up as he sees you enter the room. This ability to connect emotionally begins the interplay of your relationship with your child. It is the first step in becoming a true partner in a social relationship. Developing joint attention is one of the most difficult and coordinated tasks an infant must perform. He must be able to understand and respond to sensory cues to attain and maintain joint attention. If your child has difficulty sustaining joint attention, it will be a challenge for him to engage with others.

Delays in social relating are usually noted first through nonverbal interactions. Your child may have fleeting eye contact or respond slowly with his facial expressions and gestures. He may not develop spontaneous verbal and nonverbal interaction with you and others. He may not show you toys, bring things to you or point to objects of interest. In addition, he may not respond to your emotional overtures or when you point to things. A child with ASD will display at least two of these symptoms of social delay.

It is not that your child does not want to interact with you. Rather, he has not yet developed the necessary skills that allow him to join in a two-way interaction. The lack of joint attention is what most parents are referring to when they say, "Something is not right." Although you may not be able to put into words what you are experiencing, you know in your heart and by the sinking feeling in your gut that something is wrong. You are not "connecting" with your child. You are not feeling joint warmth and joy. This can be especially confusing for first-time parents who haven't previously experienced the typical responses and behavior of a young baby. The devastation and feelings of helplessness can be immense. My number one goal during my first visit with a child is to help parents to have a moment of joy that connection with their child can bring. Dr. Greenspan refers to it as searching for the gleam in a child's eye. I also look for the mutual responsive gleam in Mom and Dad.

Some professionals believe that children with ASD do not make eye contact. We now know, for example, that if you are in the visual space of a child with ASD, he might make great eye contact and maybe follow up with an excited smile! To say that a child is not on the autism spectrum because he can hold someone's gaze is not always true. On the other hand, some children with ASD have the uncanny ability to visually absorb an enormous amount of information with only darting glances or by using their peripheral gaze.

WHY EYE GAZE MAY BE OFF

In March 2009, the Yale Child Studies Center published a study focusing on toddler response to biological motion. It was noted that young toddlers with autism were not sensitive to biological motion, including facial expressions, speech and gestures in social interaction. Instead the toddlers with autism were drawn to highly synchronized movements, which are not characteristic of most human movements. This may explain why toddlers with autism often do not make eye contact or pay attention to what others are doing. In fact, children with ASD as young as two years of age show a preference for watching people's mouths rather than their eyes. Because infants in the first few days of life have been detected paying attention to biological motion, perhaps this behavior could potentially be useful in identifying infants at risk for autism very early in life. In addition, therapeutic strategies emphasized in the DIR model that help draw toddlers' attention to people, including facial expressions and gestures, may influence brain and behavioral development in children with autism, so that more typical development occurs and the symptoms of autism are reduced.

You may feel that you share some aspect of the core symptoms of ASD with your child. Many of us have some of these same symptoms and behaviors. The key is that all three categories of symptoms must be present, and your child must exhibit features of major delay from each category. Although symptoms must be present in your child in all three categories, the individual manifestations vary. Thus, no two children with ASD are exactly alike.

Symptoms Beyond the Core Features of ASD

When first taking medical histories of children with ASD, I was dismayed to find that many of the symptoms parents described were not found in the medical literature. These symptoms were generally related to unusual ways a child responded to sensory stimuli, difficulties performing even the simplest of gross and fine motor tasks and many unresolved medical problems. Over the past decade, however, these symptoms have gained prominence as they can influence a child's well-being and may possibly be linked to the core features of ASD.

Unusual Sensory Responses

An unusual response to sensory information—including taste, smell, touch, sight, sound, sense of balance and position in space—is considered a common symptom but is not yet required to make a diagnosis of ASD. In my experience, most children with ASD have sensory processing delays that affect (to varying degrees) the way in which they relate to their world. In fact, because of these unusual interpretations through their sensory systems, they can experience the world as a very painful and anxiety-provoking place, further isolating them from necessary and desired social interaction. Sensory disturbances can be the most pervasive and often the most debilitating symptom for your child.

To better understand how your child's sensory perception can affect his behavior, think about your own sensory sensitivities. For example, I have an acute sense of smell and can't stand being in a room when onions are being prepared or served. I enjoy crowds and can tolerate a lot of noise. My husband, on the other hand, loves the smell of simmering onions but is very sensitive to noise and avoids crowds. We all have sensory issues that can attract or repel us. In ASD, however, the ability to perceive and interpret sensory input appears to be well beyond these typical variations. What is foreground information to you may appear to be background for your child, and vice versa. Your child may not be able to filter the sensory input from his environment—sometimes letting in too much (becoming overwhelmed) or too little (becoming unresponsive or overcompensating by overreacting). He may do both at the same time through differing senses. These atypical ranges of sensory processing result in over- to underresponsive behavior in your child, depending on the situation. Some of the differences in each sensory pathway that your child may be experiencing throughout his day include the following:

Auditory (Hearing)

The auditory range of a child with ASD is truly puzzling. You may have noticed this with your own child. You might stand behind him and call his name and get no response. Yet when an airplane flies high overhead, he is the first to hear it and look up. On the other hand, one of my older patients told me that the pitter-patter of rain on the roof sounded more like nails being pounded. Your child may disconnect from your interaction to pay attention to sounds coming through walls or air moving through cooling ducts. One adolescent boy told me he hears every conversation in his house from his bedroom. Imagine the difficulty this creates for him and his family when he relates private conversations the next morning!

Visual (Seeing)

A child with ASD may have a visual ability that is more acute than usual. When visual acuity is measured in these children, it is not unusual to find that they can see things nearly twice as far away as is typical. As a result, your child might have difficulty focusing on relevant visual information. When he can see so much at once, he can become constantly distracted and it can be difficult for him to determine the important visual elements around him. He may then have difficulty staying engaged with his immediate surroundings.

Evaluating where objects and people are around him (known as visual-spatial processing) can also be very difficult, frightening and anxiety-provoking. He may be unable to judge spatial relations well enough to navigate stairs or pass easily through a doorway, or he may wander aimlessly around the room. Your child may not be able to determine the relationship between the big picture and the details within that picture. Therefore, he may be more interested in small pieces of a toy, such as the wheels, than he is in the whole toy itself. Often visual-spatial difficulties are under-recognized and undertreated in children with ASD.

Tactile (Touch)

There are two types of touch sensors in our bodies: one for soft touch and another for deep pressure. Children with ASD may be overly sensitive to one form of touch but underreactive to the other. Johnie, a five-year-old with ASD, has great sensitivity to labels in clothes and to wool, and he won't let his parents hold his hand, because it is uncomfortable for him. At the same time he craves deep pressure and regularly seeks this out by rubbing his chin hard on his mother's forehead or pushing his back against his father's leg. The opposite can also be true—soft touch may be fine but deep pressure may feel terrible. Any combination of over- and/or underreactivity to touch can be seen in ASD.

Taste

Taste sensitivity is particularly difficult for children with ASD (and their families). Children with ASD are known to be picky eaters, and it has always been interesting to me that they crave similar foods—particularly carbohydrates and salty items. Additionally, their lips and tongues may be overreactive to food textures and can find a tiny lump in mashed potatoes, which they will gag on or spit out.

Smell

Children with ASD rely heavily on their sense of smell. Your child may smell your hair and clothing or plants and flowers excessively. This behavior is reminiscent of individuals who are blind and use senses other than their eyes to understand the world. It is also quite possible that your child gets an increased sense of security when in the presence of a familiar smell. Children with ASD may also have an unusual range of smell sensitivity, making typical situations, such as a visit to a restaurant, a difficult, even painful, experience for them.

Proprioception

Proprioception helps us to understand where our body is in space. (Balance, governed through the vestibular system in our inner ear, requires proprioception.) Processing this information can be very difficult for those with ASD. You may have noticed that your child likes to spend a lot of time spinning in circles. Moving like this may help increase his sensory input, which then allows him to better orient his body in space. Not being able to judge the relative location of my body in the world was a difficult concept for me to understand, until I switched from driving a sedan to a minivan. Suddenly I had difficulty judging my space on the road as I drove my new vehicle. So I pulled my seat belt extra tight, and then I adjusted my huge side mirrors and the rearview mirror to get the best view of the road beside me and behind me. At first I was very nervous and drove slowly, parking as far away from other cars as possible. I continued these compensations until my system adjusted to the size of my new car. Imagine how children with ASD must feel as they navigate through the world without the support of mirrors or seat belts or the processing ability to adjust to change quickly (if at all). This difficulty can result in increased fear and anxiety for your child.

Motor Planning and Sequencing (Movement)

Motor issues are often noted in physical descriptions of children with ASD. Your child may be clumsy or have problems with both large and small motor movements. This clumsiness may lead to difficulty printing, coloring, painting, eating with utensils, using scissors or manipulating toys. Handwriting tasks may also be incredibly difficult for him.

Muscle motor control influences more than body movement—it can have an impact on speech as well. Multiple fine motor skills and coordination are required to make the precise mouth, lip and tongue movements to form words. Children with ASD can have oral apraxia (total inability to properly articulate) or oral dyspraxia (partial difficulty). Spoken (expressive) language can be impacted long after an understanding of language (receptive) improves with therapy.

Your child may also be described as having low muscle tone, or hypotonia. This is not hypotonia in the true medical sense, due to muscle or nerve disease. He may lack the sensory information or motor memory to control or coordinate his muscles. Your child may appear limp like a sack of potatoes when sitting on the floor, or he may actually prefer to lie on the floor rather than sit. While the tone of his muscles may appear to be very low, if you tickle his feet, he will probably immediately jump up and have very strong muscle tone and strength for a period of time after the sensory stimulus.

Sequencing Motor Steps

Remember when you learned to ride a bike, throw a ball or sink a basket? You practiced and practiced until you acquired the long-term memory for the sequence of steps required to perform this skill. With ASD, you may have taught your child to do something (such as toilet training) over and over, yet he still can't do it on his own. He may want to use the toilet but lacks memory of the steps he needs to take to complete the task.

Medical Issues

In my early days of treating children with ASD, I consistently encountered medical concerns—often unrecognized and untreated in the medical community—that were noted by groups of parents who saw similar issues in their children, including persistent gastrointestinal distress, feeding issues, hyperactivity and sleep problems.

When a referral for diagnosing ASD was often delayed, I encountered children aged five to seven who never had had a solid bowel movement in their lives. Feeding issues were frequent—spanning the range from picky eaters to those with an inability to chew or swallow. Food and environmental allergies were also often significant in the families, as well as in their children. In addition, the children's sleep issues were the most pervasive and difficult to solve that I have ever encountered in pediatric practice. It was not unusual to hear of seven-year-old children who had *never* slept through the night. This meant that not only the children were sleep deprived but also the families. It was clear that medical needs abounded for these children. In fact, to date, ASD is thought to be a system disorder with a potential influence on the health of your child. Because medical well-being is a necessary prerequisite to effective therapy, these challenges must be addressed.

Dysregulation—Response to Change

Children with ASD may respond to changes in their external (sensory) and internal (health) environments by becoming dysregulated. In many children this dysregulation is evidenced by an increase in their ASD behaviors—anything from flapping, rocking or spinning to having tantrums, withdrawing, becoming startled or acting out.

Any one of us can respond in a dysregulated fashion to a new situation. Imagine yourself moving next door to a busy fire station. At least once a night, sirens scream outside your window. You bolt out of sleep, with your heart pounding and adrenaline surging, and find it difficult to get back to sleep. But by the end of the week, you are rolling over at the sound of sirens and during the second week you sleep right through. Your system has adjusted to the noise (stimulus) around you.

Children with ASD have difficulty adjusting to changes in their environments. For them it's not just a firehouse siren that is going off. It is the tag in their shirt, the radio in the room next door, the person speaking to them and more. Your child can become dysregulated often if he is not getting the proper cues from his environment. Imagine how you might feel if you were lost in a country where no one spoke English and you didn't speak the local language. Because of your inability to communicate, you would likely experience fear, anxiety and stress. Feeling this way might lead you to act out in anger or to shut down and become incapable of figuring out what to do. It's the same for your child, except that he encounters these problems in his very own home and environment. No wonder he may hand flap, rock or withdraw from a situation. These behaviors, often labeled as inappropriate, may be the best he can do to help himself given the information as he perceives it. Your child's behaviors are a coping mechanism. Once he gets help to interpret his environment, he will become more efficiently and effectively regulated.

With all these symptoms, the challenge becomes how to identify the way in which your child learns about his world and then to work with his capabilities to help reduce his challenges and decrease his dysregulation. When your child is regulated, he will be much more available for interaction, which, in turn, can help him make progress. The key to helping him is to first try to understand his unique sensory-motor system. Chapter 5 will help you become a detective and closely observe your child to get a clear picture of how he interacts with the world. With this knowledge, you can ease his burdens of daily living and begin to take steps toward a better life and improved interactions for him. A child who is regulated, attentive and engaged is a child who is more capable of learning.

Other Common Features of ASD

In addition to the core features and expanded symptoms that are present (to differing degrees) in each child with ASD, there are a few consistent trends that have been noted.

- Four out of five children with ASD are boys. This male-to-female ratio has remained consistent over the years.

- Physically, the diagnosed children have very few visible anomalies that suggest clear genetic disorders. Generally, they are beautiful babies who become adorable children. This lack of major external physical manifestations may, in fact, be one of the reasons why this disorder was not historically studied by medical specialties other than psychiatry.
- It has been noted that children with ASD have large head circumferences (greater than 97 percent on growth charts), providing one clue for researchers looking at the neurobiological underpinnings of ASD.
- It has also been shown that children with ASD develop epilepsy in approximately one-third of cases, most often when young or in adolescence.
- Until recently, children with ASD were consistently characterized as having mental retardation. Rates as high as 75 percent have been claimed—a statistic that many now agree is closer to half that.

A Spectrum Disorder

Autism is considered a spectrum disorder, meaning that, although all children diagnosed with an ASD will have elements of the core features, the degree of challenge in each of these core areas defines where on the spectrum a child is placed. The full umbrella under which all the ASDs are included is Pervasive Developmental Disorder (PDD), reflecting the serious challenges these diagnoses bring to children. The *DSM* IV-R also includes Rett syndrome and Childhood Disintegrative Disorder (CDD) under the PDD umbrella.

Rett Syndrome

Rett syndrome is a rare genetic disease caused by a change in the MECP2 gene that results in features of autism, but eventually it becomes clear that there is a motor-based deterioration in the child. This disorder occurs in females (but may be carried by males). Children with Rett syndrome are described as having a normal early development. Generally between five and forty-eight months of age, they have a decrease in the growth of their head size. This is accompanied by a loss of social interaction and a loss of previously developed hand skills, which are replaced with repetitive hand movements (hand-wringing or hand washing). Eventually these children have impaired language as well as very poor motor function (poorly coordinated gait or body movements), which can be progressive throughout their life. Children with Rett syndrome are most often initially diagnosed with ASD. All girls diagnosed with an ASD must also be evaluated for Rett syndrome through specific testing for the MECP2 gene.

Childhood Disintegrative Disorder (CDD)

This is a condition that also has developmental symptoms described as autistic-like. It occurs in children over the age of two after a significant regression. Children with CDD are described as having absolutely normal development in all areas for at least two years. Before they reach ten years of age, they regress and have a significant loss of previously acquired language, social play, motor skills or bowel and bladder control, often accompanied by repetitive behaviors. Of course, children diagnosed with CDD must be thoroughly evaluated for underlying medical causes for such deterioration.

Autism Spectrum Disorder (ASD)

The majority of individuals diagnosed with PDD have an ASD. They include Autistic disorder, also known as Classic Autism; Pervasive Developmental Disorder Not Otherwise Specified (PDD-NOS); and Asperger's disorder. All three of these diagnoses exhibit the three core issues of ASD but with varying severity.

The most challenged children are diagnosed with Autistic disorder or Classic Autism. These children demonstrate all three core features of autism as well as many sensory-motor processing issues. They may also be diagnosed with mental retardation. I don't necessarily agree with the diagnosis of mental retardation in these children, and fortunately, this perception is changing. However, they are often seriously impaired by sensory-motor coordination issues affecting their ability to communicate in all ways, making IQ measurement very difficult.

Pervasive Developmental Disorder Not Otherwise Specified (PDD-NOS) is the diagnosis used to describe children who have many features of ASD but do not fulfill all three of the core categories. This diagnosis is often given to very young children and can be confusing for parents. One parent called PDD-NOS "Physician Didn't Diagnose" because he felt that he was left in limbo, not knowing how to help his child. A child with PDD-NOS will either develop clear-cut symptoms of an autistic disorder or gain strengths over time to meet his specific challenges.

Many consider Asperger's disorder to be equivalent to high-functioning autism, but there is controversy over the applications of these labels. Children with Asperger's will show delays in social interaction and develop repetitive patterns of interests and activities that are often quite different from their peers (such as focusing on clocks, reptiles and train schedules and categorizing the birthdays of everyone they have ever met). Although language acquisition in Asperger's is often not delayed per se, the practical use of language for social interaction and communication can be impaired. If not addressed in an appropriate therapeutic program, this may then severely impact the child's growth and development as well as social and occupational options. Many parents welcome a diagnosis of Asperger's, as opposed to autism, as it seems less debilitating. In fact, the multiple challenges in Asperger's disorder can be severe on an individual level.

As you begin the journey that will lead to your child's improved relating and communicating—the goal of all therapeutic interventions—set aside the label. Don't focus so much on where on the spectrum your child may fit, but rather on his full individual profile that describes his strengths and challenges. Look at *your child* to find the clues to help him move forward.

Debunking the Myths

The study of autism has resulted in enormous advances in our understanding of the disease, but some misinformation persists. One can hardly pick up an article or book about ASD today without encountering within the first paragraphs at least two statements about ASD that cut through the hearts of parents and families. The first is that 75 percent of all those diagnosed with ASD have mental retardation. The second is that children with ASD have little or no empathy. Both of these statements are ingrained myths that in many cases have become self-fulfilling prophecies.

Myth #1: Mental Retardation and ASD

Over the years, I've evaluated many children with measured IQs that indicate that they are "severely mentally retarded," yet I find that these same children can be creative problem solvers when provided with proper sensory–motor-supported interactions. This was the case when I met Steve and his family.

Steve is a six-year-old boy who was diagnosed with ASD at age two. He had been immersed in multiple therapeutic interventions over time, without much progress. He was nonverbal, self-absorbed and preoccupied with repetitive behaviors most of the time. His IQ had been measured as 50 (in the mental retardation range). His parents were discouraged and brought him to see me for a second opinion about school placement. I asked about his ability to play with toys or problem solve. His parents had never seen him do either. While playing with him on the floor, I noted he occasionally looked at the toys on the shelf. If I was very animated and used a lot of gestures, he showed interest and responded with gestures, and I encouraged his parents to try this as well. Doing this supported his attention and engagement, but it was difficult to sustain the interaction for more than a few seconds. If we asked a question, Steve did not respond. If we asked again, he disengaged. I suggested pausing after a question until he responded.

That pause led to great results! Steve picked up a fire truck that had a hose lodged in the wheel. He tried to get it out but couldn't. He was visibly upset, which provided an opportunity for his dad to ask, "Do you need help?" He then waited eight seconds (I counted out the pause to myself), and Steve gave the truck to his dad and smiled. Dad, of course, was thrilled. He tried, unsuccessfully, to dislodge the hose. He asked Steve with great animation, "What can you use to fix it?" Steve remained seated but began to look around, bypassed the toolbox and pulled the stethoscope from a doctor kit nearby. Dad looked puzzled but I encouraged him to wait and see. Steve then pulled the tubing from the stethoscope, unhooked it and handed it to Dad. Unsure what Steve wanted, Dad asked (with animation), "What is this for?" Steve took the stethoscope tube and tried to use it to replace the hose on the fire engine. The new tube didn't fit. So Dad asked, "What else might work?" and waited while Steve looked around the room. Steve then grabbed the fire truck and brought it to me, taking my finger and indicating that I should use my nail to dislodge the hose. It worked! Steve's smile, along with the joy on his parents' faces, made my day. This interaction took over fifteen minutes, but during this time Steve was totally engaged.

When we adjusted to Steve's unique rhythm and timing, he was able not only to respond to us but to show us that he was a much more resourceful problem solver than indicated by his IQ scores. The key was creating an environment in which he could excel.

Like for most children with ASD, the situation during Steve's initial IQ test was probably not ideal. Most likely, his parents were absent, and the person testing was new to him and unaware of his sensory, motor, rhythm and processing needs. In an environment that doesn't support his needs, Steve is not able to do his best. Standardized testing, such as IQ tests, require standardized techniques, which can be difficult for many children with ASD profiles. And, although there are tests that are designed to measure children who are nonverbal, such as the Leiter International Performance Scale-Revised (Leiter-R), they will not be accurate for a child who is anxious during testing. It has always amazed me that children with ASD can double their IQ scores after years of treatment. In reality, their IQ probably does not change but their ability to perform on the test does.

For that reason, I don't find that standard test measurements provide useful information about a child with ASD. I rely instead on history and observation. However, you should know that most school districts require IQ testing for funding purposes, and you should be prepared for the results—which may be poor. I encourage you to look beyond the score. Do not let test results determine your child's potential and abilities. Believe what you feel and see when interacting with him. Let your child's therapists and teachers know about those "aha" moments with your child. I think that these moments are the true measure of your child. They can spark hope and help you to continue supporting your child while gently challenging him to move further up the developmental ladder. After playing with a child, I usually look directly at him, telling him how smart he is! The response is uniformly a positive one— from a fleeting glance to a huge smile to excitedly jumping up and down. Many have later told me how meaningful it was to get positive feedback— often for the first time in their lives.

Science may be catching up to clinical observations. Recent studies have shown a decrease in the incidence of mental retardation occurring with ASD. Reports from the California Department of Developmental Services documented a major decrease in mental retardation in the state's population between 1987 and 1998. In 1987, 15 percent of children with ASD had no mental retardation and 16 percent were in the mild category. By 1998, 42 percent of those diagnosed with an ASD had no mental retardation, and another 18 percent were considered to be in the mild category. In fact, this research has been confirmed by 2009 CDC statistics showing nearly 60 percent of children with ASD have IQs greater than 70 by age eight. This significant change may be related to several factors. While the broadening of the ASD definition may account for some of this, it is possible that the methods for measurement and the expertise of the clinicians have improved. It could also be possible that the causes of ASD have changed in our modern society, resulting in differing profiles.

I suspect that, over time, this field will advance to the point that these assumptions about the intelligence of individuals with ASD will change and that their innate intelligence will be revealed. Many of the "lowest-functioning" children with ASD actually have at least an average, if not above average to superior, intellect. What is low functioning in these children is their motor-planning sequence, rhythm and timing systems—all affecting their ability to respond appropriately to test questions.

Myth #2: Empathy and ASD

A lack of empathy is often considered characteristic of ASD. My experience tells me, however, that the capability to understand another's intent or emotion is underestimated. Generally you know that another person is empathizing with you or your situation based on his response—how he looks at you, what he says to you or by his body language. The other person not only must understand what is happening to you but also must be able to plan and sequence appropriate responses. Because children with ASD have difficulty with sensory processing and motor output, their inability to respond or emote the same way we do doesn't necessarily mean they lack empathy. For emotion to show on your face, you need to have a well-developed range of expression. Due to motor-planning difficulties and the tone of their facial muscles, children with ASD often lack expression. Think of the motor control required when an infant puckers up to blow kisses or raspberries. These two actions are very difficult for a child with ASD.

I realized how much we are impacted by facial expression when I had the opportunity to spend time with identical twins. Both brothers had ASD, but with different challenges. Tim had major motor difficulties. His twin, Andy, had fewer motor challenges. When they were quiet, it was difficult to tell them apart. When active, Andy was happy and animated and had a wide grin and deep dimples, while Tim's face barely registered any expression. Because he lacked facial expression, I might have assumed that Tim was disconnected if I had seen him alone. Watching him with his twin, I realized they were communicating with each other. Tim was just as engaged as Andy; he simply expressed it in a slower and less dramatic fashion.

This experience reinforced for me one of the basic rules in working with children with ASD: what you see may not correlate to what the individual child is thinking or feeling. In fact, many of the children I have followed over the years are among the most empathetic children I've met. A measure for empathy is having theory of mind, which is defined as the innate ability to see the world through another person's eyes, another person's point of view. While your child may not pass testing procedures for theory-of-mind evaluations, watch him respond to the mood or emotional state of someone he loves and knows well. You can quickly tell he is a barometer of the other person's feelings. Your child may have difficulty in situations of conflict and respond with a behavior pattern of increased anxiety. He may have a temper tantrum, cry, hug or cling to you, seeking safety and relaxation. His identification with you, family members, caretakers, teachers and therapists is an especially strong tie—often a major lifeline. A child with ASD is not detached from life—quite the opposite—and he craves everything that life has to offer. It is his sensory processing, motor systems and rhythm and timing issues that seem to derail him most often from attaining this goal—a fact he is probably well aware of.

CHAPTER 3

What Causes Autism?

UNTIL THE 1960s, the primary cause of ASD was thought to be psychodynamic. The most popular hypothesis, coined by the psychiatrist Bruno Bettelheim, was that autistic behavior resulted from a cold and distant "refrigerator mother," who was unable to bond with her child, resulting in the child's rejection of all physical and emotional contact. Although this ludicrous theory has since been replaced by scientific facts, when I entered this arena in the 1990s, old notions still prevailed. I often encountered families where the mother was being treated instead of her child. Little emphasis was placed on developing a treatment plan or providing services for the child himself. Blaming the mother meant the child did not get the help or support he needed. Imagine the helplessness parents must have felt when their child made little progress. Fortunately, this perception is no longer the case. Although we may not have all the answers, research into the cause of ASD has significantly moved into the realm of modern science.

What follows in this chapter is a broad overview of biological influences relating to your child's symptoms. As a student of autism research over the past two decades, I have been pleased to see that the pace of discovery and potential answers to the causes of ASD has never been more accelerated than at the present time.

ASD: A Disorder of the Nervous System

Many pathways can lead to ASD. A single cause is probably not the culprit. In fact, it may be that there are many "autisms," each with different but interrelated causes that may affect brain development in similar ways. Each aspect of the pathway is a fertile area for research and can provide clues to potential causes of autism and how this may then affect brain function.

Possible Developmental Pathway to ASD

———

Genetics/Environment

▼

Structural Brain Change

▼

Underconnectivity between Neurons

▼

Changes in Learning Circuits

▼

ASD Symptoms

ASD is associated with a genetic predisposition. While the number, density and purpose of the implicated genes are not fully known, several candidates have been identified. To influence a child's development, these genes most likely require an environmental exposure (yet to be determined). These genes may lead down different pathways (genetic, infectious, metabolic, mitochondrial or immunological), each of which may predispose a child to developing ASD. These pathways may then influence the structural development of a child's brain and the creation of sufficient neural connections, resulting in less neuron-to-neuron transmission of information. Underconnectivity in key brain areas could then result in the child's difficulty processing key sensory information, learning, communicating and relating, as well as in typical behavioral symptoms of ASD. The role of the brain immune system as well as seizure disorders (see Chapter 16) also garner much interest as potential mechanisms that can further alter brain development and connectivity.

Whatever the exact pathway, many more children are being identified with clinical symptoms of ASD. Most likely all these factors will play a role. Therefore, multiple avenues of research may unlock a variety of potential treatments geared to each child's individual needs.

Genetic Research in ASD

Evidence for a strong genetic predisposition in ASD came from several sources. First, ASD has been associated with several known genetic disorders. Fragile X (the most common cause of inherited mental retardation) was discovered in 15 percent of ASD cases. This rate has decreased remarkably to 1 to 2 percent of all cases, probably due to improved diagnosis of Fragile X. Tuberous Sclerosis has been estimated to be associated in 3 to 9 percent of all ASD cases. Other chromosomal disorders may be present in as many as 5 percent of all ASD cases. Once these known genetic issues have been "ruled out" through proper testing, the remaining patients are said to have idiopathic (no known genetic cause) ASD.

In addition, data from twin studies suggest a 90 percent ASD concurrence rate for identical twins who share 100 percent of their DNA. If one identical twin has an ASD, the other has a 90 percent chance of also having an ASD, although the challenges presented may be different for each twin. The fact that the concurrence isn't 100 percent suggests that there are other contributing factors (such as environmental influences). The risk of concurrence for ASD in fraternal twins (nonidentical twins who share 50 percent of their DNA) is about 40 percent, depending on the study. This, too, suggests some interplay between genetic and environmental factors in these families.

It is well-known that if one sibling has ASD, the risk for each additional sibling is greater than the general population (2 to 7 percent), also suggesting genetic susceptibility. Family studies of ASD also show family members without ASD who may have some autistic traits, as well as increased prevalence of other neuropsychiatric disorders, such as mood disorders or Obsessive-Compulsive Disorder (OCD). Perhaps if a family member inherited only a few of these genes, he would exhibit some symptoms but not have ASD.

Earlier genetic studies suggested that the genetic heterogeneity (one disorder being caused by more than one gene) in ASD resulted from as many as five to seven genes. Today that number is thought to be as high as twenty to thirty genes. The interaction of these different genes could compound the likelihood of developing ASD. This genetic complexity speaks to the variability in symptoms among individuals with ASD, thereby making it difficult to determine the exact genetic causes of the disorder.

Autism Speaks Autism Genetic Resource Exchange (AGRE) is the largest private collection of genetic and phenotypic (behavioral) data for families with ASD that is available to researchers. Many of the genetic advances in the last five years using large databases, especially this one, involve identifying particular genes that are responsible for neural development and synaptic communication in the brain. Mutations in these genes, possibly related to environmental triggers, may be responsible for the changes in brain wiring present in individuals with ASD. It is important to note that most of these findings have been reported in family studies where there are multiple individuals affected with autism.

Intense genetic study of ASD has not yet found a set group of genes resulting in ASD. However, a group of researchers from Cold Spring Harbor in New York proposed a unified genetics model predicting two different risk patterns for ASD in the *Proceedings of the National Academy of Sciences* in July 2007. One pattern was for clear inherited susceptibility genes from parent to child (the same pathways that lead to blue eyes); the other was from new spontaneous, de novo mutations (a random occurrence that may be influenced by environmental factors). These researchers proposed that the new mutations occur in unaffected females who have no family history of autism. The females then pass the gene to their sons in a dominant fashion. This hypothesis came from the observation that girls are more resistant to the influence of the possible genes influencing ASD and that boys are affected in much greater numbers.

Another piece of interesting genetic information came from Harvard researchers Dr. Eric M. Morrow and his colleagues, who in 2008 identified families in the Arabic Middle East, Turkey and Pakistan who had considerable shared ancestors. In looking at this population, Morrow and his co-researchers searched for genes that must be inherited from a healthy mother and a healthy father for their child to have ASD. Mapping genes from these families confirmed many previous findings in genetics research, including missing DNA regions affecting at least six genes that play a role in ASD. Importantly, these six genes influence synapse development, which is the means of connecting one nerve to another. Synaptic connections among nerve cells allow the brain to form circuits that result in learning. When the information is not passed through these circuits as expected, learning differences can occur. This lack of synapse development could also correlate with the appearance of ASD symptoms in the second year of life. It is at this time in a child's development when synapses rapidly form connections. ASD could be caused by a genetic susceptibility that interferes with developing synapses. It is also possible that this missing DNA may represent missing on/off switches for autism-related genes. This development may have been turned off in ASD. Because learning and interaction can foster brain development, it is possible that intervening with appropriate treatment for your child can turn on what was genetically turned off, thus creating new pathways in his brain.

When synapses are underconnected, deficient amounts of neurotransmitters or chemicals are available for nerve-to-nerve communication. This lack of neurotransmission produces the behaviors we see in ASD. Many neurotransmitters may be changed in ASD and we attempt to modulate them through medical treatments (see Chapter 20). The key neurotransmitters include acetylcholine, dopamine, norepinephrine, GABA, glutamate and serotonin. Serotonin was one of the first neurotransmitters to be implicated in ASD. Abnormally high blood platelet levels of serotonin, as well as mutations in genes related to serotonin production, have been found. Dr. Diane Chugani has documented deficient amounts of serotonin and abnormalities of serotonin distribution throughout brains of children with ASD compared to their typical siblings. These genetic serotonin changes reproduced in mouse models have resulted in abnormal behaviors in the mice. This progression of studies links the genetics to what we observe in children. It is clear that this line of research will have a direct impact on treatment.

EPIGENETICS, OXYTOCIN AND ASD

Epigenetics refers to those factors that regulate genes, turning them on and off when needed. Epigenetic factors may alter the expected course of genetic expression, changing the way our systems function. In fact, a disease suspected to come from a gene alteration itself may not involve changes to the DNA sequence but rather may be due to changes in gene regulation. In fact, an epigenetic change was recently found to strongly correlate with ASD in a region of the genome that regulates oxytocin receptor expression. Oxytocin is a hormone that, when released into the brain, acts as a neurotransmitter influencing social interaction, having been linked to reading social cues as well as levels of trust. Studies have shown that oxytocin given to adults with ASD can improve social engagement and repetitive behavior. The epigenetic change recently discovered (higher methylation of the oxytocin receptor gene) may result in a person being less sensitive to the hormone and could be a factor in the social delays in ASD. This phenomenon may not be specific to ASD but awareness of it may prove valuable as a marker to individualized treatment with oxytocin or especially if future research reveals specific medications to modify this increased methylation.

Understanding the genetics of autism continues to be a primary research focus in ASD that will greatly inform parents and doctors about how to help children with ASD. Knowing the genes that predispose to ASD not only allows treatment to be developed but also will hopefully lead to preventative approaches. This knowledge allows your doctor to search for known ASD genetic associations (see Chapter 15).

Structural Changes in the Brain

No matter the genetic susceptibility, if your child has ASD, each potential cause appears to be related to a similar set of structural brain changes. Drs. Margaret Bauman and Thomas Kemper studied brain tissue from those who had died from a variety of causes but also had ASD and found that individuals with ASD had brains that weighed more than those of typical people. In addition, they identified individual neurons in the brain limbic system (the seat of emotional thinking and sensory processing) of those with ASD that were much less interconnected than usual. Fewer connections among these neurons were related to more symptoms of ASD. Also, the neurons in the cerebellum (the area of the brain involved in coordinating movement, walking and proprioception, as well as sensory processing) were much fewer than expected, making the brain appear more similar to a brain that is at an earlier stage of development. The good news is that neurons are present, making it possible for your child to develop new neural pathways through therapy.

Research in ASD continues to investigate brain anatomy and possible structural changes that might affect function. One finding that has been replicated many times is the clinical observation of larger than expected head circumferences in children with ASD. This large head circumference was thought to result from brain overgrowth in the first year of life. Studies by Dr. Eric Courchesne and his team at the University of California, San Diego, using MRI scanning studies to compare children with ASD to typical children have given us much insight into brain architecture. Their studies showed that children with ASD have slightly decreased head size at birth, followed by rapid acceleration of head growth at six to fourteen months. The researchers found that the larger the head circumference, the more challenges the child faces. Children with autism have bigger heads than children diagnosed with PDD-NOS and those children with PDD-NOS have bigger heads than normal infants. By two to four years of age total brain volume continues to be increased in children with ASD; however, at later ages, brain volume tends to normalize. This emphasizes that the course of brain development rather than the final product may be different in ASD.

The question that remained was whether the children's brains were bigger overall or whether there were certain parts of their brains that showed evidence of abnormal growth. Dr. Martha Herbert and her colleagues at Harvard Medical School performed MRI scans on boys ages seven to eleven with ASD and another group with developmental language disorders and found an increase in white matter in these subjects compared to unaffected children. The white matter is the part of the brain responsible for carrying information from one area to another. These findings suggest an ongoing process that occurs after infancy that impacts the connections within the brain. They also suggest to the researchers that these developmental brain white matter abnormalities in ASD either could be a result of abnormalities in brain growth or could indicate that the brain was not pruning unneeded connections—a process that happens in typically developing brains. Recent MRI studies have highlighted the frontal lobes, amygdala (part of the limbic system) and cerebellum as brain structures that can show abnormal growth patterns in children with ASD.

The Underconnectivity Theory of ASD

With the knowledge of these abnormalities in brain structure, the other related and key bits of information came from actual functional brain studies.

There is considerable research documenting clinical evidence of an alteration in neuronal function in ASD. Examples include a child's delay in executive planning (organizing, sequencing), language and reading comprehension or face-processing abnormalities (difficulty in recognizing people and understanding facial expressions), found in children with ASD compared to typical children.

The theory of underconnectivity in ASD was reinforced by the studies of Drs. Marcel Just and Nancy Minshew and their colleagues. Using fMRI studies, which monitored brain function while a subject performed a particular task, areas of brain activation were measured, as well as the degree of synchronization or correlation between various areas of the brain. The study looked at sentence comprehension in adolescents with high-functioning autism (HFA) with normal IQs compared to typical adolescents. The brain network in adolescents with HFA was found to be less synchronized and the integrating language center in the network much less active than typical. However, the center that processed individual words was more active in the brains of the HFA group than in those of the typical adolescents. In addition, the connectivity between the different brain areas was significantly lower in ASD than typical. It is likely that the underconnectivity results in difficulties with comprehension (complex skill) but enhanced superior ability in a localized simpler skill. It is well-known clinically that some with ASD can read (that is, decode words) beyond their expected age norms. However, when tested for comprehension of those same passages, they score far below expected levels. This is known as hyperlexia. Even if a child with ASD does not have hyperlexia, understanding differences through these types of brain studies begins to demystify why he may have simple abilities (such as knowing math facts or spelling) but great difficulty with more complex thinking processes, such as solving math word problems or writing paragraphs. It may also explain why children with ASD may have "splinter skills," such as the child who can hyperfocus and excel in one specific area, such as art or the memorization of certain facts, yet finds daily self-care activities most difficult.

SPLINTER SKILLS

Splinter skills are talents or abilities that don't necessarily relate to or connect with the other abilities of a child with ASD. Examples include extraordinary abilities in math, music or art. Children with a splinter skill are often called savants.

Follow-up studies by this research group showing this same pattern of underconnectivity in children with ASD for sound, vision and posture perhaps explain the difficulty with sensory processing, motor planning and learning and comprehension for children with ASD.

An important factor here is that each area of the brain shows activity, even though the functional connectivity in ASD may be less than expected. The human brain is incredibly plastic. Studies of individuals who have suffered traumatic brain injuries have demonstrated that the brain can adapt and be shaped through learning and experience. It is important for studies such as these to be conducted over the lifetime of individuals with ASD to document how their improved abilities, following individualized treatment, correlate with changes in brain function connectivity.

Other Potential Influences

There are many other factors that influence brain function, including diet, medications and hormones. The high tryptophan content in turkey, for example, may cause you to become drowsy following a large Thanksgiving meal. This amino acid is needed to manufacture serotonin, which gives you the feeling of well-being, even sleepiness. You may also have experienced the effects of low blood sugar (dizziness) or become groggy or hyper as a side effect of a medication. If you are a woman, perhaps your hormonal cycles affect your body regulation, including how you think. Diet, medications and hormones exert their influence in many different ways but eventually impact our thinking, learning and relating. Children with ASD are not exempt from these influences and, in fact, may experience greater and more unusual reactions. For example, a teenage girl with ASD may experience great difficulty with her mood during her menses.

Many nutritional factors have been thought to be especially important in altering developmental pathways. For example, vitamins such as B6 (folate), B12 and D are all needed to produce neurotransmitters. Magnesium, zinc and many other heavy metals are required for brain electrical conduction. Deficiencies or excesses of these nutrients can trigger symptoms. It is not known if nutritional factors are a primary cause of ASD or if a deficiency leads to symptoms that can include features of ASD. Such has been the case in a rare disease known as cerebral folate deficiency. Deficient amounts of brain folate result in developmental delay, motor regression, seizures, mental retardation and autistic features, which improve when treated with folinic acid.

Parent reports of remarkable improvements in their children treated with vitamin B12 (methylcobalamine) led researchers at the MIND Institute to investigate the effects of methyl B12 treatment in children with ASD. Vitamin B12 is an antioxidant that is needed in the metabolic pathways for cellular function. Although preliminary results of the study found no statistical difference between those children with ASD who were treated and those who were not, there were a few in the treated group who did show improvements in language and socialization. Further studies are being conducted on vitamin B12 and many of the other vitamin nutrients key to brain functioning.

The Role of the Environment

Environmental risks that may result in ASD susceptibility are a major concern for all. There are many types of potential environmental triggers—including chemical toxins and various infections that can influence genetic expression and/or immunologic responses, or cause direct damage to the developing brain—that could possibly predispose a fetus or infant to develop ASD.

The structural changes described in ASD suggest that whatever is causing the disorder is most likely taking place during fetal development and the first year of life. During these two critical time periods neuroimmune responses are most likely to be influenced by genetics, as well as maternal and environmental factors. Altering these responses in turn could modify the development of neurobiological brain pathways, which could result in abnormal anatomic changes, such as abnormal synapse formation, neuron connections and brain growth. To date, research has not discovered a direct environmental trigger that results in ASD. However, several environmental associations with ASD have been studied, including possible influences in the fetal environment as well as childhood vaccines.

The fetal environment is of special importance. Hypotheses for potential negative effects on fetal development include maternal vitamin deficiencies, immunologic alterations or exposure to toxins. An example of a link between maternal vitamin deficiency and abnormal fetal neural development is the connection between folate deficiency and neural tube defects, like Spina Bifida. Discovery of the connection between vitamin deficiency and the birth defects resulted in the preventive addition of adequate folate to maternal diets. There has been an interest in the study of the relationship of B and D vitamins to fetal brain growth and ASD. Maternal infection, especially viral, has been on a list of potential causes for ASD for decades. Examples of this association include fetal rubella infection and ASD susceptibility. Fetal response to an infection could be caused by a direct insult to the fetus by a virus transmitted across the placenta or by a reaction to maternal antibodies produced by a maternal infection. These antibodies can cross the placenta and affect fetal brain development through fetal inflammatory responses.

It is often said, "Genes load the gun. Environment pulls the trigger." To date, research has not discovered a direct environmental trigger that results in ASD. However, many plausible hypotheses are being actively studied. Hopefully, results of research with this emphasis will move the field much closer to discovering the cause as well as the prevention of ASD.

Vaccines—MMR and Mercury

The debated link between environmental toxins and ASD is probably one of the most controversial. The discussion has been generally focused on particular infant vaccines and their role in the development of ASD. Targeted in the debate are the mercury-containing substances (in the form of thimerosal) in vaccines, as well as the particular vaccines themselves (such as for measles).

Epidemiologic studies have yet to reveal any data implicating specific vaccines, especially the MMR (measles, mumps and rubella) or those containing thimerosal, as having a real risk of causing ASD. Specifically, research data on the MMR-autism connection show that there was not a major increase in ASD when the MMR vaccine was first introduced. The timing of an ASD regression has not been found to be clustered around or related to the MMR vaccination dates, the MMR vaccination rates have remained stable while the ASD diagnoses have increased, and the relative risk of ASD is not increased in vaccinated versus unvaccinated children.

Early in the debate a group of researchers led by Dr. Andrew Wakefield published findings in the journal the *Lancet* suggesting that virus particles in the MMR vaccination cause inflammatory reactions in the gut that increase toxin absorption and blood circulation through a "leaky gut." This connection to ASD has been refuted by several researchers. In fact, the *Lancet* recently stated that this research was flawed and pulled the article from the literature.

Mercury and Thimerosal

The mercury theory suggests that a mercury-containing preservative (thimerosal) in vaccines may have caused the increase in the numbers of children with ASD. Although a very small amount of thimerosal was used to preserve each vaccine vial, it was theorized that given the increase in the number of vaccines given to infants over time, the cumulative level of thimerosal for each infant in the first six months of life exceeded the Environmental Protection Agency (EPA) limit for methylmercury. This hypothesis appears reasonable given that methylmercury poisoning has symptoms resembling autism; that mercury can cross the blood-brain barrier into an infant's brain, where it could have potential toxic results; and that studies with genetically altered strains of mice have shown that they are more susceptible to thimerosal toxicity. However, there is no published evidence from scientific studies of increased mercury in children with ASD. In addition, the lack once again of any epidemiologic evidence proving a link between an increase of ASD with thimerosal-containing vaccines makes this hypothesis less likely. Currently, all pediatric vaccines in the routine infant immunization schedule are manufactured without the preservative thimerosal. As of January 14, 2003, the final lots of vaccines containing thimerosal as a preservative expired and were destroyed. Other vaccines (for example, influenza, tetanus and diphtheria vaccines for older children and adults) continue to be manufactured using thimerosal as a preservative—although influenza vaccine without the thimerosal preservative is also available.

The most compelling information refuting the mercury association with ASD came from 2008 California Developmental Services System data that showed an increase in ASD in California despite the exclusion of more than trace levels of thimerosal in nearly all childhood vaccines. Still unknown is whether a very small subset of individuals who develop ASD could be more vulnerable to the toxic effects of a compound such as mercury because of the way their system handles toxic products, either by limiting the body's ability to excrete the toxin from the body or to repair the toxic stress, such as with a mitochondrial disorder (see page 221).

Immunization Decision

From my days in general pediatrics, I know that a child getting shots can be stressful for the entire family. In some cases, there can be a reaction to the shot (swelling and pain at the injection site) but time and acetaminophen can take care of that issue. At other times a reaction can be more severe—hours of high-pitched crying or a seizure. I once gave a DTP (diphtheria, tetanus, pertussis) injection to a three-month-old baby and that night he had a seizure. We decided not to repeat this particular vaccination for him. When his younger sibling came to me at three months, because of the family history, we decided to hold off on the DTP. Much to everyone's surprise that night the three-month-old younger sibling had a seizure—without having had the vaccine. The vaccine and the seizure were not cause and effect, although with the older child it seemed to be so. Vaccines and ASD may also appear to be cause and effect, but this is more likely to be coincidence. In fact, I have seen many cases of regressive autism in children who have never been vaccinated.

I am alarmed that parents are choosing not to immunize their children— this happens especially with younger siblings of a child with ASD. In reality, when it comes to immunization, there is no win-win strategy. If you immunize your child, there are potential risks. If you don't immunize your child, there are definite risks. After generations of immunization we, as a society, have what is called herd immunity—enough of the population is immunized to protect those who are not. However, if that balance shifts, diseases that have not threatened the population for decades can emerge. There have been recent outbreaks of measles, for example, especially in communities where many children are not immunized. Some of these childhood diseases can be deadly, and at the very least, the illnesses themselves can be prolonged and uncomfortable. Some of the diseases affect neurological functioning, leading to severely debilitated children. A pregnant woman who is exposed to measles runs the risk of her child having birth defects. Schools, playrooms, playgrounds and pediatricians' offices are all places where children come in close contact with one another, as well as with other adults. Infectious diseases can spread easily from one child to another in these situations. When a child is not immunized, parents must be diligent to prevent exposure to any of these childhood illnesses, often limiting their child's ability to travel and socialize.

Each family has to weigh the risks and benefits of immunization. However, I believe we should always immunize. There are no scientific data that prove that immunizations cause ASD, but we do know the risks of infectious diseases that immunization can prevent. One technique that I have found to be useful is to immunize a child and follow up with blood tests to see if he attains immunity. If his immunity level is adequate, then these levels can be followed over time to decide whether further immunizations are required. The immunization schedule developed by the American Academy of Pediatrics was set forth to obtain herd immunity. However, on an individual basis, an immunization schedule can be set up to meet the needs of a particular patient. I understand how difficult this decision can be. Be sure to discuss this issue thoroughly with your doctor so you can work together on this critical issue while maintaining your child's well-being.

Is There an Autism Epidemic?

In 2009, the Centers for Disease Control (CDC) estimated that 1 in 110 children born in the United States has an ASD. At this rate nearly thirty thousand children are diagnosed with ASD every year. Because four out of five are boys, just over 1.5 percent of all males born could be affected. It is estimated that there are nearly six hundred thousand individuals living with ASD in the United States. When I first met Ryan and his family in 1989, autism was thought to be a very rare disease. Today public awareness of autism is clearly on the rise. Hardly a week goes by without media coverage of the issue, and most people know either a family or a child that is affected.

Some view this increase in ASD as an epidemic. Whether or not the number of children now diagnosed with ASD represents epidemic proportions stimulates much controversy. Some feel the increased numbers are due to improved case finding and expanded diagnostic criteria. Others believe today's increased numbers of children affected by ASD are due to a myriad of causes, including vaccines, medical conditions or environmental toxins. However, if the increase is due to improved diagnosis, then it stands to reason that there would be 1 in 110 affected older adults who had never been treated. Yet, we do not find a large number of underserved older individuals with ASD. In fact, it has only been over the past twenty years that all public systems have been impacted by individuals with ASD needing services. Schools, government systems, health plans and community organizations, as well as families and friends, have taken notice of the increased numbers of affected children. It is important to note that these increased rates have not been documented only in the United States, but studies in Europe, including Scandinavia, have also found as many as 1 in 84 children with an ASD. Most likely, these rates will be repeated worldwide once research tools are adapted to meet the needs of differing cultures and languages throughout the world's populations.

Studying Autism Spectrum Disorders: Future Directions

Aggressive research is needed to explore the reasons for the increased numbers of children affected with ASD over the past twenty to thirty years. Research must continue into all potential causes of ASD. Studies need to clarify which treatments are best suited for different challenges to help you and your doctor decide on the appropriate treatment approach for your child. There is much hope that all of this is possible.

- Today there is increased funding for research (one billion dollars in NIH funding in 2010).
- There is increased government understanding of the needs of this population. Whether there truly is an increased number of individuals with ASD or not, at least we do know there is a great number of children and adults with ASD who are underserved and require much more intensive services across the board.
- There is a large body of researchers educated in ASD and interested in solving the puzzle. Increasing numbers of articles are published daily on the causes and treatment of ASD, spanning the spectrum of possible research.
- Although there is a need for more manpower, the numbers of professionals who understand and treat individuals with ASD continue to increase.
- Autism Speaks (AS) sponsored the Autism Treatment Network (ATN), which is now educating doctors from many disciplines and developing treatment centers of excellence, where all professionals can provide care, pursue clinical research and train new professionals interested in ASD. I

hope this collaboration between medical centers across the United States and Canada can provide answers and treatment similar to what the childhood cancer treatment centers have accomplished.

■ Through multicentered treatment trial networks, such as those conducted through the ATN, the Research Units on Pediatric Psychopharmacology (RUPP), and ACTN (Autism Speaks–sponsored Autism Clinical Trials Network), possible medical conditions associated with ASD will be better understood and improved methods and use of medication will be developed.

■ Finally, ongoing research into possible environmental triggers, as well as complementary and alternative medicine approaches, will also aid you and your doctor in choosing from the huge number of existing treatments and approaches.

Over the past decade, there has been a tremendous amount of important and significant research about the causes of ASD. Research supports the theory that implicates alterations in brain wiring at the level of the synapse. Better understanding of the biological pathways helps researchers determine the types of treatments that may help your child and the preventive strategies that could be employed. The good news is that significant technological advances in the fields of genetics and neuroscience continue to move the research on autism forward at lightning speed.

PART II

Before Your Child Is Evaluated

CHAPTER 4

Understanding Social and Emotional Development

Because ASD is essentially a disorder of relating and communicating, it will be helpful for you to understand a typical infant's social and emotional growth. By understanding this typical course of development, you can better appreciate what doctors are looking for when they evaluate your child. This will also help you gauge his developmental progress. Your child can be assisted to meet social-emotional milestones—even if they do not occur on the usual timeline.

If I were to ask you, "What is the typical movement or language development of an infant?" you would have no trouble responding. We all know that an infant must sit before standing and stand before taking a step. Likewise, he babbles before uttering syllables and puts syllables together, such as "mama" or "dada" or "baba," before words, and words come before sentences. When it comes to the usual progression of social-emotional capacities, however, most of us have had little education in the development of social interaction and expect it to occur without effort. In fact, social and emotional development occurs in a similar way to any other ability—step-by-step. Research providing evidence for this gradual development and the influence of emotional responses on learning and personality began in the 1940s. Over the past twenty-five years, Drs. Stanley I. Greenspan and Serena Wieder expanded our understanding by showing the influence of emotions on the development of language and intelligence.

Typical Social-Emotional Growth

The Greenspan Social-Emotional Growth Chart, designed for typical infants and children, reflects a systematic development. It is similar in appearance to a child's height and weight growth charts in measuring changes over time. It was created by tracking the emotional growth of over one thousand infants in their first four years to assess the time frame during which they acquired the developmental capacities that supported their ability to relate and communicate.

Included in the Bayley Scales of Infant and Toddler Development (a tool that measures infant mental and motor development), the Social-Emotional Growth Chart documents the growth over time of the functional emotional developmental capacities (FEDC) in infants. The FEDC are represented by sequentially attained social-emotional abilities in children from birth to forty-eight months of age. These abilities begin with attention to and engagement with another person, move to developing simple emotional to-and-fro communication, progress to using these interactions to solve problems, eventually shift to using words as symbols or ideas to convey intentions or feelings and, finally, by thirty-one to forty-two months of age, give way to creating logical connections between emotions and ideas. When the social-emotional milestones are attained in a progressive fashion, several patterns emerge. The dark line on the chart in Figure 1 plots the median (average) growth for most typically developing children. The line above the median plots a course of more rapid social-emotional developmental progress, as would be seen in a precocious child who is an early talker. The three lines below the median show slower progress and indicate that a child may have increasing problems as he ages, either by losing ability (regression) or failing to make further progress (plateau). A child's growth below the median needs to be assessed.

The First Six Stages of Social-Emotional Developmental Growth

Six stages of early social-emotional growth generally occur in the first forty-eight months of a child's life. (Three advanced stages continue into adolescence and are covered in the following section.) These stages are briefly described, but for a complete discussion of each stage, see *The Child with Special Needs* and *Engaging Autism,* both by Stanley I. Greenspan, M.D., and Serena Wieder, Ph.D.

Stage One: Regulation and Interest in the World (Birth to Three Months)

This first developmental milestone occurs in the first three months with an infant's ability to maintain his attention and behavior while being interested in the full range of sensations (sounds, sights, smells and movement patterns) around him. Joint attention, the ability to enter into a state of shared attention with another person, is at the core of any meaningful communication. In infants, joint attention begins when a baby tunes into the sound of his mother's voice by quieting, becoming alert and turning toward the sound. This complex movement pattern shows attention to something happening in the moment. Initially, attention may be fleeting but over time it will extend

Figure 1: Patterns of Social-Emotional Developmental Growth

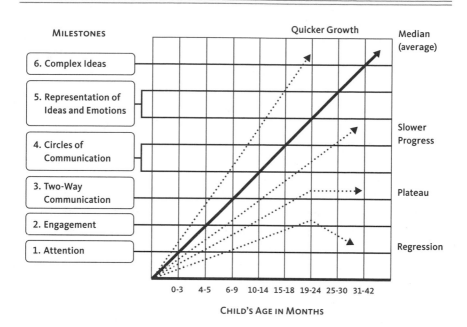

CHILD'S AGE IN MONTHS

for longer periods. An infant learns to use this interaction with his parent to self-calm and respond emotionally (known as co-regulation). He remains calm without over- or underreacting to what he hears, sees, smells and touches or to how he feels during this connection. Each infant has his own pattern of reacting to these external and internal stimuli: some jump and cry when a door slams; another may sleep through a party; some respond quickly to our overtures; some take more time. Parents naturally learn the best ways to help their infants soothe themselves and attend to their interactions. Through these interactions, infants learn about those close to them, distinguishing their sound, smell and feel.

We are well aware of the importance of shared attention in our social interactions. Have you ever entered a room, talking excitedly to a good friend or your spouse, who is reading the paper or a magazine? You are hoping for a reaction to what you've said, and he just looks up and says, "What?" You did not have his attention and realize you have to start over from the beginning. When we are in a conversation, if a friend looks away while we are talking, we might pause and ask, "Is everything okay?" We know instinctively that we must have shared attention first before we can engage someone in a conversation or any interaction. If your child is unable to sustain attention to you or to respond to sights and sounds in his environment, that might be what is causing your gut feeling that something isn't right.

Stage Two: Engaging and Relating (Two to Five Months)

This second developmental milestone describes an infant's ability to engage in relationships—especially with you, his loving caregiver. This ability for mutual emotional engagement can be seen through your infant's gazes, smiles, laughs and excited arm and leg movements that are synchronized with any exchange between you. This connection occurs with increasing depth and range over the first four to five months of life. For example, if an infant who has followed his mother's voice finds and makes eye contact with her and they both smile at one another, that internal sense of pleasure and warmth (experienced by both mother and child) is a true moment of engagement. Eventually, an infant uses his eye contact, sounds and movements to call her to him so he can feel the connection again and again. In fact, engagement (whether it is happy, sad or angry) dictates the stability of the relationship. If an engagement elicits pleasure, we will pursue it further. If it elicits fear or other discomfort, we will often retreat. In sharing these emotional connections, infants begin to learn patterns and understand what each pattern means to them. Getting Mom's attention, seeing her smile and getting fed, hugged or tickled bring the baby pleasure. On the other hand, an infant may have felt his grandfather's rough beard grazing his cheek, which causes him discomfort. Emotionally based interactions provide long-lasting memories so the next time he sees a man with a beard, he might cry. Childhood memories are created through sensory-motor and emotional experiences. If I mention Thanksgiving, you might smile while your spouse cringes. For some, holidays and family get-togethers were exciting, fun and pleasurable. For others, they were contentious and difficult. Even certain scents (such as a turkey cooking or a scented candle) can evoke memories of a situation, no matter what our age. This is what is meant by the dual code of experience: emotion and sensory input equals information.

If your child cannot sustain attention, he will have great difficulty experiencing engagement, because both capacities go hand in hand. This does not mean he can't experience this connection, but it may be fleeting or occur only under certain conditions. He may be self-absorbed when left alone and not respond to your voice, but when you throw him up in the air, he may look at you and giggle. How encouraging this can be! The goal is to support experiences that elicit his engagement as much as possible.

Stage Three: Two-Way Intentional Communication (Four to Ten Months)

Once your infant is able to sustain attention and engagement, he can enter into a two-way, purposeful, back-and-forth communication. This communication involves your child's opening and closing a circle of connection between you to convey his intentions. If he looks at a toy, you follow his lead by picking up the toy and showing it to him. He may smile, reach for the toy and thus close the circle. He has communicated a need or desire, and you have responded appropriately to that request, even a nonverbal one. Two-way communication is similar to a tennis match, except the goal with social communication is to keep the ball of interaction in play for as long as possible. An infant at this stage should be able to string two circles together—a series of back-and-forth communications. As time goes on, children are able to string more and more circles together. It's not uncommon by twelve months of age to have five to ten circles in a conversation throughout the day. Initially, two-way communication is done with gestures rather than words. If a baby wants to be picked up, he lifts up his arms, and then his mom reaches down to pick him up. The baby may not like being held face-to-face with Mom and wiggles until Mom turns him around to face forward. Thus, several circles of communication have been completed. This interaction requires fine tuning of the sensory-motor system, together with appropriate rhythm and timing on the part of Mom and baby in order to make these actions fluid and timely. For children with ASD, this is not an easy task. Their behavior may actually be random or impulsive rather than purposeful. It is not unusual for me to see a three- or four-year-old with autism who is not yet able to communicate his intentions in order to develop beginning circles.

Stage Four: Shared (Often Nonverbal) Problem Solving (Ten to Eighteen Months)

During this fourth stage infants make huge gains in their abilities as they learn to string together many circles of communication into a larger pattern (often more than twenty circles in one sequence) in order to solve a problem, often using gestures. You see this when your child takes your hand, walks you to the door, points that he wants to go out and perhaps vocalizes the sounds or words to communicate his intentions. This is a critical point in a child's life. During this time he not only practices shared problem solving but he also learns how to negotiate to get what he wants (such as pointing to a favorite item). In order to do this, he must use his understanding of what he sees, hears, smells and feels, as well as coordinate his movement and his body, including his mouth, to get the desired result. By solving these small problems all day long, infants learn patterns they can use in new situations. These interactions also help them regulate their emotional responses. If a child wants a favorite toy yet can't reach it, but is able to get his mom's attention by a sound, a look or pointing to it, and she gets him the toy, he may learn purposeful ways of getting something he wants before getting upset or frustrated. This, of course, requires a quick response by Mom, or the child may indeed begin to cry. During this stage, children become quite adept at using emotional signals as precursors to their use of language. Many children with ASD who have language are still unable to maintain the flow of the two-way communication, which is necessary for negotiating many of the most important emotional needs of life (like being close to others, exploring and being assertive, limiting aggression, negotiating safety and so on.) They require much practice at this stage of development.

Over time, the patterns become more complex. In order for a child to get you to take him outside, he has to have a goal and sustain many circles of interaction that were planned, sequenced and prioritized. Children with autism usually cannot consistently negotiate this level of social reciprocity to maintain a continuous flow of interaction. In general this is because it requires a great deal of self-regulation to maintain the required attention, engagement and prolonged reciprocity. Behavior patterns instead become repetitive and interests remain narrow. Fortunately, fostering emotionally based experiences with your child can help expand his interactions, setting the stage for further development.

Stage Five: Creating Symbols—Using Words to Express Ideas (Eighteen to Thirty Months)

By eighteen months, a child is physically able to produce words beyond sounds. In order for him to have language, words must have meaning for him. He will develop the connection through experiences that lead to creating ideas. These ideas create mental representations or symbols—also called symbolic thinking. This is seen when he engages in make-believe play or uses words, phrases or sentences to convey intention. When your child reaches this milestone, he begins to understand that symbols can be added to gestures to connect his thoughts and feelings to another's. For example, he understands that saying "baba" will get him something to drink and that it works consistently. Symbols (words) become connected with intent, which is a critical component of human behavior. The seeds for his attaining this ability are sown when he is thirsty and gestures to his bottle and you respond "bottle." These early patterns allow connections to be formed and give your child an example and means to express his needs. If a child is delayed in developing the earlier patterns, it would not be surprising to see an eventual delay in language. Your child's language development won't occur unless his earlier social-emotional levels are in place and in practice. Early representation can occur as soon as eighteen months of age. As symbolic thinking becomes more developed, it correlates with the explosion in language and expression of emotional feelings seen in most children around thirty months of age. During this stage, a child learns that words not only label items ("What's this?") but express desires ("I want"), actions ("Swing please") and feelings ("Hungry," "Tired").

Examples of early signs of symbolic thinking can be seen when your child begins to engage in pretend play and share ideas or experiences from everyday life, such as picking up a toy phone and talking into it or feeding you toy food. This develops into more complex pretend-play scenarios, often incorporating familiar emotional themes of nurturing and dependence. He may feed his teddy bear or put him to bed, or take the toy to the park to play. As your child's play continues to grow during this stage, even more complex problem-solving patterns will emerge involving his wishes, ideas and feelings, as can be seen in setting up a tea party where he chooses which stuffed animals get to attend or arranging farm animals that need to be taken care of by the farmer.

Stage Six: Emotional Thinking, Logic and Sense of Reality (Thirty to Forty-Two Months)

This milestone occurs when a child is able to make connections among different internal representations or emotional ideas—that is, to form complex ideas. This capacity is a foundation for higher-level thinking, problem solving and dealing with many of the emotional issues of childhood, such as separating reality from fantasy, modulating impulses and mood, and learning how to concentrate and plan. Although present in the early years, over time this skill becomes much more sophisticated and allows for the development of the higher-order thinking skills required for lifelong learning and interacting in relationships.

At this stage, your child will be able to think in concepts and abstract ideas, each linked to another in a logical fashion. He also demonstrates his capacity of emotional awareness of himself and others. He will explore the "how," "what," "where" and "why" of a situation, emphasizing time and causal relationships among themes. Pretend play in this stage becomes much more advanced as your child not only sets up a situation but also begins to review, compare and contrast, as well as build on what he has learned. Motives and consequences of actions are anticipated while your child also considers others' feelings and the lessons to be learned. As he acts out emotionally based themes, he begins to understand the relationships between experiences and feelings of his own and those of others. Playing tea party with family and friends expands into good guy/bad guy scenarios complete with pretend jails for those exhibiting bad behavior. "Magic" can occur: flight on a magic carpet is possible; fairy-tale heroes and superheroes battle evil stepmothers and bad guys. During this stage of development, separation, being lost, disappointment, fear and danger, rescue and safety, joy, anger and sadness are all explored in play and through interactions. Learning about how one feels is the first step to understanding what others might be feeling in similar situations (also called perspective taking or theory of mind).

Social relationships and advanced learning both require a capacity for emotional awareness, perspective taking, flexibility, expanding ideas, information gathering, hypothesis making, risk taking and a willingness to learn through experience. The foundation for all these that was begun during the early developmental stages is solidified during this particular period.

Advanced Social-Emotional Stages

Once the foundation for these first six stages is accomplished, your child is set to move into the higher-order thinking skills characteristic of the next three stages. Brief descriptions follow and full descriptions can be found in *Playground Politics* by Stanley I. Greenspan, M.D.

In typically developing children the first six stages will be achieved by age four to six. The next three stages develop on less of a timetable, sometimes requiring experiences throughout adolescence to fully acquire mastery.

Stage Seven: Multicausal and Triangular Thinking

This stage goes beyond concrete cause-and-effect relationships. It takes into account that there can be many reasons why things happen. During this time, a child must be able to imagine multiple possibilities. Theory of mind, or understanding how another might feel or act in any given situation, becomes clearer as children learn to "triangulate" in relationships. "I want to play with Ann, but she likes to play with Amy, so if I play with Amy, I can also play with Ann" is a subtle thought process children develop during this period.

Stage Eight: Gray Area Thinking

Beyond reasons for the how or why things happen, children begin to qualify and rank their ideas and feelings in this stage. "I like playing with Danny because he's better than I am at basketball, and I learn from him." "I need to act bold around Tim but quiet around Joe since it's more fun if I'm this way." Relativity, modulation, adapting and manipulating, as needed, are skills children learn when playing with others. In fact, playground time gives them the opportunity to practice and fine-tune these skills.

Stage Nine: Reflective Thinking

During this advanced stage, children begin to think about their own reactions to situations (through reflection) and change their behavior accordingly. "I am more anxious than usual. I wonder why and what I should do about it?"

Beyond these stages, children become more practiced at these skills as they experience more diverse opportunities that require thinking, novel thoughts, preplanning and so on. Eventually, they are able to strategize and play out various complex scenarios in their mind as they take on more responsibility. All of this is possible when there is healthy growth through the first six stages of social-emotional development.

Social-Emotional Developmental Milestones in ASD

If an infant has difficulty meeting any of the early milestones, his development can stall. Children with ASD, depending on the degree of challenge, especially in sensory processing and motor response, may miss not only the experience of these interactions but also the practice necessary to improve and expand their responses. The good news is that intervention has shown that proper support can help a child experiencing these delays to gain and develop all these stages.

Understanding these developmental levels and what gets in the way of your child's attaining them is essential to getting him the help he needs. Understanding his individual sensory and motor profile and the way in which he responds and learns from his world will help you connect and share with him to solidify his developmental milestones. By understanding typical social and emotional growth patterns, you can better determine where your child is having trouble and how best to help him. To see these stages in action, you can view videos (at www.icdl.com) demonstrating the range of responses in typically developing preschoolers as well as in children with ASD during treatment sessions.

CHAPTER 5

How Your Child Experiences the World Around Him

The Sensory-Motor System in Action

WHEN TOMMY, a three-year-old, first came to see me, he immediately began licking the edges of the tables and chairs in my office. "Dr. Ricki, I just don't get it," his mother said. "Tommy has such a need to lick—but it's not just that. He will only wear a few shirts. He throws major tantrums during haircuts, so I have to cut his hair and nails while he's asleep. Loud noises make him frantic. He's so uncoordinated, he can't hold a pencil or a spoon and he's always bumping into furniture. How could autism be the cause of all of this?" If you have similar concerns about your child, you are not alone. These confounding behaviors can profoundly impact the quality of your child's life and get in the way of your emotional connection with him. Many of these behaviors are often due to challenges with your child's sensory-motor system.

As shown in Figure 2 the sensory-motor system operates as a feedback loop. We receive sensory input through all our senses: vision, hearing, taste, touch, proprioception (feedback we get from our muscles and joints), smell, vestibular (balance and how we experience our body in space) and interoception (from our internal organs), and then react to that input. Sensory information is processed through the sensory pathways in the brain and is then connected to the motor system. Motor pathways, also found in the brain, stimulate the nerves and spinal cord so that muscles will move in an appropriate response. This system can operate very quickly—think of touching a hot stove and how immediately you recoil. Now imagine if you couldn't properly interpret what you had just touched or if you didn't feel pain from the heat. You might not respond appropriately. While this is an extreme example, the inability to process sensory information—either misinterpreting the input or

Figure 2: Sensory-Motor Feedback

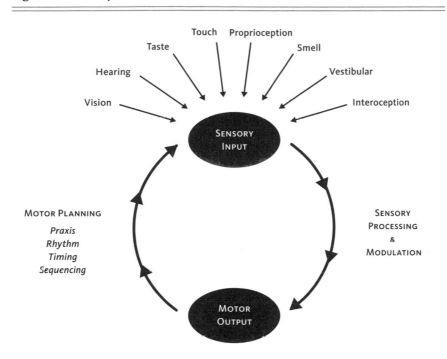

having a delayed response—is what happens to children with ASD all day long. Appropriate responses to sensory stimulation are learned. Every time we receive new sensory input, it helps us refine the physical or motor response to that input. We become more skilled over time with practice. Athletes are finely tuned in this area. Prima ballerinas or golf pros have an excellent sense of their bodies, where they are in space, and can maneuver accordingly. In contrast, many children with ASD have difficulty with movement and often have trouble simply sitting properly in a chair.

Types of Sensory Input

Sensory processing or sensory integration refers to the way we make sense of and use sensory information—the sounds, sights, smells, tastes and movement around us. Sensation provides us with information about our environment and our bodies so that we may respond purposefully and successfully. Sensory integration provides a foundation for motor and social skills. It is also responsible for our ability to maintain attention, as well as organize participation, in daily activities and routines. A child's sensory processing and integration is assessed by examining his pattern of responding to the sensory information around him. There are two primary categories of sensory processing: sensory modulation and sensory-based motor planning (praxis).

Sensory Modulation

Sensory modulation describes how well our response is matched to the sensory stimuli we experience. If your child is overresponsive to sound, he may get extremely upset when he hears a lawn mower in the neighbor's yard and may run around the house covering his ears and repeatedly crying "eeeee." If your child is underresponsive to sound, he might not flinch at extremely loud noises or may turn up the volume on the television beyond what others in the house can tolerate. A balanced response to sound (and other sensory information) allows your child to maintain a calm, alert state for learning and participating in various activities throughout the day without being unduly distracted or disturbed by the sensory information around him.

Sensory processing has an impact on emotional functioning. Emotions and sensory stimuli can predispose a person to respond more strongly to an

How Your Child May React to Sensory Information

	Overresponsive	Underresponsive	Seeking Out Sensation
Tactile	Dislikes being touched or hugged, hair cutting or washing, teeth brushing, nail clipping; avoids touching messy substances; complains about tags and/or seams in clothing	A hard fall causes no reaction; not always aware of touch	Bumps into people or furniture to get physical contact/sensation; seeks out messy substances, such as finger paints
Auditory	Puts hands over ears to block out sound; shows extreme fear to sounds like vacuum, sirens, toilet flushing, coffee grinder and so on	Difficult to get child's attention; seems oblivious when spoken to; doesn't look around for the source of sounds	Craves loud noise or music; likes to talk, hum or make noise
Movement and Motor Planning	Afraid of heights; dislikes spinning, swinging or sliding; needs continuous physical support from an adult	Does not object to being moved, but doesn't initiate much movement; once movement starts, can keep going for a long time; does not realize he is falling and makes no attempt to break fall	Needs to keep moving as much as possible; may repeatedly shake head, rock back and forth or jump up and down; craves intense movement experiences, such as bouncing on furniture; likes active play (teeter-totter, swinging)

Continued...

How Your Child May React to Sensory Information, *continued*

	Overresponsive	Underresponsive	Seeking Out Sensation
Visual	Overwhelmed by moving objects or people; avoids direct eye contact; complains of sunlight or that lights are too bright; may squint in ordinary light	Unaware of light/dark contrast; unaware of movement; bumps into moving objects; delayed response to visual information, such as an obstacle in his path	Seeks visual stimulation, such as finger flicking or spinning; seeks bright lights, including direct sunlight; stares at moving fans
Olfactory	Complains of strong odors or smells that may not be evident to others	No response to typically offensive odors	Seeks strong smells; sniffs everything, including hair and clothing
Food Taste or Texture	Aversion to certain tastes/ textures of foods; gags often	Eats most foods; no reaction to unusual textures or tastes	Licks nonfood objects; seeks items to put in mouth
Pain	Light touch can cause a major reaction	Does not react to pain or notice extreme hot/cold temperatures	Engages in skin picking, scratching, self-injurious behavior
Proprioception, Vestibular (orientation in space, balance)	Prefers not to move; avoids weight-bearing activities, such as running, jumping	Awkward motor movement abilities; fatigues easily; appears weak, floppy, loose-limbed; poor grip; has low tone	Bumps or crashes into objects or people; rubs hands on tables; craves active movement, such as pushing, pulling; likes being squeezed or swaddled
Interoception (internal body stimuli)	Tantrums easily when hungry or thirsty; prefers wearing as little clothing as possible	Unaware of hunger, thirst, toileting needs; no sense of satiation; will keep eating beyond hunger; oblivious to body temperature (won't remove jacket if too warm)	Craves strong tastes, such as very spicy or sour; may prefer foods (or bathwater) to be either very hot or very cold

event regardless of whether the situation is primarily emotional or sensory. One child may throw a tantrum about getting dressed because he doesn't want to go to school. Another child may throw a tantrum about getting dressed because the tag in his shirt bothers him. Some sensory stimuli can be calming and comforting, which will allow your child to better handle upset caused by sensory stimulation. For example, if loud sounds upset him, gentle touch may help him to calm down.

Sensory response patterns can vary for each sensory input and, particularly for children with ASD, can change moment to moment. See pages 52–53 for examples of overresponsive, underresponsive and seeking out sensation.

Sensory-Based Motor Planning (Praxis)

Sensory-based motor planning (praxis) is the ability to use the hands and body in a skilled task, like playing with toys, using a pencil or a fork, building a structure, cleaning up a room or working in the yard. A child with praxis issues can have great difficulty with any of these simple tasks. Praxis includes knowing what to do as well as how to do it. Motor planning involves making adjustments as needed to plan and fine-tune, sequence and time body movements. New activities require more praxis than routine daily activities. Praxis helps your child master repeated tasks so that they become habits and routine. Praxis depends on the accurate processing of sensory information. When you sit in a chair, you don't think much about how you do it. It's an automatic response, and until someone asks, you don't pay attention to the pressure of your back against the backrest, your bottom on the cushion or your feet on the floor. When you think about sitting in a chair, you become aware of the sensory input that is keeping you there, stable and comfortable, as well as what would be required to shift your body and stand up. If your child has insufficient praxis or sensory processing to adequately inform his motor system, he will have difficulty getting into and sitting in a chair with ease. He may lie in the chair or continually squirm or try to climb, perhaps unsuccessfully, into the comfort of your lap. Praxis allows us to get our needs met. If we are thirsty, we will find a way to get something to drink—sometimes without much thinking about the steps or planning required to get a glass of water. A child who does not have adequate sensory-motor modulation (praxis) might be thirsty and know he wants something to drink, but won't know how to make it happen. His being thirsty and unable to satisfy his thirst may result in a tantrum. Praxis allows our intentions to become purposeful. Children with poor praxis may make slow developmental progress. It may be that one of the earliest signs of ASD—not pointing for desired objects—is due to difficulty with praxis.

Some children with ASD learn a skill but need to relearn it every time they attempt it. Their "body map" does not retain the information they need to effectively and efficiently move through the tasks they face throughout the day.

The Body Map and the Brain

Scientific study has shown that our sensory-motor processing systems are laid out systematically in our brains in a body map in which areas in the brain correspond to our sensory input and motor output. These body maps are complex and interconnected throughout the brain. No two people's are exactly alike.

The cerebral cortex is where the majority of the body maps are located. (See Figure 3.) The key areas of the brain for body maps include the following:

- The **occipital lobe**, located at the back of the brain, is where visual input is processed. This information is then sent to the parietal lobe. Between these two lobes the vision-based body maps are located.
- The **parietal lobe** is filled with many body maps that deal in physical sensation (sensory processing), the space around the body and three-dimensional spatial relationships.
- The **frontal lobe** is where voluntary and skilled movements are coordinated. It also is responsible for all the "executive functions," such as planning. It is the location for higher-ordered thinking skills, which include moral reasoning, self-control and parts of language. Many body maps are located in the frontal lobe.
- The **temporal lobe** processes auditory input. In addition, it connects many of the language and emotional processing functions.

The sensory input that comes from the system of touch and proprioception was first mapped out in the 1930s by neurosurgeon Dr. Wilder Penfield, who conducted careful experiments to locate the neural pathways that related

Figure 3: Brain Structure and Function

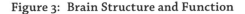

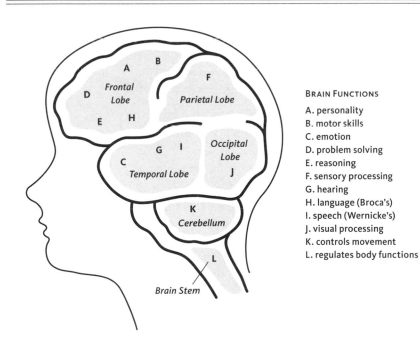

BRAIN FUNCTIONS

A. personality
B. motor skills
C. emotion
D. problem solving
E. reasoning
F. sensory processing
G. hearing
H. language (Broca's)
I. speech (Wernicke's)
J. visual processing
K. controls movement
L. regulates body functions

to sensory inputs and motor outputs. He then drew the sensory-motor areas on a schema of the brain that seems fairly consistent from person to person. This "map" shows the relationship between the neurons and their related body parts. For example, sensory input and processing from the fingers are all located near each other. We would expect this to be the case because extreme fine-tuning is required to be able to coordinate the fingers for maximum use of the hand.

A recent study done using functional MRI (fMRI) scanning of the brains of children with ASD who have severe motor-planning issues has suggested that their brain maps may be so underconnected that the neurons of the fingers are actually far away from the neurons of the thumb. This could be why your child may have difficulty holding utensils or pencils and with handwriting. All children with ASD have some degree of motor-planning issues. It is likely that their body maps are incomplete, and this lack of connection results in difficulties in coordinating movement.

Sensory Processing Disorder (SPD)

Sensory processing disorder (SPD) is caused by the inability to use information received through the senses in order to function as expected in daily life. In children with ASD (unless they have an additional medical problem), sensory information is sensed normally through the usual body system (such as ear, eye, skin) but it is processed (and interpreted) abnormally. Unlike a sight- or hearing-impaired child, a child with SPD experiences the sensations from sight, sounds, touch, taste, hearing and movement, but they simply don't interpret them accurately or respond appropriately.

There are three types of sensory processing disorders:

■ **Sensory modulation disorder** causes problems with timing and synchronizing simultaneous sensory messages. If your child overreacts to a stimulus, he has a low threshold for that stimulus; if he underreacts to that stimulus, he has a high threshold. If your child is overreactive, you may feel like you're walking on eggshells trying to avoid igniting an explosive outburst or tantrum. Your underreactive child could have a large piece of furniture fall next to him and not react. If your child is sensory-seeking, he craves sensory input and will seek it through making contact with the objects and people around him, including crashing into furniture, touching anything within reach or leaning on other people.

■ **Sensory discrimination disorder** describes children who have difficulty distinguishing between sensory inputs. A child may have problems distinguishing foreground from background, auditory from visual and, in particular, three-dimensional (visual-spatial) cues. He may also have difficulty coordinating the proper sense with motor output in order to catch a ball or to play hide-and-seek. He never really understands how he fits or moves in his environment and may not know if his next step will cause him to fall. This inability to judge space and distance can be frightening and make him feel anxious.

■ **Sensory-based motor disorders** include postural disorders and dyspraxia. Postural disorders cause a child to have poor posture. He may not understand how to coordinate his body movements or integrate his right side with his left (poor bilateral coordination), making it difficult for him to pass an item from one hand to the other. He may be unable to get both sides of his body working together as needed to jump rope or ride a bicycle.

Dyspraxia is caused by a disconnection between sensory processing and motor planning. Children who have dyspraxia have difficulty planning and executing a sequence of actions—particularly complex ones. A child may know what he wants to do (intent) but is unable to perform the steps to get it done. If your child has dyspraxia, it can be difficult for him not only to use toys but also to organize them into a pattern, for example, setting up for a tea party. Praxis/motor planning can affect the gross motor skills that govern large muscles or the fine motor skills of the hands, which are needed for gestures and things like buttoning and unbuttoning. Praxis can also affect facial and oral muscles, which are required for forming facial expressions and expressing language. Apraxia is a term that is used for when expressive language is so disorganized that a child can produce only sounds or utterances instead of syllables. He cannot progress to words and sentences. He may have plenty to say but lacks the muscle coordination necessary to express himself verbally.

Autism and Sensory Processing Disorder (SPD)

Children with autism have difficulties in all sensory processing areas: modulation, discrimination and motor planning and sequencing. However, the degree of challenge in each of these areas is highly variable. The more challenged your child is with sensory processing, the more challenged he may be with autism. All children with ASD have SPD, including those with high-functioning autism and Asperger's. Their SPD makes it more difficult for them to take in, organize and plan in order to interact and develop relationships, as well as to respond appropriately to the various stimuli in a constantly changing environment. Author Temple Grandin describes a major sensory modulation disorder that caused her to be so overloaded by sensory input that she created a "squeeze machine" as a means of calming herself during these periods. The squeeze machine (which she invented) allowed her to give herself a total body squeeze that she could control.

Some children with ASD will do whatever they can to screen out incoming sensory input. This may be what your child is doing if, while watching a favorite video, he covers his ears in anticipation of a stimulating scene. Decreasing the sensory input will make the scene more tolerable. If your child squints while being pushed on a swing, he may be decreasing his visual input in order to deal with the changes to his balance he experiences while swinging.

Donna Williams, in her books *Nobody Nowhere* and *Somebody Somewhere,* describes what it is like to have sensory discrimination issues. The inability to filter the sensory and visual-spatial information around her led her to spend days inside, unable to leave her house. Many of the most challenged children with ASD say they cannot process two senses at once. They describe being able to hear but not see, or to see but not hear. For children with autism, trying to use more than one sense at a time is often very confusing and painful.

Recent research by Dr. Stuart Mostofsky and his colleagues shows that children with ASD, even if designated "high functioning," are profoundly dyspraxic compared to typically developing children. The result is that these children have impaired motor imitation (waving goodbye) as well as difficulty with skilled gestures, such as using utensils (hammering a nail, cutting with scissors or writing with a pencil), and this directly relates to their degree of difficulty with socialization. These researchers suggest that dyspraxia may indeed be a core feature of ASD or at least a significant marker for a child's underlying brain processing difficulties.

Sue Rubin, who is showcased in the Academy Award–nominated documentary *Autism Is a World,* demonstrates what it is like to be locked in a body with a severe apraxic sensory-motor disorder. Sue was diagnosed at the age of four. Her challenges were so overwhelming that she could barely complete simple tasks and had difficulty producing words. As a teen she was given a keyboard and assistance, and it was discovered that she had been learning all along. She immediately started doing age-appropriate schoolwork, which eventually led to her attending college.

Many children with autism are described as having underreactive muscle tone. From a medical point of view they don't have hypotonia, which is a muscle disease, but they do seem floppier and looser limbed than their contemporaries. If your child lies on the floor like a sack of potatoes, he is getting poor information from both his proprioception and vestibular sensory functions. This leads to a decrease in motor-output information into his muscles to instruct them to increase their tone.

I often feel that children with ASD are so overwhelmed by sensory-motor issues that I might not be seeing them if not for these issues. In addition, their unique profile of sensory-motor processing often defines the behaviors we see. For example, if your child has a poor body map and is a sensory seeker, he might run into chairs and people in order to get needed pressure. This sensory stimulation activates his body map, giving him a better sense of his body and relationship to the world.

It is important for all of us who work with children who have ASD to understand that the behaviors we see can often be explained by these underlying sensory-motor processing issues. Whether your child is avoidant, hyperactive, self-absorbed or repetitive really depends on his response to sensory inputs. Your job (and that of his therapists) is to help him manage these processing issues by supporting him and approaching him in such a way that he can circumvent these challenges. For example, if he is overloaded by sensory input (too many loud sounds), you can counter the input from the environment by interacting with him in a soothing, calm manner. When this occurs, you will be much more able to get him regulated, interactive and spontaneous. When you are armed with information about how your child experiences the world and can share this with others who work with him, it is a huge step for helping him move forward and helping him deal with the natural ups and downs that occur in daily life.

Rhythm and Timing

We all understand, often subconsciously, the dance of our interactions with others. In fact, we expect it of adults we connect with on a regular basis. When all our systems are working in concert, we can be relaxed, spontaneous, creative, humorous, compassionate and respectful all at the same time. The ability to receive information from the world and others, and successfully act on it, pulls together the full complement of our cognitive, emotional, sensory, proprioceptive and motor abilities.

When these systems are not coordinated, we make errors. As children, when we make a misstep (like blurting out in the conversation), we may receive a wide range of reactions—discipline from a teacher, frustration from friends or family or redirection from an adult. As an adult, these social errors are less tolerated and can disrupt the flow of communication between two people engaged in conversation or a relationship.

A number of elements combine to make this exchange flow smoothly. A few of the most obvious include a sense of space, sensory processing and motor-planning abilities. We all know our comfort zone regarding personal space. We understand who we can be close to (a loved one) and what the customary distance is for light social talk or to conduct business. When our comfort zone is infringed upon, we may feel threatened and will, in most cases, step back. Our sensory systems will be on high alert, picking up visual, auditory or olfactory clues to help us understand how comfortable we are (such as retreating if we pick up an unsavory smell) and assessing the non-verbal clues for us to judge if the content we hear is adequately reflected by the speaker's intonation and gestures. This multisensory processing can be thrown off if one sensory pathway is compromised, for example, speaking with someone who does not make eye contact.

Motor planning is required to match another's rhythm and timing (pace) in a conversation. In fact, if both are not in sync, the reciprocity quickly falls apart. Coordinating inputs and outputs—and the sheer complexity of that coordination—causes problems for children with ASD. While their difficulty with interaction is often ascribed to not having a theory of mind, the ability to see things from another's perspective, I find that adjusting my speech and movement to match a child's unique sensory profile enables him to engage and connect with me. This reciprocity can be difficult for your child—he may need more time to process input or output or both. Patiently waiting for his response can help maintain communication. Jumping in to fill the pause or reframing the question before he has had a chance to answer may overwhelm him, and he may retreat. Learning your child's particular response time will help in your communication with him. When you exercise patience and try to match your child's particular rhythm, he will visibly brighten and two-way communication can begin to flow. It's not always easy to adjust your innate response time. However, if you are mindful of your child's response time and are careful not to overload him with information, by engaging in a nonverbal or verbal conversation (at his own pace) you will help him to build on his ability to communicate. With practice, he can increase the speed of his responses.

Early Movement Difficulties in Children with ASD

Early signs of praxis delays in infants later diagnosed with ASD were identified in studies by Dr. Philip Teitelbaum. He evaluated movement by reviewing videotapes of children with ASD that were taken when they were infants. He noted consistent motor-planning-related concerns in these infants that included a characteristic "tent shape" of the mouth as well as decreased facial expression due to reduced facial muscle tone. He also noted that they had difficulty rolling back to front at four to six months, sitting up without falling over at six to eight months and delayed crawling after eight months of age. If a child was crawling, he would favor one side. Dr. Teitelbaum also described a delay in the development of protective motor responses when walking after twelve months. There was a tendency in these children to fall directly to the floor rather than extending their arms to stop the fall.

Dr. Teitelbaum, without knowing the current status of the children, reviewed videotapes of them as infants and was able to identify those who would later be diagnosed with ASD. In addition, when looking at tapes of identical twins, both of whom had ASD, but one with more challenges than the other, Dr. Teitelbaum was able to discern which twin would eventually become more challenged based on the difference in motor-system development between the two children at six months.

I have seen identical twin brothers with differing motor patterns and challenges as well. I was most struck by the difference in their facial expressions: I could easily read emotion and feeling in the brother with less challenge and was less able to read the face of the more challenged twin. Being able to understand the expression that we see on someone's face is essential to our emotional relationships. No wonder early therapists in this field interpreted these children as not wanting to interact—because they could not read affect (expression) on the children's faces. We now know that children with ASD wish to be part of the world but their bodies do not coordinate enough to make it possible for them. It would seem from these studies that sensory-motor integration is not only a key feature of ASD but also is present very early on—well before the red flags of loss of language and lack of social reciprocity are noted. In fact, difficulties in sensory-motor integration often underlie these losses.

If motor planning is a very early feature of autism, it is easy to see how early communication would be impacted. Babies communicate with us in nonverbal gestures before they have language. In fact, these gestures become complex in the first couple of years of life and parents rely on them in order to figure out what an infant is thinking and feeling. If a baby is not developing a system of gestures that is linked to his sensory needs, then this early form of two-way communication between parent and child will not develop as expected. Without these early stages of communication further progress can be derailed.

Auditory Processing

Auditory processing is a challenge for the majority of individuals diagnosed with ASD. It involves understanding speech (receptive language) as well as using speech (expressive language). Although many children with ASD are eventually able to use words, they don't often use them correctly within the appropriate context. Your child may have an apparent strong command of language (sometimes those with Asperger's syndrome are called "little professors") and can use sophisticated vocabulary to talk about preferred subjects, but he may be more challenged when it comes to a conversation in which he must interpret another's social, physical and verbal cues. He may have an enormous vocabulary but may be less likely to be able to "read" another person.

Receptive language requires not only proper functioning of the ear and its connection to the brain, but the information must be processed accurately through neurons in order to give an appropriate response. You may have thought that your child was deaf because loud sounds didn't trigger any reaction. However, other sounds that don't register with you can elicit a response from him—such as the hum of the refrigerator. While he may be missing foreground noise, he may process a good deal of the noise occurring in the background. These subtler noises may affect him in the same way that a loud noise affects you—they can cause discomfort or be a distraction. The term for the inability to process sound is verbal auditory agnosia (VAA). It is interesting to note that children with ASD who have VAA are more likely to have abnormal EEG patterns that reveal slow or inadequate processing of information through the temporal lobe (the location of the sensory body map for hearing, speech and language). Once given appropriate treatment, these children can have improved receptive language abilities, and the degree of VAA can be reduced remarkably. If your child has decreased receptive language, it is imperative to have him evaluated for possible deafness or hearing loss due either to middle ear dysfunction (often caused by fluid produced by ear infections) or to damage of the hearing nerve itself. Hearing function can be assessed through traditional hearing tests that measure ear drum function as well as stimulated nerve evaluations known as the auditory brain stem response (ABR). If you discover that your child has a hearing problem, it does not rule out the fact that he may also have an ASD. But correcting his hearing issue can help in his receptive language abilities.

Over the years, parents have told me that they feel that their child's receptive language is fine. Yet when I see the child in the office, it is clear to me he is having trouble understanding what is being said. The child may be compensating for his lack of auditory skills with enhanced visual ability. Many children later diagnosed with an ASD may not respond or understand when the person is speaking behind them, but if they can see the person talking, they become attentive and engaged and respond appropriately. Your child's visual system may help compensate for the delay in his auditory pathway. Using visual cues when you speak to him can help him better understand what you are trying to say. If he has auditory delays, it is important to always speak to him when you are in his line of vision. It also helps to use gestures and facial expression to enhance what you are saying.

Research has shown that auditory processing timing can be delayed due to many conditions, including dyslexia, which has minor delays in processing, and ASD, which has much more significant delays.

Sight and Vision

Sight is what our eyes see. Vision is what our mind understands about what we see. Children with ASD often learn more about their world through their visual system than their auditory system. Author Temple Grandin describes this in her autobiography, *Thinking in Pictures:*

> *I think in pictures. Words are like a second language to me. I translate both spoken and written words into full-color movies, complete with sound, which run like a VCR tape in my head. When somebody speaks to me, his words are instantly translated into pictures. Language-based thinkers often find this phenomenon difficult to understand, but in my job as an equipment designer for the livestock industry, visual thinking is a tremendous advantage.*

Acquiring a functional visual system is also a developmental process. A newborn baby may not readily see very much beyond his hands. When you take your finger and touch his palm he may grasp it. Eventually he begins to look at your finger. Thus tactile sensory input guides his sight, beginning to organize his visual system. With time the baby can visually locate a desired object, reach for it and pick it up. By six months he begins to move a toy with his hands using his visual system to examine it from many angles. By twelve months he can see the toy from any direction and know it is his toy. Over time the visual system learns to direct both his brain and his body—first seeing then understanding, remembering and using what is seen. This requires integration with his other sensory and motor systems. For example, he learns to visualize his toy and connect with his auditory system to say "car." Eventually in middle childhood the visual system is fully connected with the brain network so that he can see an object such as a hot stove and know it could be hot without touching it.

While children with ASD may depend on their visual abilities, these may not be as developed as would be expected in a typically developing child, resulting in visual behavior patterns that interfere with their ability to react and interact with their environment. In fact, visual development is unpredictable in children with ASD. For example, when a five- or six-year-old must touch or taste everything in order to understand what it is, then his tactile or oral sense is directing his body and brain rather than his visual system. This narrows his world to only objects he can handle or taste. His visual system may be functioning at a level of an infant. Delays in visual development then form the basis for visual patterns seen in children with ASD. These include poor eye contact, use of peripheral or central vision, visually sweeping the room rather than looking at or finding specific items and looking past, rather than at, people and objects.

Understanding how your child sees is the first step to evaluating his visual ability. To see accurately our eyes (including their brain connections) and the muscles that coordinate eye movement must be fully functional. **Visual acuity** describes how accurately we see an image. This is measured when your doctor determines how precisely you can read an eye chart. The goal for most eye exams is 20/20. This means that if you have 20/20 sight, you can see clearly at twenty feet what should normally be seen at that distance. Children with ASD often have super-acute sight. When tested, they could have 20/10 sight, meaning they can accurately see images at twenty feet that could normally be seen at ten feet—twice as far as typical. If your child's sight is acute, he could be distracted by all visual stimuli. He may be drawn to what he can see in the distance rather than what is right in front of him, or he may be so focused on all items in his space that his eyes may flit distractedly from one thing to another. It is interesting to note that if a child with ASD and this acute sight later develops myopia (nearsightedness) and needs glasses, he is often more able to attend to his immediate surroundings.

Precise coordinated eye movements are needed for focusing, eye tracking and binocular vision (eyes working together). All are required for maintaining eye contact and spatial awareness, even hand-eye coordination. All are potential concerns for children with ASD. However, if these skills are delayed, they can be learned.

It is important to also determine your child's **field of visual attention.** *Visual field* is a medical term that describes how much of the retina is used in sight. While the visual field in children with ASD is generally intact (they have full use of their retina), it often appears that they are not seeing in all directions. For example, when they play with toys or other objects, they often narrow their focus centrally to seemingly exclude all around them. It is not due to a problem with sight, but the difficulty they have coordinating their sight and body movements to look around. If your child seems to behave this way, it is important to determine the dimensions of his visual space. In most cases, you can define an area to the front, to the sides, above and below him—a box—where he will focus his attention. Once you explore these dimensions, use that information to engage him in this space. Start by always getting in front of him, bringing your face into his box. This increases his chance of seeing you, at which point you can then engage him more readily and begin interaction. It's possible that he is too distracted beyond the box or it is too difficult for him to sustain his attention beyond these dimensions. He may also perceive too much sensory input outside of this area, which could be painful for him. As a result he might retreat to his narrow focus. But it is much more likely that he is having difficulty following and focusing on what you want to share with him. It is vital to know the area where social interaction is the most comfortable and successful for him. Knowing his range preferences, whether central or peripheral, also gives you an opportunity to prolong his emotional connection. Expanding his visual range must be done very gradually and in very small steps. If you move a foot or two away, you may lose his attention, but by moving a few inches at a time, he can be drawn gradually into larger and larger areas of interest. Expanding his range will increase his flexibility and spontaneity during any interaction.

The greatest visual challenge for children with ASD is **visual-spatial thinking and logic.** This ability is related to understanding where you and others are in space, and then being able to imagine them not in a two-dimensional but a three-dimensional way. Visual-spatial thinking requires connection and integration of many brain neural pathways. It is not surprising that children with ASD might find these concepts difficult to understand and perform. This skill is incredibly important for understanding the meaning and use of numbers, figures, formulas and scientific concepts. It has been said that the area of visual-spatial processing in Albert Einstein's brain was developed in overabundance compared to the rest of us, perhaps allowing for his genius understanding of space and motion. If your child has difficulty constructing (for example, he might shy away from building blocks) or copying block designs, or if he has difficulty playing hide-and-seek in contrast to completing a puzzle that has a specific location for each piece, he might have visual-spatial processing challenges. If he has a severe impairment in understanding where he is in space, he may not judge where the descending steps are or how far or close the oncoming car is. When I first set up my office to see children with ASD, I had a Persian area rug. That was a huge mistake! After having many children immediately throw a tantrum upon entering the room, I realized that the busy carpet was too overwhelming and they were unable to orient and guide themselves across the space. Most knew what direction to walk in once I replaced the rug with a plain carpet.

A child with serious visual-spatial challenges truly feels "lost in space," resulting in excessive frustration and anxiety. Since he is not able to direct his vision in a purposeful way, instead he may wander, be repetitive or line up items. For example, it is most challenging for him when he needs to move his body in a purposeful way while there is other movement occurring in his environment. His world becomes rigid because he can't understand even small changes from the fixed picture in his mind. In other words, he is bound to what he knows and relies on this memory. In fact, he may spend a good deal of time trying to reset his surroundings to match that picture—closing doors, changing the placement of toys and so on. One can only imagine how frightening the ever-changing world around him must be. Just think about his difficulty turning around in the mall or dodging a ball coming toward him.

In addition, children with visual-spatial challenges may narrow their focus on one aspect of their environment. You may see this as your child plays with his toys, lining up objects in a certain order that makes sense to him, showing interest in the wheels of the truck instead of the whole truck or lying on the floor, watching the wheels go by. If your child has these difficulties, he may lack the ability to take in the big picture. For some children, difficulties with transitions may also result, such as changing stations in a classroom or going outside for activities because he can't picture where they will be. Helping your child picture where he is going will help him understand transitions in space. This information is often provided through pictures, visual schedules or words to remind him of where he will be moving and therefore possibly preempting his anxiety. Your child will need as much information and support as possible to plan for transitions (see Chapter 25).

A developed visual system can direct the body in space. For this to happen automatically, the motor and visual systems must develop together and synchronize simultaneously with all the sensory systems. Writing, drawing, cutting, using two hands to open a bottle cap, close a button, tie a shoe or even catch a ball are some examples of visual-motor integration. Children with ASD find it especially difficult to perform even the most simple of these tasks.

Multisensory Processing

When we process information, we are often using multiple sensory inputs in order to comprehend what we are experiencing and formulate an appropriate reaction. Think of an apple. You know what an apple looks like, and you know its texture, taste and smell. To imagine an apple, your sensory information coordinates across all systems to complete the picture of the apple.

Most of what we experience and do involves multisensory pathways. For example, reading generally requires both visual and auditory processing for us to understand meaning. Phonetic readers sound out an unknown word and get its meaning because they hear it or say it. Whole-language readers understand a word when they see it because the word evokes an image that then triggers understanding. Some individuals with autism are whole-language readers. No one describes this better than Temple Grandin in her book *Thinking in Pictures*. However, if the auditory pathway is not clearly coordinated with the visual pathway, one can read a word but not understand its meaning. Such is the case for children with hyperlexia. They can decode vocabulary (read words) that is above their age-expected ability, yet their comprehension of the words is incomplete. The multisensory processing required for reading comprehension is often underconnected in ASD. In fact, children described as having "low-functioning" ASD have been found to have the most difficulty with multisensory processing. When studied using advanced scanning techniques, it is clear that they can process only through one sensory system at a time. If such a child is using his auditory path, he may close his eyes to decrease the visual input that might detract from his auditory processing. These patterns of sensory processing may relate directly to the underconnectivity between neural systems seen in ASD.

Your child, too, may find it difficult to process and act on information through his senses. This creates challenges in sustaining interactions, performing countless everyday tasks and learning. Knowing his individual differences and how they might be impeding his developmental progress is the key to helping him move forward. Armed with an understanding of how your child's development should progress and where things can go wrong can help you to better understand the diagnostic process and what evaluators are looking for in your child.

A Comprehensive Evaluation and Treatment Approach—DIR/Floortime

WE WERE driving through snow that had begun during the night. Tom and I were in the front seat of the car, and Diana and Ryan were in the back. Ryan was so cute, bundled up in his warm coat and red-and-blue-striped hat and mittens, prepared for his first cold-weather day! At the suggestion of Dr. Greenspan, we were on our way to Dr. Serena Wieder's office. "She'll help you learn how to connect with Ryan," he had assured us. When we arrived, Ryan timidly entered the office. Everything was so new and different. I could only imagine how overwhelmed Diana and Tom were feeling but knew we were all filled with hope. "How wonderful to have you here," Dr. Wieder said as she welcomed us with a wide smile and kind eyes. Squatting down to Ryan's eye level, she greeted him with an emphatic "Hi!" I noticed he gave her a longer than fleeting glance. Immediately relaxing, I thought, *Okay, we're off to a good start.*

Dr. Wieder spent nearly two hours with us. She pointed out not only Ryan's challenges but also (most important) his strengths, which would help all of us better understand the best ways to support him while playing. She called this technique DIR/Floortime. "Ryan is underreactive to the world around him," she said. "He is not responding to what he hears, but did you notice how he perks up with visual input? Diana, try increasing and varying the tone of your voice. Sit in front of Ryan and put an object where he can see it. Let's see what he does."

Diana moved into Ryan's line of vision. Her face lit up, and she was more animated than I had ever seen her. With exaggerated movements she slowly placed a favorite Disney character on her head, being certain that Ryan followed her every move. With a huge smile and excitement in her voice, she said, "Let's play." To our surprise Ryan looked at her face, grabbed the toy and jumped with glee. I had never seen such a response from him before. Diana must not have, either. She looked up with a smile and tears welled up in her eyes. The first connection with her son had happened. Within moments, and without words, Diana and Ryan were moving and exchanging the Disney character figures from Ryan's beloved movie. Their shared attention and joyful excitement mounted as they passed the figures back and forth, connecting with each other.

The first appointment with Dr. Wieder was so successful, we scheduled another for first thing the following morning. We were staying with a friend who lived in the area, and Diana rose early to get Ryan ready. Her shrill cry for help jolted me out of bed. Bolting into the hallway, I saw Diana run by, yelling, "Ryan's not in his bed. I can't find him." We scattered in search of him. I ran to the pool area first, relieved to find no one there. Running back into the house, my heart beating fast, I heard Ryan's eight-year-old sister calling, "Mommy, he's here." Following the sound of her voice, we all arrived at the front door at nearly the same time. There, sitting quietly by the door, was Ryan, fully dressed with his coat, hat and mittens on. Who cared if they were on the wrong hands! It was the first time he had dressed himself. Ryan was waiting patiently to return to Dr. Wieder's office. He had experienced a connection with his family, just as they had with him. It was all about the relationship—and he was ready for more. As for me, I was ready to learn more. If DIR/Floortime worked for Ryan and his family, I wondered if I could help others in the same way.

Diana's tears were the first of countless times I have seen this response when parents experience the warmth of a connection with their child with ASD. Connection is at the core of what it means to be human. Not feeling this bond is what usually triggers concerns about your child. In fact, the attention and engagement that are developmental milestones most children accomplish early in their first year can be missing when a delay is present. Knowing that children with ASD experience this type of delay and observing the power of DIR/Floortime interactions to change children's lives, I decided that developmental approaches offered the best opportunity for the children I was seeing. Developmental approaches in ASD may have differing names, such as DIR/Floortime, the Denver Model or SCERTS (Social Communication, Emotional Regulation and Transactional Support). (See Chapter 8.)

The DIR/Floortime Model

The Developmental, Individual Difference, Relationship-based (DIR/Floortime) model is a framework that helps clinicians, parents and educators conduct a comprehensive assessment of and develop an intervention program tailored to the unique challenges and strengths of children with ASD and other developmental problems. The objective of the DIR/Floortime model is to build healthy foundations for social, emotional and intellectual capacities, rather than focusing on skills and isolated behaviors.

The DIR/Floortime approach to evaluating and treating children with special needs has been extensively developed by Stanley I. Greenspan, M.D., and Serena Wieder, Ph.D., over decades of observation and research into the nature of the social-emotional development of infants and children and is built on the work of Jean Piaget, Erik Erikson and T. Berry Brazelton, to name a few. The work of Drs. Greenspan and Wieder went beyond solely looking at the typical developmental path, to understanding how children with developmental delays could be supported. They examined both the functional developmental capacities of these children and also the individual differences. DIR/Floortime is a comprehensive, multidisciplinary approach to evaluation and treatment that emphasizes the needs of each individual child and his family.

To correspond with the Social-Emotional Growth Chart (see Chapter 4), *D* represents a child's developmental abilities; *I*, his individual differences, such as sensory, motor, language and cognitive function; and *R* is engaging in learning relationships that are tailored to his unique profile. These three key principles of DIR give guidance for the evaluation of and treatment planning and implementation for children with special needs and are particularly effective in children with ASD.

When I was first introduced to this model, it appealed to me because it was the most similar to my own approach to pediatric medicine. Pediatrics has always been grounded in developmentally appropriate approaches for children. Because no two children develop exactly alike, in wellness or disease, there are individual differences. And, although medical texts describe particular illnesses or syndromes, no two patients have the exact same response to an infection, trauma or illness, and this requires that there be a wide array of treatment choices available. Developmental models have a long history in pediatrics and child psychology. Pediatricians are always aware of a child's developmental progress in all areas and base any suggestions on a child's differing abilities. For a child with ASD who has social developmental delay as the core issue, developmental approaches made the most sense.

In addition to the developmental needs of children with ASD, it was also clear to me that these children had severe unmet medical challenges. The DIR/Floortime model was, therefore, also attractive because it emphasized the interplay of well-being with behavior. It provided an opportunity to combine my expertise in pediatric medicine and working together with families over a child's life span to support the physical and emotional health of children with ASD.

When I began working with children with ASD, the existing treatment approaches originated in large part from a strictly behavioral-based protocol (Lovaas's approach of applied behavioral analysis). These behavior modification treatment approaches were neither broad-based nor took in the bigger picture to consider all the challenges a child with ASD and his family might face.

This gap was filled by the DIR/Floortime model. Especially unique was its emphasis on relationship (R) in every interaction with a child, all day long. This is important because at its core, ASD is a developmental delay of social-emotional abilities. However, developing these social-emotional capabilities is directly influenced by challenges in sensory-motor processing. The brains of children with ASD have shown a pattern of underconnectivity between neurons but not a lack of connectivity (see Chapter 3). Because the connections are there—although not strong—there is an opportunity for learning to take place and with learning comes more neural connections. In order for this growth to happen, we must learn each child's particular profile of processing, and then work to support and expand on his abilities. This approach is based on the affect-diathesis hypothesis of Drs. Greenspan and Wieder, proposing emotional connection (affect) as the glue that organizes all the jobs of our brain and coordinates the nervous system from the brain outward. Affect (emotion) lends purpose and meaning to the information we take in through our senses. This hypothesis suggests that the more a child has emotional-based learning interactions, the more he will experience the warmth and pleasure of relationships. This becomes an internal reinforcement that motivates him to become even more spontaneous and interactive. This results in his moving more quickly up the developmental ladder, improving his ability for thinking, feeling and experiencing deeper relationships.

No relationship is more important than that between parent and child. Relationships are the central organizing factor in the DIR/Floortime model. It is in the context of all our relationships that developmental growth and learning occur. The relationship allows us to practice responding to another's emotion and initiate a response ourselves. Through relationships, your words become actions when cued by emotion. Think of the response and behavior of your body and your words when you disagree with someone as opposed to when you agree, or how differently you respond when asked to do something you enjoy versus something you dislike. Words lead to affect (emotion/ expression), which in turn leads to action, as feelings provide the link between thoughts and actions. By working together with your child in emotionally based interactions, you will better understand his intentions and abilities. Working with him during high states of emotion, even a temper tantrum, can open the doorway for developmental growth. Helping him work through the situation can increase his ability to calm himself, and then spontaneously problem solve similar issues that arise under other circumstances.

Examining Floortime

In the DIR model, Floortime is the technique you use to support development for your child. Typical infants experience their world through their sensory-motor system. An infant hears, smells and sees his parents, then moves his body in response. He learns to expect these moments, developing patterns of sensory-motor behaviors. Eventually, these patterns build on one another, especially when the moments are connected by shared emotion and interest. The connections that lead to shared problem solving continue to stimulate a child's interest in the world and he will, along with others, further explore his environment. As he becomes more experienced, he will become more practiced and will coordinate ideas, emotions and intentions with his motor abilities. He learns that he can make things happen and that he can develop mastery. Learning occurs through sensory interpretation, movement and reciprocal interactions. We are most practiced in this type of interaction with typically developing children, who are wired to not only be available but also to crave and seek out interactions with us.

Defining Floortime

Floortime is a crucial technique for children with developmental delays, such as ASD, who have similar cravings but whose individual differences inter-fere with their interactions. If they have difficulty with sensory processing and they struggle to understand what is happening around them, delays in development may begin as early as infancy. If their motor planning does not match up to sensory input, they can lose the connection of emotion to their intention, which is so critical to learning and interactions. They may never reach the point where they have mastery, making things happen on their own. Instead, they may develop the restricted interests, echolalia (repeating sounds or words) and self-stimulation so often seen in ASD. Through DIR/Floortime practice, however, you can help your child learn these pathways. In DIR/Floortime, you and your child's treatment team engage with him in spontaneous play that follows his interests (in other words, he leads) and aims for as continuous a flow of reciprocal interactions as possible. This may be done in a variety of settings, using different approaches as needed for your child (see DIR/Floortime methods, page 111). In all cases, you and his therapists can work with him at his functional developmental level, always keeping in mind his individual profile. Knowing the "D" (development) and "I" (individual difference) of your child will guide you to the best way to capture the "R" (relationship-based); (see Chapter 8). Always play so you both have fun and enjoy sharing with each other. Through these experiences of emotional connection, your child will have continuing opportunities of connecting his thoughts and ideas to action.

The process of identifying these issues takes considerable time, but it is well worth the effort. Ultimately, a profile of your child will emerge, from which further evaluation and treatment programs can be planned and implemented. Parents often tell me that this description of their child is one of the most useful tools they have to help inform family, friends and therapists about their child. Not only does it help to explain their child's uniqueness, but it also can aid in explaining the best ways to interact with him whether for learning or play.

I believe in taking an eclectic approach for your child that encompasses his strengths and challenges. By examining all aspects of his health, development and behavior, ranging from his social-emotional abilities to how he interacts with his environment and processes, the many types of sensory information available to him (auditory, visual-spatial and so on), you will have a clear picture of how to modulate his relationships. You will have a clear sense of your child, how he interacts with the world around him and how you can best help him.

The DIR/Floortime approach is a comprehensive method of assessing where a child's strengths and challenges lie as well as working with him to build on his strengths to overcome his challenges.

The Four Goals of DIR/Floortime

The social-emotional milestones (see Chapter 4) are the six progressive levels that a child masters in order to think, communicate and understand his world. Although these milestones are acquired over time in a step-by-step fashion, mastery requires a great deal of practice and is attained at different times for each child. As your child develops, you may notice advanced islands of ability before mastery of earlier milestones is completed. This is true of all developmental capacities. For example, while learning to take his first steps, he may get down and crawl if he needs to get across the room quickly. The same is true with social-emotional development. A child may have some words, but in order to find a lost object, he may solve the problem by gesturing to get help. DIR/Floortime interactions encourage achieving each of the milestones, but there is overlap because the overall skills are not necessarily attained separately as your child develops and learns. The purpose of DIR/Floortime is to enter a shared world with your child based on his natural instincts, where he becomes self-motivated through practicing meaningful interactions.

During a DIR/Floortime evaluation, the professional observes the quality of the relationship and seeks out ways to support interactions. He can then coach parents on how to best sustain and capture even more of their child's abilities. It is not unusual to find a child who has some ability moving up the social-emotional developmental continuum in a first session. When parents experience success during the evaluation, they will become empowered to try this method on their own. Many of the parents in my practice have told me that as they become experts in DIR/Floortime, this technique helps them improve all their relationships.

Four goals to help direct interactions with your child during DIR/Floortime are discussed in the following sections.

Goal One: Encouraging Attention and Intimacy

For this first goal, you concentrate on maintaining your child's mutual attention and engagement. By calmly joining in his activity and gently connecting with him, he will not only enjoy having you in his space but will also invite your company. You can work to connect and maintain attention and that, in turn, strengthens the bonds of engagement and intimacy.

Goal Two: Two-Way Communication

The next step builds on attention and engagement to establish communication. At first you can open and close circles nonverbally, using facial expressions, hand gestures and tone of voice, as well as expression and attitude, to help connect with your child. Communication through gestures is the foundation for later language. It is also important for your child to move into initial problem-solving situations that will be the basis for further creativity and thinking. As new neural connections are formed and solidified for him, it will be easier to support his ability to open and close many circles of interaction in a complex problem-solving dialogue.

Goal Three: Encouraging Expression and the Use of Feelings and Ideas

Once your child is able to sustain complex circles of interaction, he has set the stage for learning how to express his feelings or intentions, not only in words but in pretend play. At this stage, the symbolic world is emphasized, perhaps by engaging in dramas and make-believe. This type of play gives your child the opportunity to express his needs, wishes and feelings, as well as engage in emotional problem solving that is essential for further social interaction.

Goal Four: Logical Thought

The last goal helps your child connect his ideas with feelings to not only understand how the world works, but also to allow him to respond to his situation by creating new and inventive ideas and solutions for any problems he encounters.

The length of time spent practicing at each level depends on your child's unique profile. Those who are less challenged will often progress at a faster pace as long as other issues don't interfere. It is more difficult for children with major motor-planning issues to move as quickly, as they struggle with bodies that often don't respond as they would wish. It is important to follow progress critically and support your child as dictated by his needs and to determine alternative ways of working with him when progress is slow.

Which goals to work on will depend upon your child's abilities. If he is delayed at all levels, DIR/Floortime requires concentration on the first two goals. If he has fairly good attention and engagement, participates in continuous two-way interactions and is beginning to use words spontaneously and with meaning, his DIR/Floortime may begin with goal three (encouraging expression and the use of feelings and ideas). No matter what goal is the focus, all four goals should be considered at all times.

The DIR/Floortime model, while not extensively researched, does have evidence for success. Drs. Greenspan and Wieder have reported a retrospective review of two hundred cases followed for at least two years (some for eight years) of children who met *DSM* IV criteria for autism. They all were evaluated and treated using the DIR/Floortime model and ranged in age from twenty-two months to four years at the beginning of the evaluation. Of these children, 58 percent had good to outstanding outcomes, evidenced by joyful relating, simple preverbal gestures and a variety of facial expressions. They were able to engage in purposeful, organized, problem-solving interactive sequences involving over fifty circles of spontaneous verbal communication and to sustain shared social attention for various social cognitive or motor-based tasks. They had the capacity for creative pretend play and could hold logical two-way conversations. They were able to separate fantasy from reality and to anticipate consequences. On the CARS autism rating scale, all children in this group shifted to the non-ASD range. A second group (24 percent) made significant gains in their ability to relate and communicate with gestures. This group had relatively good mastery of early developmental skills, and their symbolic abilities were emerging. The third group (17 percent) continued to have significant difficulties in both the early functional abilities and later levels. It was difficult for them to attend to and enter into simple and complex sequences of gestures. For those in that group who had some symbolic capacity, they were unable to imitate and use these abilities in an interactive manner (like sing songs or do puzzles). Looking at the individual profiles, these children who still met criteria for an ASD had major muscle tone, motor-planning and sensory-reactive problems. They were often self-absorbed, had significant motor-planning issues and displayed mixed patterns of reactivity—overreaction in some areas and underreaction in others. These are the children who have the most challenged body maps (see Chapter 5). Although they may have ideas and intent, it is very difficult for them to implement them and, therefore, let us know what they're thinking and feeling, whether through gestures or speech. This would indicate the need to identify children with characteristics of this third group and devote much therapeutic time to these sensory, motor and planning challenges.

There are a multitude of potential therapeutic interventions for children with ASD. The beauty of the DIR/Floortime model is that it helps you discover the right therapy at the right time for your child. All potential therapies are available to use when and if your child needs them. The DIR/Floortime model offers a way to think about your child to best put all the pieces together. One of the most appealing features of this developmental approach is that it is multidisciplinary and inclusive of all therapeutic treatment approaches. While DIR/Floortime is the technique used to support your child's interactions, developing his interactions through his relationships is the mainstay that can and should be generalized to all his therapeutic settings. In this way, any idea or therapy from each discipline that will help meet all your child's needs is utilized to help him improve. No longer do you have a one-size-fits-all approach, but a very specialized, individual, need-driven plan that can be flexible enough to keep your child moving forward.

PART III

Determining Whether Your Child Has Autism— and Knowing What to Do

CHAPTER 7

The Evaluation Process

THE EVALUATION process can be complex and confusing, but a proper diagnosis is the first step toward getting your child the treatment he needs. It is important to assess everything about your child, including his behavior and medical concerns. Being as educated as possible about his relative strengths and challenges will help you best determine appropriate treatment. In my practice, the parents and their child are fully engaged in this process, allowing them to learn important ways to foster connection and interaction with each other. This evaluation is often the beginning of the therapeutic intervention.

Could Your Child Have Autism?

You may have had a gut feeling that something isn't right with your child and sought answers from your pediatrician. Searching for what may be wrong can be a time of anxiety and uncertainty, and it's important to be able to communicate effectively with your doctor. The following section offers a list of red flags that can give you the language you need to describe what you are seeing and feeling in interactions with your child. The red flags identified fall in the three developmental areas that form the core issues in ASD—communication, behavior and social ability. If you are unsure of how these behaviors would look in a child, Autism Speaks (www.autismspeaks.com) has a video library of many of them.

Communication Red Flags
- No babbling by eleven months of age
- No simple gestures (like waving bye-bye) at twelve months
- No single words by sixteen months
- No two-word phrases by twenty-four months
- No response when his name is called
- Loss of any language or social skills at any age

Behavioral Red Flags

- Odd or repetitive ways of moving fingers or hands
- Oversensitivity to certain textures, sounds or lights
- Lack of interest in toys, or playing with them in an unusual way (for example, lining them up, spinning them, opening and closing parts rather than using the toy as it was designed to be used)
- Compulsions or rituals (has to perform activities in a special way or certain sequence)
- Preoccupations with unusual interests, such as light switches, doors, fans, wheels
- Repetitive vocalizations or words

Social Red Flags

- Doesn't point to show things that he is interested in
- Doesn't make attempts to get his parents' attention; doesn't follow or look when someone is pointing at something
- Doesn't play peekaboo
- Rarely smiles socially
- Seems to be in his own world
- Rarely makes eye contact when interacting with others
- Prefers to play alone
- Doesn't respond to parents' attempts to play, even if relaxed
- Avoids or ignores other children, even when they approach

More information on red flag behaviors can be found at www.firstsigns.org and www.earlyautismstudy.org.

Research has shown the best predictor of ASD is parents' concern about their baby by one year of age. Therefore, if your child exhibits any of these red flags, it is urgent that you see your doctor as soon as possible. At the very

---

FOLLOWING UP ON YOUR CONCERNS

- Observe for red flag behaviors.
- Ask your doctor to check for ASD with an ASD screening test.
- If there are positive signs and symptoms, get an evaluation from an ASD specialist to find out if your child has an ASD.
- Discover how your child learns about you and his world—his strengths and challenges.
- Determine if he has any medical issues.
- Shape his treatment plan to match his unique profile.

least, your child should be evaluated for possible developmental delays (which may or may not be an ASD) through screening and a possible referral to a specialist. Early intervention for any developmental delay, especially ASD, can significantly improve your child's social, emotional and developmental growth.

Screening Children for ASD

By observing a child, parents and educators, as well as doctors, can watch for signs of an ASD. By eighteen months of age, most toddlers can engage in warm, joyful interactions that involve continuous back-and-forth patterns of emotion and gestures that may be nonverbal yet are absolutely understood between a child and his parents. He can engage his caregiver by consistently using nonverbal gestures to get something he wants (such as using his index finger to point and get attention from a parent or picking up a toy and bringing it to someone to initiate play). We also look at a child's ability for joint attention (tuning in to someone by sight or sound) and early symbolic use of toys, such as playing appropriately with cars or blocks.

Fortunately, the 2007 American Academy of Pediatrics (AAP) guidelines for pediatricians recommend all children be screened for ASD at eighteen and twenty-four months. These screening tests do not make a diagnosis of ASD but will help you and your doctor determine whether your child might have a significant developmental delay that warrants a full evaluation. Although there are many screening tools for possible ASD, the Modified Checklist for Autism in Toddlers (M-CHAT) is often chosen because it is easy to administer. This screening test, which is used on toddlers between sixteen and thirty months of age, is usually administered and scored as part of a well-child checkup, but may also be used by specialists or other professionals to assess risk for ASD. The M-CHAT (see Appendix 2) consists of twenty-three yes-no items that evaluate a child's ability for attention and pretend play, and the ability to use gestures (like pointing) to communicate with others. Cutoffs have been established for typically developing children as well as for those with possible developmental delays characteristic of ASD. If a child meets this latter criterion, a further extensive evaluation for autism must be done as soon as possible. I tell doctors that developmental delays are not a wait-and-see proposition, but one that requires immediate medical attention, because early intervention significantly improves outcomes for children with ASD (or other developmental delays). When the delays are mild, the chances of normalizing development with early intervention are much greater.

If your child fails the M–CHAT (two of the critical items specifically identified on the test or any three items of the test) or any other ASD screening test, a referral will be made for him to have a comprehensive neurodevelopmental evaluation, where further observation and testing will take place.

Before You See the Doctor: Information Gathering

The more information you can provide to the team performing the evaluation, the more useful the visit will be. If your child does not pass a screening examination and is suspected of having an ASD, I recommend the following to help you and the doctor prepare for your visit:

- Review baby books or other chronicles of your child's developmental milestones to remind you of his past behavior and experiences.
- Collect all old medical records, especially laboratory reports; previous evaluations; and your child's growth chart and immunization records. Prior to your visit, send copies for the doctor to review in advance.
- If your child is currently in therapy, bring a copy of his most recent report/evaluation. If he has had an Individualized Education Program (IEP), bring a summary of that report, as well.
- Review the content of a typical medical history as described in the following section. Discuss the questions with all caretakers and family members who know your child. Going through this process prior to your visit will give you time to remember important medical issues or family history and will free up time during the doctor's visit for attending to your child's present issues.
- Review videos/DVDs of your child that may illustrate certain behaviors you wish to show to the doctor. While it may be difficult to watch them, it can be helpful for the doctor to see specific behaviors or to determine if your child has had a subtle regression in his abilities. I always find it extremely helpful to see a child's behavior at home, outside of a doctor's office.

Who to Bring to the Evaluation

While who attends the evaluation is up to the family, parents, of course, are present for the whole evaluation. Having other family members or caregivers with you can help in a number of ways—they can be a second or third set of ears for you to help clarify or verify what has been discussed; they can learn how to support therapies and treatment approaches; they can also look after your child if he needs a break or if you and the doctor need to speak out of your child's presence.

The Neurodevelopmental/Medical Evaluation

A neurodevelopmental evaluation for your child is typically performed by pediatricians, developmental and behavioral physicians, neurologists or child psychiatrists. The goal of this evaluation is to ascertain the extent of your child's developmental delay, to verify if he has an ASD and then to help develop a therapeutic plan to meet his individual needs. In some communities, several professionals may do part of the total evaluation. Rarely is one able to complete the entire evaluation, and often the diagnostic work is supported by psychologists, speech pathologists, occupational therapists and educators. Reviewing your child's full history provides the practitioner with a complete picture of all concerns. The ASD diagnostic tools (discussed in the rest of this section) are used to help make a diagnosis. Your doctor will also include a physical exam, which will complete the initial evaluation and direct, together with the history, further therapeutic procedures. The following sections summarize the key areas reviewed in these sessions and may help you think about these concerns as they relate to your child.

Present Symptom History

Prepare as complete a history of your child's symptoms as you can so that your doctor can fully understand your concerns. Think about ASD-specific behaviors relating to his ability for attention, repetitive behaviors, play skills, daily functioning skills and so on. Make a list of issues currently facing your child. In this way, your doctor can be certain to address all your concerns.

Family History

Knowing your family's medical history is extremely helpful in thinking about your child's medical issues. A child with autism is a child who is part of a family that has given him not only his physical characteristics, such as hair color, but also any genetically determined medical disorders. By exploring medical issues in your immediate family (both sides, going back two generations as completely as possible), these potential concerns can be identified. Of particular interest are disorders that are often associated with ASD (such as autism, mental retardation, Fragile X, Tuberous Sclerosis) and other neurobiological disorders that seem to be present in family lines where autism is diagnosed (mood disorders, metabolic disorders and autoimmune disorders). If these disorders are present in your family history, it may give clues about pursuing both a diagnosis and a treatment for your child. In addition, a child with autism can be affected by any other inheritable diseases, so a complete review of all medical issues within the immediate and extended family is critical.

Developmental History

To get a sense of where your child is today, it is important to know about his development in the areas of gross motor skills (such as running, jumping), fine motor skills (finger, hand control), social skills and language. This helps determine whether he has delays in one specific area or if it's more global. The review also allows your physicians to understand the chronology of his functional developmental capabilities—in particular, regression, or loss of skills, is important to determine. To assess whether a regression has happened during a child's development, videos and DVDs can be extremely helpful. Because a regression represents a loss of skills an infant or young child has previously achieved, pay particular attention to a child's ability at a younger age to maintain joint attention and hold engagement, as well as his ability to sustain back-and-forth communication with another, whether through words or gestures. If he had more skills at an earlier age than at the present time, a regression has most likely taken place.

I learned this technique when I evaluated two-year-old Paul for a possible ASD. His parents told me they thought he had not regressed but rather had failed to make further developmental progress after ten to twelve months. At the time of the visit, Paul had only fleeting shared attention and rarely engaged with his parents. Reviewing a video taken of Paul at six months, I observed him engaging in behaviors he no longer did at age two. While playing with his mother and sister at six months, he was joyful and maintained long periods of warm, reciprocal vocal interactions. He easily made eye contact and had multiple linked back-and-forth exchanges with them using gestures and sounds. At several points, if he lost their attention or if they walked away, he would call out sounds and babble to entice them to come back and resume their interaction. As difficult as this was for all to see, it added a critical piece of information to our medical investigation of Paul's regression.

Past and Current Medical History

Your child's complete medical history will help identify issues in pregnancy, birth, infancy and early childhood that may be influencing his behaviors today. Your doctor will review questions in the following areas to help prioritize issues of concern.

- **Feeding patterns** (such as an infant's ability to nurse): Children with motor-planning delays often have difficulty suckling at the breast. What was he fed in his early months? What was the progress and timing of milk changes (such as breast to formula to cow's milk)? When were solids introduced? Did he have difficulties swallowing? Is he a picky eater? If so, what does he eat? It is especially important to review current nutritional issues.

- **Immunization record:** Was there an untoward reaction to immunizations? Is he fully immunized?
- **Acute illnesses:** Has he had a significant number of upper respiratory, ear, lung or skin infections? Does he have a chronic illness requiring daily intervention? When and for how long has he required antibiotics?
- **Neurological:** Does he have "spacey" episodes or frank (obvious) seizures? If he has been treated for seizures, what medications have been used? What are his responses?
- **Allergies:** Does he have any allergies to food or medication—or any general allergy symptoms, including allergic rhinitis, eczema or asthma?
- **Gastrointestinal symptoms:** What is his pattern of bowel movements? Typical or diarrhea and/or constipation? Does he frequently spit up or vomit? Does he have bloating? Has he been jaundiced? Does he seem to have abdominal pain?
- **Skin:** Does he have frequent rashes? Are there any over- or under-pigmented spots on his body?
- **Kidney:** Has he had any urinary infections? Is he circumcised? Is he interested in toilet training? If so, how is it coming along?
- **Cardiac:** Has he had any episodes of fainting or blue lips? Any history of heart disease as an infant?
- **Respiratory:** Does he have a chronic cough? Does he wheeze?
- **Sleep patterns:** When does he go to bed and fall asleep? Does he wake up in the night? If so, what is he like at those times? Awake and alert or sleepy? Does he fall back to sleep easily? Does he snore?
- **Prescription and over-the-counter medications:** This includes any vitamin or mineral additives, plus health food products, he may be taking. Bring in a list of any current medications, vitamins, supplements or additives to share with your doctor.
- **Any past issues:** Consider past issues with, for example, his respiratory, cardiac, gastrointestinal, skin, kidney, liver and other systems (such as ear infections, recurrent upper respiratory infections, snoring, wheezing, loose stools, constipation or skin rashes).
- **Hospitalizations:** Your doctor will be especially interested in those requiring overnight stays.
- **Injuries:** These range from broken bones to falls to head trauma.

Sensory-Motor History

A review of Chapter 5 in advance of the visit will help clarify what sensory-motor strengths and challenges your child is experiencing. Looking at your child from this perspective will help you discover how he learns about his world through his sensory system, and then coordinates his movements. How he reacts to sensation will determine whether he is overreactive, underreactive, sensory craving or has a mixed response. I recommend *The Out-of-Sync Child* by Carol Kranowitz for information on sensory issues and Sensory Processing Disorder.

The Physical Examination

Following a complete medical history, your doctor will take a look at your child. In this part of the evaluation, he will look for physical signs associated with ASD and related conditions that may have physical manifestations—for example, the typical skin markings seen in Tuberous Sclerosis. This examination contains standard features of a physical exam (such as listening to the heart and lungs; examining the ears and throat), as well as components of a more extensive neurological exam, which is completed depending on the functional level of a child. Typical items that your doctor will focus on with your child specific to ASD include:

- Measuring his height, weight, blood pressure, pulse and head circumference (observing for large head size as plotted on a growth chart)
- Looking for neurocutaneous abnormalities—growths or discoloration of the skin; often a Woods lamp (a special light used to see skin changes) is used to check for Tuberous Sclerosis
- Identifying any dysmorphic features your child may have (such as unusual placement of facial features, over-rotation of ear placement, unusual whorls in the hairline and scalp), which may suggest genetic abnormalities
- Observing cranial nerve functions
- Evaluating peripheral reflexes
- Assessing muscle mass and tone
- Observing his gait, posture, facial movement and generalized movement

Making the Autism Diagnosis

The goal of your child's evaluation is to make a diagnosis, which will then help determine the appropriate therapies. The overarching questions that need to be answered are:

- Does your child have an autism spectrum disorder?
- If so, what are his strengths and challenges?
- Does he have a medical complication?
- How do you find the right treatment plan for his needs?

The first step in making a formal and definitive diagnosis of autism is to determine whether the three core features of ASD outlined in the *DSM* IV-R are present (see Appendix 1). In order to quantify these symptoms, standardized questionnaires, known as the Autism Diagnostic Interview (ADI) and the Autism Diagnostic Observation Schedule (ADOS), have been developed that define the *DSM* IV-R symptoms in more precise terms.

When you or your doctor has raised a concern about whether or not your child has autism, these above procedures will be followed to gather information and potentially rule out other causes for his behavior or delayed development. To determine whether your child has autism, your doctor may use several diagnostic tools. Which test is given depends on your child's age and general ability level. General characteristics of the most common tools used to make an ASD diagnosis are reviewed in the following sections.

Autism Diagnostic Interview (ADI)

The Autism Diagnostic Interview (ADI) is considered the gold standard for diagnosing ASD in the research setting but is not used consistently in the clinical setting.

- The ADI entails a parent interview; the child is not present.
- It is used for children over the age of three with mental ages from about eighteen months and above.
- It can take several hours to administer.
- It contains ninety-three items that focus on behaviors in the three core areas (see Chapter 2).
- Questions relate to *DSM* IV-R definitions of ASD and deeply explore a child's ability for development in receptive and expressive language, social functioning and repetitive behaviors. This tool also examines a child's unusual sensory responses, as well as his pattern of development of autism (assessing if a regression has occurred or not).

Autism Diagnostic Observation Schedule (ADOS)

The ADOS has become the gold standard for assessing and diagnosing autism and Pervasive Developmental Disorder across ages, developmental levels and language skills. It also includes a component of free play, where a child can interact with his parent or caregiver to demonstrate the quality of their relationship.

- This play-based tool is used by the administrator and the child.
- This assessment can be used to evaluate almost anyone suspected of having an ASD, from toddlers to adults.

- The ADOS is individualized to a child's expressive language level and chronologic age. This assessment takes thirty to forty minutes to administer.
- The ADOS was developed for research but more recently has been adapted by clinicians. It contains various activities in which the examiner observes social and communication behaviors related to the diagnosis of Pervasive Developmental Disorder. The ADOS gives a measure of possible ASD that is not affected by a child's language. It does, however, require training to learn how to perform and then code the interactions.

The following semi-structured interviews are also designed to elicit information about the presence and severity of features characteristic of ASD. I find the Childhood Autism Rating Scale (CARS) or the Gilliam Autism Rating Scale (GARS) useful in the clinical setting because they include a child's history as well as direct clinical observation for evaluation. Both tools can be used through age twenty-two.

Childhood Autism Rating Scale (CARS)

CARS is commonly used because it is a reliable test that is easy to administer in the clinical setting.

- It is given to children over two years of age.
- It takes less than ten minutes to administer (following an observation period).
- Items are scored from one to four in each of fifteen areas. The CARS includes items drawn from five prominent systems. Each item covers a particular characteristic, ability or behavior. After observing a child and reviewing relevant information from parent reports and other records, the examiner rates a child on each item. Using a four-point scale, the examiner indicates the degree with which a child's behavior varies from that of a normal child of the same age. By using a scaled system, cutoffs have been determined above which are general indicators of ASD.

Gilliam Autism Rating Scale (GARS)

GARS is a newer scale that, like CARS, is very useful in the clinical setting.

- It is given to children over three years of age.
- It takes five to ten minutes to administer.
- There are forty-two items in the categories of stereotyped behaviors, communication and social interaction that describe the characteristic behaviors of people with autism. Scores from these three categories are then rated on the likelihood that an individual has an ASD. In addition,

the specific scores in each category help estimate the severity of the disorder.

Each of these tests results in a score for your child that will tell you the likelihood that he has an ASD. Parents have told me how hard it was to hear the dreaded "A" word. However, the next step of the evaluation will bring you hope, as you will learn how your child navigates the world and how you can begin interacting with him.

LIMITATIONS OF STANDARDIZED ASSESSMENTS

Standardized assessments are useful in evaluating children with ASD. However, there are certain limitations to these tests, especially when administered by a professional and not through an interaction between child and parent or caregiver. Examples of pitfalls in this testing include:

■ A child with ASD may not be able to perform at his best with an unfamiliar tester who does not understand his strengths and limitations. For example, if your child has severe auditory sensitivity and the tester has an overly loud voice, he could be overwhelmed before the testing begins and results may not then reflect his true ability. Often, evaluations are done without a parent present. A child with ASD could have overwhelming anxiety in this circumstance and not perform anywhere near his capabilities.

■ Often standardized evaluations do not include an opportunity to see how your child responds to his parents or caregiver. Because this is a child's most trusted relationship and often the one in which there is the most connection, it's crucial that the evaluation include observation of this relationship.

■ If the evaluation requires a verbal response to questions, a child who has apraxia/ dyspraxia may not be able to respond, although he may know the answer.

■ If the testing requires that a child manipulate objects with his hands (putting a peg into a hole) or use hand-eye coordination (catching or throwing a beanbag), a child with motor-planning challenges may score lower, not because he doesn't know what to do, but because his motor control is lacking.

Assessing Your Child's Strengths and Challenges

Determining that your child has ASD is only the first step. The ASD diagnosis is important on many levels as it defines the core features that are challenges for him. However, knowing that your child has autism does not always inform you or therapists as to the best way to interact with him. This requires determining his individual strengths and challenges that affect the way he learns from his environment. I find this information to be most valuable in directing individualized therapy as well as in helping the family know how best to support him.

This part of the evaluation will identify:

- Your child's social–emotional abilities
- Your child's specific sensory-motor strengths and challenges

I believe the pattern of a child's response and learning capabilities is best evaluated through the DIR/Floortime model (see Chapter 6). By questioning parents about their child's ability to connect with them and maintain his composure or to engage in reciprocal communication or interaction, one gets a picture of the child's functional developmental capacities, which can then be seen in an actual face-to-face assessment. A sensory-motor history can also identify and clarify challenges. During this visit, I observe the child as he interacts with his parents or caretaker, determining his strengths as well as the challenges he faces. Coaching to help parents learn how best to support their child begins during this evaluation. It is not unusual for a child to connect with his parents for the first time as we search for the mutual gleam in their eyes. These observations, together with the history, help determine all the components necessary for the child's treatment.

Your Child's Social-Emotional Abilities

A tool known as the Functional Emotional Assessment Scale (FEAS) can be used to determine a child's social-emotional developmental capacities. The FEAS is divided into two parts: parents or caregiver and child, with six subtests in each part directly related to the social-emotional developmental milestones (as shown on the Social-Emotional Growth Chart—see Chapter 4). Children with autism are by definition delayed in social development (attention, engagement, initiation, reciprocal interaction, problem solving, use of words and logical thought). Their FEAS scores will, as a result, be lower than would be expected from a typically developing child. The FEAS assessment is less structured than the ADOS and functional levels are determined based on a child's spontaneous interactions with his parents or caregiver, thus overcoming some of the limitations of standardized testing procedures. During the FEAS observation, the clinician can assess a child's individual profile, taking into consideration his sensory- and motor-processing issues, (possibly) identified in the sensory history, that can interfere with interaction.

I have found this tool to be one of the most productive in helping children with ASD. Challenges identified in this process clearly determine whether further evaluation is required and shape appropriate treatment. Often these evaluations are videotaped and compared to subsequent tapes as the children make developmental progress. Parents or caregivers can also use the tapes to review sessions and ask questions about interactive techniques to help shape interactions with their child.

What I Look for in the DIR/Floortime Observation

I can't think of another situation in medicine where observation plays a bigger role than it does in evaluating a child with a possible ASD. While observing a child at play with his parents or caregiver, I ask myself whether each developmental level is fully present as expected, is delayed or is not there yet but is emerging. I also consider at which level a child needs increasing support and what interactive techniques work best to sustain longer and longer interactions. If a major delay or emerging abilities are present, I determine what unique characteristics either help maintain (a child's strengths) or interfere (a child's challenges) with his moving up the developmental ladder. For the challenges, I look to discover what can help improve the quality of his interaction.

The observation is a gauge of all the foundation steps necessary to support a child's interactions and relationships. I look for a child's age-appropriate ability to:

- Attend to the relationship with his parents and caregivers
- Emotionally engage
- Participate in either verbal or nonverbal (gestural) communication
- Use language or gestures to express feelings and ideas and think creatively and logically, as noted on the Social-Emotional Growth Chart (see Chapter 4)

Information gleaned from this observation allows me to complete the FEAS, describing a child's social-emotional developmental abilities as well as his sensory-motor strengths and challenges. Next comes understanding his unique profile. Techniques to support his emerging interactions can be suggested and practiced during the visit.

Your Child's Specific Sensory-Motor Strengths and Challenges

The individual profile describes a child's unique combination of strengths and challenges in his sensory and motor systems. In other words, it describes how he gets input from the world through his sensory system, processes this input and then produces an output (reaction) through his motor system. During the observation, I pay particular attention to the areas discussed in the following sections, always questioning how he is doing and what is helping or hindering his ability to interact.

Auditory/Language

Questions I consider to determine how a child processes what he hears include:

- What are his receptive (understanding) language abilities? Without visual input, can he respond if you speak to him from behind? Does he turn his head to the sound of his name? What are his receptive abilities when we give him visual input? If we call his name in front of him while looking into his eyes, does he respond?
- How does he communicate his wishes? Does he use gestures rather than words? Is he using his hands to point, offer or take? If not, is he taking his parent's or caregiver's hands to complete the task? Does he have facial expressions that match what he wants to express verbally? What happens to his gestures with prompting (for example, if he doesn't point, but we say to him, "Can you use your pointer finger to show me what you want?" will he respond)?
- Does he use language in addition to gestures? If so, is he using sounds, words, sentences or paragraphs? If he has language, is it repetitive (echolalic, that is, he repeats the last word that you say) or is he spontaneous, using words to get something done? If he has spontaneous words, are they appropriate to the situation? If he is using words, are they understandable? Again, are the understandable words repetitive or are they spontaneous? If the words used are spontaneous, are they understandable? (Children with good auditory memory have echolalic words that often sound better than their spontaneous language. In this case, the spontaneous language is often used with meaning, whereas the repetitive language is not.) If he does not have understandable language but does have vocalization, does it appear that there is intent either in his movement or in his eyes? If he is using words to get his wishes or desires met, what is the quality of the language? Are verbs being used or just nouns? If verbs are being used, how is the tense? Is there pronoun reversal? (If he is asked, "Do you want a cookie?" does he answer, "You want a cookie," when *he* clearly wants one?) Is he able to pick up the meaning of another's body language?
- Is he following a verbal direction without visual input? Can he get a toy from the shelf without being shown which one?
- If he is using language, is there anything different about the quality of the rhythm of his voice? The intonation of the voice and the lilt and singsong nature that we recognize as our dialect is known as prosody. Children on the spectrum often exhibit a difference in this cadence and sound more repetitive or robotlike.

Vision

How a child processes what he sees can be evaluated with the following observations:

- If a child doesn't respond to his name from behind, does he light up and come to you if he sees you calling to him with outstretched arms? Is he a visual learner? Is his vision informing his auditory path, or is his auditory path informing his vision?
- Is he visually attracted to parts of toys (such as wheels) as opposed to the whole toy? Does he line toys up in a repetitive manner?
- Does he seem anxious as he scans the room? Is the room overwhelming for him?
- In what area of vision does he have best attention and engagement in the relationship with his parents? Is there a limit to his effective visual field of attention? Can we sustain longer attention and engagement if we enter that visual space and then catch his eyes? Can the visual space that is used to sustain relationships be increased in all dimensions? If so, what works? Is the visual space bigger when he is engaged in physical activity than in toy activity—or vice versa?
- Under what circumstances do we get the greatest gleam in his eye?
- Is he a visual seeker? Can he find hidden items? Does he explore a toy? Is he a little engineer, exploring all the ways in which a toy works mechanically?
- Is he visually distractible? Does he move from thing to thing after he glances at them? If so, how can we best join him to improve the interaction?
- Can he move toys around to tell a story?
- How does he move through space?

Smell

Smell is sometimes one of the best ways for a child to interpret his environment if it is not making sense to him. To better understand how he uses his sense of smell, consider the following:

- Does he sniff things, such as hair (especially his mother's), clothes, toys? Does he seem to do it to help understand something or to calm himself down?
- Are there specific smells that trigger a certain behavior?

Mouth/Oral Motor

The mouth is a big issue in autism, both in the way a child senses things in his mouth, as well as how he moves his mouth to create sounds and speech.

- Does he lick toys or people? Is he drooling? Is his mouth open or closed?

- Is he able to make understandable sounds, or does his language sound like a run of vowels? If he is making words, are there clear sounds that are not understandable?

Proprioception/Vestibular

How well your child orients himself to people and objects around him impacts on his relationships and behavior.

- Is he able to negotiate easily around the room? Is he walking aimlessly while bumping into things?
- Is he lying on the floor or slouching in the chair? If sitting on the floor, is he slouched over like a sack of potatoes? When stimulated by tickling, does he sit up?
- If he engages in active exercises or big movement or if he's thrown into the air, does his motor tone increase? Does he do better with small movements—like quietly rolling a ball back and forth?

Motor Planning

A child's ability to organize his big muscle movements, as well as his fine motor control, can be assessed by asking the following:

- What is his rhythm and timing? What does it take to establish a rhythm with him and to support the back-and-forth exchange?
- Do we need to slow down or to speed up? If his timing is slow and his verbal response time is slow, can we count silently one-one-thousand, two-one-thousand and so on until he responds? How long does it take for a response? Can we slowly speed up the response time and his engagement with us through interaction?
- How many steps can he complete in a sequence when playing with toys or getting something he wants?

Sensory Modulation

Knowing how your child will react and respond under certain situations is important so that you can prepare him for, and help him navigate, what comes his way.

- Is he overreactive, underreactive or mixed in his reactions?
- Is he self-absorbed or sensory-seeking? (Does he keep to himself or seek out sensory input by bumping into things or rubbing his face against textures and surfaces?)
- What sensory supports (things like picture cards or physical assistance) help improve interaction? Likewise, what seems to cause him to disconnect or lose interest?

Following these observations of a child, in conjunction with talking to his parents or caregiver and reviewing evaluations made by other professionals (OT, speech therapist), an individual profile can be developed. This will help guide the choice of DIR/Floortime team members who will best "fit" with a child's profile and give him the greatest support. Remember, the relationship that a child develops is an important factor in working with these challenges. This evaluation process also gives us clues as to how to sustain longer and longer interactions with him in a regulated and reciprocal manner. In this way, we can present problems for him to solve—especially those requiring emotional thinking.

Does Your Child Have a Medical Complication?

Your child needs to have a complete medical evaluation if he has a developmental delay or has been diagnosed with ASD. The medical evaluation can be done simultaneously or separately from the neurodevelopmental evaluation. Your child's medical history is reviewed and a physical exam performed to identify medical issues that might be a cause of an ASD and to determine whether he has any additional health issues associated with the disorder. There are many health-related issues associated with ASD that need to be addressed so that the whole child can be treated for his specific needs. Medical concerns range from allergies to seizures to gastrointestinal issues. Part V thoroughly reviews the health concerns for a child with ASD, including appropriate evaluations and treatment.

The medical evaluation is also used to identify behaviors or illnesses that may be interfering with your child's development. These can include tics, mood disorders, self-injurious behavior, anxiety and attention deficit. In many cases, treating these issues (which may not specifically be due to ASD) may allow your child to learn and develop. Basically, taking away one problem will make treatments and interventions for the other problem potentially more successful.

The notion that a child with ASD can also have any other childhood illness is not revolutionary but is often overlooked. The difference in ASD is that because of communication issues or delays, if your child has a strep throat infection, he might engage in increased repetitive or tantrum behaviors rather than the usual complaining that it hurts when he swallows. What may look like "just the autism" is your child's reaction to his health being out of balance. What is going on with him physically and medically is just as critical as his surroundings, therapies and teaching methods in influencing his ability to feel, think and express his thoughts and ideas. It is important to make a thorough medical investigation of possible health issues, as well as diligently watch for any medical issues as your child grows and develops.

Treating associated and/or acquired medical problems is imperative for your child to maintain his ability to learn and develop.

I often tell parents that my job is to be like Sherlock Holmes—to discover every clue possible to ascertain the medical, emotional and social issues for their child and family. In addition, each new issue that comes up requires the same curiosity and diligence to uncover solutions to best help the child.

Finding the Right Treatment Plan for Your Child's Needs

A diagnostic profile is a summary of how your child navigates in the world. It not only highlights how he learns and interacts with others; it also delineates what developmental or medical issues or other challenges may get in his way. This comprehensive summary is unique to each child and is the opposite of the one-size-fits-all approach that is characteristic of so many programs designed for children with ASD. By identifying these different components, you will get a clear picture of how a treatment team can be constructed to best suit your child's needs. This summary also provides a guide to possible further evaluations, as well as medical tests that either relate to ASD or have been raised through a medical history or physical exam. It should also be noted that health and nutrition concerns for your child are the same as those for typically developing children, and that health-related issues such as diet, exercise and safety must be considered, and then modified as needed, for the individual child with ASD.

This process underscores the pressing need to look at children with special needs as individuals, as well as to treat the whole child and not simply the autism. This integrated summary treatment plan will help determine not only the form of treatment but also the fit of the treatment environment and therapists, while keeping in mind a child's individual profile.

Over the years, I have transformed the evaluation into a comprehensive process, performed in large part at my office. Families have shared with me how enlightening and hopeful this process was for them. Parents want to know what they can do to help their child, how to do it and what resources they need to get it done. My job and focus are to help them understand their child and feel supported in the journey they are taking to improve their child's life. To illustrate this process, a brief description of Alex, a three-year-old with ASD, is provided in the following sample.

A Sample Diagnostic Profile: Alex

The following profile illustrates all aspects of an evaluation. As you will see, at the end of the process a complete picture of Alex's abilities, areas where he needs support and issues that need further consideration will emerge.

History

I first met Alex when he had just turned three years old. He is the first child of then thirty-four-year-old parents who were high-school sweethearts—a warm, engaging couple who took aggressive action once they realized something wasn't quite right with their son's development. By eighteen months of age, he had no gestural or verbal language. He could not point, respond to his name or interact. He was diagnosed with ASD at twenty-four months. A special preschool for children with ASD was recommended. However, Alex was not making progress. If anything, he was more self-absorbed than ever. He had become a very picky eater and was perseverating on toys, and especially wheels, to the exclusion of interacting with others. Alex was a healthy child who had mild eczema and seasonal allergies. He disliked making eye contact, loved watching videos and was interested in computers. He would not willingly put his hands into sand or paint. In addition, he appeared to have low muscle tone, slouching and lying on the floor while gazing at the wheels on his cars and trucks. Although extremely concerned about their son, his parents were energetic and eager to do whatever they could to help him move forward.

Observation

Alex, a brown-haired child with sparkling green eyes, was clearly attached to his parents, giving them frequent, big, warm smiles and hugs. Yet it was difficult for them to sustain his attention and engagement for any length of time. He quickly reverted back to his self-absorbed perseveration with car wheels. However, when his parents became more animated, using broad gestures and expressions, he responded. When his parents paired their words with eye contact, his response was very positive. He looked up, gazed into their eyes, smiled and paused. It was a very warm moment. It was clear that Alex was navigating in a visual space about eighteen inches wide and directly in front of his face. As long as his parents were in that space, they could connect. An amazing reciprocal, gestural conversation then took place involving multiple toy cars. When Alex was totally supported by strong gestures, high drama and a lot of expression, he could utter phrases and sounds, some echolalic and some spontaneous. Although Alex enjoyed looking at different parts of a toy (such as opening and closing windows and doors in a dollhouse, moving the elevator up and down), he did not seem to grasp the purpose of the toy in pretend play. He had great difficulty catching or rolling a ball. After playing with toys, it was time for sensory-motor play. When his parents swung him by his arms and legs, he was the most animated. Using a start-and-stop motor game, Alex eventually was able to use sounds and gestures to signal to his parents when he wanted them to swing him, creating multiple circles of interaction.

During the two-hour observation, several episodes of "spaciness" were noted when Alex stopped mid-interaction and became very quiet. He would drop his arms to the side and gaze to the right. This lasted for several seconds, at which point he would resume his play.

Based on these activities and interactions the FEAS was performed.

Physical Examination

Normal with the exception of a large head size and several dry skin patches.

ASD Diagnosis—Autistic Disorder

Alex displayed all three features required for *DSM* IV-R ASD criteria (scoring in the ASD range on both the CARS and ADOS). In addition, he has the large head circumference often seen with ASD. He did not have any physical exam findings to indicate the possibility of a Double Syndrome (medical issue) associated with ASD.

Individual Profile

Social-Emotional Developmental Level: Alex scored in the deficient range on the FEAS for a three- to four-year-old, which correlated with a diagnosis of ASD. He was constricted in the early social-emotional stages of attention, engagement and two-way communication and had not yet reached the age-appropriate next levels. However, when his sensory-motor needs were supported, he displayed much more ability to sustain attention, engagement and reciprocal interaction. Once engaged, his affective enjoyment was also heightened.

Sensory-Motor Profile: Alex has an underreactive sensory system. He has very poor auditory processing, resulting in receptive and expressive delays. He also has oral apraxia, which makes it difficult for people to understand him and respond appropriately. He does, however, have echolalia, and that may represent a good auditory memory. His visual system is a definite strength, yet he has a very small field of visual attention, allowing him to become hyperfocused. When things are out of his visual range, he tends to be visually distractible. His visual acuity appears typical, while his visual-spatial-motor coordination is poor. His motor planning and sequencing, as well as rhythm and timing, also are underdeveloped, making this a major challenge for him. Another challenge is his decreased proprioceptive vestibular control—his poor body map—which affects all his responses.

Intelligence: Although not officially measured, with proper support, Alex was able to become much more creative in his problem-solving abilities, indicating a strength that will be discovered through therapeutic intervention.

Mood: Alex was warm and engaged when supported.

Medical Concerns

Health Maintenance: A review of Alex's full dietary intake, including vitamins and minerals, will help determine his nutritional needs. Alex continues to see his pediatrician for regular well-child visits.

   General Medical Health: Alex is healthy. Both his eczema and possible nasal allergies are under control.

ASD Medical Associations

In order to rule out disorders associated with ASD, the following were concerns for Alex. There is a family history of autism as well as immunologic diseases. This requires a thorough laboratory evaluation to rule out appropriate disorders. His spaciness or absence-like episodes require appropriate evaluation for seizures. Medical disorders that may relate to a seizure disorder, and genetic, immunologic and metabolic causes of autism, will be thoroughly investigated. These investigations will then determine appropriate treatment and follow-up.

ASD Target Symptoms

The significance of his symptoms requiring treatment will be determined after Alex has had the benefit of individualized therapy.

Family Systems and Resources

Alex has an incredibly supportive family. His parents were thrilled with his response to their support and were eager to follow up with interactive techniques learned in the observation.

Community Opportunities

Alex is eligible for services provided by the California Department of Developmental Services. His family is very active in their local church and community ASD-outreach organizations.

Final Diagnoses

- ASD (Autistic Disorder)
- Sensory Processing Disorder
- Apraxia
- Allergic predisposition
- Eczema
- Hay fever
- Rule out possible seizure disorder

The Treatment Plan

This part of the evaluation process provides the "marching orders" for a child's treatment. Every diagnostic issue is reviewed, recommendations are made for further necessary evaluation and specific therapeutic plans are created that will help a child progress along the developmental path. The makeup of the team is also reviewed so that it will best meet his individual needs. Practical means of implementing therapeutic prescriptions must be addressed, including financing as well as emotional support for his family. Finally, follow-up plans are determined. Treatment plans are discussed in detail in Chapter 8, including the plan constructed for Alex.

After the Evaluation

After the evaluation process, depending on whether or not a diagnosis of autism has been made, questions immediately arise. Although the range of questions varies case by case, parents want to understand what the label really means, and if their child hasn't been definitively diagnosed, they want to know what comes next.

What Does an "ASD" Label Really Mean?

If your child has been given a diagnosis of ASD, you may be devastated and confused. You not only have to deal with what this diagnosis means for your child and your family, but you are also confronted with a wide range of opinions on how best to proceed, a paucity of resources for help and, simply, grief.

I think it is very important to demystify this label from the beginning, to see it for what it really is—a label. Because ASD is so diverse and because the label itself doesn't necessarily direct you toward the best path for treating your child, I suggest that you take a very practical approach: it is only a label—it is not your child. Use the label for what it can give you and your child: funding, information and support systems. Any treatment plan for your child will be very expensive, and the ASD label is required for obtaining coverage. Sources of payment for services can include medical insurance, educational systems, state-funded programs and private sources. Using the ASD label also helps you to research potential treatments, as well as identify the professionals who are best qualified to help you evaluate your child's abilities and needs and find appropriate treatment. Eventually, you may want to seek out others who have been in your shoes. By connecting through autism parent support groups, internet sites and so on (see the Resources), you can find needed support for the journey. Getting the ASD label is just the beginning of the process for knowing your child. I urge you to accept the label if your child meets the criteria for the broader umbrella of ASD and to then take full advantage of all the services and support that accompany that label. At the end of the day, however, remember that your child is not an autistic child, but a child who has autism.

Getting the ASD diagnosis can trigger the grieving process. While you may have had suspicions and fears about your child, this diagnosis often confirms your worst nightmares and it is important to acknowledge this loss. It is as if a death has occurred in the family—the death of your dream of having a normal, healthy child. I urge you to allow this grieving process to occur and to allow the emotional steps that are part and parcel of a grieving period to take place—denial, anger, bargaining, depression and acceptance. Having a person (perhaps a health-care professional or person from one's faith community) whom you trust and respect to discuss these issues with is integral to working through your grief. However, I encourage you to not let your child get lost in the grieving process. There is a loss, but there is also your child who needs help. The dreams you had for your child prediagnosis may not come true as you envisioned them, but there will be other achievements to be gained. Expectations may need to be realigned. You can give your child the gift of time, to allow him to have enough support to continue to grow at his own pace. When I talk about the gift of time with parents, I ask them if they can tell the difference between a three-year-old and an eight-year-old. They all say yes. Then I ask them if they can tell the difference between a twenty-three-year-old and a twenty-eight-year-old. They will look at each other and say, "Not always." We now know that by using intensive programs that are targeted to your child's specific needs and abilities and giving him the gift of time to catch up in communicating and relating, there is genuine hope that eventually he will make huge developmental strides.

I have seen parents' attitudes shift during the evaluation process when they see how their child can function with appropriate support. When a connection occurs in the session, often for the first time in a long time, parents find themselves empowered to continue to do the hard work necessary to help their child. As they commit to this path, they are working together to create a meaningful life for their child where a new dream can emerge. Once hope returns, each parent can mobilize his resources for the journey ahead. As one mother said, "At the beginning, of course, I was so worried about him and so sad, often crying myself to sleep. But I woke the next morning ready to do whatever was necessary. Each time we connected, I felt another brick had been laid on the path to helping him be all he could be."

What If It Isn't Autism?

With increased awareness of ASD, many children are being identified as having red flag behaviors that could indicate autism. It is clear that a percentage of children may have major challenges but do not fulfill diagnostic criteria for an ASD. Of course, it is extremely important to be aware of the red flags, and if a child exhibits these, he must be evaluated. However, while not getting a diagnosis of autism may be a relief at first, it can also be confusing. You may have had major concerns identified about your child's behavior and development, such as language problems and sensory-motor issues, but if it's not autism, then what could be the cause? In some cases, it may be a severely challenging Sensory Processing Disorder.

While all children who have an ASD have a Sensory Processing Disorder (SPD), not all children who have an SPD have autism. When sensory input and motor output are impaired, as is seen in a child with an SPD who is severely challenged, social communication will also be affected and in this case a diagnosis of autism may be given. When children with these severely challenged SPDs are calm and operating at their best, they often have social capabilities and can play and communicate effectively with others. Children with autism may only have fleeting social interaction, even when regulated.

SPD can also be categorized as Regulatory Disorder. Regulatory Disorder has been described in many ways and has been defined (for clinicians and medical professionals) by the *DSM* IV-TR. These disorders are first evident in infancy and early childhood. The infant or young child has difficulty with behavior, attention, and motor or emotional processes. Their distinct behavioral patterns often affect their daily interaction and relationships. They may be diagnosed as having SPD or a more formal attention diagnosis like ADD/ADHD. Although they have major challenges, they typically display age-appropriate cognitive skills and can be warm and connected, especially when not experiencing challenges to their sensory systems.

New research from STAR Center in Denver, where SPD is being studied, reveals that children with SPD process multisensory information differently from typical children. Event-related potentials (ERP) data used to measure brain functioning under particular conditions are beginning to show that children with SPD do not use the same areas of the brain to process sensory information and send it to the motor cortex. The sensory information does not follow the same pathway as it does in typical children and thus impacts the way these children react to sensory stimulation. This research may explain why we see children with SPD who become very distracted by their sensory environment rather than acting upon it. As they refine this type of research, it will be instrumental not only in informing us about what is happening in the brains of children with SPD, but also in guiding us as to how to better match our therapeutic programs to these needs. Because all children with ASD have SPD, this will also be very informative for those with ASD.

There are degrees of SPD/Regulatory Disorders—some more challenging than others. Also, there is no consensus of what diagnosis should be given to children with these types of disorders. Your child could be evaluated by several professionals, each giving him a different diagnosis. It is helpful to remember that psychiatric diagnoses are descriptions of behavior that is caused by underlying brain function. Not all patients behave exactly as described in diagnostic criteria and can fall through the cracks of the medical definition system. For children without a specific diagnosis, there has been little research and no funding provided for these gray area categories. It is clear that these children are challenged and need therapy, but without a diagnosis, finding appropriate treatment and obtaining funding (or medical coverage) for treatment can be very difficult. Parents are often sidetracked from getting help by spending most of their time trying to find a definitive diagnosis.

It is important to move beyond the diagnostic label itself and look at an individual child's functioning abilities, identify strengths and challenges and then devise a treatment program that is tailored to his individual profile. In general, children with SPD have fewer challenges than children with ASD, and they may actually have a learning curve that trends upward at a faster pace. This occurs only, however, after we know how each child learns and what challenges are getting in the way of social and emotional growth and developing social interaction. For me, the process for both these disorders is similar, and the treatment teams should have similar abilities and approaches.

Typically, treatment for these children follows the same protocols as those for children with ASD. The good news is that most children with SPD typically fit into the less challenged categories than most on the ASD continuum. Therefore, they tend to respond well to treatment, often requiring fewer treatments over time. Once their underlying issues are treated appropriately, they are eventually able to sustain continuous relationships and develop strong friendships. Although children with SPD may move toward a more typical developmental trajectory, they may eventually exhibit other disorders, such as ADHD or mild learning disabilities. The key is that they must have intense up-front treatments based on their particular developmental profiles in order to assure the best outcomes. Parents also need to be supported by professionals and not ignored because their children don't meet the strict criteria for ASD.

Autistic-Like

The diagnostic dilemma of ASD and SPD is beautifully illustrated in the movie *Autistic-Like: Graham's Story*. Graham's parents first noticed his unusual behaviors when he was one year old. He was fascinated by lines and would spend hours crawling along lines in carpets or floors or watching wheels spin. His behavior was inconsistent, however. When not focusing on the lines, he could be socially responsive and reciprocal—he was beginning to interact and babble with his parents. Over several months, however, the time he spent in his repetitive pattern of lines and wheels began to eclipse the time he spent interacting. His behavior concerned his parents, so they had him evaluated and were told he had red flags for a possible ASD. He was recommended for appropriate ASD intervention, using a behavioral approach, applied behavioral analysis (ABA). Graham was in this program when I first evaluated him. At that time, it was clear to me that he had extreme visual-spatial and motor-planning challenges that made ordinary interactions difficult. He was attracted to lines on the rug but did not make the connection as to what the lines were part of or what they formed—he didn't get the bigger picture of the rug and its placement in the room. Additionally, the input from his body did not inform him as to his place in space. Because this was disorienting, he would lie down and stare at wheels to get focused input to his body the best way he knew how. When he had focused interaction from another source, for example, when his father crawled into his crib with him to play, Graham was very engaged and socially reciprocal. When left to his own devices, however, he would immediately fall apart, reverting to what made sense to him, which was lying on the floor and following straight lines. At these times, he was very difficult to engage in any type of reciprocal interaction, and he simply became more and more repetitive.

Although he had major sensory processing challenges, it appeared to me that when he was supported, Graham was able to interact socially as expected for his age. It was clear that he did not meet the complete criteria for ASD but rather had a complex sensory-motor processing challenge. He received therapy to help him organize his perception of his body in space and improve his visual-spatial organization. Graham was put on an intensive home program. He also attended an integrated DIR/Floortime-based preschool. His parents became expert "Floortimers" and advocates for him. His progress has been remarkable. Because he received early intervention starting when he was eighteen months old, he was ready to enter a typical kindergarten when the appropriate time came. While his early intervention was similar to what we would do for a child with ASD, he has made relatively fast progress because his program fit his particular challenges.

The most important factor of this evaluation process is that parents and children are encouraged to continue working toward the joy of communicating and relating. Even without a complete evaluation, you can begin this process with your child on your own (see the "When Does Therapy Start?" box). Remember, the relationship between you and your child is of utmost importance. You and your family can become true experts in how to foster that relationship and help your child.

WHEN DOES THERAPY START?

As soon as possible! If you get an evaluation right away, that will be your start. Every time your child interacts is an opportunity. Ask the evaluators what techniques worked best to help you with your interactions at home.

Because wait lists for evaluations can be as long as three to six months, you can begin therapy at home even before an evaluation or diagnosis is made. If your child has any delay in social interaction, early intervention will be supportive. You can begin to help your child by using DIR/Floortime-based interactions with him at home.

- Get down on the floor and join him in his space. Look at him, catch his eyes and use nonverbal gestures (such as putting a toy on your head or rolling a soft ball toward him) to get his attention. Follow his lead. If he plays repetitively with a toy, join him. Give it a go! The parent–child interactions are the key to DIR/Floortime.
- Read books about DIR/Floortime by Drs. Stanley I. Greenspan and Serena Wieder (*The Child with Special Needs* and *Engaging Autism*). See the Resources section at the back of this book.
- Look for a P.L.A.Y. Project in your area. Visit www.playproject.org to get help learning about these DIR/Floortime-based techniques.
- Go to the Interdisciplinary Council on Developmental and Learning Disorders (ICDL) website (www.icdl.com) for information about supportive professionals in your community and ideas about getting DIR/Floortime started in your home.

Getting to know your child via a thorough evaluation is a critical step, especially as you begin to consider his therapeutic team and treatment options. I find that the observations gained through this approach serve children and families well and subsequently provide much guidance for the whole team.

CHAPTER 8

Treatment Plans

FOR YEARS it was believed that the brain was hardwired for certain actions and behaviors and was incapable of change. Neuroscientists questioned that belief, and as a result of their inquiries, we now know that the brain is more adaptable than originally thought. Brain plasticity is the ability that we have to not only learn but to retrain our brains to perform different functions. For example, following a stroke that has caused the loss of speech and language, through rehabilitation and much hard work, different areas of the brain can be trained to take over these language functions. A similar process can take place in ASD. It requires concerted effort, creativity, some repetition and much practice, but the connectivity in the brain can be encouraged to grow, resulting in developmental progress. Treatments, particularly those that target social-emotional and sensory-motor functions, are geared toward capitalizing on brain plasticity. In fact, research on early intervention for children with ASD shows that treatment significantly improved the lives for these children. While early intervention is ideal, it is never too late to start. In my experience, children make gains no matter what age they begin therapeutic intervention. Brain plasticity occurs throughout our lives and learning should be supported for individuals with ASD throughout theirs.

The thing to keep in mind is that once you have your child's profile identified, that drives all other decisions. By identifying the way he interacts with his world and noting any sensory sensitivity, you can tailor your interactions accordingly. His profile is the key to making the most out of any treatments. He must always be met where he is developmentally, and then work from there. As always, the relationship between parent and child, child and caregiver, and child and therapist is paramount.

That said, there are certain guidelines to follow so that your child is treated with the dignity and respect that he deserves.

- The relationship is central to any interaction. Try to keep his interactions going as much as possible all day long. He cannot practice too much.

- Always talk to your child (not about your child). Be engaging. Use facial expressions and nonverbal gestures to illustrate your words, if needed.
- Never talk negatively about your child. Be careful when speaking in front of others, including therapists. If you need to talk about your child with therapists and your child is with you, keep it positive and always inform him that you're talking about his progress. As he gets older and his receptive language increases, ask his permission to speak about his progress in front of him or if he would like to be excused.
- Never allow others to speak negatively about your child—especially if he is in the room. Always be careful if your child is in the vicinity, because many children with ASD have acute hearing. Even if you are discussing how the day went with his teacher, remember that your tone of voice and content may be taken out of context by your child.

WHAT YOUR CHILD MAY BE HEARING

Although you may not think your child is listening to what you are saying about him, in my experience, children with ASD are emotionally sensitive and can easily pick up on your tone of voice or your emotions. I often see this happen in my office. If you are discussing your child and you notice a change in him (ranging from increasing self-absorption to obvious facial and body language changes to anxiety with outbursts), it is imperative that you provide him with a simple explanation of what you are speaking about to help him better understand what is going on.

There are many techniques that can be used (such as DIR/Floortime activities, sensory soothing, directly speaking to your child). In my office, I use age-appropriate language to let a child know that he appears upset and that we understand that adult talk can be confusing or hurtful. I let him know that we did not intend to upset him and that we are sorry. I also let him know that it is okay if he wants to leave the room while the adults continue to talk. (I have a supervised playroom at my office.) Addressing a child's fears and speaking to him in an age-appropriate manner will generally help calm and relax him.

- Give your child responsibilities to feel a part of the workings of your family—simple chores or tasks can help him feel he is contributing something to the household (see Chapter 22).
- Treat your child in an age-appropriate manner (see Chapter 22).
- Give your child boundaries that will help guide him through an often uncertain world.
- Always let your child know how you feel ("I feel angry when _____"). Naming your feelings can help him better identify his own.

- Let him know you understand how difficult situations may be but that you and your team will always be there to support and encourage him.
- Praise him in abundance for his successes, no matter how small they may be.

The Treatment Team

Early multidisciplinary intervention is the standard of care for children with ASD and provides the most hope for improved outcomes. Early intervention programs are intensive and begin one-on-one (child and therapist) for thirty to forty hours per week. In terms of intensity and cost, it is a lot like sending your three-year-old to college. The payoff is that when early intervention succeeds, your child is more likely to be able to attend college (if he wishes), find a career and follow his dream as a young adult. I cannot emphasize how much immersion into an interactive program can benefit children with ASD.

Not only does your child's treatment plan require a team for it to work, but also the team must be integrated and have an established communication network. The treatment plan should be multidisciplinary, family oriented and unique to your child. At the end of the evaluation, you should be able to summarize the key points that will let everyone on the team know what is needed to help your child become engaged and maintain the gleam in his eye. You will also be able to describe your child's unique profile, how best to interact with him, what the personality fit of the therapist should be and what you need to set up his space during therapeutic times to get the longest, most sustained interactions so he can move up the developmental ladder. His program must be flexible and dynamic, changing as required to meet his unique characteristics and his situation. Services need to be coordinated, often with the source of financing, schools and insurance.

Coordinating the efforts of a range of professionals in a variety of fields can be a complex job. I urge doctors to take on the role of team leader/case manager who will oversee the multiple layers of treatment. As case manager your doctor can provide leadership for others on the team as well as actual case management for your child. The doctor should treat all your child's coexisting medical problems, be influential in helping with medication plans if needed and be responsible for ongoing monitoring and longitudinal follow-up and support-team coordination. Often the doctor can take a leadership role in providing support to parents and other family members. For many years, I have been encouraging doctors to embrace this role, and it is gratifying to note that there has been a shift in the willingness of some to provide longitudinal case management. Clearly, we are not as far as I would like in this regard but I do see the situation improving.

In the absence of a doctor fulfilling this requirement, parents often take on the task of team leader. It can be challenging, but I have found that parents can often be the best ones to manage their child's program while getting support from professionals.

Expertise to provide the support needed for a child with ASD comes from a variety of different professionals, including a speech therapist, occupational therapist (for sensory integration), nutritionist, physician, psychologist, educator, case worker, advocate and in-home program specialist. If a doctor and parent share the role of team leader, I suggest that they become like a coach and a quarterback. The coach (parent) works with all the team members, keeping them motivated and on track every step of the way. The quarterback (doctor) helps lead the overall design of the treatment plan, calling the individual shots and modifying plans as quickly as necessary to be certain all needs are covered. Coach and quarterback work together to connect with the range of therapists, implementing the treatments plans, evaluating treatment plans and keeping the lines of communication open among the team members. Of necessity, many parents take on both responsibilities.

When a team is working together, if one therapist discovers a technique that works well for your child, that information can be passed along to the other professionals so that they may incorporate (as appropriate) that technique into their therapy for him. In this way, there is no lag time in learning about what works well, nor does anyone spend an inordinate amount of time pursuing a less effective method. Having common goals and objectives and sharing successes (as well as failures) can lead to the most progress. Each therapist can bring his or her unique perspective to those goals and objectives, as well as be informed about what is happening for your child in other arenas.

When there is a child in the family with autism, I suggest to everyone that this is clearly going to be a case where "it takes a village" to provide all the necessary support. Parents, of course, are always the mainstay, but you need help. This is the time to mobilize all those in your family, extended family, friends and others within the community (whether professional or nonprofessional) who can learn the keys to interacting with your child. Trained in-home therapists are in great demand and often parents find that they need to search for those who are willing to learn how best to interact with their child and who can then provide parts of the intensive therapy. You may have many more resources than you realize. Help often comes from religious organizations, community schools (including community colleges) and friends.

Treatment Prescriptions: An Integrated Plan

Parents like to know about every available treatment and they are willing to try as many as possible if they think it may help their child. It's important to keep in mind that choosing treatments should be based on your child's needs. From there you can prioritize when, where and under what conditions each treatment program would be used.

Most children need to draw on several programs to best address their needs. It is important that all the programs be considered as a whole, factoring in the confines of available time, finances and available personnel. A comprehensive treatment plan can be daunting. You need support to implement this program for your child while meeting the needs of the whole family, your jobs and your community.

Treatment consists of the central approaches that provide the building blocks for your child to make developmental progress. Usually this consists of relationship-based interactions, speech therapy, occupational therapy (OT) and educational programs. When your child is under the age of three or four, treatment begins as an intensive home program, thirty to forty hours per week, provided one-on-one (child and therapist). Ideally, the intensive program will conform to his unique profile while promoting his ability to sustain longer and longer interactions and engage in creative problem solving.

Be prepared to engage in these necessary approaches for the long term. The components of each program should progress as your child develops. Eventually you may consider augmenting his core program with targeted treatments for specific challenges. Too often, I have seen programs remain static and children become bored. It's very easy to get lulled into routines. A large part of a case manager's job is to help families periodically evaluate their programs and to be certain that they are dynamic, flexible and challenging enough to keep their child on a growth curve that trends upward.

Many of the treatment categories available for children with ASD are covered in the Treatment Approaches section. This is not an exhaustive review of all therapies in each category, but it targets those that are most familiar to me and accessible to those I see in my practice.

Following your child's evaluation, potential treatments should be reviewed and prioritized so a plan can be developed to address his most pressing issue or need as soon as possible. In order to prioritize what approach will best help your child, you can rate the treatments on a scale of one to four as follows:

1. Arrange immediately
2. Consider in the next four to six months
3. Consider within the year
4. Consider eventually

I suggest prioritizing treatments, because choosing the next steps can be overwhelming and this process will help you to determine where to focus your time, resources and energy. There is a wide range of options available and the internet can introduce you to an enormous range of treatment options without imparting much advice on determining whether the treatment is appropriate for your child. Understandably, you do not want to leave any stone unturned. However, pursuing multiple avenues simultaneously makes it difficult to evaluate what treatments are effective, so taking a step-by-step approach can be useful for making these kinds of decisions.

It is also important to know that there are many different treatments available that might be very important for your child. Having a plan of attack, so to speak, can help you have confidence that his health care professionals will be with him every step of the way in determining, evaluating and choosing treatments.

Treatment Approaches

The following approaches are typical components of a treatment prescription for a child with ASD. A child might not need all these services, or he may cycle through them one at a time. They are included here to show the most common approaches to treating ASD.

- Relationship-based interactions: DIR/Floortime
- Speech and language therapy
- Occupational therapy
- Educational options
- Behavioral therapy
- Nutritional management
- Auditory augmentation therapies
- Other learning augmentation strategies (including visual/spatial)
- Additional social-emotional enhancement strategies
- Further medical evaluation
- Medical recommendations
- A sample treatment plan
- Follow-up considerations

Relationship-Based Interactions: DIR/Floortime

The primary resources to help you understand the basics of DIR/Floortime and how to implement it for your child are *The Child with Special Needs* and *Engaging Autism,* both by Drs. Stanley I. Greenspan and Serena Wieder. Information about this dynamic approach and how it works with the DIR/

Floortime model can also be found at www.icdl.com. The credit for the DIR/ Floortime approach, including many of the implementation suggestions I have put forth here, goes to Dr. Greenspan and Dr. Wieder, my teachers and mentors for many years.

DIR/Floortime is a relationship-based technique that supports a child's social interaction and developmental progress. As a specific therapeutic approach, Floortime is designed to be done on the floor. We are not used to being at a child's level, but for a child with extreme difficulty processing sensory and motor information, it's important that we do our best to accommodate to him rather than force him to accommodate to us. A typical session is initially done individually with one child and one adult and lasts twenty to thirty minutes, and eight to ten sessions are done per day. Sessions occur at home but can happen anywhere, including in therapeutic environments such as OT, speech or school.

At home the sessions can be incorporated into daily routines whether it's while getting up and dressed in the morning, during breakfast or dinnertime, during family time or playtime or at bath time and bedtime. All are opportunities for lengthening reciprocal two-way interactions. One of the mainstays of DIR/Floortime is the recommendation to "follow your child's lead"— which really means following his interest. If his favorite toys are cars, those can become your favorite toys. Following your child's lead means not only being near him but engaging with him, as well. For example, if he is lining up cars, then you can take a car and gently put it into the lineup—this turns solo play into a reciprocal play by taking turns and determining who's going to line a car up next. In other words, you are using his interests to foster a shared experience.

Interacting with your child is what is most important. There is no specific game here; there are no rules. All that matters is that you feel emotionally connected to your child. Each time the scenario can be played out in different ways—in fact, we hope that will happen. The key is to first meet your child at his developmental level to begin the interaction. This happens most often when he's doing something that interests him. It pays to be persistent. Don't take no for an answer. If he turns his back on you, he may simply feel overwhelmed and need a break. It is neither a rejection of your attention nor a cue for you to disengage. If you think of your child's behavior in the context of how he reacts to sensory input, then you can adjust your response accordingly and not take it personally.

Getting DIR/Floortime Started

Although it may seem daunting, the best way to begin DIR/Floortime is simply to get down on the floor at your child's level, follow his lead and go. Following are a few suggestions to get you on your way:

- Start interacting at your child's current developmental level.
- Match your interactions to his sensory profile.
- Use your emotion, gestures and facial expressions to help sustain his interactions.
- Be observant! What are his interests? Join him in what he likes to do.
- Play with him. Follow his lead while being careful not to direct what he's doing. Support what he wants to do.
- Help him organize what appears to be aimless play by getting him to include you in his play.
- Match your movements to his rhythm and timing. Pace your responses to match his.
- It's all about the interaction—not the rules of the game. Use toys as props but keep yourself, and his interactions with you, central to your play. Look for the gleam in his eye.
- Gentle, playful obstruction on your part will set up problems for him to solve.
- Remember, opportunities for interacting occur all day long wherever you are.
- Enjoy! DIR/Floortime is mutual.

These suggestions were in mind when I saw Jack, an underreactive, low-toned, apraxic three-year-old whose visual capacities were stronger than his auditory abilities, but he had major difficulties sustaining even fleeting attention and engagement. He was lying on the floor, aimlessly pushing a truck back and forth while his parents sat next to him.

"I'm not certain what to do," Mom said cautiously.

I suggested to her, "He seems to prefer using his vision to connect. See what you can do to gain his attention. Then see how it feels to get into his rhythm."

She immediately lay prone on the floor, facing him, slowly rolling another car into his visual space and giving him time to respond.

"Now that you have his attention, see if you can use your facial expressions and nonverbal gestures to maintain a back-and-forth interaction."

Mom tried but could only get a fleeting response from Jack.

"Since that doesn't seem to keep his attention, let's try some sensory games, like lifting him up and throwing him into the air to engage his body. Let's see what happens if he's energized."

Mom threw Jack into the air several times. Following the second toss, he started giggling, improved his eye contact and maintained much more attention. Eventually Mom expanded the sensory interaction by waiting until Jack prompted her to toss him in the air for as many times as she could. Using these techniques, Jack eventually was able to sustain several circles at a time while joining his mom and dad in rolling a ball on the floor back and forth to each other while giggling, waiting excitedly for each time one of his parents would roll the ball to him and joining all of us in a round of clapping and yelling "Yeah" when he got the ball. All of this occurred while he was gazing directly at his parents. They were amazed to see how understanding their child's unique profile helped. Once he was connected, he was able to join them, leaving his cars and wheels behind. As soon as we stopped the intensity of our interaction and talked to each other, Jack disconnected. He returned to his previous, more aimless, self-absorbed pattern, emphasizing how much this interaction had mobilized his abilities.

A session with Jack can feel like a workout. But, by attending to his sensory needs and engaging his body, Jack was transformed from a self-absorbed child to a much more energized, interactive and joyful one. I assured Mom that continuing to interact with her son in this way would greatly support his spontaneity and abilities.

On the other hand, Eddie, an overreactive, oversensitive, easy-to-tantrum child, requires a different approach. Although he could sustain brief periods of simple interactions, when he is overstimulated, his movements become quite large and increase in intensity, often resulting in destructive behavior. People "walk on eggshells" around him, hoping not to disturb and upset his emotional well-being. For Eddie, a less stimulating environment is usually best and DIR/Floortime is most effective if he is approached very softly and slowly. A soft, whispery voice works better than normal tones with him. Movements should be slow and deliberate so as not to overwhelm him. Expressions can be softer and less animated than usual. With Eddie, as we tone down our responses, we may feel him calming as he slows down and becomes much more ready and able to interact. Eddie needs to know what's going to happen next. While the underreactive child might enjoy crashing trains or toys together accompanied by vocalized crashing sounds, an overreactive child like Eddie needs to not only be prepared for the collision but also to have it happen in a much smaller way. I suggested that his parents let him know what to expect by using a soft voice and saying, "I think we're going to crash.... We're going to crash soon." With this extra support Eddie was able to anticipate what was going to happen and responded by first looking up at Dad, then saying, "Fix." This was markedly different from his usual reactive response. Because Eddie may respond to overstimulation with a major meltdown, the worst thing for him is to add fuel to the fire with loud noises, raised voices, over-the-top action or overwhelming sensory input. If a meltdown does occur (and it usually will), it is important that he learn to self-calm—at first while supported and eventually on his own.

Expanding the Circles of Communication and the Theme

In DIR/Floortime we always try to build on where a child's developmental abilities are and expand the circles of interaction (and eventually the theme) by starting in simple ways. If your child can consistently sustain five circles back and forth, inserting another tiny challenge (essentially anything that might prompt a response from him) may prolong the exchange.

In **spontaneous DIR/Floortime** sessions you take any opportunity to establish the relationship and discover your child's innovative ways of thinking and feeling. When he goes to the door, clearly wanting to go outside, you can open the door and let him out, or you can use gentle, playful "obstruction" to expand on the situation by going to the door and asking (and gesturing), "Do you want to go outside to play or stay inside?" If he gestures out, you can then ask, "Through this door or that one?" When he points to a door, you can then ask, "Who will open the door? You or me?" If he points to you, you can ask, "Should I use this hand or that hand?" When he points to a hand, you can say, "Can you help me? It is hard to do this alone." When he comes to help, you can ask, "Which hand will you use to help?" You can continue on by asking whose hand will go on the handle first, which way to turn it and whether you can count down together to opening the door and so on. In this way, a simple task can be transformed into a multistep process that has the two of you interacting with one another while problem solving together. A child can practice experiences like this throughout the day to strengthen his developmental capabilities.

If your child likes two particular toys, you can try to introduce two more similar, yet different toys and see if you can get him to play with them in a new way with you. As his comfort level increases, and as he strengthens his developmental capacities, he will then be able to engage in more emotionally-based ideas as well as some role playing.

Once your child can sustain a continuous flow of circles, you can also expand your interactions by using a theme that is familiar and loved by your child. Many children with ASD have favorite movies, often wanting to watch them repeatedly. While some children are able to repeat entire sections of a movie, it's usually not useful language. In fact, it becomes stereotyped, which is the opposite of the spontaneous original communication we are striving for. Use this interest in your DIR/Floortime sessions. For example, if your child loves the movie *Aladdin,* the entire session can be devoted to that theme. Family members and therapists can all be involved and the session can be focused on your child setting up everyone to act out a scene from *Aladdin*. From a basket filled with *Aladdin* toy characters, choose one and ask him, "Who will be Aladdin? Who will be Jasmine? Who will be Abu?" and so on. If your child is nonverbal, he can take the toy figure and give it to the person who will play that role. You can ask your child to set up the play area. "Where will the castle go? Where should the carpet go?" and so on. In doing so, you will be expanding on the theme in a way that is fun and entertaining. You've taken something he loves and turned it into a fully interactive session, allowing him to use his interests in a novel way rather than as a part of his repetition.

If your child is ready, emotional content can be added. One of the participants can say, "I don't like my character. I want a different one." Your child will then learn to deal with emotional content and conflict and to problem solve. As the negotiation continues, thirty minutes may pass and no actual theatrical play has occurred—but it's time well spent because it's fully interactive. This is what DIR/Floortime is all about! It's not the play or the acting out that's important—it's the interaction.

Although DIR/Floortime is instrumental in helping develop your child's ability to engage in a two-way relationship, it is also important to know that children need structure. The DIR/Floortime model includes helping children understand what behavior is expected of them and what behavior is unacceptable. As with any child, we need to help them to understand the consequences of their actions. This understanding can be explored and expanded on during DIR/Floortime through play-based interactions.

Although DIR/Floortime, as described earlier, is a spontaneous interaction, it can also be done in other ways:

- **Semi-structured DIR/Floortime** is designed to be more content driven yet still interactive. Parents can draw on what is being done in school and reinforce it during semi-structured DIR/Floortime. If your child's class is learning about color, and he is able to sustain several reciprocal circles, you can gather toys of differing colors and place them around the play area, along with matching colored baskets. You can then initiate a game of putting the colored toys into the correct basket—most children love to throw the toys into the basket. If he makes a mistake, you can pull the toy out of the basket and ask, "Is this the right color for this basket?" and observe his response. Not only can you see if he knows his colors (even if he is nonverbal) but you can have fun at the same time. Once you know your child understands the issue at hand, it is not necessary to dwell on the subject and you can move on to more advanced concepts.

- In **sensory-motor-based DIR/Floortime** it is important to be aware of maintaining engagement and interaction while doing activities that will best stimulate your child's sensory and motor systems. If he has a very poor body map and is underreactive with delayed rhythm and timing, the following techniques could be helpful: jumping (on a trampoline or on the bed) or helping him use his full body (such as Dad throwing him into the air and doing other gentle roughhousing types of maneuvers that will deliver deep tactile pressure). These big motion activities can energize him, and he will then be ready to roll balls back and forth, run together and change directions, swing (in this case you'll want somebody in front of him as well as in back) and practice rhythm and timing (if your child is on a swing, the person in front could catch the swing and wait for him to say "Go" to push back). Activities for your child could include perceptual motor challenges, such as stringing beads or catching soft (Nerf or Koosh) balls or walking on a balance beam.

Visual-spatial processing and motor-planning games include obstacle courses, hide-and-seek or building block games. These are all fun games that your child will enjoy and they also increase an emotional connection while maximizing the interaction. Because his sensory-motor needs are clearly being attended to in this format, he will produce the most gesturing and language. For children with severe sensory-motor challenges, much of DIR/Floortime is initiated in these types of exercises. It is also critical to understand what works for your child to help regulate him so that on those days where other factors are interfering with his abilities to function you can revert back to these tried-and-true methods.

Following the evaluations, the goals for DIR/Floortime are established for you to implement sessions with your child at home, at school and in therapeutic settings (see Chapter 6). The DIR/Floortime prescription of eight to ten sessions per day with twenty to thirty minutes per session may be initially daunting; however, once the connection is made with your child, the time can pass quickly. The type of DIR/Floortime session, whether spontaneous, semi-structured or sensory-motor, and the emphasis in the session itself will be guided by your child's individual needs on a daily basis. When starting out, often families concentrate on the first two goals (see Chapter 6), supporting their child's attention, engagement and two-way communication. Of course, this prescription will vary over time as he gains strengths. DIR/Floortime is generally home based and often parent directed. If you happen to be in a community with DIR/Floortime professionals (see www.icdl.com for listings), clinic and/or home-based therapists can greatly support your efforts.

Speech and Language Therapy

A speech therapist must understand the language deficits of ASD as well as be able to connect with your child. Ideally, the speech therapist will be well versed in many techniques that can help support your child's needs. Speech therapy can address the core issues of receptive and expressive language delays, as well as oral motor issues (difficulty using the tongue, lips and jaw to produce sounds), which are often so characteristic of children with ASD. Additional speech and language techniques to address oral apraxia should be combined with the more traditional speech and language curricula. There are many types of speech and language programs, each of which needs to be considered for its applicability to an individual child. Often the choices offered will depend on the experience of the therapist. Because autism is characterized by developmental delays, speech and language specialists who are skilled in developmental language therapeutic interventions bring added expertise to the therapeutic experience.

Your speech and language therapist will help determine why your child is having difficulty understanding and producing language. Some of the issues that could be problematic for him include difficulty with:

- Understanding spoken words (he may not be processing what he hears)
- Connecting words to objects (mapping)
- Coming up with words (word finding and word retrieval)
- Saying the words (he knows the word but has difficulty with muscle coordination)
- Connecting the visual picture to the spoken word (primarily using visual strategies to decode words)

A child's first language is nonverbal and comprised of gestures but, if successful, can be fully understood by both parent and child (such as when an infant points to a toy and his mom responds). By twelve to eighteen months of age, a child responds to his name, understands single words or names for familiar objects and performs some actions when asked. By eighteen to twenty-four months he understands two-word combinations that he also can say (such as "Daddy up" or "Get milk"). He even understands words for objects that aren't in sight and can respond to simple "who, what, why, where" questions. His vocabulary can be as high as five hundred words. Between twenty-four to forty-two months, this becomes much more expansive. He understands complex directions as well as simple causality. By forty-eight months of age he understands up to three thousand words and can respond appropriately to "when, how and why" questions.

Speech and language therapy for your child needs to be geared not only to his language ability but also to his social developmental levels. Traditional speech therapy often uses prescribed exercises and may not be as comprehensive as a developmental approach that addresses your child's sensory-motor challenges and fosters interactions based on his interests. Some find the most successful language interactions occur in joint speech and language occupational therapy sessions (such as swinging on a platform or swimming in a pool while working with a therapist).

If your child is at the early state of social development, some ideas to consider while encouraging his language comprehension include:

- Be careful not to overwhelm him with language. Increase your gestures. Decrease the number of words you use as well as their complexity. Match your tone to meaning. Maintain reciprocal flow as much as possible.
- Pair your language and tone to his actions while gesturing. If you ask, "Do you want to go up?" gesture up while your voice goes up. Do the opposite for down.
- Use words/vocabulary in multiple settings to reinforce meaning. For instance, talk about and show flowers in a garden, in a vase, in a grocery store and discuss artificial ones and real ones.
- Pair words with your facial expression.
- Associate words with objects (pair auditory and visual). For example, say, "Would you like a banana?" while showing him one.
- Try not to tell your child what to do. Use language to give him clues. Don't say, "Show me _____." Try "Can you tell me?" instead.

As your child's language advances, match your vocabulary to his, but gradually increase its complexity. You can reinforce your child's ability for reciprocity by answering his question with a question. For example, if he asks, "What toy?" you can answer, "What is your idea?" If he responds, "Push truck," you can reply, "Oh, the truck. That's your idea. What a great one" as you begin to play.

I usually recommend one-on-one sessions with a speech and language therapist and two to three one-hour sessions per week (or the equivalent—for younger children some therapists suggest half hour sessions more frequently). These can be performed in either home or clinic/school-based settings.

Occupational Therapy/Sensory Integration (OT/SI)

OT/SI is another foundation treatment that is necessary to help support the sensory-motor system—another major concern of ASD. The OT/SI professional needs to be experienced in sensory integration techniques. Your OT/SI therapist can help you understand your child's unique sensory-motor profile. Your therapist will have the expertise to also create appropriate programs for him so he can better understand and deal with his sensory environment. The therapeutic program will be individualized to the sensory and motor challenges identified in his profile. Your child's OT/SI therapist is a member of the team who can help you develop an in-home sensory-motor program, often known as a "sensory diet." These are fifteen to twenty exercises that should change on a quarterly basis and that will be useful for the DIR/Floortime sensory-motor component. Parents and in-home therapists will also be able to use these techniques at home or in school to help when a child becomes dysregulated, especially in anticipation of transitions. For example, if a child is highly anxious, he may need a break just before a transition to become calm and prepare—such as swinging or rolling on a large ball. Others who have difficulty with soft touch may find they need to be brushed all over prior to changing clothes for gym class. Many parents find readily accessible mini in-home trampolines are useful for sensory breaks between therapeutic sessions. Your OT/SI therapist will help you determine the best approaches for your child.

Your OT/SI specialist can also help you create a "sensory rescue" kit. Much like an emergency preparedness kit, this can be a box or bag filled with tools and toys (such as brushes, weighted vests, favorite soft stuffed animal, balls) that you can put into the trunk of your car for use away from home. A rescue kit can also be sent to school. Having this rescue kit can prove invaluable to your child and your family.

OT/SI is recommended in one-on-one sessions for two to three hours per week. These exercises can be performed at home but a more complete session can occur in a large, gymlike clinic setting where a therapist often has sensory-motor props available (such as circular swings hanging from I bars, large hammocks, slides, water basins, vibrating boards, huge mirrors and so on).

Exercise

As your child gets older, OT/SI sessions can develop into exercise regimens. I find that children with processing delays can have difficulty participating in organized team sports, because athletics typically require multisensory processing along with the utmost coordination. On the other hand, children with ASD can excel in individual sports, as they are often better suited to meet their sensory-motor needs. Swimming is an excellent example. Many children with ASD can thrive in the pool, where the pressure of the water gives constant feedback to their sensory-motor systems. In a warmer climate, such as California, speech and OT/SI therapy sessions can be conducted in the pool and are often some of the most regulated interactive sessions the children have. Consider getting your child involved in swimming. It will allow him to be a full participant in an activity while also meeting his needs.

Martial Arts and Movement

The martial arts (tae kwon do, judo and so on) are extremely well suited to children with ASD because they are individual sports that are done in a group setting. Children are taught by instructors who show, rather than tell, what is to be done. There are many mirrors around the room, where the participants can see what they're doing. In many of the martial arts, in order to gain the next belt standing, children learn sets of "movements" with repetitive prescribed steps. Your child's natural inclination for visual memory gives him an advantage over typically developing children. The set movements also support his proprioceptive and motor-planning needs. The bonus again is that while these are individual sports (often the group is made up of ten children each working at a different belt level), they are interactive and social, as well. Your child has a greater chance to be successful as he gets regulated through the sport. I have seen numerous children with ASD who, as they go through their adolescence, are able to achieve as high as "black belt" status in their chosen martial art.

Hippotherapy

Another sensory-motor-building technique that is quite helpful to most children with ASD is hippotherapy (therapeutic horseback riding, www.americanhippotherapyassociation.org). Many children find this experience one of the most joyful of their entire program. The stability of a horse to support proprioceptive and motor planning can sometimes be phenomenal for them. Research in 2009 with children with ASD who experienced hippotherapy during a twelve-week horseback riding intervention showed that they had more social motivation, improved attention, less distractibility and fewer sedentary behaviors than children with ASD on a wait-list control group. These programs are increasingly available across the country and are often underwritten by local support groups, making them more accessible.

Because the absence of structure outside of school (such as over the weekend or during school holidays) can lead to dysregulation for your child, these programs can provide him with fun experiences, often providing lasting effects throughout the break.

Visual-Spatial Processing

If a child is suspected of having visual-spatial processing issues, an excellent resource for augmenting his in-home exercise programs is the book *Thinking Goes to School* (see the Resources). This book describes hundreds of exercises that support visual-spatial learning. These exercises can be implemented at home and can become a major component of his sensory-motor-based DIR/Floortime. Some children will need to be evaluated for their visual-spatial capacities. This is generally performed by a developmental pediatric optometrist. From such a thorough consultation specific exercises can be prescribed for your in-home program that will be directed toward the specific needs of your child. For more information on visual-spatial issues, see *Hidden in Plain Sight: Visual-Spatial Challenges in Autism and Learning Difficulties* by Drs. Serena Wieder and Harry Wachs, available at www.icdl.com.

Educational Options

Finding the right school setting for their child is generally high on any parent's list of concerns. Ideally, the school setting should be one that can be customized to allow individualized instruction as well as the necessary opportunity for normal peer interactions. It should be a multimodal (using more than one way to teach something) language-based curriculum with visual cues and appropriate sensory-motor opportunities available when needed. This ideal is not always available. Each state has (often within cities or counties in each state) implemented programs for special needs children in different ways, making broad-based comparisons difficult. Parents also have to consider family needs, including siblings' education and financial concerns, when exploring potential educational settings.

Finding the right educational experience for your child can be a daunting task but there are several things to keep in mind as you search. An educational program should:

- support the goals you have for your child
- foster communication and social skills
- encourage play (including imaginative play)
- support developing cognitive skills
- work toward giving your child independence and responsibilities
- provide traditional academic curricula
- work with your child's profile to reduce episodes of dysregulation and supply and support coping strategies
- provide structure, a system for evaluating progress and support for attaining and maintaining new skills
- have a low teacher-student ratio and opportunities for typical peer interaction
- encourage parents/family to be a part of the process and provide information for a home program

National educational guidelines were developed by a panel of the National Academy of Sciences (www.nationalacademies.org). This panel synthesized the best multidisciplinary information to guide not only diagnosis but also educational programs for children with ASD. Specifically, the panel determined that children with ASD require twenty-five hours of structured interventions per week by trained professionals to address their communication, social and adaptive behavioral challenges.

Educational Models

There are three types of educational models. They include Applied Behavior Intervention (ABI, also known as Applied Behavior Analysis or ABA), structured teaching and developmental models. ABI includes discrete trial training, incidental teaching and Pivotal Response Training techniques (focuses on two particular behaviors, motivation and response to information, that impact the overall behavior of children with autism). Often external reinforcement (such as food or tokens) is used to help motivate the children. The research about these programs indicates gains in IQ and specific academic skills, but is not clear about the value of these programs and their ability to meet all the needs of children with ASD, especially their social-emotional growth. That said, ABI-based methods for teaching children with ASD have become widely accepted. In some communities it is often one of the only modalities available. Many children do best with structure to help them organize and focus and they improve while in these programs. Parents often prefer ABI approaches because their child's progress is measured by data-driven information. If an ABI model is the only option available in your community, consider augmenting your child's program to include what is not covered through the ABI program, especially relationship-based approaches. In fact, more modern approaches to ABI include taking into consideration the individual child's social abilities.

Structured teaching is also called the TEACCH approach (Treatment and Education of Autistic and related Communication Handicapped Children) and emphasizes improving skills of individuals with some modification to their surroundings to accommodate their challenge. The physical organization of the educational space, visual schedules, work systems and task organization are key components of structured teaching.

The third category, developmental models, includes DIR/Floortime and the newer Relationship Development Intervention (RDI), based on the tenets of DIR/Floortime but often implemented within a structured context; Social Communication, Emotional Regulation and Transactional Support (SCERTS); Hanen/More Than Words; the Son-Rise Program; and the Denver Model. The Denver Model combines most elements of the developmental models (including family at the center of treatment, individualized approaches, the social basis of ASD as its core concern, the interdisciplinary team, play-based) while adhering to structured teaching methods.

Similarities Among All Developmental Models

Similarities among all developmental models for ASD include:

- Parents and families are at the heart of their child's treatment.
- Children are unique—each should have an individualized treatment program.
- Children with ASD can and do learn.
- ASD is a disorder of relating and communicating. Fostering relationships is the basis to making developmental progress.

- The warmth and pleasure of relationships stimulate a child's internal motivation and become a natural reinforcement, encouraging even more spontaneous interactions and learning.
- ASD is complex and requires multidisciplinary team expertise.
- Treatment is based on a child's interests, his developmental levels and unique profile.
- Treatment is play-based in naturalistic settings to promote his self-motivation.
- Treatment is intensive, emphasizing initiation, spontaneity, social interaction, attention, engagement, reciprocal interaction, pretend play, communication and language.

All the developmental models focus on supporting a child's social-emotional developmental growth, fostering social communication and looking to emotional relationships as the basis for strengthening cognitive abilities and creativity.

Often what best fits a child's needs is an eclectic approach. Unfortunately, when dealing with families of a child with ASD, professionals too often become polarized, following one educational technique at the exclusion of another. Pitting one program against another is counterproductive. We don't have research to definitively prove that any one approach is the best. If one program was best, it would be widely known because all children with ASD would respond to it. The truth is there are so many components to each program that it is often difficult to sort out individual impact. I recommend that you stick to the basics: Always evaluate the social-emotional development and sensory-motor regulation of your child to put together the most appropriate program. I believe it is important to have as much relationship-based learning as possible available for your child 24/7. I am practical and understand that this is not always available in a school setting. Evaluate what types of experiences your child receives at school and then supplement and support what he gets at school by developing a home-based program to help meet the rest of his needs.

Once your child has developed the capacity for reciprocal interactions and is beginning to form mental representations with thoughts and ideas, he will have the emerging skills necessary for an educational setting. After your child reaches the age of three, you will need to develop an Individualized Education Program (IEP) at his school. I recommend that you go through this process even if you are planning on private school education. It is possible that other services can be financed through the school system that will help round out your child's total program.

The right age to start kindergarten is an issue for many families. Most public school systems admit children to kindergarten at age five and have a cutoff date by which a child should be that age. I think it's much more important that a child enter kindergarten when it is developmentally appropriate. Giving him more time in pre-K allows him to move further up the developmental ladder as he learns through his intensive program. The result is that he can enter kindergarten much more able to sustain social interaction. Check with your local school district about cutoff ages. In some areas, if a five-year-old takes an extra preschool year, he will not be placed in kindergarten when he enters school but will go into first grade. Private schools can be more flexible about the age/grade issue.

Choosing the right school placement requires that you do a major search, keeping in mind your geographic parameters. I recommend that you investigate developmental preschools and elementary schools. These educational settings are based on the understanding that even typical children develop cognitively and emotionally on individualized trajectories. School programs are generally designed to meet the needs of the individual child and support his social-emotional growth as the key factor to promoting further cognitive growth. This, of course, is more ideally suited to a child with ASD, who will then be recognized for his strengths and challenges and be offered the opportunity for a variety of learning experiences. Due to the configuration of most classrooms for children with ASD, a therapeutic helper will often be supplied to accompany your child in the classroom. When this helper or aide is well-informed about your child's individual profile and understands the best ways to keep him regulated and interactive and also knows how to foster peer interactions, the ground will be set for your child to gain the most from his classroom experience.

When thinking about education, many of us focus on academics. The intensity of the academic curriculum in many school programs is far more accelerated than in earlier generations. Currently, the desire to get the best education in order to get into the best college underlies much of parental expectations for their children. It is important to explore the overall goals of education. I spend time talking with parents about these expectations as they search for the proper school setting for their child. I evaluate a child's complete program and look at what we think the school program will add. By doing this, it will become clear what programs need to be included during nonschool time. Since a delay in social ability is a core issue of ASD, increasing social experiences for your child is a major goal while he is at school. A setting that has less emphasis on academics and greater emphasis on social interaction may most benefit your child. This does not mean that academics are not important for him. There are many goals of education and academic achievement is only one of them. Social-emotional development is another large part of what children learn in school. Adolescent patients I see rarely ever talk with me about academics. What causes them the most anxiety and pain is when social situations do not go smoothly. If they are struggling and anxious about social issues, they are not getting much out of their academics. It is important to pay particular attention to your child's social-emotional needs. It impacts his ability for peer interaction and developing and sustaining friendships, which is essential to his growth and development. It also underlies his ability to express his feelings and ideas and encourages cognitive growth. For more on educational issues, see Chapter 23.

Behavioral Therapy

There are many forms of behavioral therapy that address the needs of children with ASD. As mentioned in the previous section, behavioral programs are frequently adopted for use in the public school systems. Behavioral therapies rely on repetition and reinforcement to teach particular skills and concepts. If your child's school program includes a behavioral component, I recommend augmenting this with DIR/Floortime at home. For example, if the behavioral educational program is working on categorizing fruits and vegetables, you can use plastic fruits and vegetables in a semi-structured DIR/Floortime session to provide a meaningful context or story. Interact with your child to determine if he can identify particular fruits or vegetables. Then ask if he would like to use his beloved toy truck as a grocery van going around and picking up different kinds of fruits and vegetables. You can ask, "Who is going to go pick up the banana?" Your child may say "Me" or simply take the truck over and choose a banana from the basket, at which point you can be assured he understands what a banana is.

In addition to behavioral educational therapeutic programs, behavioral methods can be used as indicated by the needs of an individual child and can be useful for potty training, some feeding problems and standardized bedtime routines.

Nutritional Management

Nutrition needs change over time and need to be addressed in your child's treatment plan. His basic dietary needs as well as supplementary vitamins and additives should be reviewed. Issues related to feeding also fall under this category. See Chapter 13 for more information on nutrition.

Auditory Augmentation Therapy

There are many ways to augment your child's receptive and expressive language abilities. Receptive augmentation techniques usually involve improving information understanding through the visual system by using visual cues, hand signs, the Picture Exchange Communication System (PECS; www.

pecs-usa.com) or computer-based learning programs. For a child who has receptive understanding (often the auditory processing is better than the visual) but apraxia, then techniques that will support the motor system to help facilitate an alternative means of communication can be successful (see Chapter 12 on Augmentative and Alternative Communication).

There are several therapeutic techniques that may help auditory-processing timing. The most studied is Fast ForWord, which requires that a child be able to use a mouse on the computer and is recommended after the age of five. Fast ForWord is a brain training program that uses computer technology to elongate spoken words and sounds so that they can be understood much more easily by someone who has slower processing timing. Using visual as well as auditory input, the program is able to keep a child's attention during training. Your child may see four pictures on the screen and be directed to pick out the picture of the word that he hears through headphones. The word will be drawn out to several hundred milliseconds in length (someone who processes in the normal range will have difficulty understanding this word). As your child gains mastery through computer technology, he will be able to gradually shorten his processing timing. A child with dyslexia may come into the normal range within six weeks of treatment. In my experience children with ASD require double or triple that much training time to begin to approach normal processing ranges.

Other programs designed to help children with ASD improve their auditory processing fall under the category of auditory integration training (AIT), although there is not as much research to recommend this form of treatment. It does not appear to work as consistently for children with ASD. However, when it does work, one can clearly see improvement in auditory-processing timing. That these systems generally use only auditory input may be one reason why they are not as effective as the Fast ForWord system, where multiple sensory inputs are included. However, many parents and children describe how much less affected they are by differing sounds after AIT. If I recommend AIT, it is important to determine if a child has a normal EEG because this technique may have the potential of stimulating seizures in a child. I generally recommend that children with ASD become computer literate and able on the mouse so that, if needed, they will be able to use brain training programs such as Fast ForWord (www.scilearn.com).

AUDITORY INTEGRATION TRAINING (AIT) TECHNIQUES

There are many AIT approaches that you might hear of as you are researching therapists and programs. Some are considered alternative and have not been subjected to rigorous testing or evaluation as to their success rates. I include them here because you will most likely hear of all or at least some of them during your child's treatment. All the techniques will have your child listen (typically while wearing earphones) to music or other sound recordings meant to alter his auditory processing, often while performing sensory-motor activities. They differ on where (home, clinic), how long and what (content of listening material), as well as on how individualized their program is for your child.

- **Berard AIT** seeks to normalize hearing and the way the brain processes sound.
- **The Listening Program** is designed to help, balance, strengthen or restore the ability to listen and process sound.
- **Tomatis AIT** uses auditory stimulation to activate learning.
- **Samonas AIT** is an auditory training system.

Other Learning Augmentation Strategies

As you design treatment intervention approaches for your child as he progresses, you will find many techniques are now available to support his learning. These techniques target specific ways in which your child may learn best (such as visual prompts for a visual learner) or support his individual challenges, such as auditory delays. These techniques include educational, often one-on-one interactions, as well as those that use computer-based support. Any program, of course, is strengthened when used in the context of relationship-based interactions.

Educational-Based Interventions

Children who have incredibly strong visual learning abilities and not as well-defined auditory processing often learn to read through whole language reading techniques. Whole language reading is when the picture on the page depicts the words below. A classic example is the book *Brown Bear, Brown Bear, What Do You See?* by Bill Martin, Jr. and Eric Carle, where the text and the pictures are coordinated. A child who is a visual learner will envision the picture of the bear from the book each time he hears or sees the words "brown bear." Whole language readers can also be hyperlexic (the child can read above expected grade level but does not have corresponding comprehension). They do not need to sound out a word phonetically—they just know it by sight. They can know these words outside of the context of a picture. However, without first seeing the picture, they may not be able to comprehend what the word by itself means. For these children I encourage whole language reading as a means of supporting their comprehension. Whole language books can be used in conjunction with semi-structured DIR/Floortime. You can read a book about a certain topic to or with your child and then play with the items described in the book while on the floor. In the example of *Brown Bear, Brown Bear,* the animals and birds depicted in the book can be represented by puppets or stuffed animals in a fun DIR/Floortime exercise.

Many children with ASD are able to incorporate basic educational concepts, including sight words (words they know when they see them) and math facts (addition, subtraction, multiplication, division), because these skill sets draw on their ability for visual memory and rote learning. Where children with ASD often fall behind is with comprehending what the facts mean—the higher-order learning abilities that require much more typical brain connectivity. Some of the more difficult tasks that impede their ability to learn in a school setting include understanding stories, composing their own narratives and being able to do math word problems.

Because of his challenges, your child may eventually hit a "comprehension wall." It is not unusual for a child with ASD to have reasonable success in early elementary grades, where fact-based learning is required (math facts, spelling and sight words—the "what"). Your child's anxiety may increase, however, as the academic challenges of later grades require more understanding (comprehension—the "who, when, where and why") and the abstract application of the facts (math word problems, book reports or essay questions). A child with ASD often can get the facts but not the meaning behind them. Your child may be able to speak to someone but not understand how to have a reciprocal conversation. Unless social-emotional comprehension has matured, quite often difficulty comprehending social situations goes hand in hand with difficulty comprehending academic concepts. This "comprehension wall" can be a significant barrier to further progress.

Your relationship-based interactions will support your child's abilities for higher-level abstract thought. Because it is so exciting when he begins to know about things and people, it is easy to get into the trap of staying fact-driven with your child. Asking him (often repeatedly) "What is this or that?" so he can label items allows you to share with him his growing information. However, he may be ready for more of a challenge to support his thinking about the underlying meaning or reasons for what is happening and especially how he feels about it.

Aiden, a six-year-old with Asperger's, was excited about playing with cars in my office. "These are minicars," he declared proudly. "Just like we have at home. Right, Dad?" "You bet," his father answered. "Which one is this?" Dad asked as he pointed to a red and blue one. "A Chevy," Aiden responded. "And this?" "A Ferrari." They continued in this fashion, with Dad asking and

Aiden responding, for the next fifteen cars. There was no doubt in my mind that they had done this time and again at home. When they finished with the cars, Aiden approached me, moving on to his next favorite topic: tornadoes.

"Did you know tornadoes come through tornado alley?" he began.

Assuming I was about to hear yet again everything he knew about tornadoes, I asked Dad if he could use the topic that Aiden loved and expand his facts into an emotionally-based dialogue.

"I really try, Dr. Ricki. It's so hard to do. Can you show me?" he asked.

"Wow, you really love tornadoes, don't you?" I said, turning eagerly to Aiden.

"Yes," he replied.

"Why?"

He thought a moment. "They have a huge wind that blows and makes a loud noise."

"Yes, they do. What do you think that might feel like?" I asked. I was worried because this was a difficult type of question for Aiden.

He thought for a minute, then said, "Tornado Alley goes through several states at certain times of the year. Would you like to know what they are?"

As Aiden returned to his more comfortable facts, Dad glanced at me with a huge smile on his face as if to say, "It's not as easy as you'd think."

Not letting Aiden off the hook, I said, "I think I get that. But what I really want to know is if you lived in one of those states and it was tornado season and one day the wind started blowing, how would you feel?"

"I'd want to go to the tornado."

"Oh my," I replied, sounding worried and furrowing my brow. "I'd sure be scared if I heard a tornado and it would scare me if you were near one. You might get hurt."

He said, "Not me. I'm strong."

"Wouldn't you be scared just a bit?"

"Well, maybe just a little."

"How scared do you think I would be?"

He pondered the question without answering.

To keep things flowing, I gave him some encouragement. "Do you think I would be scared a little or a lot?"

He quickly responded, "A lot!"

"You're right. So if I was in a tornado and I did get so scared, what should I do?"

"Find your mommy. She'll take care of you," he answered while looking at his mother.

By keeping the interactive flow going, we were able to move from Aiden's comfort with facts into emotional-based multivaried dialogue. I encouraged his mom and dad to help Aiden practice these skills throughout the entire day by continually nudging him to be as creative and thoughtful as possible. Not all conversations work out as well as this one. I was actually prepared for Aiden not being able to veer off his script. However, upon reflection I realized that Aiden was incredibly comfortable that day having the full attention of both his parents during our visit. This again emphasizes the importance of meeting a child's sensory needs while challenging him to climb over the comprehension wall.

Educational programs designed to help augment the intense interactive work that you are doing with your child should be considered. One of these programs is Lindamood-Bell Learning Processes (www.lindamoodbell.com). These programs stimulate basic sensory functions related to learning and have been recognized as being effective not only for dyslexia and learning difficulties but also for hyperlexia and autism. They target the ability to decode the written word, comprehend written language, comprehend oral language, spell and think critically. When it is appropriate for a child, I will suggest that he do a program like this during vacation or summertime for an intense period where the skills taught through this program can be solidified. He can then continue with the program when school resumes. This solid foundation can provide the practice needed to help move him beyond this comprehension barrier. Because the brain is underconnected in ASD, it is significant that many of the children I see have been supported by Lindamood-Bell Learning Processes over many years. They teach visual learners to make the connections between what they see and what they read. This integration of imagery and language is crucial for full comprehension but may have other benefits. I often see children who excel at this program improving their social comprehension. This program can work synergistically with DIR/Floortime methods for moving a child up the developmental ladder.

Computer-Based Learning

There are many reasons for children with ASD to become computer literate. Once they are able to word process, the computer can become a major communication tool and greatly support written assignments in the classroom (as can calculators for math problems). Children with ASD, who often have major delays in expressive language, can develop email friendships and eventually use computers to support their educational and career efforts. For young children with ASD, computer-based learning modules are used in speech and language and educational programs. I encourage you to help your child to become comfortable with a mouse (and eventually a keyboard) so that this avenue is open not only for these reasons but also for the therapeutic component. Many of the children I see have increased their understanding of the world through internet resource sites. Others have been able to develop their creativity through art-based computer programs. When your child is on the computer, however, you and your child's therapists need to work hard to keep it as interactive as possible, as he may have a tendency to fall into a repetitive mode. Following computer-based programs with a spirited DIR/Floortime interaction will keep him from perseverating at the computer. I also suggest choosing computer programs that promote problem solving rather than video-based learning. Short video loops can become favorites and children with ASD will often fall back to repetitive watching rather than actively engaging with computer-based material.

Two computer-based programs that target specific brain function and may potentially augment learning are:

■ **Interactive Metronome (IM)** is a neuromotor assessment and treatment tool used in therapy to improve the neurological processes of motor planning and sequencing. The IM program challenges a child to match a rhythmic beat with repetitive movements. An audiovisual guidance system provides him with immediate feedback that further refines his motor planning and sequencing. I generally suggest this program for a child who is able to follow directions as required for the IM program. After completing this program, some parents have noted that their child is more able to participate in sports. (www.interactivemetronome.com)

■ **Cogmed Working Memory Training** is a software-based program designed to improve attention. This home-based program helps children with attention problems by training and increasing their working memory capacity. Children improve their ability to concentrate, control impulsive behavior and better utilize complex reasoning skills, resulting in improved academic performance. This is one of the programs that I may recommend as a child with ASD gets older and academic concerns become paramount. (www.cogmed.com)

Additional Social-Emotional Enhancement Strategies

There are many relationship-based strategies that parents and therapists can use to augment an individual child's program. Once your child moves up the social-emotional ladder, and is able to have a continuous flow of back-and-forth interaction with a peer, playdates can be meaningful and can become part of his therapeutic program. These can be facilitated by your in-home helpers or professionals. The goal is to foster your child's increasing comfort and capability with a peer. There is a special skill involved on the part of the adult to help promote the interaction without overwhelming the playdate with adult-directed ideas. Parents often need expert support in this area. I suggest that you think of a couple of children from your child's classroom as potential play partners. As these children learn more about your child and how he behaves and functions, they will intuitively become his helpers at school, integrating him more and more into their social circle. I also suggest that you make playdates as fun as possible so that the guest child asks his parents for a repeat playdate. Having one or two friends that a child can rely on is an essential part of learning to navigate friendships, as well as to appreciate and desire to continue them.

Social Stories and Story Movies

This program, developed by Carol Gray, Ph.D., helps families, therapists and caregivers describe a situation, skill or concept in a structured format that is not presented simply as fact based but uses terms supporting a child's, adolescent's or adult's ability to understand social cues, perspectives and typical social responses. There are books (see the Resources) that contain scripts for social stories about common experiences, like eating a meal, sharing toys, speaking up in class and more, that can be adapted for your child. These stories can be an adjunct to your program and can help with difficult situations. A social story about raising your hand in class can be followed up by DIR/ Floortime practice that sets up a pretend school classroom at home (recruit other family members to play the role of students!). Ask your child to assign the role of teacher, determine where everyone will sit and decide who should be the one to raise his hand. Don't forget to expand the circles and the theme. Before your child goes to school again, review the social story with him to help him be as prepared as possible. You can have him practice raising his hand in the car on the way to school—more DIR/Floortime in action!

Social Skills Groups

Social skills groups are often offered by professionals from speech and language, OT and psychology. They can be very valuable, especially over time. The important factor is how the children blend with each other, matching their strengths and challenges. This mix may vary over time and reevaluation can be made as to the fit of the group for your particular child. The curricula in these groups will change depending on the skills of the children and adolescents, often covering the usual challenges experienced by their age-appropriate peers and modified as needed for the group.

Play has long been known to be one of the best places for children to experience developmental growth. The National Association for the Education of Young Children describes play for all children as a key means for a child to develop self-regulation, language understanding and social ability—all precursors of school success. Children with ASD often spend so much time in therapy that natural opportunities for play can be missed. When the time to play does occur, depending on his developmental level, a child may also miss social cues with peers. By joining a regularly scheduled peer social group, your child can receive the needed structure and consistency with a defined group of children. In this group he can learn and practice spontaneous social interactions with trusted peers. Studies of these groups for children with ASD report major social gains, especially when "group work" is necessary—games, discussions or role play. Gains occur when emphasis is placed on sustaining relationships while practicing perspective taking, conversation skills and building friendships.

Additionally, you may find these groups to be fertile ground for your child to develop friendships offering opportunities for extended playdates. Some friendships have been supported through typical peer-mediated groups (sometimes referred to as "buddy" systems). This can be particularly effective for a child with ASD who has developed a friendship with a typical peer who can then ease social transitions while at school. His peer can often be the one to open further opportunities for socialization, even in the school playground setting. A study in 2009 of a thirty-week social skills group for seven- to eleven-year-olds with ASD showed that these children improved significantly in the areas of anxiety management, joint attention and especially improved flexibility and transitions—all significant challenges for children with ASD.

If your child has difficulty in a social skills group, one factor that may be derailing his interactions is excessive fear and worry regarding social situations. This is similar to what you may feel if you have excessive anxiety that gets in the way of your athletic, musical or public speaking performances. Yet for a child with ASD, it could lead to complete withdrawal and avoidance of social situations, allowing him to become even more self-absorbed. If you feel this is happening to your child, you may need some help from your doctor to alleviate your child's social anxiety (see Chapter 20).

Further Medical Evaluation

In general, once a child has been diagnosed with ASD, any further evaluation will include whatever is needed to rule out any of the double syndromes or associated medical illnesses that could be related to ASD (see Part V for information on health issues). In addition, any unmet health maintenance needs may be evaluated and recommendations will be made for possible "non-ASD" medical conditions. There are literally hundreds of possible laboratory tests that examine blood, urine and cerebral spinal fluid, as well as brain wave studies (EEG) and scanning techniques, that have been suggested for children with ASD. Potential standard laboratory tests are shown in the Standard

Medical Testing Procedures for Children with ASD box and are described further in Part V.

STANDARD MEDICAL TESTING PROCEDURES FOR CHILDREN WITH ASD

- Hearing evaluation
- Laboratory testing:
  - ▶ Blood
    - — blood survey (CBC, iron, ferritin)
    - — chemistry panel tests
    - — genetic tests (karyotype, Fragile X DNA, CGH microarray, MECP2)
    - — thyroid function tests (TSH, T4, free T4)
    - — metabolic screening (plasma amino acids)
    - — heavy metal screening (mercury, lead)
  - ▶ Urine
    - — metabolic screening (urine organic acids)
- 24-hour EEG, if indicated
- Appropriate X-ray and scanning procedures (such as MRI), if indicated
- Tests to help confirm specific coexisting conditions or diseases

---

You may be aware of medical conditions that you fear may be interfering with your child's progress. I find it useful to rule out these conditions by conducting appropriate lab tests, while at the same time pursuing treatment for your child's current issues. Keep in mind that extensive medical testing can be limited by insurance coverage or funding constraints. A list of other possible lab tests can be found in Appendix 3.

Medical Recommendations

Following the evaluation and review of appropriate laboratory tests, your doctor will make recommendations for treatment, further evaluation and follow-up. These concerns, of course, will be ongoing throughout your child's lifetime. The doctor will also spend time discussing the role of medications that may help modify your child's symptoms that may be getting in the way of learning and developing relationships. (See Part V for further discussion of health issues in ASD and specific treatments.)

Complementary and Alternative Medicine

The National Center for Complementary and Alternative Medicine within the National Institutes of Health describes CAM (complementary and alternative medicine) as "a group of diverse medical and health care systems, practices and products that are not generally considered part of conventional medicine." CAM includes potential therapies of various types: high vitamin usage, extra supplements (nutritional and otherwise), Eastern medicine techniques (Traditional Chinese Medicine, acupuncture, acupressure, cupping and homeopathy), as well as many other alternative systems, including manipulation and body-based methods, chiropractic/osteopathy, hyperbaric oxygen and mind-body interventions like prayers/blessings. Studies have shown that anywhere between 25 and 92 percent of all children with ASD have been treated using some form of CAM. Interestingly, children with ASD in the United States, Canada and Hong Kong are more likely to use CAM than children with other disorders. It has also been noted that CAM treatment is more likely in patients who experience longer wait times before seeing conventional doctors—perhaps due to parents' frustration with waiting while wanting to take action to help their child. Studies have shown that most primary care doctors, including pediatricians, are much less likely to directly prescribe CAM for ASD (unless the doctor specializes in CAM). A recent study of 539 physicians revealed their general desire for CAM education, specifically for children with ASD. The challenge in prescribing CAM treatment for children with ASD comes from the lack of scientific research available to guide medical decisions. Surveys of parents that review which treatments work and do not work give medical researchers hints at what to study but do not specify whether a particular treatment works. It is important to understand as much as possible about CAM treatments because some are potentially harmful.

CAM treatments can be divided into those that are proven but harmless biological treatments without theoretical basis (such as vitamin B6 or antifungal agents), those that are unproven yet harmless treatments with some theoretical basis (such as vitamin C, a gluten-free diet or hormones) and those that are unproven, potentially harmful treatments (such as chelation, hyperbaric oxygen, high-dose antibiotics, high-dose vitamin A, immunoglobulin or withholding immunizations).

The potentially harmful treatments obviously require the most research. Potential errors in judgment and use of these treatments can lead many parents and professionals down a dead-end path. Such was the case with the use of secretin, which was once suggested to be a miracle treatment for ASD (see Chapter 17).

My approach to CAM therapy in the overall treatment protocol is a practical one. Although I'm not a practicing CAM physician, it is important to have mutual trust and respect between a doctor and family. I discuss my clinical strengths and biases with parents yet emphasize that the team needs to be informed about all treatments a child is receiving—CAM or otherwise.

Medical decisions are generally made after considering all the substances in a child's regime, including vitamins, additives and so on. Medications can be impacted by supplements and a doctor needs to know everything that a child is taking. Medication treatment plans should be made without altering other therapies so that the effectiveness of the medication will be clear.

Research into effective CAM treatments has finally begun. Some suggestions for CAM usage for children with ASD actually come from studies done suggesting CAM treatments for the population at large. Such is the case in the use of omega-3 fatty acids, which are now recommended for everyone who does not get enough fatty fish in their diets. In a small group of thirteen children with ASD, a pilot study found that omega-3 fatty acids were better than placebo for alleviating hyperactivity symptoms in these children. Omega-3 fatty acids have been beneficial in a range of disorders, including schizophrenia, depression, bipolar disorder, ADHD, dyslexia and dyspraxia. It may well be that CAM therapies that have been shown to be valuable in other neurodevelopmental disorders will be applicable to children with ASD.

In medicine our number one rule is "First, do no harm." Using CAM that is harmless is generally not a problem. All vitamins and supplements should be reviewed with this in mind. However, if there is a serious concern that a treatment is potentially harmful—for example, with regard to chelation, there have been deaths reported of children with ASD—proceed with caution. Research-driven proof in these cases must show us that the benefit far outweighs the risks. The difficulty with some cases is that treatment success is reported after longer periods of time, often three years. Keep in mind that all children with ASD should improve over a three-year period, or something has gone amiss with either the evaluation or the program.

FAMILY EMOTIONAL SUPPORT/RESPITE CARE

Parents go through an incredible barrage of emotions when they have a child with ASD. An ongoing grieving process colors the whole experience. The welfare of your child and how you are going to put together a program for him, as well as finance it, are serious concerns. Your extended family may not live nearby, leaving you without a safety net. You may have little time left to devote to your relationships, friendships and other children. You and your spouse each bring your individual profiles and ways of processing information to the experience, as well. All these challenges can eat away at a marriage, or the very family structure. It is critical that health care professionals, especially doctors, are aware of this and include this topic as part of the planning process for families. Depending on the resources of the parents and family, I explore means of developing excellent respite care for the child so that the parents can have time alone to recoup some of their energy and emotional strength, as well as to attend to the needs of their marriage. (See Chapter 10 for more on how ASD impacts the family.)

A Sample Treatment Plan

The last part of the evaluation process for Alex and his parents was an extensive review of his diagnostic profile. The information from this review and observation was used to develop Alex's treatment for the next four to six months. Each item was prioritized and the characteristics of the team members who would best be able to support Alex's needs were considered.

Relationship-Based: DIR/Floortime
- Eight to ten sessions per day of 20 to 30 minutes
- Use all three types of DIR/Floortime interactions but begin with sensory-motor to "gear up" his system. Put toys aside, because Alex had much improved interaction without them.
- Target the first three social-emotional levels together
- Concentrate on the following goals for the next four to six months:
  - ▸ Encourage attention and engagement
  - ▸ Encourage two-way communication
- If difficult to engage, return to sensory-motor interactions
- Characteristics of team members: highly dramatic, speaking with their hands and facial gestures. Need a lot of energy to keep Alex motivated.

Speech and Language Therapy
- Home or clinic-based, two to three one-on-one hours per week
- Oral motor exercises for apraxia
- Speech and language curriculum adapted for home DIR/Floortime sessions

Occupational Therapy/Sensory Integration
- Home or clinic-based, two to three one-on-one hours per week
- Sensory-motor home-based program
- Sensory rescue kit
- Exercise focused on increasing Alex's visual field of attention, on motor planning and on Alex's proprioceptive challenges (hide-and-seek games, gradual expansion of his visual field, stop-and-go games, swinging and so on)
- Visual-spatial evaluation in the future

Educational Placement
- Change setting to a DIR/Floortime home program temporarily
- Parents to interview at specialized developmental preschools in the area

Nutritional Management
- Three-day diet review
- Addition of omega-3 fatty acids

Behavior Management
- Toileting discussion in the context of Alex's developmental level

Auditory Processing Augmentation
- Initially support Alex through gestural language and visual prompts (like visual schedules)
- Reassess for other augmentative strategies in six to twelve months

Social-Emotional Enhancement
- Primarily through his intensive DIR/Floortime interactions with family, therapists and siblings. These will be expanded once he is established in an appropriate preschool setting. As he gains more developmental ability, playdates can be considered.

Medical Evaluation (diagnostic workup to include):
- Overnight EEG to rule out seizure disorder
- Blood laboratory testing to evaluate for genetic metabolic, mitochondrial, immunologic disorders related to ASD (see Appendix 3)

Medical Recommendations
- Allergy management—including allergen control. Proper use of creams and lotions reviewed.
- Further recommendation will follow results of lab tests
- Brief discussion concerning the target symptom approach for medication use. Depending on the results of the EEG, there is a possibility that motor planning and sequencing are major challenges that might eventually lend themselves to medication treatment.

Family Support
- Identified family members and potential babysitters to help in the home and become involved in DIR/Floortime
- Parents were referred to the California Department of Developmental Services for respite support
- Recommendations were given for local parent support groups and appropriate reading materials

Follow-Up Considerations

Once I've completed an evaluation, I have a sense not only of a child and how he experiences the world but also of the many strengths and challenges of the family. Most families are searching for medical professionals who will work with them not only as they begin their journey but also as they travel down the road. I generally like to evaluate a child at least once every quarter. In that period of time I expect to see some change, and if not, I will begin to problem solve why he might not be improving. I find that with these intervals I can often see change that parents have grown into with their child and no longer recognize. We plot out progress and identify issues that are now challenging their child, tweaking his program as needed. By the end of each session, priorities have been outlined so the road map is clear for the next steps. It is important to insure that children with ASD progress up the social-emotional ladder to become creative thinkers and problem solvers. Sometimes this will result in minor changes. Other times a major change is needed. Of course, being available as needed for sudden change in behavior is essential. Families need a health care professional who is responsive and creative. This reassurance is an integral part of helping parents move forward with their children.

Alex and his parents returned eight weeks after his evaluation with me. He had progressed and was consistently sustaining five to six circles of communication with sensory-motor play. His parents were much more confident in their abilities. His speech/OT and psychological evaluations were complete. The team had been chosen and work had begun. His mom and dad were now assisted in Alex's DIR/Floortime program by two local college students—one majoring in psychology and the other in drama. A master therapist was on board to train the DIR/Floortime players and supervise the home program.

The blood lab results had returned and all were normal—especially his genetic profile. His parents were thrilled and open to discuss the implications for their having additional children. His overnight EEG, however, was positive, exhibiting sharp waves and slowing (often seen in children with this profile; see Chapter 16). We discussed at length whether or not he should be treated for these findings because he was exhibiting "spacey" episodes in addition to the EEG abnormalities. His parents opted for a medication trial. An antiepileptic drug was identified, potential side effects were discussed and a follow-up was scheduled. While leaving the office, Alex brushed by me. He stopped, turned his head, quickly glanced at me and gazed into my eyes. I raised my hand in front of him, saying, "High five." He briefly touched my hand with his. Mom, Dad and I hugged as they left the office, energized and hopeful for the next step of their journey.

CHAPTER 9

Staying on Track

FOLLOW-UP IS a crucial component of your child's treatment. Keeping his program current and appropriate for his developmental level will help him progress up the social-emotional ladder. Keep in mind that the critical factor in his progress is establishing relationship-based interactions in all encounters, therapies and treatments. A relationship must first be established if your child's goals are to be achieved. From that primary relationship, he will develop the ability to maintain and enjoy interactions with family members, peers and others outside of therapy.

DIR/Floortime—How to Keep Things Going

As your child gains more skills, you will spend much of follow-up navigating through any stumbling blocks that may arise during DIR/Floortime. DIR/ Floortime does not always go as planned and one of the common questions that arises is what to do if interactions become derailed. In the course of therapy, or during the course of a day, things will happen that will interfere with the success of a DIR/Floortime session. Your child may be out of sorts, as could the person working with him. Events occurring in your child's life and the environment (siblings, weather and so on) could also influence the relative success of DIR/Floortime. Sessions may be more or less successful on a daily basis and this is to be expected.

You may reach a point when you feel that your child's treatment is not consistently moving forward. He may be repeating previously mastered tasks rather than advancing to more creative problem solving. You and his therapists can start by considering any issues that may be hindering his progress. Reviewing your child's profile and examining his functional capabilities to see if certain patterns arise are a good place to start. Some of the common issues that I see that you might consider include:

- He has not met a developmental step and is being asked to perform at too high a level.

- He is bored because he is working at too low a level and is not being challenged.
- His stereotypic or repetitive behavior patterns—stimming, vocalizations and so on—are getting in the way of his interactions with you or his therapists.
- A sensory-motor challenge (such as auditory processing challenges, visual-spatial difficulties or motor-planning delays) has not been clearly identified and treated appropriately to help him begin to overcome that challenge.
- You fall into repetitive routines with him.
- He has an underlying medical issue that has not been addressed (see Part V).

Any of these issues can result in his feeling anxiety, leading to frustration, tantrums, acting out, aggression and/or self-absorption.

If your child's appropriate developmental level has not been assessed, it is important to observe once again his emerging capabilities. In addition, you need to observe your own behavior as well as that of your therapist—how you use language with him, how you give him information and how you set up creative problem-solving situations. Be certain that your actions match his developmental level and needs while at the same time adequately challenging him. Remember to use his natural instincts as opportunities for interaction and learning throughout the day. If your child loves wheels, think of all the situations that he might love to explore! Find a tire swing in the park. Go to a tire store. Watch someone change a tire. Visit a bike shop where he can see and feel different types of wheels. Get a toy wheelbarrow and let him push it in the yard while you pick up leaves together. The opportunities are endless. When we are doing what we love, we are on top of our game and most capable of success. The same is true for your child. When he is doing something that he thinks is exciting, he will be using all of his interactive and sensory-motor abilities to work together with you.

Two crucial steps on the social-emotional developmental continuum can be more challenging for parents and therapists to figure out best ways to help their child. One is the ability to understand and use words (symbols). The other is moving from symbolic representation into abstract thoughts and ideas. When your child can think abstractly, he can take individual ideas and build bridges between these ideas to come up with his own novel solutions to situations or problems. There are many ideas presented by Drs. Greenspan and Wieder (such as in their works *Engaging Autism* and *The Child with Special Needs*) to help facilitate achieving these aspects of social-emotional development through DIR/Floortime. (See Chapter 6 for the discussion of DIR/Floortime.)

When it comes to helping your child with symbolic thinking, it is important to remember that children with ASD often need to have visual reinforcement for what they hear, underscoring the importance of using gestures while you speak. When speaking and working with your child, you must be dramatic, showing your emotions as you convey the meaning of the spoken words with your hands and facial expressions. You can also give verbal guidance to go with physical action. For example, to warn your child, you might say, "Uh-oh" as you take his hand to keep him from touching something he shouldn't. If motor planning is an issue, you can help him handle a situation not by telling him what to do but by gesturing and verbally prompting him. For instance, you could ask, "Could you use your hand to open the door?" You can also help him by commenting on his ideas or when he successfully completes a task. Telling him, "What a great idea" or "You are so smart" will often bring out the gleam in his eye. Any encouragement will support your child as he begins to find solutions for situations on his own.

Emotional exchanges can make your child feel anxious. Therefore, using DIR/Floortime to emphasize things that feel good, such as happiness, or situations where we're taking care of things (like feeding a doll or putting a doll to sleep) or repairing things may be less anxiety provoking than playing out something that is fearful. As he becomes more able, you can help him by setting up situations that require more imagination. The ability to understand symbols and to think symbolically develops from experience and practice in different situations, which are often limited for children with ASD. The range of scenarios that can be acted out in DIR/Floortime are limitless and can occur all day long in a variety of settings. It can be a time for your child to figure out (symbolically) how to cope with something that has upset him. For example, DIR/Floortime sessions could involve a situation that has been causing him anxiety, such as going to the zoo. By acting out a trip to the zoo with dolls where one assumes the role of a frightened child, he can learn how to cope with the situation and to control his anxiety. By supporting him as he works through emotional content, you help him gain the ability to respond appropriately when confronted with an emotionally charged situation.

Behaviors That Get in the Way

One of the major issues parents mention that derail DIR/Floortime is the stereotypical and repetitive behavior patterns of children with ASD—stimming, vocalizations and the like. These behaviors could occur because of anxiety, boredom or your child's inability to control his body once these repetitive motions have started. In fact, children who have repetitive behaviors tend to increase these behaviors when anxious. If repetitive behavior is getting in the way of DIR/Floortime, it is time to step back and assess why your child might be anxious and address that issue before moving on to any others. The DIR/Floortime approach supports him in a fashion that should help regulate his sensory-motor system, decrease his anxiety and allow him to make progress.

Stimming (Stims)

We all have stims or ways of self-calming. We doodle, twirl our hair, tap our fingers on the table, fiddle with a pen or pencil, bounce our leg—the list could be endless. For the average person, these repetitive behaviors don't get in the way of social interactions or the ability to learn and grow.

Stims in children with ASD can be a symptom of a variety of issues. It's typically a basic pattern that could emerge as a response to anything from anxiety to fear to pain to boredom. Repetitive behavior in ASD is generally sensory and motor based. It is possible that sensory behavior (repeated stims) may help to stimulate a child's undefined motor map for him. Stimulating his motor map may give him a better sense of his body position in the world.

Because children with ASD have a high level of sensory and physical challenges (coordination and so on), they also have a high level of anxiety (see Chapter 20). Their stims may be a way they can self-calm, or they may serve as a distraction from whatever is bothering them. Sometimes they engage in these behaviors because they are bored. Without an activity to occupy and engage them, they may revert to prior behaviors. Of course, if the degree of stimming increases, medical issues must be considered as an underlying trigger (see Part V).

If there are no underlying issues that must be addressed when your child has increased stims, this is a good time to increase your DIR/Floortime component. Using all three interactive components (spontaneous, semi-structured and sensory-motor) helps both you and your child move beyond the stims into interactions that often meet the needs that increased the stims in the first place. For the times when he is in a more structured environment, such as school, he may need a sensory diversion (a tennis ball to squeeze, small rocks in his pocket to feel or rubber tubing to chew on).

Sensory-Motor Challenges

When discussing barriers to making progress, sensory-motor challenges can be daunting. Frequently issues arise because of the mismatch between receptive and expressive language, difficulties with rhythm and timing, as well as visual-spatial processing.

Expressive and Receptive Language

Often expressive language can be more advanced than receptive language, meaning your child will be verbally adept but will not understand what he hears or reads. The opposite can also occur, where he has receptive language that is greater than his expressive language, meaning he understands much more than he can communicate. Both of these imbalances will impede his movement up the social-emotional ladder if they are not addressed by you or his therapist. If your child has expressive language that is greater than his receptive language, he may miss out on getting the help he needs because there is a natural tendency to evaluate what he is thinking and feeling based on what he is saying. If your child has this language imbalance, he could be very chatty and others will speak to him at that level and assume he understands them. In truth, however, he is unable to have a reciprocal conversation because he is not taking in the contextual meaning of what is said to him. He may also have a very good auditory memory, and may actually have echolalia (repeating sounds, words or phrases said by others), but have an auditory processing delay affecting his receptive abilities. Many techniques have been discussed (see Chapter 8) to augment auditory processing. In DIR/Floortime it is important to be certain that you are using the language level and gestural level that match your child's receptive abilities and to not be overly influenced by his expressive abilities. In order to overcome the expressive/receptive language imbalance, he must first strengthen his ability to use and understand nonverbal gestural language as he engages in back-and-forth interactions. By building on this early developmental language stage, he will eventually gain the ability for expression and comprehension. It is easy to think that a child with a strong expressive ability understands everything around him, but with a child with ASD, it is important to not take his ability at face value and to determine if his receptive ability matches his expressive strength.

On the other hand, a child whose receptive ability is greater than his expressive output also fools us. Your child may have a very deep understanding of what's happening around him, but because of motor-planning and sequencing issues, he is not able to let anyone know. These motor-planning issues are often some of the most challenging, especially when he has intent and ideas but is unable to act upon them because he has difficulty speaking due to poor muscle/motor control. If he lacks the ability to express himself, he may be desperate for some form of expressive outlet (see Chapter 12 for information on assisted and augmented communication). He needs to be evaluated for his special needs early so that therapy for oral motor planning and expressive outlet can be put into place.

Rhythm and Timing

Your child may have a slower response time than typical children. This is often due to prolonged auditory processing through the auditory areas in the temporal lobe of the brain, the underconnectivity to the motor cortex and delayed motor output caused by slower and inefficient motor planning and sequencing. "Patience" is the watchword when speaking with your child because it takes him longer to process the information (a question) and provide a response (the answer). While it may seem as though he has not heard or understood you, he simply needs more time to formulate a response. Resist filling the pregnant pause by repeating the question or asking another, because that additional input will more than likely derail or overwhelm him. Therapeutically, this requires slowing your pace to give your child time to respond. I suggest that you silently count one-one-thousand, two-one-thousand, three-one-thousand and so on to determine how long a delay is needed in order for him to respond. During this time maintain a lively expression and use gestures—such as pointing toward the toy you're talking about—to give him visual clues to support what you have asked. Connecting the visual and the auditory eventually helps promote faster auditory processing.

Visual-Spatial Issues

If your child has visual-spatial issues, he will be challenged in moving forward with sequence learning and visual motor tasks, which are so important in a child's life (think of the process involved in catching a ball and throwing it back to a friend). Visual-spatial problem solving is complex and yet is required in much of a child's ordinary play—turn taking, climbing up and going down slides, playing tag or hide-and-seek, figuring out how a toy works or how to fix something. Integrate exercises that support these skills into his DIR/Floortime. As he develops more visual-spatial skills, his fine motor coordination may improve. However, when he is bored and not engaged, he may revert to old patterns of behavior that appeal to his profile (such as lining up toys, lying on the floor, watching wheels go around), underscoring the need to keep him engaged and active in child play as much as possible. Improved visual-spatial processing also helps him emotionally navigate the world. When he can correctly interpret the three-dimensional space around him and when he is oriented in that space, his fear and anxiety will decrease, allowing him to be more receptive to a wide range of learning.

Rigidity

Rigidity is one of the core issues in autism. For that reason, it is imperative to help your child develop flexibility. Functioning in the social realm requires flexibility to adjust to others' needs, tone of voice, nonverbal cues and so on.

If he is unable to do this, keeping this notion front and center during therapeutic and daily interactions is important. Flexibility can be fostered in small
ways all day long.

Sarah is a three-and-a-half-year-old girl who had a diagnosis of PDD/
NOS and had made terrific progress in her first year of intensive multidisciplinary therapy. Her challenges were milder than those of most typical
children with ASD. She was a strong visual learner, had a great attitude, was
engaged from the beginning and was intelligent and creative. However, she
had poor auditory reception and visual-spatial difficulties, along with some
motor-planning and sensory issues. It is not unusual for a child with visual-
spatial issues to have less flexibility and be more rigid in his behavior, because
interpreting the world around him is very difficult. To compensate, a child
may adhere to rules and engage in repetitive patterns, such as lining up toys.
Sarah had made wonderful progress in therapy and was beginning to talk in
sentences linked together in paragraphs. Her auditory reception had improved
remarkably and she was able to follow through on multistep directions and
was using "who, what, where, when" questions. However, her mother said
that they were having a hard time dealing with Sarah's need to do things the
same way. "It especially occurs when she's playing with other children, and
if she can't do it the way she wants (repetitive way), then she will get up and
walk away—content to play by herself. What can we do?"

We reviewed why Sarah would want to continue being so rigid and we
considered how to refine her visual-spatial practice. We also discussed small
ways to help increase her flexibility throughout the day. Because she was able
to have social reciprocity and lots of back-and-forth conversation with different themes in mind, the task was much easier. I urged her mom and dad to
try to respond to her as if they were a child at play and to negotiate like they
imagined a child would. During DIR/Floortime if she always wanted to use
the blue car, they could ask, "Why? Can't I use the blue car? You always have
the blue car. Can't I have the blue car?" emphasizing the need for turn taking
and cooperative play. If she grabbed the car and said, "*No,* I have to have the
blue car," then the next step would be for the parents to respond as another
child would and let her know how her behavior made them feel. "It makes
me mad (or sad). You always get the blue car and it's my turn. I want to play
with the blue car and you always do."

It is important to be sensitive to how your child reacts to tone so that you
won't aggravate the sensory system. It's also important to be gentle and get the
idea across as you negotiate. Keep in mind that you are challenging your child
in small ways to think about something that is difficult for him. Remember
to always ask a question that requires him to respond with a question. Each
question you ask means that he has to think about another creative answer.

Suddenly concrete play with cars becomes an opportunity to practice creative problem solving and learn negotiation and compromise.

Temper Tantrums

All children have temper tantrums—they have them because they are tired or hungry or angry, or for any number of reasons. A tantrum is a physical expression of their internal feelings, usually involving frustration. Typical children move beyond having tantrums when they become verbal because they can then express in words what it is that they are feeling. Children with autism are more likely to be set off by the sensory information around them or due to frustration over their inability to control themselves in their environment. Limitations in terms of expressive language can also be a factor in tantrums.

The overreactive child can have a tantrum because he has an idea but is unable to express it or follow through on it due to language delays. He can become more excited or aggressive if his behavior is met with shouting or big gestures. By soothing him with a soft voice, gentle movements and an overall slow and thoughtful manner, he can get the needed time to cool down and reregulate. Once he is calm, you can help him learn the consequences of his actions to help him eventually take responsibility for them.

Jeffrey is an almost six-year-old boy with Asperger's whose challenges are due, in large part, to his motor-planning issues and difficulty with expressive emotional language. He has an overreactive sensory profile. If people get into his space or don't do what he thinks they should do, he hits them. The first thing to do for a child like Jeffrey is to use a soothing voice in responding to him so he can calm down. Once he has calmed down and can pay attention to what you are saying to him, you can then help him understand the consequences of his actions. If he's hit you, respond appropriately with "Ow" and show pain in your expression. You might also say, "Oh, my. I've been hurt. Help me." He will make the connection between your expression and his having hit you.

Interestingly, as I was explaining this technique to Jeffrey's mom, complete with sad voice and wounded facial expression, Jeffrey looked up at me and said, "You're sad."

I asked him, "Why am I sad?"

And he said, "You were hit."

I responded, "Yes. Don't hit me if you're mad. Tell me you're mad."

At which point he looked at me and said, "I am mad."

I built on what he said by asking, "Oh, you're mad. What is it you want to have done?"

He then said, "Go to the potty."

I said, "Oh, you want to go to the potty. Which one?" He pointed to the bathroom just outside of my exam room, which he recognized by looking at the restroom sign on the door.

His mom offered, "He loves signs."

So, we gave Jeffrey signs that said I Am Angry and I Am Mad that he could use in the heat of the moment rather than hitting. The idea here was to enable him to convey his emotions in a communicative manner rather than acting out his frustrations.

Expanding the Theme

It is easy to fall into routines and repetition in play and conversation with your child. You play the same games, ask the same questions and get rote responses. It is important to realize that you must always be aware of expanding your child's experiences, especially building on familiar themes to promote thinking and creativity. It is essential to bring some creativity to all your interactions. For example, if you are in a grocery store, you can ask your child, "Where are the apples?" If he easily answers that question, you can then ask him, "Do you want red or green or yellow apples?" If he identifies which color apple he wants, you can then ask, "How many do you want?" If he can't answer a particular question, you can lead him to an answer by giving him a choice, such as "Do you want two or three red apples?" and then let him choose. Every time you go to the grocery store, you can engage him in this way. Additionally, in anticipation of grocery shopping you can expand on the theme by having him make up his own grocery list. If he's in charge of the fruit plus his own special snack, make him responsible for finding these items when you shop together. Create the grocery list at home before you go, using both words and pictures—stickers can be very helpful. If he is in charge of three red apples, two bananas, one orange and a favorite snack, make a picture list that has the words for the items written on it, as well. Once you have the list, you can decide who will hold it and which list will be used first (his or yours), and you can generally prepare him for what will happen on the shopping trip. You could expand on this theme further. If, for example, he is beginning to learn math concepts, you could ask him to add up how many pieces of fruit he has in his cart and see if it is the same as the number on his list. When you get home, if he is able, he can be in charge of putting away his groceries. Not only have you created many circles incorporating many different ideas around a central theme, but your child also will develop an increasing sense of responsibility as he helps out with family chores. This example underscores the importance of expanding themes in ways that are fun and exciting for your child. Try to follow his lead to help him think more broadly about what interests him. This task requires creativity on your part, too!

What if Nothing Is Working?

What do you do when it seems nothing is working, despite your, your child's and the team's best efforts? Take heart. The truth is each and every child I have seen has made progress. The difficulty is that the rate of progress for some children is slow and, because it is incremental, hard to assess. Because progress has its own pace, I prefer to see my patients at least once every three to four months. In that time frame, I generally can see improvement, whereas it is more difficult for those who live or work with the children on a daily basis to see that change. Periodic videotaping helps evaluate growth as well as make comparisons when a child may regress, or take a few steps backward. If it isn't possible to document progress over time or if the team collectively notes a decrease in abilities, the rule of thumb is to take a fresh, comprehensive look at your child. This requires starting from the beginning with a complete evaluation, including current history, a physical examination, appropriate lab tests and determining possible treatment options and plans. Don't lose any time in starting the process. Often a reassessment requires the whole team advocating for your child in order to figure out what issues are getting in the way of his progress. It is important to determine if your child has had a true loss of skills across the board (as seen in regression) or if what is happening is a loss of motor skills. If progress is blunted or has stopped in one setting but not others, then you need to consider what might be happening in that particular situation—such as a poor school placement or wrong fit with a therapist. Whatever the result of the investigation, the entire treatment plan must then be revamped to accommodate what you and the team feel will fit your child's needs, a new plan must be put into practice and your child must be monitored for improvement. This approach has worked well for me.

One day Carole, a good friend and psychology colleague, called about one of her clients. She was very concerned about Russell, a six-year-old who had a very intensive multidisciplinary team working with him and had made significant gains. Although he was nonverbal, his gestural system had been developing and his creativity and interest in the children in her therapeutic group had increased to the point that he was interacting with them in various activities. Over the past several months, however, he had gradually had a major change. His mood, while usually neutral to outgoing, had become sad and self-absorbed. If stimulated, he responded in an overreactive fashion, sometimes interpreted by his teachers as aggression. Although toilet trained, he started having stool accidents and was taking his stool and smearing it on the school walls. He was described as so uncooperative and aggressive at school that his parents had been asked to consider another placement. His therapists were discouraged. They felt their best efforts no longer resulted in a response from him. Russell's parents were frightened, not knowing what else they could do to help their son. Carole was very concerned that this regression could have a medical basis and called me for guidance.

My first question was whether she felt that Russell had lost his intent. In other words, had the light in his eyes dimmed? "No, I don't think so," she replied. "In our group sessions I still find that I can connect with him, even if it is fleeting. In fact, I think he still understands a good deal of what we are saying but he is definitely much more aloof."

"Okay," I answered. "That is a significant clue." In general, I find that a true regression involves loss in all areas, including receptive language. I agreed that he needed a full medical evaluation but I also felt from what Carole was telling me that perhaps he was responding to something happening in his environment. I asked her if she could think of anything.

"Yes," she replied. "There are many family factors going on at the same time, with job changes for both parents requiring them to be away from home, and I've always felt that the school he's in is not the proper setting for him—that he just doesn't get the right support."

"My approach would be to find out what he's thinking and feeling. He needs an expressive output perhaps through augmentative techniques, including supported typing. It may be that if the school is not meeting his needs and he's bored, he is smearing his stool as a comment on what's actually happening in the school setting. Talk to him like you would talk to any six-year-old. Let him know that something must not be right for him to be showing us this behavior. Tell him that you know how smart he is and that he knows that six-year-old boys should not be smearing their stool and should be using the toilet. Tell him you really think he can do this and that you'll help him. In the meantime I'll help you arrange to get the full battery of medical testing. Please discuss with his parents about giving him a break from the school setting, which may be influencing all these behaviors."

Carole went to work with her team. At first they were doubtful about these suggestions but put many changes into place. Carole was able to institute sessions for Russell with a computer to facilitate his communication. His mom decided to take a break from work and homeschool Russell for a short period. Carole instructed the team to intensify DIR/Floortime interactions and expectations all around for Russell. By the time the results of the full medical battery returned (which were normal), Russell had not only stopped having stool accidents (once Carole and his mom had a talk with him and removed him from school, they stopped) but he was making progress communicating his intent and wishes through the augmentative communication device and DIR/Floortime. Within weeks he was calmer and much more available for interaction with his home team. His mom said, "My son has returned to me. Once again we are sharing laughter and joy. Hope has returned."

There have been a few difficulties over the years with individual patients resulting in similar episodes and in retrospect they were probably predictable. These situations often involved either extreme periods of aggression or suspected regression but usually represented major underlying family issues, such as an impending divorce, an older sibling going away to college or a death in the family. It can be frightening for a child to lose skills but the causes are usually multifactorial and require significant investigation and follow-through. No matter what the situation, by using your skills to look at everything going on in your child's environment while determining what might be happening as you interact with him, you can begin to consider those factors that may be influencing his behavior. From this you will be better prepared to address each situation as it arises.

CHAPTER 10

ASD and the Family

Having a child with ASD can and will have an impact on your immediate and extended family. While it is easy to be distracted by your child's often overwhelming needs, it is important to carve out time for your family and friends. Often they can be your best support. Additionally, you may need help dealing with many concerns, including those that are emotionally charged, such as how to tell others about your child, whether to have more children, how to incorporate siblings into his program, and practical ones, such as financing, finding respite care and just organizing your life and family, as well as getting your own job at work done.

Parent Concerns

There is no question that having a child with special needs adds to parental stress. Not only must you work through the grieving process once your child has been diagnosed with ASD, but you also have to do battle with health care, education and financing in order to put together a program for your beloved child. With all these family pressures it is easy to put your own life and emotional needs on the back burner. While this is understandable, I must remind you that the journey you are on with your child with ASD will be a long one and that you must pace yourself. If you do not attend to your physical or emotional self, you will have less to give to your child—and your spouse and other children. I recommend that you work with a counselor or therapist to address any stress, depression or grief you may have.

You may even be overcome by guilt, worrying that perhaps something you have done may have caused your child's autism. Frankly, guilt is part of our parental job description—no matter what. But, I can assure you that most concerns you may have—every fall, every high fever, every accident that may have occurred in your child's life—most of the time are unrelated to your child's having autism. Any issues related to pregnancy and delivery can be put into perspective with what we now know about autism and its development.

As individuals, as a couple and as a member of your community you must determine your own path—one that is best for your family and for your child. All parents must find their own way but there are common concerns that arise, including grieving for the loss of the initial dream of what it might be like to parent and grow a family, adjusting the expectations for their child, developing coping mechanisms for raising a child with special needs, navigating the health care and education systems, parenting the siblings of their child with ASD and coping with the added stress for themselves and the family.

Coping with Stress

In working with families, I like to explore what behaviors in the children push the parents' "stress" button. Knowing what can trigger a negative response is the first step in developing a coping mechanism so that you can turn a highly charged situation into a learning experience. In the DIR/Floortime methodology, parents are taught to understand why their children behave the way they do by learning about how their children learn and interact with their environment. It is important to realize that each parent can have different reactions to their child's behavior. A recent article has shown that mothers are more often concerned about regulatory matters (times when a child is not calm and available, like when he shows anxiety, aggression, tantrums and so on) and fathers get stressed with their child's external behaviors (repetitive actions, like stimming, that make him look autistic). Both mothers and fathers can have extreme emotional distress when dealing with their child's difficulty with social connections.

How you respond to stress and anxiety, especially when they are connected to your children, is largely dependent on your individual patterns of behavior. Remember, we all have our own strengths and challenges! Understanding through the evaluation the best ways for each of you to reach your child can be a huge help.

Often parents are so stressed with simply getting through the week, completing job requirements and fulfilling household and family responsibilities—including all the special therapies required for a child with ASD—that there is little, if any, time left for their relationship. Although many studies indicate an increase in divorce among parents of children with ASD, when parents are able to keep their lines of communication open and have a little bit of time for themselves individually as well as for their own relationship, chances are greater for their ability to sustain the energy required to continue down this long journey together. There is no question that having a child with special needs will put a strain on your relationship, but something that can help alleviate the stress (on you as individuals and as a couple) is having resources outside the family that you can rely on. Extended family, friends, religious institutions and more can become the source of assistance, respite and support.

SUPPORT FOR YOURSELF AND YOUR FAMILY

- Acknowledge your feelings: sadness, grief, worry, anxiety. Get professional help as needed.
- Meet others who have worn your shoes.
- Read stories of challenge and success (see the Resources).
- Be as informed as possible. Read!
- Keep yourself healthy and fit (exercise, even if at ten-minute intervals)!
- Stay organized. Plan ahead. Use schedules. Keep internet listservs of therapists for ease of communication.
- Pamper yourself. Schedule breaks.
- Join parent support groups. Stay connected as much as possible.
- Don't ignore your relationship with your spouse. Touch base daily. Celebrate together your child's successes no matter how small.
- Schedule date night.
- Remember that humor is important!
- Relax when possible. Pursue your passions—even if it's window-shopping!
- Keep immediate and extended family members involved. Don't shut anyone out if possible. Be open about difficulties and successes.
- Ask for what you need. They may say no but most likely will say yes!
- Schedule family meetings. Involve all in duties and fun.
- Plan vacations and time off (modify these for children with ASD as needed).
- Celebrate the small steps for all.
- Continue traditions and family times.
- Validate siblings and give them individualized attention.

Respite Care: Getting Away

In order to maintain your relationship while also attending to the needs of your child, you might want to consider respite care. Respite care is short term or temporary care provided for your child in order to give you the opportunity to have some time together as a couple or time with your other children, or to manage any issues surrounding your child's care (meet with school administrators, visit schools or educational settings and so on). Unfortunately, studies have shown that respite care is an essential yet still unmet need for families with special health care needs. Families who have children with long-term needs are stressed economically, often with both parents working to fund their child's program. They are also mentally and physically exhausted from all that is required to keep the family going. Many people do not have extended families to provide a safety net for critically stressed times. Finding individuals to provide respite care so that you can have time away, even if for an hour or two, as well as occasional evenings out with your spouse to help nurture your relationship, requires not only funding but also available competent resources. I urge you to identify possible individuals who could provide some respite care and to decide what steps they need to take and experiences they need to have in order for you to be comfortable leaving your child with them. Funding for respite care is sometimes available from state agencies (this varies by state) and should be explored as another means to provide these services. Of course, parents can get some time for themselves if family members are available or if friends are willing to help out (sometimes several parents can form a support group, allowing one couple to go out while the others sit for all the children). Another possibility is finding talented therapists or teachers who would be willing to look after your child for an evening. I believe that professionals need to help find ways to support parents so they get this necessary time to regroup and find the energy to enthusiastically continue with the challenges and joys of family life.

Support from Other Parents

Parents need to be in contact with others who have experienced what they are going through. Input and aid from peers who also have children with ASD can become part of your support system. It can be very difficult to discuss issues with friends who come from the world "before the autism diagnosis" and who can't grasp all that you are experiencing. Parent support groups are very strong throughout the country and often parents form lasting friendships with other families. See the Resources section for a list of organizations and advocacy groups that offer support to parents of children with ASD. You can also check with your child's therapist, doctor or school for any local support groups.

Telling Others about the Diagnosis

Deciding what and how much to tell others can be difficult, especially if you are still in the process of understanding what autism means for your child. You may be afraid of how your child will be accepted or labeled when others know about his ASD.

Parents' comfort level in telling others about their child's autism varies greatly. Some tell everyone they know; others are much more reticent. If telling will help your child develop his interactions with a particular person, then by all means let that person know. On the other hand, if people express concerns about your child but you are not prepared to share your story, you can simply thank them for their interest. Whether or not to tell them specifics about your child depends on their relationship to him. If these individuals spend time with him, teach him or are responsible for his welfare for any or part of the day, then the more information they have, the better equipped they will be to work with your child.

In my experience it does not help your child if you withhold information. If your child's teachers realize that he is falling behind and are unaware of his diagnosis, then their focus will be on how to suggest that he get an evaluation rather than using what you know to help your child. Having a diagnosis/label is typically required in schools to get special services, but sharing with the teacher what you know about how your child learns or where his particular challenges lie will be invaluable in getting him the help he needs. The bottom line is if your child has significant enough delays to meet the ASD criteria, eventually others will know there is a problem. Tell those who can aid and support your child in his school and community.

Telling which family members and how is as individual a matter as the family you are in. Explaining the situation to siblings requires some thinking and advanced planning. Children can pick up on your worry and concern and can only be helped by being told what is going on—always in an age-appropriate manner. Too often siblings can be uncertain as to how to interact with their brother or sister and become "little parents," picking up the same tone of voice and the same phrases that parents use with a child with ASD. Children know at some level that they are having difficulty interacting with their sibling and they, too, are trying to find answers. It is better for a child to hear about his sibling with ASD from you than from someone else, who may not deliver the information in a sensitive manner. (See below for more on the sibling relationship.)

Financing Your Child's Treatment Program

One of the most pressing issues you may encounter when working through the evaluation and treatment plan for your child is how to pay for his programs. Multidisciplinary programs are very expensive and can run tens of thousands of dollars per year. Unfortunately, most are paid "out of pocket" because insurance companies and educational systems have not embraced them. In general, insurance requires evidence-based scientific backup in order to fund a particular treatment. Given the intensive needs and the broad-based program that is typically provided for children with ASD and their families, it has been difficult to perform the longitudinal studies required to inform health professionals about "best practices."

One program most often cited as evidence-based has been the behavioral approaches that include ABI, although there have been publications and recent reviews evaluating the effectiveness of ABI that have not found ABI to meet the gold standard for an evidence-based study. It is, however, one of the more researched methodologies, which may be because behavioral-based therapies lend themselves to a structured format. Because they are one-size-fits-all structured formats that can be well outlined and followed, they are the preferred format for research, allowing them to be more frequently studied. Because the children studied have received the same intervention, it is easier to compare outcomes and compare results to a control group. The DIR/Floortime model encompasses whatever approaches a particular child requires in order to help support his developmental progress, so no two programs are exactly alike. Progress is measured on a case-by-case basis, with the program changing to meet the child's needs. This is wonderful for the child but is not always ideal for the research paradigm, thus making a study of this model much more difficult. In order to study the DIR/Floortime model outcomes, different approaches may be used. For example, newer brain-scanning techniques can document changes in brain processing following an intervention. In addition, funding may now be available to provide support for the long-term group studies that will be required in order to show the value of this approach while also meeting the criteria for evidence-based practice review.

Funding Resources

Funding resources vary by state. Early intervention services are mandated by federal law and provided in each state until a child reaches the age of three. The content of these programs also varies state by state and some programs may not be appropriate for a child with ASD. After age three the state will provide federally mandated educational programs that are considered appropriate for the child. The Individuals with Disabilities Education Improvement Act (IDEIA) mandates that the state provide all eligible children with a free and appropriate public education that meets their unique individual needs. Autism is specifically mentioned in the IDEIA as a condition that constitutes a disability. Thus school districts are required to provide an education "appropriate" to your child's special needs, including "appropriate" placement that will allow your child to progress educationally. The key word here is "appropriate"—which leaves much room for interpretation by states and local school districts. It is clear that the number and hours of services offered to children with ASD vary across the country. My advice is to become a "squeaky wheel." No one can advocate more passionately for your child than you. Given the financial constraints of governments, they often resist going much beyond a minimal interpretation of the law. On the other hand, through advocacy I urge you to do what you can to help put together the program that is most appropriate for your child's needs. In some states special needs advocates are trained to specifically address these funding issues. You may need to hire a lawyer with expertise in special needs to go through a fair hearing process with your school district in order to get a judgment to provide the correct program for your child. My recommendation is to leave nothing on the table and to press the system as much as possible in order to provide for your child. For information on services and legal counsel, see www.wrightslaw.com.

Insurance

For insurance purposes, reimbursement for out-of-pocket expenses related to your child's treatment will depend on the diagnosis, time spent and provider reimbursement coverage. This, too, varies by state, as well as by insurance carrier and plan. Insurance help for autism specific to California can be found at www.insurancehelpforautism.com. If you do not live in California, the site may prove helpful in providing information that you can follow up on in your own state. Included on this website are diagnostic codes that can be used for medical diagnoses, as well as diagnostic codes related to OT, speech and language, and behavioral approaches. Although not all states have laws that mandate autism insurance coverage, there have been several initiatives at the state and federal levels to mandate such coverage (www.autismvotes.org). In considering which diagnostic codes to use when requesting coverage, it is important to remember that many of your child's visits to his doctor are for issues that can be considered separately from the autism and they should be used if possible. For example, if I see a child with a seizure disorder, allergies or GI dysfunction in addition to the autism, I may use these diagnoses as the primary reason for the visit (which may improve chances for reimbursement for the visit) and autism as the secondary one. Knowing the terms of your insurance policy—including what is covered, both diagnostically and therapeutically—can be very helpful to your health care professionals as they support you in the process of claiming reimbursement.

Autism Speaks has made efforts to enact legislation on the state and federal level that would require mandatory health care coverage for ASD for all evidence-based therapies, including ABI. Several states have passed these laws (varies by state), which call for health insurance coverage up to certain amounts per year and for a certain number of years until a child is eighteen. The federal law would require that federal-based systems (Medicaid) provide similar coverage. See www.autismvotes.org for more information.

Should We Have Another Child?

One of the most frequent questions I discuss with families is whether or not to have more children. Many parents will also get a consultation with a pediatric genetics specialist to further understand the implications of this decision. Occasionally parents are already expecting when their child is diagnosed with ASD, which adds anxiety and stress to the pregnancy itself. There is no doubt that a genetic predisposition to developing ASD means an increased percentage of siblings might meet the diagnosis. That's the tough news. On the other hand, once you have a child who is diagnosed with ASD, future children will be followed extremely closely, and my philosophy is to begin intervention at the first sign of any sensory or motor concerns. If a younger sibling of a child with ASD displays difficulty with regulation in infancy (such as increased irritability, colic-type symptoms, a slightly slowed development of motor ability, and especially a decreased response time to auditory and/ or visual input, all of which can be associated with slightly delayed social-emotional milestones), I recommend appropriate sensory-motor intervention, even in a six-to-eight month old. This type of intervention is very common for children born prematurely and should not be withheld from siblings of children with ASD, especially if there's a suspicion the sibling might also be susceptible for an ASD. When a child is dysregulated, anything that will help him become regulated will be beneficial, not only to the child but also to the family. If a child is able to assume a typical developmental trajectory, that is a great result and the therapy can stop. If a child continues to have challenges, then treatment is in place, and because it has been started early, it gives him a head start on the journey.

Families must also watch for possible developmental issues in the siblings of the affected child. Many siblings may not have ASD, but they may have a mild expressive language delay, a learning disorder or attention issues. I see many families where one child has ASD and another an attention deficit disorder. Often there is so much energy put into the child affected with ASD that it is not until the other child exhibits great difficulty in school or with relationships that parents become aware of the non-ASD child's underlying issues that also need attention and possible treatment.

Sibling Concerns

If you have more than one child in the family and one is affected by autism, you may be concerned about how to ensure that the needs of your more typically developing children are met. All family members' lives are complicated by the therapeutic schedules and the moment-to-moment needs of the affected child. In fact, the impact of raising a child with ASD on the family, especially on siblings, adds yet another layer of responsibility and concern for you. Common sibling issues include how to discuss autism, how to handle sibling-to-sibling conflict in order to support a relationship between the children, how to help typically developing siblings handle their level of stress relative to their affected sibling and how to help siblings and affected children become integrated into the functioning of the whole family so that all family members feel they have a role and purpose.

How to Talk to Siblings about Autism

Many parents struggle with how to explain autism to their unaffected children—some wonder if anything should be said at all. The truth is that typically developing siblings instinctively know that something isn't right with their brother or sister; they pick up on the same lack of response or unusual behaviors that got parents started down the road toward diagnosis. Although they may not be able to put into words what they feel or observe about their sibling, they will be concerned and may experience stress over this issue without knowing why. They may feel uncomfortable about what they may be thinking about their sibling. Therefore, it is best to talk with your other children as soon as you feel they can understand a simple explanation of ASD. Having the diagnosis out in the open is helpful as they may hear you talk within the family about the ASD or their sibling and misinterpret the situation. They are likely to pick up on your feelings as well—seeing you in pain or grief and not fully understanding the circumstances can be upsetting and confusing. They may blame themselves for their sibling's condition and/ or your suffering.

Speaking with your other children can ease their discomfort and confusion, as well as support them in their interactions with their sibling. Although it is helpful to use clear-cut definitions ("Your brother has autism"), it is also important to emphasize that this is just a label and doesn't define their sibling. They will gain a better understanding of their brother or sister if they have a handle on their sibling's particular challenges as well as strengths. Explaining a challenge to siblings must be done at their level of understanding. I suggest that you think about a challenge that was most difficult for your typical children. As you talk with them about their sibling, have them reflect on that challenge. For one sibling it might be doing cartwheels. For another, it might be learning to ride a bike. Everybody has difficulty learning something. Once you've had them reflect on this, then you put into perspective that for their brother or sister to learn to play with toys and to talk is one hundred times harder than their having to learn to do a cartwheel or ride a bike. The next step is to talk with them about the best way for them to interact. You can engage them by asking questions: "Did you ever notice that Johnny responds more quickly when you're looking at his face?" You can then go through all the things that will help improve their relationship.

For younger siblings who won't understand, helping them play together, making it as successful as possible, can be the key to strengthening their relationship. If this is hard for you, use your team to support these sibling-based interactions. With older children you can be more specific in your explanation about what ASD is and how it affects their sibling, always being sure to inform them, as best they can understand, about their sibling's unique profile and how best to interact with him. The key is to always gear what you're saying to the child's or adolescent's level of understanding, both intellectually and emotionally.

Sibling-to-Sibling Relationships

Sibling adjustment to a special needs child is another concern that comes up again and again. Having a sibling is a gift to a child with ASD because a brother or sister will often be persistent in the pursuit of a relationship with their sibling and will generally interact like a peer. Siblings can become best friends. With older siblings there is a risk that they will fall into a more parental role—adopting the language of the parents to become more directive with the child, telling him what he can and can't do, calling behaviors good and bad and essentially becoming another boss. It is important to encourage siblings to be siblings and not become another parent. If you have siblings yourself, I suggest you reflect on your own memories of typical sibling behavior to help you guide your children in their relationship. Our experiences with our siblings (whether love-hate or best of friends) are a huge part of who we are today. Children with ASD as well as typical children learn and grow based on sibling interactions. House rules about behavior toward one another, cleaning up toys and so on should be clearly established so that all children understand them and are able to comply. Within the framework of those house rules children need to learn to negotiate with each other and the child with ASD has to learn to stick up for himself without the support of his parents. If we expect him to develop any level of independence in the future, the sibling relationship must be a proving ground for him to learn to hold his own with peers.

One of the biggest issues for the typically developing sibling is the concern that parents don't have enough time for him. Siblings naturally vie for their parents' attention, and no matter how much actual time is spent with each sibling, each will feel he has been shortchanged. When there is a special needs child, however, because of the time and attention that child needs, siblings can feel angry and resentful, as well as guilty about feeling that way. You may

ASD AND THE FAMILY

inadvertently feed into this situation by focusing attention on the fact that you have less time for your nonaffected children. The issue of time can become very difficult in a single-parent home or in a two-parent home where both parents work outside the home. The truth is that in most families there is very little extra time to devote all around. To alleviate the situation, you can help your nonaffected children understand that their feelings are normal, and you can also endeavor to make every effort possible to carve out "special time" for each child by each parent. Special one-on-one time devoted to a child's needs will reassure him that he is cared for and valued, supporting his own developmental needs. Often typically developing children are involved in team sports, hobbies and educational pursuits that will allow you to become their supporter and advocate in those situations.

Although they often are very good at interacting with the child with ASD, siblings should be siblings, not therapists. That said, I have seen siblings become some of the best DIR/Floortimers when they are supported in having fun with their sibling. When the unaffected sibling understands what the challenges are for their brother or sister, they can become excellent helpers to support their sibling. If therapists integrate siblings into DIR/Floortime, emphasis must be placed on the unaffected sibling having just as much fun as the child with ASD. Learning how to play together in sensory-motor exercises is a great way to begin. Interactive games that not only fit the needs of many children with ASD but are enjoyed by all children include hide-and-seek, Simon Says and the beanbag toss. Physical activities, like jumping on a trampoline, can support motor-system issues, as well as bring forth the typical nonverbal interactions of childhood. When a child with ASD has his sensory-motor system regulated by the appropriate input, he is more able to be a vital part of the interaction. Warmth and connection between siblings can be incredibly positive and reinforce the sibling relationship.

Handling Sibling Stress

It goes without saying that there is stress in the lives of all children in modern society. The stressors in each household vary but life today is stressful in general and children are not immune to these issues. When there is a child with ASD in the family, the focus of stress can be on that child, his program and the financial constraints raised by his care and family members' fatigue. Discussing the role of stress in children's and adolescents' lives needs to be carried out with the typically developing children so that they understand that they are not the only ones experiencing stress—and that they can get help in coping with it. Childhood has never been worry or stress free and parents can help children navigate through these periods of stress and learn from them so that they will be able to deal successfully with these issues when they are adults.

There are unique issues related to autism that could be potential sources of stress for siblings. These include embarrassment around peers, sadness over not being able to fully engage with their sibling and concern over the "acting out" or aggressive behavior of their sibling.

Eventually children may develop concern for their parents and what they are going through, and by late adolescence they will be trying to determine their role in the eventual caregiving of their sibling. These are all very real concerns and must not be minimized. Often acknowledging that these concerns exist and putting them into the context of the family and situation can be very helpful. Children need assurance that there will be support for the short and long term. Over time you can help them be aware of what the future might hold emotionally and economically. Depending on your child's or adolescent's needs, I suggest that the sibling have an opportunity for his own therapeutic work, exploring his feelings with a person who is neutral and not emotionally connected to the family. This can help him develop perspective and sort out his needs versus the needs of his affected sibling. This differentiation and learning to accept responsibility for oneself without using the affected sibling as an excuse may be critical to his own personal growth, especially during the more difficult adolescent years.

DIR/Floortime approaches were initially developed for all children and later were applied to children with special needs. Remember to use your interactive skills with all your children. They become especially important when working with children on stressful issues. Being certain that you have attention, engagement and reciprocal communication while talking with your child at his level to explore his thoughts and feelings can be one of the most open and supportive interactions you experience with your child. These types of experiences go a long way to helping children feel acknowledged and understood by their parents.

Studies have shown that siblings who have brothers or sisters with ASD often learn to cope quite well. For many, learning to be a helpful member of the family becomes second nature. In fact, as an adult they may pursue one of the helping careers. Having been immersed in a family situation where the value of the relationship is held in highest esteem, they may become more skilled than their peers in responding positively to their own emotional needs.

Your Child's Role and Purpose in the Family

It is critical that children with ASD be included in family activities, especially if their siblings are involved. I suggest that all members of the family have chores and, once children are old enough to participate, that family meetings occur to help make decisions about family activities and problem solve issues within the family. Of course, responsibilities will be modified for a child with ASD in a way that will allow him to be successful. But the whole family must be prepared to let the child with ASD take part. Raising the bar of expectation must also occur between your typically developing and special needs children. Siblings must learn to step back and allow the child with ASD to do for himself. The rule of thumb I use for siblings is they need to watch the back of their special needs sibling but they must also give him room to grow and develop.

Religion

If your family life includes participating in faith-based experiences, your child with ASD should also be included. In some settings the religious staff may not be educated or prepared to meet the needs of children with special needs and your child's participation may require some extra effort or participation on your part. Religious education and experiences can be adapted for children with ASD—whether it be Sunday school, Hebrew school, preparation for communion, confirmation, a bar mitzvah or simply attending services. Your religious community can provide great support and comfort for your family. I highly recommend continuing this family tradition and including all your children.

One of my most moving experiences was at a bar mitzvah for one of the children I see. Noah, a teenager with ASD, also had a seizure disorder, motor-planning issues and auditory processing challenges. He had significant difficulty in school, especially with math and reading comprehension. His mother had been told by school staff that his academic potential was limited. Although he had receptive and expressive language delays as a younger child, his teenage years were marked by a major improvement in his understanding and expressing language. A tall, handsome, dark-haired boy with a ready smile, Noah prepared for his bar mitzvah for months, working with a Hebrew teacher who was able to adapt the Torah portions for him. A bar mitzvah, one of the most meaningful experiences in Jewish family life, can be an intimidating experience for most thirteen-year-olds, yet Noah was able to read his Hebrew passage from the Torah, expressing humor and grace. He also wrote his own interpretation of his Torah passage, which related to the Ten Commandments. In his speech he spoke about his favorite commandment, which was to honor his mother and father. His father had passed away two years before and Noah poignantly discussed what his father meant to him and how much he missed him. He then went on to speak of his mother, whom he loved and cared for deeply. As one can imagine, there wasn't a dry eye in the house when he finished. Later at the celebration with more than one hundred family members and friends, the dinner tables were decorated with

Noah's artwork, and movies that he had written and animated were shown. It was an impressive event, especially considering that Noah had been totally underrated by his school.

Noah's bar mitzvah is an excellent example of how advanced a child's thinking and feeling can become when he is allowed to participate in his family's experiences. Include your child as best you can in your full family life. Whether going to a movie or on a family vacation, with preplanning it can be accomplished. The internet is replete with suggestions and recommendations for family-friendly special-needs resources, especially for travel.

Animals

Animals can play an important role in any family. For a child with ASD, having a pet in the home or participating in a program such as therapeutic horseback riding can provide wonderful experiences. There's a special bond that animals form with all children and this is even more obvious for children with special needs. Depending on the temperament of the animal, children can become involved with feeding and caring for their own house pets. They can accompany you on trips to the grocery store to buy dog food and can clean the dog dish and scoop poop. Caring for an animal is a huge responsibility and can be a major factor in building your child's self-esteem. Many of the children I see are very proud to be the dog walker in their family, and family members derive a sense of security from the fact that their dogs are protective of and watch out for the children. In some communities companion dogs for children and adults with ASD are available, and they can be a wonderful addition to a child's therapeutic program.

The connection that many children with ASD feel while on a horse's back can be one of the most exhilarating and reinforcing experiences for a child who struggles so much to be connected all day long. Often a child will become extremely verbal once settled on his horse, as his sensory-motor system seems to work in concert with the animal. For more information, see www.americanhippotherapyassociation.org.

Grandparents and Extended Family

It can be wonderful to have extended family to help share in daily activities and celebrations. Grandparents especially can be a source of support in looking after children and giving you a welcome break. However, sometimes it can be difficult to convey to grandparents the realities of the situation of having a child with ASD. Parenting styles have changed over the generations and grandparents may be critical of how their children parent. ASD was not as prevalent when they were raising their families and may indeed be a new concept. In their era some of the ASD behaviors (such as hyperactivity, not following through with directions, not appearing to listen, not appearing to be respectful) were interpreted as disrespectful and "bad" behavior. The notion that behavior is communication is most likely a novel one for them.

An interesting phenomenon that I have seen in grandparents is that they have often forgotten the trials and tribulations of raising children. They may not be as aware of the daily challenges that can arise in homes when young children with one or both parents work outside the home. The key, of course, is to help grandparents (and extended family members) become educated about the individual profile of your child with special needs and to give them the special tools that you have learned that help foster your child's interactive relationships and work on his challenges. Many grandparents are quite interested in reading materials and learning all that they can. I am always open to any grandparent who wishes to attend their grandchild's visit with me or to set up a separate appointment. At these visits the grandparent's own concerns and emotional needs can be addressed. Grandparents can feel incapacitated or bewildered by the ASD label and may not feel comfortable becoming a caretaker for their grandchild because they do not want to step on the toes of the child's parents. Once your child's grandparents have a better understanding of the issues, you may find them to be strong forces in supporting your family. They may be in a position to lend financial support, but more importantly, they may also have the extra time to do research into community resources and, if they are physically able, become part of the respite plan. Some grandparents want to do more and become active in parent advocacy groups. Autism Speaks (AS), for example, was founded by Bob and Suzanne Wright, themselves grandparents of a child affected by ASD.

A GRANDFATHER TAKES TIME TO CONNECT

Carrie is a four-year-old with ASD who was also diagnosed with a seizure disorder. Treatment for the seizure disorder improved her receptive language ability. Carrie's grandparents had always been integral parts of the extended family and were eager to learn more about how to interact with their granddaughter. Carrie has major motor-planning challenges that greatly impact her rhythm and timing in interacting with others. Her grandfather, in his eagerness to connect with her, responded to all her gestures with an almost continuous line of questioning, which derailed Carrie from what she was thinking and feeling. I pointed out to her grandfather that in his eagerness to connect he was overwhelming his granddaughter and he needed to give her time to respond. I suggested that he silently count seconds while waiting for her response to get an understanding of how much time she needed to react. In most cases he had to count between six and eight seconds before Carrie responded.

Once he slowed his rhythm and timing to match Carrie's, they were able to build many circles of communication. Because of the success of communication between Carrie and her grandfather, all family members slowed their interactions to match her pace. The result was a wonderful increase in her expressive language. This was an "aha" moment for Carrie's grandfather, and he later sent me a letter describing his experience and how tweaking his interaction with his granddaughter not only helped to develop a stronger bond between them but also opened up the possibilities for her future in his eyes.

Hope for your child, both his small steps and developmental leaps, will always be found in his family. In all my years in pediatric medicine, I have found that families with a child with ASD are extremely resourceful and resilient. Despite sometimes huge challenges, they find joy, humor and deep love with their children. They are survivors. I am confident that you will be, too.

PART IV

Your Child's Communication Issues

CHAPTER 11

Behavior as Communication

O NE OF the most difficult issues faced by parents of a child with ASD is their child's behaviors. These behaviors may exist in patterns, some persisting over time, others changing as a child grows and develops. While there are some who categorize these behaviors as good or bad and seek to work with the parents and child to eliminate the bad behaviors, my approach is different. In my view, the behaviors we observe are a child's response to a disturbance in his internal or external environment. Therefore, a behavior is an opportunity for you, caregivers and therapists to help your child problem solve and to work out whatever issues are stimulating this response. (Medical considerations that might cause unusual behaviors are reviewed in Part V.) However, many other issues can also be involved. Assume that a child's behavior is his means of expressing his emotional feelings of need or discomfort, often due to a sense of dysregulation or assault on his system—essentially it is a cry for help. Punishing the behavior is a missed opportunity and often makes things worse if the initial problem that stimulated the behavior is left unresolved. Typically, if the initial issue is not addressed, the behavior can escalate or a new, more intense behavior can take its place.

Getting a Clearer Picture

Always assume the behavior is not willful because your child likes it, wants to torment or is mean-spirited. The behavior may begin as a response to a particular situation and then become uncontrollable for him depending on his individual profile. When children with ASD are aggressive and act out in a manner that causes harm, once calm they generally regret their actions and are full of remorse. We've all had the experience of becoming very angry and saying something we later regret. We also engage in small behavior changes to soothe ourselves when we are anxious or bored. Some of us fool with our hair; others rhythmically rock a foot or leg; some doodle. For children with ASD an emotional response to anger can set off not just an outburst but also a series of patterns that can become aggressive or self-injurious. Likewise, if they are anxious and need to soothe themselves, they may increase repetitive patterns. Children with ASD will often become more self-absorbed or return to typical patterns of behavior, such as flicking fingers or rolling toy cars.

Exploring what the issues might be for your child requires thoughtful investigation. Learning as much as possible about his environment (both internally and in his external world) and what may be stimulating his behavioral pattern will often provide the necessary clues to help him. If your child increases his behaviors, the following suggestions may be helpful:

■ **Identify the behavior:** Keep a log of behaviors on a calendar or in a day planner to identify when this pattern of behavior occurs. Is it only during the week, or is it on weekends, as well? Is it in the summer months or the winter? Does it occur annually, such as might happen with the transition from his summer program to school each fall? Identifying patterns of behavior relative to time can be very useful to determine the cause. For example, if a child has the same behavior each time a strep infection occurs, a medical diagnosis of PANDAS (see Chapter 21) might be considered. If a teenage girl has particular patterns of behavior that occur at the same time in her monthly cycle, responses to hormones might be the culprit. If your child becomes anxious or aggressive only in a certain classroom, then he may be having trouble understanding the subject matter and may need extra support. If you can identify these patterns, it allows you to become proactive and help your child anticipate these changes and to better understand his reactions.

■ **Is this a new or old pattern of behavior?** If it's old, what did the behavior do for your child in the past? Did repetitive motion soothe him while stressed? If this is a new pattern of behavior, could there be changes in his health that may be influencing his response? Is he ill, or has he developed a chronic medical problem? Just as we may feel irritable if we are not feeling well, so may your child, and he may only be able to express his irritability or discomfort through his behaviors. Has something been missed while assessing his individual profile that might affect his behavior? (Visual-spatial processing difficulties are often underestimated for children with ASD, yet even mild problems can be anxiety-provoking when things move or change for a child.)

■ **Is it seasonal?** Seasonal allergies might influence a child's behavioral patterns. I have seen several children with seasonal affective disorder (SAD) that occurs around daylight savings time in the fall. This change creates a unique pattern of behavior that is often recognized only after it has occurred over several years.

▪ **What has happened in the family?** Have family members been ill? Has a favorite nanny or therapist left? Has there been a death in your family? Has there been a major emotional upheaval within your family and thus could increased family stress be affecting your child?

▪ **Has your child's environment changed?** Has there been a move to a new home? Have members left your family home (an older sibling moved out of the house or went to college)? Has there been a remodel at home or outside landscaping changes that could alter his perception of his world? What has been happening with his educational program? Has a transition occurred? Have his teachers changed? Have seating arrangements changed? Is there a new child in the class who is acting out? Has the academic challenge been increased? (This is especially significant if your child has not been appropriately challenged in the past.) Has he been bullied at school? Has his therapeutic program changed? Has there been a change in therapists or increased challenge by the therapies? A key issue that can lead to your child developing behaviors is whether the therapist provides the right fit to your child's individual profile and whether the therapeutic program itself is appropriate to meet your child's needs. I often find that the programs get boring and repetitive for children with ASD, which can be a key factor for acting-out behavior, including aggression and self-injurious behavior.

▪ **Have there been changes in his sensory environment?** Have new lights been installed that may affect a child with visual sensitivities? Have new sounds entered his environment? I find that children with ASD respond very poorly to fire alarms at school. If alarms ring on a regular basis, this increases a child's fear and anxiety as he is unable to anticipate when the next alarm will go off, resulting in increased behaviors. Is there construction outside work or school that is providing intense stimulation to the sound-sensitive child?

▪ **Has there been a developmental spurt?** If there has been a sudden improvement in his receptive language and your child is now taking in all kinds of new sounds that he must interpret, he might experience increased aggression until these new sounds make sense to him and he becomes much more comfortable. Puberty triggers many brain changes that may impact behavior. Puberty can also change a child's reactions to fear, anxiety, frustration and anger, which can result in self-injurious behavior. On the other hand, adolescents with ASD often experience a greater awareness as they strengthen their brain pathways during this time. This change may heighten their awareness of their difference from their peers, which could lead to frustration, anger and untoward behavioral patterns. Sometimes children with ASD are reluctant to grow up and become teenagers. This fear may actually stimulate behaviors that are much more childlike.

■ **Has the behavior become a means of getting attention?** This requires an insightful examination of your responses to his behavior. See if you are unwittingly reinforcing the behaviors he may be using to get your attention. If he needs your attention, teaching him how to get it in a constructive manner is central to problem solving these issues.

■ **Is your child aware that the behavior is occurring?** When I asked a child with ASD who was able to type fluently why he was vocally repeating the same phrase the entire time he was typing his thoughts and feelings, he appeared puzzled and then told me that he had no idea he was doing it. Upon reflection, he thought maybe it was helping him stay regulated so that he could type, which was a very difficult task for him.

Once a clear picture of the pattern of behavior has been identified, further investigation may be required. Obviously, if your child is ill, a visit to the doctor may be necessary. If you have concerns about school, further fact-finding with the school and your child's aide to determine the source of his increased discomfort may be required.

Difficult behaviors were the topic of conversation when fourteen-year-old Neal and his family came for their quarterly visit. The preceding week had been particularly stressful for everyone. Although Neal is very challenged with ASD (nonverbal, apraxic, with sensory and motor-planning issues), he was able to communicate in brief sentences using his voice output computer. He was very frustrated when asked to cooperate and help around the house. His parents felt as if he was continually pushing back at their requests. With his parents' agreement, we decided the time had come to address this behavior directly with Neal.

I started the dialogue by suggesting to Neal that I knew it was tough becoming a teenager—especially because his body was changing.

"I don't like that," he responded.

"What does it mean to become taller?" I asked.

"I am going to miss home when I get taller," he replied.

"Do you think that by getting taller you'll no longer be sleeping at home?" I asked. "Would you like to ask your mother how she feels about that?"

His mom responded, "No matter how tall you are, you will always be welcome to sleep at home. When you do move out, you can still stay with us a few nights a week if you want."

"I want to be a baby longer," Neal answered.

I asked him why he wanted to be that small, at which point he went to the toy shelf and took down the dollhouse. Opening the dollhouse, he started setting up a bedroom with a bed and desk.

"Is that your bedroom?" I asked.

"Yes," he typed.

"What does baby Neal do all day? Does he have chores?" I asked.

"No."

"Does he do homework?"

"No."

At this point Neal needed a break and went to the other room for a snack. It was clear that Neal was dealing with typical adolescent issues—especially related to independence. Although his reluctance to do chores or homework could be seen as typical teenage behavior, Neal was also dealing with the fact that he has special needs. He was linking the changes in his body with his fear of leaving home. The thought of accepting responsibility and moving on is indeed a frightening one. In his view it was less anxiety-provoking to reject responsibility and stay young. This conflict increased his anxiety, resulting in the behaviors that were disrupting the family.

His parents agreed to rethink their approach with Neal. They needed to give him reassurance that he would be able to meet the demands that accompanied growing up. At the same time, he needed practice being more self-sufficient to develop confidence in his ability to do things for himself. This new direction for Neal and his family was made possible once they truly understood what was driving his behavior.

Helping Your Child Deal with Emotionally Charged Behaviors

If a child is engaging in aggressive behavior and is unable to stop, fear and anxiety may be driving him to continue the pattern. Helping your child understand the behavior is important for his well-being. Explain that you understand that the behavior is happening in response to some change he is experiencing and you will do whatever you can to help him. Use appropriate language, gestures and tone of voice. He may not get every word, but he will understand that you are there to help.

Calm Down

First help your child calm down by using whatever techniques you know that will soothe and reregulate his system. You need to control your own emotional response to the issue that has triggered his behavior, as well as your response to the behavior itself. I advise family members to do their best to not add fuel to the fire. Anger and aggression will often elicit an angry, aggressive response. By taking a deep breath, downplaying your tone of voice and using calm and controlled movements, you will also relax yourself and assure that you can better help your child. It is easier to resolve the issue if you help him to calm down first and allow him to be part of the problem solving, rather than jumping in and taking it on yourself.

Take Action

Once the behavior has been identified, a plan needs to be developed to address the situation. Let your whole team know what works and what doesn't work in each situation. Prepare a behavioral rescue kit that contains appropriate items to help soothe your child (brushes, weighted vests, favorite toys, music, videos and books) and can be carried in the car or left at school for emergencies.

Anxiety and Stress

Anxiety is a normal reaction to stress. It can help one deal with a tense situation in the office, study harder for an exam or keep focused on an important speech. In general it helps one cope. But anxiety can become excessive. If it becomes an irrational dread of everyday situations, it can become a debilitating disorder. There are five major types of anxiety disorders. They are:

- Generalized anxiety disorder
- Obsessive-compulsive disorder (OCD)
- Panic disorder
- Post-traumatic stress disorder (PTSD)
- Social phobia (or social anxiety disorder)

Certainly individuals with ASD have symptoms that are similar to those of these anxiety disorders. Anxiety in children with ASD may result in difficulties in family, school and social functioning. In fact, studies have shown that 35 percent of children with ASD have increased anxiety. Children with ASD especially experience generalized anxiety (leads to everyday worry and may be associated with tension, irritability, sleeping difficulties, stomachaches and more), separation anxiety (leads to dependence on adults) and social phobia (leads to social isolation and few peer friendships). A recent study of ten- to fourteen-year-olds with ASD reported social anxiety disorder in 30 percent of the adolescents.

I often feel that most of the children with ASD I treat are doing whatever it takes to get through a day in an environment that is extremely frightening and anxiety-provoking for them. It is amazing to watch how well they actually perform given their high level of anxiety. Not only are they living in this frightening world but they are often aware that they're not interpreting their surroundings as they should. This heightens their anxiety even further. Their individual profiles are often characterized by uneven and poor comprehension of what people say, with delays in processing that information. Weak visual-spatial processing and/or poor motor planning further exacerbates their processing and comprehension challenges. If a child falls apart, it may be because he is scared, worried or in pain, or because he realizes that his body doesn't respond the way he would like it to. A child with ASD may also have increased anxiety when he has an idea but he can't convey it or act on it. Reducing anxiety can significantly improve your child's well-being. When this debilitating symptom is treated, progress can resume.

Anxiety may be primary or secondary. Primary anxiety is an underlying biologically-based disorder that may or may not be a response to a situation and may simply be "free-floating." Secondary anxiety has many possible causes. Whether primary or secondary, the heightened state of stress caused by the anxiety drives the behavior you see. This behavior, whether aggression, self-absorption or repetition, may then further increase your child's anxiety, driving even more behavior, and the vicious cycle continues. This is especially true if, at these times, others in his environment respond to him in ways that add to his confusion or distraction. For example, if a child can't solve a problem, he may become anxious and aggressive. If this happens to your child, relieving the underlying issue (for example, medical discomfort, a processing disorder and so on) will decrease his anxiety and help him get control of his behavior. One of the generally overlooked causes of anxiety in children with ASD is difficulty with visual-spatial processing. Children with these challenges live in a fearful world where they have difficulty understanding movement and spatial relationships, and judging foreground from background. They can be rendered helpless when faced with moving objects, when tracking objects (including words on a page) or when recognizing and identifying objects. Often, unless the visual-spatial issue is addressed, anxiety can result.

Treatment is not always simple. Determining the source of your child's increased anxiety generally takes much thought and may take the help of your doctor if you suspect medical issues play a role. If your child is experiencing anxiety:

- Learn his pattern of responses to anxiety
- Determine the cause (such as medical, undiagnosed processing difficulty, environmental)
- Help your child understand what is happening
- Treat or eliminate specific problems
- Target the anxiety using calming DIR/Floortime and sensory-motor techniques known to work for your child

When anxiety is excessive, despite increased DIR/Floortime and sensory-motor techniques, medication may give additional support to your child.

Medications used to treat anxiety, such as SSRIs, tricyclic antidepressants, benzodiazepines and beta-blockers, are discussed in Chapter 20 and Appendix 6. However, these medications should be used only in combination with appropriate sensory-motor and relationship-based techniques.

Anxiety is a significant but often overlooked issue for children with ASD. Recent interest in the issue has sparked research into medication choices (such as mirtazapine) for children who experience side effects from the more usual medications. In addition, there is a direct therapeutic program that helps children learn to alleviate their own anxiety when it occurs, no matter the cause. Known as cognitive behavior therapy (CBT), this program has recently been adapted for children with ASD. In CBT techniques address dealing with anxiety so that the child can become more available for social interaction and learning. In fact, unless a child learns to deal with his anxiety, many of his other therapies won't be as effective, because he may be using all his strength to cope with his worry or fear. In a current CBT program being studied in a randomized controlled clinical trial at UCLA, children with ASD learn about anxiety by learning their body cues (such as increased heartbeat, headache, stomachache, butterflies, sense of dread), as well as skills to relax (such as self-talk when anxious). This program then offers the opportunity to practice what is learned through interactive play to develop confidence and mastery.

Anxiety was a concern for Liam and his family. He was first diagnosed with ASD at eighteen months and came to see me for this issue when he was six and a half years old. He has a mixed reactive sensory profile and often overreacts to sensory stimuli, which in turn increases his anxiety. When he is anxious, his repetitive behaviors, including stimming, increase. He does reasonably well in school despite some difficulty with motor planning, sequencing and visual-spatial processing.

Liam has had many gastrointestinal problems throughout his life, including major feeding resistance and intermittent constipation. He also has absence (petit mal) seizures, which are being treated with the appropriate medication. He takes medication for his anxiety and his poor motor planning.

His mother contacted me early in August. Although Liam had enjoyed camp and other summer activities with his sister, his behaviors had increased over the past few weeks. She noticed more stimming than ever and felt that he was clearly much more anxious. She also noticed that he had not been having regular bowel movements. He had not been ill, but his sister had had a strep infection several weeks before and had been very sick. In addition, his family recently had moved into a rental home while their house was being remodeled. His mom explained that she had set up Liam's bedroom the same way it had been done in their primary home, but the environment surrounding his room and the home was different.

Many of Liam's issues needed further investigation. It was important to confirm the degree of his constipation and to test for an untreated strep infection. While searching for answers, I encouraged Liam's mother to use the techniques we knew helped him calm down and reregulate, including swinging, swimming, massaging and brushing. We also devised a "moving home" calendar, filled with family photos of fun activities around their own house, so that Liam would be able to anticipate his return.

Liam's blood test results for infection were negative. However, an X-ray of his abdomen revealed significant constipation. His mom changed his diet to relieve the constipation and Liam was given medication to help soften his stools and to help increase his gut motility. With these sensory, emotional and medical adjustments in place, his mother continued DIR/Floortime and the sensory techniques that were most helpful. Six days later she reported that his stimming had markedly decreased and his bowel movements had improved. He was looking and feeling much more relaxed.

By early September Liam's mom reported that he was back to his usual self, with minimal behaviors. He was excited about starting school and the transition this year was easier than in the past. The whole family was looking forward to returning to their home by Christmas. By following through on what his increased symptoms were "saying," his mother was able to get Liam the help he needed.

Transitions

Transitions can provoke anxiety for all of us. For children with ASD these situations provoke not only usual physiological and emotional changes (such as increased heart rate, butterflies in the stomach, headache) but can also increase behaviors (such as repetition, aggression, tantrums).

Transitions large and small, anticipated or unexpected, can occur throughout the day—all can be jarring to a child with ASD. Those that are the most difficult to handle are the larger transitions that involve moving to a new school, meeting a new teacher, moving to a new home or city, going through a divorce or accepting a death. If the transition affects the entire family, the parents or caregivers may not be as available for their child as they are coping with the change on their own terms. This may lead to the child acting out even further because his usual support system seems unavailable.

Anticipating Transitions

Fortunately, most situations that require transitions can be anticipated. Children with ASD often respond adversely when things happen suddenly or if they have difficulty understanding what is happening. Situations that will overwhelm a child's sensory system should be avoided if at all possible. A child with visual-spatial processing issues may have difficulty with places with visual complexity (such as an arcade or play space with bright lights, loud sounds, highly decorated carpets and unusual smells). If your child is not prepared for a transition, he might become anxious, resulting in a temper tantrum or a meltdown. Therefore, you, your family, his teachers and therapists need to help him through transitions using techniques that are compatible with his individual profile.

If transitions are difficult for your child, do your best to keep him informed. Visual schedules can help in advance of any transitions. To prepare for a Saturday morning errand run, you could show him pictures of all the places you will go, working with him to develop a visual schedule of the day's stops. This will help him not only predict where he's going but also understand where he's been. You could add further interaction by helping him understand what he will do at each stop or who he will be with (if you are picking up the dry cleaning and he will stay in the car with his nanny, he should know about it). Children who are particularly sensitive to transitions need to be forewarned as they move through their day. Many children become used to multiple transitions in the schedule during the school day but lose that structure while at home at night and during the weekend. Structure and preknowledge help them to organize and anticipate and can certainly ease the movement from playtime to mealtime to bath time to bedtime at home.

Any major changes require major preplanning. If you are planning to move your child to a new school, I recommend that you and your child visit the school, ideally at a time when there are no children present to overwhelm him. You can take pictures of all areas of the school where he will be—classroom, lunchroom and bathroom—along with photos of his teachers, aides and school principal, and put them in a book for him. He will then have his book to refer to and review many times before the actual transition takes place.

You can use DIR/Floortime to help prepare for transitions. Play areas can be arranged to look like the new rooms at school. Depending on your child's developmental level, the steps of the transition can be practiced through pretend play. A countdown calendar can be made for home, so your child can further anticipate the day the new school begins.

If you are leaving on a trip, there are some things you can do to help maintain some stability in his schedule. You can create a calendar for your child to count down to your return. You can tape videos of yourself that your child can watch while you're away, or you can call over the internet using Skype.

Always check in with your child to see his response during transitions. If the transition has been successful, be certain to remind him how well it went.

Saying "You did an awesome job!" can go a long way to reinforce positive behavior for the next time.

Planning for Transitions

Successfully navigating transitions is a high priority for many of the families that I see. A discussion with six-year-old Katherine's parents revolved around her difficulty in school. She had made significant progress and was now in first grade. However, she insisted that everything go her way. When it didn't, she became aggressive, pinching or hitting teachers and fellow students. The discussion revealed that her behavior was triggered by transitions. Katherine's aggressive behavior could occur with small transitions, such as a seat change in the classroom (which happened on a weekly basis), as well as with larger changes or transitions, such as when a large group of younger children unexpectedly came to her classroom. Katherine was working on visual-spatial challenges and she tended to be overreactive. When situations changed, her anxiety increased, resulting in her behavior. Her mom noted, however, that when Katherine had time to process the situation, she would calm down and return to a more regulated state. We discussed how to prepare Katherine for transitions and how to use DIR/Floortime interactions to help her get ready for what was coming. For example, if there was a predictable transition (like the weekly seat change), the night before the transition was expected, Katherine and her parents could act out the change in their playroom at home. For a larger transition, as was expected to happen at an upcoming Easter egg hunt in their backyard that would be attended by many children, DIR/Floortime could also provide an opportunity to act out and prepare. The different scenarios of sharing eggs with a small group or a large group of children were practiced in the office. Katherine became the director of the Easter egg hunt, helping place eggs around my office and then helping us look for them. Her mom later reported that the Easter egg hunt was fun for all and incident free.

Since that time, Katherine's mom and dad have discussed how preplanning has eased her through so many difficult situations. At the same time, it isn't possible to prepare ahead for everything. Use DIR/Floortime interactions to help your child learn to adjust to the unexpected. Doing this in the DIR/Floortime setting, where it is calm and secure, will give him practice dealing with change, coping with the resulting anxiety and realizing he can get control over the situation. Developing coping skills is important for all children and particularly children with ASD. When a child has coping mechanisms, he can break the vicious cycle of anxiety that leads to behaviors and more anxiety. These skills that we all use as adults are practiced repeatedly as we grow and learn. Giving this extra emphasis as DIR/Floortime progresses, creating new and different situations that your child can solve together with you, will lead to independence and more success for your child.

Help for Specific Behaviors

Given that behaviors can be seen as a form of communication for a child with ASD, how might you interpret common behaviors? Perseveration, aggression, temper tantrums, anxiety, scratching and picking and high-pitched screams are all common behavioral symptoms that affect the well-being of your child and your entire family.

Perseveration (extensive repetitive behavior) is a core feature of autism. However, depending on your child's individual profile, it can wax and wane or dramatically increase under varying circumstances. Perseveration is often extremely difficult for families to endure. A child can become so self-absorbed in the repetitive behavior that productive interaction can be very difficult. Perseveration can increase when a child is ill (as noted in post-strep phenomena when children exhibit OCD-type behavior—see Chapter 21). It could be a result of increased anxiety from an environmental stressor, it could be a calming technique for the child or it could represent motor-planning issues, where he is getting stuck in a pattern of behavior while attempting to do something complex. Treatment guidelines will depend on the triggers and how the behavior is interpreted. For a child who uses perseveration as a coping mechanism, it would be counterproductive to try and eliminate it. For a child who is severely anxious because of a new sound in his environment, removing the sound may markedly decrease his perseveration.

A new behavior or one that suddenly increases in intensity requires a full investigation, often in consultation with your child's doctor. Occasionally these situations are true emergencies requiring immediate help. This occurred with Simon, a three-year-old with ASD, who was extremely underreactive. He had a severe motor-planning delay and a seizure disorder, as well as chronic sinusitis, ear infections and nasal allergies. To address these issues, he was given a treatment program along with medications for his health issues. Within eight months he changed from a poorly responsive, self-absorbed child who often preferred lying on the floor into a charming, interactive boy who was easily engaged, creative and full of ideas. His progress was truly exceptional.

Simon's crisis came following an illness that required antibiotics. In reaction to the antibiotic he developed severe diarrhea, resulting in painful diaper rash. The diarrhea and rash resolved, but a week later Simon became incredibly dysregulated, covering his ears and scratching and picking at his skin. His sleeping patterns changed, he began verbal stimming and it was difficult to connect with him—much like his behavior before treatment. Simon's parents were frantic when they arrived at my office. They feared that he had lost everything he had worked so hard to achieve. Most of all they were worried that he would not be able to improve. By looking for potential causes for Simon's behavior, two significant changes became obvious. His medication to support motor planning had been increased to a new dose, and due to his diarrhea, his nanny had begun attending his class in order to change his diaper. Once the diarrhea had resolved, she continued coming to class with him. His teachers thought her presence disrupted Simon, because he was relying on her for many things he had learned to do for himself. Her presence may have signified to Simon his inability to perform on his own.

Subsequently, the nanny left the classroom and his medication was adjusted to its previous level. Within several weeks Simon was back to his charming self and able to resume his relationships. Simon's parents were greatly relieved when they realized that his cognitive ability and memory had not been affected. What happened to Simon is no different from what happens to a typically developing child if he becomes ill and is irritable, distracted or stimulated. Yet children with ASD have much more vulnerable systems. Pointing this out following Simon's improvement with the proper approach helped solidify his parents' confidence in the strength of Simon's advancement.

I suggested that Simon's parents maintain a calendar to document changes or events that occur in his life so they can more easily identify the cause of any future problems. They were urged to keep a calendar year after year as it was also a way in which his team could help anticipate seasonal or particularly difficult transitions. By being able to anticipate certain patterns, team members could help prepare Simon for the more difficult times (such as the transition from summer vacation to school).

This episode is also an example of the importance of monitoring effect versus side effects of medications. Because Simon's parents had a clear picture of his behavior at each dosage level for his medications, we were able to determine how much to decrease the dosage. Simon's target symptoms and side effects are now clear and provide good markers to watch for in the future.

Your child's behaviors are an opportunity to learn more about him so you can help him. Use the strength of your relationship, your emotional bond and mutual love to help him move through these difficult times.

CHAPTER 12

Augmentative and Alternative Communication

W HAT WE see a child do or hear a child say may not equate to what he is thinking and feeling. He may have an idea but may not be able to plan and implement in order to share the idea. I often see this in children with ASD who are described as "low functioning" or as the "most challenged." This may be controversial, but because I live my life believing that the glass is half full, I always look for intent in the eyes of children with ASD. I have yet to be disappointed. The children with ASD who are described as "low functioning" are often those with the greatest motor-planning challenges, including oral motor apraxia. Our challenge is to provide an expressive outlet for these children so that they can communicate. This inability to express themselves can lead to anxiety; as they become more anxious and frustrated, they may engage in repetitive behaviors or act in a manner that could be perceived as aggressive.

We express ourselves through our voices, language and body movements. A child's first words are celebrated, and he builds on language and vocabulary to communicate first orally and then through writing. Children with ASD do not easily progress along this path. Those who have receptive language (understanding what's being spoken to them) but are limited in their expressive language need an outlet for their thoughts and feelings. Augmentative and alternative communication ([AAC]; with or without support) can give them a "voice."

WHO SHOULD USE AUGMENTATIVE AND ALTERNATIVE COMMUNICATION?

I consider using AAC (with or without support) when a child's receptive ability is greater than his expressive ability and no other techniques are helping to close this gap. Consider using AAC if your child has major motor-planning challenges, good receptive language, apraxia and little expressive language, along with major fine motor issues (precluding handwriting) and visual-motor processing issues. Children with visual-motor processing issues who use supported typing may employ their peripheral vision when they use a keyboard, often making it difficult for the layperson to understand that they are actually typing. Your child may be challenged during DIR/Floortime because his difficulties with motor sequencing will not allow him to keep the flow of interaction continuous and spontaneous. Despite appearances, he may be gaining much from these sessions, so keep them going.

Supported Communication

Supported communication is the term used when a child is given emotional, communicative and sensory-motor support (a parent's or therapist's hand supporting the child's hand or arm) so that he is more able to use an augmentative communication device (most often a keyboard) to point to pictures, letters or other symbols in order to express his feelings and thoughts. In the past, research into supported communication indicated that the communication was being directed by the therapist rather than the child. As a result this technique has been disregarded by many, which is unfortunate. When used properly, supported communication can be an incredibly effective resource for children with severe motor-planning challenges, especially for those who can't point reliably. Many have progressed from supported to independent typing. The most effective means of providing these children with a "voice" that I have encountered in clinical practice is supported communication on a keyboard, which the child uses to type.

Most of our output is automatic. If I ask you to write something, without thinking about it, you will pick up a pen and hold it in the writing position. Years ago, when you first learned to write, holding a pencil might have been awkward or uncomfortable, but through practice a "memory" was formed that allows you to automatically pick up and hold a pencil or pen in the proper manner. The tactile sense of the pen stimulates the learned neurocircuit, resulting in the correct movement. Something as simple as picking up a pen to write can be incredibly difficult for children with ASD. They may not have coordinated neural networks to be able to pick up a pen, let alone move it along a piece of paper in the patterns required to create letters, which therefore makes a simple task such as handwriting a huge challenge. Children with ASD who can't reliably point, initiate movement or organize sequenced steps of movement may benefit from supported typing.

Supported communication engages the motor system by stimulating the sensory input pathway. In the beginning a child's dominant hand is gently supported from underneath the wrist. His arm is held for typing while rhyth-mically or periodically being given gentle resistance, which stimulates sensory input. This gentle but consistent stimulus appears to result in increased motor tone, which the communication partner can feel in the child's arm, wrist and hand. Often the child's index finger will extend, ready to hit the key. If the communication partner stops giving the support, the child's arm, wrist, hand and finger often lose their tone and purposeful movement, only to regain them again once the support is resumed. Over time the support can be adjusted from the wrist to the elbow to the shoulder. Eventually a little tug on the child's shirt is enough to prime his sensory system to focus on the necessary steps in order to type successfully. This process takes time and is very dependent on how calm a child is during the session. Through supported expressive com-munication the child becomes more independent as he eventually learns to type on his own, but more important, he can use this form of communication for relating, developing friendships and interacting.

Supported communication requires the appropriate augmentative com-munication device, one that suits a child's abilities and needs. In addition, it is necessary to have an individualized technique that works for both com-munication partner and child to help support the child's sensory-motor sys-tem and promote a continuous flow of output through his hand and fingers. Communication devices can be as simple as a letter or picture board, or more complex, like an electronic device or a laptop computer that has been modified with voice output. Many parents find letter boards to be useful. It is important to find the tool that suits your child. It can be modified to meet specific preferences. For example, if he is more comfortable with black letters on a white background or white letters on a black background, the keyboard can be adjusted accordingly.

Augmentative and Alternative Communication (AAC)

Augmentative and alternative communication tools can range from simple picture boards to high-tech devices that generate electronic speech. Essentially it is any method that helps a child who cannot speak to communicate better at home, at school or at play (see the Resources).

The Benefits of Supported Communication

Children who have had a positive response to supported communication have shown remarkable changes. Some who were previously taught at pre-school levels begin communicating at age-appropriate levels through their typing. They show that they've been learning despite low expectations at school. Supported communication can help with language development and communication:

■ Supported communication through typing supports a "voice." Through typing your child engages in sequencing, planning, language, communication and social reciprocity.

■ Oral motor exercises complement the typing. Children are typically between six and ten years old when they start typing and have used very little language. Their speech, in addition to being difficult to understand, ranges from very soft to extremely loud because they've had no practice with voice modulation. Children who have apraxia need to practice producing language. If their diaphragm and vocal chords or voice box are stimulated at the same time they are working on typing, they can increase their language skills.

■ Supported communication is a bridge to spontaneous language. It does not replace speech—it supports it. Over the past decade I have seen children who have been typing for five to six years, many of whom are writing extensive papers and creative stories. Their ability to express themselves vocally has improved—simple words or statements have developed into longer and longer thought patterns.

■ Having a "voice" helps them control their world. This leads to decreased anxiety, resulting in decreased behaviors, such as stimming, aggression and tantrums.

One supported technique is called the rapid prompting method (www.halo-soma.org). The other comes from studies done by Dr. Biklen and colleagues at the Institute on Communication and Inclusion (http://soe.syr.edu/centers_institutes/institute_communication_inclusion/default.aspx) at Syracuse University. In both cases, the goal is that through much practice the child will eventually move toward independent typing. The story of Sue Rubin, who made this progression, is documented in the Academy Award–nominated documentary *Autism Is a World* (www.cnn.com/CNN/Programs/presents/index.autism.world.html).

Supported communication can be comfortably integrated with DIR/Floortime. Children who use supported communication successfully are often not able to have reciprocity in DIR/Floortime. If they are challenged with motor-planning issues, such as pointing, picking up a toy or handing a toy or ball back and forth, they may not be able to go beyond simple tasks in DIR/Floortime. If their cognitive ability far outstrips their sensory-motor coordinated output, DIR/Floortime may not advance. Using supported communication during DIR/Floortime can lead to improvements in both.

Jacob, who is now seventeen years old, was the first in my practice to use supported communication. Jacob has taught me so much about this technique and even more about the potential for all children with ASD, no matter the degree of their challenge. When Jacob was ten, he was consistently attempting DIR/Floortime at visits. At that time, he had such severe motor challenge that he could not successfully pick up a pencil and write or adeptly handle a toy. Jacob's play was very repetitive; he was always using the same toys—lion figures from the movie *The Lion King.* During DIR/Floortime, which he seemed to enjoy, Jacob had attention and engagement and some ability for two-way communication, completing four to five circles, yet he was not able to demonstrate a continuous flow of communication or connection between ideas. On the other hand, he demonstrated all these abilities and more when conversing through supported communication techniques. Once we added Jacob's supported communication to the DIR/Floortime scenario, we were enlightened as to what he was thinking and feeling while playing. He became creative, logical and reflective. Jacob played with the lions Mufasa, Scar (Mufasa's brother) and Simba (Mufasa's son) in an agitated and haphazard manner. They seemed to be fighting. Jacob made roaring sounds and then drew all over Scar with a red marker. When we took out Jacob's communication board, he typed that he drew blood on the mean lion, Scar. He explained that Mufasa hurt Scar because Scar had hurt Simba. While he typed, Jacob began to calm down as he wrote about how he was upset that in the movie the brother lions (Mufasa and Scar) fought. Scar was so jealous that he killed Mufasa. Jacob said he would be devastated if something happened to his father. Later in DIR/Floortime Jacob had the brothers make up so that Scar was not jealous and didn't kill Mufasa.

As he typed and played, Jacob still had to deal with his own sensory-motor issues. He would get up, roam around and calm himself with repetitive movements, before returning to DIR/Floortime and continuing his typing and playing. Through what he typed, we were able to understand that his simple motions of moving the lions around represented huge emotional conflicts that he was working out as we played. I was chagrined that I had underestimated what was happening in our DIR/Floortime sessions. When I asked Jacob whether it was worth continuing DIR/Floortime or if typing should be our primary activity, he said he wanted to continue with DIR/Floortime because it meant so much to him to have someone down on the floor interacting with him! Jacob taught me just how valuable having a voice through supported communication could be. He later told me that this interaction was a major breakthrough for him, because he was finally able to communicate what he had been working through for months. He was afraid that autism would take him away from the world. His father (represented by Mufasa) was fighting Scar, who represented autism to Jacob. "Autism was hurting me, and my father was going to kill it and rescue me. That's why I drew blood on Scar. I couldn't articulate all of that at the time, so I just talked about my father protecting me."

How to Know Whether Supported Communication Is Working

Supported communication has received criticism because it is assumed that the communication partner is driving the responses. In my experience, it is clear when a child is expressing himself. There is reciprocity of exchange, a nonverbal connection and shared feelings when you are aiding a child in his typing. As a communication partner, you can feel his muscle tone and the strength in his hand, wrist and fingers increase. Nonverbal cues often accompany a supported session. A child who may have difficulty focusing for a short period of time is willing to type for an hour. He may need periodic breaks to regroup but will always come back to finish his thought or conversation. As he gains more expertise in typing, he will devote longer and longer periods to this task. As he becomes more fluid in sequencing and producing his thoughts and ideas, his desire to communicate will greatly increase.

If you choose supported communication for your child, look for his facial expressions and body language to match what he's typing about. If expressing anger, he may type with much more force until his thought is completed. One child writing about his parents arguing got up from typing and became so upset that he became aggressive. What he had typed helped us understand his behavior, allowing us to calm him and create ways to help him reduce the emotional trauma. Another child who types went with his class to the zoo. He was so excited to go, but when they got there, after several visits to different animals, he started becoming more agitated, which escalated into a full-blown tantrum. Mom pulled out her keyboard and he typed furiously and emphatically, "I want to see the elephants!" Once he saw them, he immediately calmed down and was fine the rest of the day.

I have also seen validity in the results of a child's typing from his parent's reaction, particularly when the child reveals something that only a parent would know. The first time I used supported communication with one child, I asked him the names of his family members. I knew his parents' first names and he typed them exactly as I knew them. However, when it came to his sister's name, instead of typing the name I knew, he typed a different one. I looked up and at his mother, who had tears streaming down her face because he had just typed his sister's nickname, which Mom knew was unknown to me.

Another way in which we know that the ideas are coming from the children with ASD and not the communication partner is related to the subject matter. It generally appears to be age appropriate, as well as appropriate to their situation. Often the writing is heart-wrenching. Children ask me:

"When will I talk?" "When will I have friends?" "How can I make my body respond so I don't act this way?" If there's a family issue, such as a pending divorce, a child might ask, "Won't my mom and dad ever get back together—or are they getting a divorce because I have autism?"

Although we talk with children about having a voice through typing, they still ask when they will actually have an audible voice. When I asked one boy, "What does it mean when I say I want to hear your voice?" he replied, "You hear my voice through my typing." When I asked, "What do you mean by having a voice?" he answered, "I want to hear my voice so I can talk with my friends." For children who are unable to vocalize, there are devices that combine typing (or symbols) with voice output (such as AlphaSmart with Fusion, voice output computers [VOCs] and applications downloaded to an iPad—for example, Assistive Chat). The electronic voice can be made to sound childlike rather than robotic. Having this feature is particularly helpful for interactions with peers in school.

Often the standard for successful typing is raised higher for children who are being supported than for typical children who type. Children with ASD who also have visual-spatial processing issues may be using their peripheral vision to focus on the keyboard and will not look directly at the keyboard as they type. When I asked one of my patients about this, he commented, "Dr. Ricki, do you look at your typewriter while you type?" Of course my answer was, "No. I know where the keys are without looking." We know because of motor-planning memory. He knew the location of the keys because of his ability to use his peripheral vision while typing. Once again, what you see is not what you get with children with ASD. We have to look beyond our preconceived notions of behavior that seems beyond the typical range in these children.

Oral Motor Exercises

Using support or a communication device shouldn't take the place of your child's practicing his oral expression. It is sometimes assumed, erroneously, that if a child with ASD has not developed expressive language by the age of five, the prospects for future language development are poor. A 2009 study, however, dispelled this notion by showing that even if speech developed as late as twelve years of age, once a child began speaking, subsequent improvement could be expected. In some, language was often acquired quite rapidly. This finding emphasizes that each child must continue to practice even if challenged by severe oral apraxia. Becoming able to make sounds and say a few words can provide an important springboard for developing speech. If your child has apraxia, oral motor exercises can begin once a motor-planning challenge is identified. Encourage his breath control (necessary for speech) by having him blow bubbles, whistles, balloons or a party favor so it unfurls completely. You can also have cotton ball races (using a straw to blow a cotton ball across the table) or let him blow out a candle or multiple candles (this requires major supervision). Encourage him to make sounds by blowing into a kazoo or imitating animals. Using a timer, make a game out of how long he can sustain various vowel sounds. He can practice making sounds for speech production by working on phonemes (sounds that, combined together, make words). You could choose a phoneme theme for the week and create activities around it (for example, for *b* you could do all kinds of activities that start with the letter *b*: playing with balls, blowing up balloons and so forth).

Supportive communication can begin before he is ready for keyboarding. You can help your child in DIR/Floortime by supporting his sensory-motor needs as he plays. Simply giving resistance to his wrist as he plays with cars may result in several reciprocal sequences as he moves the cars down a ramp. Eventually this support can include work on letter boards and moving on to keyboards as soon as possible (often as young as two and a half to three years of age). Once your child is keyboarding, a communication partner can slowly reduce his physical support by letting go of your child's wrist and moving to his elbow and then to his shoulder. Many find that eventually pulling on the child's shirt at the neck or shoulder will be enough to support him and keep him typing.

Emotional Problem Solving

Opening the door to a child's ability to express himself allows him to practice all the steps on the social-emotional ladder. When augmentative and alternative communication is successful, the floodgates of your child's thoughts and emotions may be released. It's important for you and his therapists to be prepared to help him process his thoughts and feelings. Giving your child a voice allows him to express a range of emotions, from happy to sad and everything in between. Depending on his age, he may also express what he thinks about or experiences when he deals with the realities of autism.

Typing may also open the door to complex problem solving for him. Although he is typing, it can be hard for him to adjust to the needs of his peer group. One boy told me, "I am trying very hard to be independent, but I'm not, even though I type. I want to be like the other kids." "How does that feel?" I asked. He replied, "No one has to type like I do. They can just say their thoughts. They don't have to type their own thoughts. In school they give us choices in tests and we sometimes have to point to the right one. But sometimes I don't like the choices, so I get angry. Last week I ripped a page out of my book because I got so mad that I couldn't type my own thought." Until your child becomes more experienced with typing, he may have behaviors that do not match his thoughts. Over time this same boy learned to use his typing as his voice and to negotiate with others to come to a reasonable conclusion, rather than immediately responding emotionally in a way that he later regrets.

Beyond Supported Communication

True independence occurs for some after years of typing experience with a communication partner. It has been my experience that as a child learns to use these tools to express himself, his ability to sequence becomes more advanced. Over time he may attempt to speak. This is not an easy task. Asking him to talk or type independently could be similar to asking most of us to go to the top of the highest diving board and to flawlessly do a double twist into the water. It takes countless hours of supported typing and oral motor practice for him to gain independent expression. Generally, the written word will continue to be his most valuable tool for expression.

If and when augmented and/or supported communication becomes the voice of a child, he must have the necessary tools available to him at all times. (He is akin to a deaf child who signs and requires an interpreter to communicate at all times.) Your child needs many people in his environment who know how to support him and can be available to him throughout the day. I have been amazed to hear of school systems that refuse to allow children to use these techniques in school, thus limiting their ability to be an integral part of the classroom and often leading to behavioral outbursts.

Finally, it should be noted that often a child's writing and behavior are disconnected. As a child learns to use his "voice," it will take many long hours of practice for him to become competent and learn to rely on the benefits of using his voice instead of engaging in familiar behaviors to express his anger, frustration and lack of control in situations. You must be patient while your child is learning the benefit of greater communication by using supported communication.

I have also found that parents and therapists are reluctant to use this communication tool as an outlet for having discussions with a child. You will need to learn new patterns of interaction while supporting your child's use of his new "voice." This is the time for you to let him know you understand how difficult this is and that you will support him. Letting him know what a gift it is to hear his voice and what he has to say will give him the confidence to keep working hard. Your support, as always, is vital to his making progress with his new form of communication, one that gives him the voice he so desperately wants and gives you much greater understanding of his internal world.

PART V

Your Child's Health

CHAPTER 13

Keeping Your Child Healthy

W HEN THINKING about your child's health, it is important to remember first and foremost that he is a child. As such, he may experience any of the common childhood illnesses or injuries. Like any other child he needs to see his doctor for "well care" visits. He may also have medical conditions commonly related to ASD that need attention, such as sleep issues, GI distress or seizures. When all your child's needs are addressed, it has been my experience that an individualized treatment plan can be followed to assure his well-being and greatly improve his quality of life. If he's in good health, he will be able to maximize his therapies and progress up the developmental ladder.

Access to Medical Care for Your Child

As you may know, access to general health care for your child can be challenging. Research confirms this gap in service for children with ASD. The results of a National Survey of Children with Special Health Care Needs (NS-CSHCN) showed that children with ASD were the most likely of all children with special needs to have problems with access to care. A second study demonstrated that children with ASD were the least likely to have consistent access to a medical "home" of any children with chronic illness. I suspect that it's not that doctors are unwilling to incorporate children with ASD into their practices; it simply reflects their lack of understanding and experience in treating children with ASD and especially in addressing their needs across their life span. In fact, in a large survey pediatricians and family physicians recently reported a self-perceived lack of competency, a desire for more education and a need for improving primary care for children with ASD.

Finding Medical Care for Your Child

Like other children, your child may get earaches and stomachaches. Unlike many children, however, he may not be able to tell you when his ear aches or his tummy hurts. And your doctor may have little or no experience in treating a child with ASD. Given that not all doctors have every skill set needed to care completely for children with ASD, the more you know about your child's health care needs, including those specific to his ASD, the better equipped you will be to find a doctor who will support you and work as part of your child's treatment team.

Clearly, you want to have quality medical care for your child. The ideal situation would be a sophisticated and compassionate medical "home" that has the expertise to properly diagnose your child as well as to understand how to identify his individual profile. Then his treatment program could be uniquely designed to support his developmental needs. His "home" would be prepared to diagnose and treat common medical issues associated with ASD and would provide access to all medical specialties, including allergy, GI disorders, neurology, immunology and so on. Not only would this access be available, but the specialists in these areas would understand how these issues appear in ASD and how ASD can impact these issues. Above all, the ideal medical home would follow a family-oriented approach where education and training allow you to better understand your child's needs and develop the tools for you to become expert in helping to develop his relationships. In turn, by knowing your child, the medical team would understand how to help him be prepared for his visit and feel comfortable in the office.

This, of course, is the ideal situation. Unfortunately, at the present time there is an inadequate professional workforce to provide this type of care for children with ASD and families. There is hope, however. One of the newest initiatives to train doctors who specialize in the unique challenges of children with ASD is Autism Speaks Autism Treatment Network (ATN; see the Resources). It is anticipated that the sites in this network will become centers of excellence for clinical care, clinical research and training professionals. I am hopeful that as the ATN training sites across the country increase in number, many more doctors will be available to you.

Until such an ideal exists, I suggest you find a caring primary care doctor, such as a family practitioner, pediatrician or developmental pediatrician, for your child. Finding a doctor who listens to your concerns and learns the patterns of your child's behavior—especially when he is ill—is important. Look for someone willing to help you through his medical issues and find resources for him within your community. Remember, not everyone's needs will be the same. Determine in advance what characteristics in a doctor are the most important to you and your child. With the information presented here, you can evaluate in some detail the subtle differences in approaches and knowledge levels of the doctors you interview.

In working with your doctor, it is important to keep in mind that not only is ASD a chronic and complex neurological medical condition, but ASD behaviors can influence your child's symptoms that may be related to illness or other health issues. Your child may communicate how he's feeling inside his body by increasing his ASD behaviors. It's important to be aware of your child's general health, as well as the more specialized medical conditions often associated with ASD. Medical issues may be evident at the time your child is evaluated or may develop as he grows. Once you find a doctor, there are some things that you can do to better prepare your doctor to care for your child and to prepare your child for his visits to the doctor.

Preparing Your Doctor for Your Child's Visit

Just as you help your team members (therapists and teachers) understand your child, there are things you can do to help your doctor be better prepared to care for your child. You may want to consider first visiting the doctor without your child present to give you the opportunity to:

■ Discuss your child's sensory likes and dislikes and his motor challenges.

■ Note the sensory environment of the office. It should be calm and not stimulating. Let your doctor know if there is a light, sound or other distraction in the office that might need to be eliminated or adjusted for your child's visit. If this is difficult to arrange, ask for the first or last appointment of the day when the office will be less busy. To reduce waiting-room time, you might want to consider waiting in the car or someplace nearby and keep in touch with the office staff so they can tell you when the doctor is ready to see your child.

■ Share your child's profile with the medical staff if you know it (see Chapter 7). Explain to them the best approach to take during your child's visit. When I know a child is overreactive to sensory stimuli, I use a soft voice in order to decrease his sensory challenge and help put him at ease. If he has sensory skin reactivity, I am careful how I touch him and won't use a cloth or paper gown, keeping him in his own clothes. On the other hand, if a child is underreactive, I increase my energy to help him increase his energy and engagement. If he has motor-planning challenges, I try to match my rhythm and timing to his. By knowing your child's profile, your doctor and his staff can help him through the visit, gaining his confidence and trust.

■ Encourage the doctor to speak directly to your child no matter his perceived developmental level and even if he withdraws or runs around the room during the visit. Ask him to always tell your child in advance what's coming next and to use a step-by-step approach in the explanation. If possible, he should demonstrate what he's going to do. Many of my patients later told me how much they appreciated that I recognized and communicated directly with them.

■ Offer to show the doctor the way in which you interact with your child when you bring him for his first visit. Demonstrating a few reciprocal circles with your child will help your doctor take the first step in establishing a relationship with him.

■ Take photos of the doctor, his staff and the office setting to share with your child before his visit.

Preparing Your Child for the Doctor Visit

Preparing your child is also an important factor for a successful doctor visit. In addition to sharing the photos you've taken for the doctor visit, you can use your DIR/Floortime interactions to help prepare him. You may find the following suggestions helpful:

■ Using two play doctor kits, you may be able to familiarize your child with some of the instruments he may see at the doctor's office. Even if he is not developmentally ready for pretend play, he might enjoy playing with the objects in the kit. If he enjoys tapping with sticks, let him use the reflex hammer from the kit. He may also allow the stethoscope to hang from his neck, and even reach for the one hanging from yours! The fact that he has some familiarity with the tools he may see during the visit will take away some of the newness and ease his potential anxiety.

■ If your child is further up the developmental ladder and is able to sustain multiple circles of interaction with you, you may be able to take turns pretending to listen to each other's heart with a stethoscope.

■ Bring familiar items from his play doctor kit to the office visit. I often find children love to have their own stethoscope to hold on to while I'm using mine.

■ For the more symbolic child, you can set up your own doctor area at home and take turns either examining each other or his dolls. The play scenarios are endless.

You may also want to bring items from your child's sensory rescue kit that may help him get through the first visit. Be certain to add photos of your child's visit to his photo album. These can be used to prepare him for additional visits.

Discussing Special Preventative Concerns

Routine well-child visits are structured to address key areas of concern for you and your doctor relating to your child's well-being. This includes his individual growth and development, nutritional needs, regulatory patterns (sleep and toileting), immunization status, dental concerns and safety issues. While the topics will be similar for all children, some modifications may be required for your child that are tailored to his specific needs. The table below outlines the key health maintenance items covered in a well-child visit, as set out by the American Academy of Pediatrics (AAP), as well as sample modifications for a child with ASD.

Well-Child and Preventative Measures for Your Child

	AAP Recommendations	Possible ASD Modifications (in addition to AAP recommendations)
Growth and Development	Take longitudinal measurements ■ Height ■ Weight ■ Head circumference	Follow growth for nutritional impact of special dietary changes Head circumference profiles evaluated for possible changes seen in ASD
	Review developmental milestones	OT/PT referrals for gross/fine motor delays Speech and language referrals for speech delays
	Recommend developmentally appropriate activities	Recommend relationship-based interactions to support a child's social-emotional growth (DIR)
Nutrition	Review dietary intake to provide essential nutrients for growth and development ■ Protein/carbohydrate/fat intake ■ Trace elements (minerals) ■ Vitamins ■ Supplements	Review specific dietary needs, including special diets, minerals and vitamins, such as ■ Gluten-free, casein-free ■ Feingold ■ Specific carbohydrate ■ Calcium, iron and zinc ■ Vitamins A, B6, B12, C, D and E
	Encourage advancing chewing and swallowing skills as developmentally appropriate	Discuss feeding/swallowing concerns Modify for oral motor and motility issues, as needed Feeding specialist referral, if needed
	Recommend supplements	Review ASD-specific vitamins, minerals, supplements for effects and side effects
		Mealtime aids, like visual schedules (see the Visual Schedules box)

Continued...

Well-Child and Preventative Measures for Your Child, *continued*

	AAP Recommendations	Possible ASD Modifications (in addition to AAP recommendations)
Regulatory	Review regulatory patterns ■ Sleep ■ Toileting	Modify depending on specific profile needs and based on child's developmental profile Specific sleep recommendations Toileting time frame recommendations based on developmental sensory-motor profile
Immunizations	Follow up-to-date AAP immunization guidelines	Review parents' specific concerns regarding immunizations and ASD
Dental Care	Review health of teeth and gums Dental referral beginning at age three Dental hygiene maintenance Fluoride recommendations	Continue same schedules Modify techniques of care and visit, as needed
Safety	Review age-appropriate safety measures to prevent childhood accidents at home, at school, in the community and car (car seats, childproofing, stranger safety, pool safety, gun safety, poison prevention and so on)	Problem solve specific needs based on a child's individual profile (such as bolting across the street suggests developmental-behavioral techniques)

VISUAL SCHEDULES

Many children with ASD are very visual learners. Visual schedules are a wonderful way to let your child know what to expect from his day or a doctor's visit or to become familiar with the steps he needs to follow to complete a task. If your child has a limited vocabulary or oral expression, picture cards can be a helpful way for him to express what he is thinking or feeling, or simply what he wants to eat for lunch. You can take photos of your child engaging in the steps of a task and use them to prepare him for the next time he needs to toilet, brush his teeth and more. Having picture cards (photos or drawings) of the events that will happen throughout the day cannot only let your child keep track of what's next (helping him with transitions) but also let him be part of the process, for example, by choosing which errand will be run first or next. Using this method lets him know what to expect (through his visual system), prepares him for what's next, teaches him how to make his own choices and helps him to increase his flexibility if the schedule needs to change. Visual schedules are particularly suited if your child gets anxious with any variation from learned patterns and routines and has a strong need for sameness.

Growth and Development

Your doctor will document your child's growth, including his height, weight and head circumference (during the first three years of life). Measurements are then plotted on a standardized growth chart. If your child is above the 95th percentile or if his growth slows, plateaus or falls off these standardized measures, further evaluation will be necessary. Because of the unusual eating patterns of most children with ASD, it is common to find a growth curve that falls outside the standard expectations. This is particularly true regarding weight, which might be greater than expected. Eating calorie-laden food (typically excess carbohydrates), accompanied by too little exercise, is most often the cause. In addition, if your child spends most of his day in therapy, he most likely isn't getting as much exercise as a typical child. This is especially true if your child has a low-tone profile and is not inclined to exercise in the first place. I recommend appropriate exercise programs for all children with this issue. (See Chapter 24 for exercise recommendations, especially for older children.)

If, on the other hand, your child has difficulty gaining weight, your doctor may suggest you visit a nutritionist and find ways to increase his caloric intake. If he falls well below the expected weight for his age (less than the 3rd percentile) or if he fails to gain any weight at all, your doctor will review the wide range of medical issues that might be the cause.

Your child's growth rate will also be monitored at his doctor visits. It is unknown if children with ASD have more endocrine problems (such as a thyroid deficiency or growth hormone deficiencies) that can affect their growth rate. If your child's growth plateaus, your doctor may suggest a consultation with a pediatric endocrinologist to rule out any growth-related issues.

Developmental milestone timelines can be modified for children with ASD. Your child's functional capabilities in the social, emotional, language and gross and fine motor areas will be tracked by his doctor. What is important is that he continues to improve in all these areas. If he does not, it is time to reevaluate his profile and find an appropriate therapeutic program that will help him to progress. In this way you will support his development, which will hopefully, over time, approximate the developmental steps of the typically developing child. What will differ is the time frame. By giving your child the "gift of time" and allowing him to meet developmental milestones at his own pace, you should expect to see continued growth in most areas.

Nutrition

Eating issues are a common concern of all parents. How much your child eats can be influenced by many factors, including his appetite, his emotional drive and, most often, culture. Some children are not allowed to leave the table until their plate is clean, while others can pick and choose what they wish to eat. Your views about meals and eating are most likely based on your own upbringing. In ASD common childhood eating issues are compounded by the fact that quite often children with ASD are picky eaters. Their sensory and motor-planning issues can make feeding themselves difficult. Your child may limit the foods he eats to one type: sweet, sour, bitter or salty. The way food "looks" may be an issue for him. He may eat only foods of one color, such as white or orange foods. He may refuse certain foods, be unwilling to try new foods or eat only if the food is always served on the same type of plate or in the same container. All these behaviors are very common in children with ASD and affect nearly all the children I see.

If your child is limiting his diet to five to eight foods, you may question whether or not he is receiving adequate nutritional intake. Research data, however, show that the majority of children with ASD do eat adequate amounts of protein, carbohydrates and fat to sustain expected growth. Remember that the ultimate goal for your child is to get the recommended daily allowance of protein, carbohydrates and fat, as well as vitamins and minerals. It is okay if he eats the same foods every day as long as they are providing the nutrients he needs. If you are concerned about his intake of essential nutrients, your doctor and/or a dietician can help determine if what he is eating is enough. You may be required to maintain a food diary in order to provide a comprehensive assessment of what he eats on a daily and weekly basis.

Common Feeding Issues in ASD

Common feeding issues seen in children with ASD that may affect your child include:

- Difficulty breast-feeding, often due to problems with latching on and poor sucking skills
- Self-limiting the foods he eats
- Ingesting small amounts of food
- Difficulty with the transition to textures
- Increased sensory sensitivity around and in his mouth
- Refusing certain foods based on color, texture and/or temperature
- Decreased selection of foods over time
- Difficulty accepting new foods
- Difficulty taking multivitamin/mineral supplements
- Difficulty with changes in the mealtime environment
- Drooling
- Licking his lips repeatedly

If your child has any of these symptoms, it may be due to his restrictive food choice, but it could also be that he is having difficulty with the actual mechanics of eating. He may have difficulty with chewing and swallowing, especially if his sensory or motor function is compromised. Normal chewing and swallowing require processing sensation from his mouth, pharynx and larynx, followed by a complex sequence of muscle coordination in these areas that propels his food from his mouth to his stomach. The actual initiation of swallowing and protecting the airway rely on adequate sensory input to the swallowing control centers in the brain. For these reasons if a child has a neurological disease, GI issues (which can include food allergies or gastroesophageal reflux disease [GERD]), breathing difficulties or anatomical abnormalities, he can also have problems in these feeding areas. Difficulty with the mechanics of eating is often described as a delay in acquiring feeding skills, such as mature sucking, chewing or drinking from a cup.

Because children with ASD have sensory motor-based difficulties in general, it is not surprising that their eating is also affected by these issues. If your child has difficulty speaking due to poor motor coordination and is unable to move his cheeks, lips and tongue in order to make meaningful sounds and words (apraxia), this same problem may also alter his ability to eat. Sensory and/or motor-based problems may affect your child's ability to chew, drink, master utensils, as well as control food or drink in his mouth.

If your child has a sensory problem that interferes with his eating, he could have difficulty integrating sensory information related to the taste and texture of food. In addition, if he has a history of GERD and sensitivity to touch, these can be associated with sensory-based feeding problems. In this case your child's symptoms may include difficulty transitioning to textured foods and gagging and/or vomiting at the smell of foods or when food is placed on the tongue. If your child reacts this way, he most likely has an overreactive sensory profile, which may include sensitivity to light, noises and touch—issues commonly seen in children with ASD. These sensory issues may contribute to discomfort, resulting in interrupted eating, and may eventually lead your child to be highly selective about food, avoid certain textures and flavors, and possibly become reluctant to eat or refuse to eat.

Feeding problems that arise from muscle control can involve difficulty moving food from the front to the back of the mouth before swallowing. Children with low muscle tone often have weak, uncoordinated tongue movements, so it can take them a long time to eat. Difficulty chewing can also occur with weak chewing muscles. Children with developmental delays might take longer to acquire chewing skills because of a lack of experience with solid foods or their prolonged use of bottles. Your child might choke on liquids if they spill into the airway before the swallow has begun. If he gags or chokes on textured foods but consumes liquids and smooth foods easily, he most likely has difficulty chewing his food rather than a swallowing problem. If a true swallowing problem is suspected, your doctor may refer him to a specialist—a pediatric ear, nose and throat specialist (ENT) and/or gastroenterologist.

Treating Feeding Issues

There are several approaches you can consider to treat sensory-based feeding issues but you should know that it can take some time for them to resolve. If your child frequently packs food (holding it in his cheek) or retains textured foods in his mouth, he may do better with fewer textured foods during mealtimes. Some children with ASD are able to master crunchy foods while still having difficulty with soft foods, such as pasta. Highly textured foods are more likely to be rejected if he has high mouth sensitivity. To introduce textures in foods, start with very slightly textured foods and gradually increase the texture as he gets used to more and more textured foods. Start with small spoonfuls so as not to overwhelm him. Introducing a new food over time will help him become desensitized to the smell, look and possibly the feel of an unfamiliar food. If he has mouth sensitivity, there are some things you can do that might help with the desensitization process, such as massaging his gums using an electric toothbrush that vibrates.

Your child's need for sameness at all meals can be changed but it must be done in small increments. An effective approach is to try to help him become more flexible throughout his day by making a small change in other areas of his life that may also affect his eating. You may want to start by choosing a food that has a taste or texture that he already likes and that has the best sensory fit for him. If he loves salty foods, which is quite common, try a new salty food. Substituting beef or turkey jerky for chips can help turn a salt craving into protein intake. Try one new food for a long period before introducing another. When introducing new foods, following the pattern of look, touch, hold, kiss, bite, chew and spit out, chew and swallow can help ease the transition. This process can take a week or a month depending on the type of food your child is learning to eat.

If he likes to follow a routine at his meals, put the new food on the same spot on his plate every day. Letting him choose where on his plate the foods will be placed can help make mealtime more fun rather than a struggle. Help him change his visual expectation by taking a photo of his plate so that you can show it to him before the next mealtime. A picture of him at the table, eating, can also be incorporated into visual stories about his day. Use your DIR/Floortime skills to enhance mealtime for the whole family. Once your child becomes more interactive at the table, eating will become a social occasion. As your interactive therapies progress, this can be another opportunity to help build your relationship as well as give your child a healthy meal.

MEALTIME WITH YOUR CHILD

Meals offer wonderful opportunities to sustain longer and longer circles of communication. Relationship-based methods can be built on by having your child become an active participant in setting up and preparing the meal. In addition, teaching your child how to cook will give him some skills that will serve him throughout his life. Using visual cues, helping your child create a list of favorite foods and letting him be a full partner in getting a meal ready (like getting ingredients from the pantry, helping with measurements, washing vegetables, stirring the ingredients, setting the table and cleaning up) are a few of the ways your child can become engaged with you during mealtimes.

Handling more severe feeding issues often requires a multidisciplinary team assessment and treatment program. A speech-language therapist can help with the motor-planning issues and oral motor coordination between the tongue and the palate. An occupational therapist can provide appropriate oral sensory exercises. If your child also has gross motor issues, a physical therapist can be helpful. Concerns regarding his nutritional status and needs and supplements can be addressed by a dietician. Your doctor may serve as the case manager, referring to a medical subspecialist, such as a neurologist, gastroenterologist, pulmonologist (lungs) or ear, nose and throat doctor, if underlying physical problems are suspected.

Special Diets

If a food or food product is a source of irritation and discomfort for your child, he will not operate at his best if he continues to eat that food. Parents have long suspected that food allergies and/or toxic effects influence their child's behavior. Therefore, many children with ASD are placed on autism-specific diets, with varying results. The most frequently used diet is the gluten-free, casein-free (GFCF) diet. This diet has not been systematically investigated, despite the fact that many parents have seen significant improvements in their children when on the diet. Although parents are not usually concerned about why a diet works, if their child feels better on a diet, it is important to understand the relationship of the diet to his symptoms because some diets can be extremely restrictive and may affect your child's nutritional needs. Recent research has shown that children with ASD who are on a GFCF diet can be deficient in calcium, protein, vitamin D, folic acid and B vitamins, all of which are vital to your child's health. Currently, there are ongoing treatment trials to help parents and doctors determine if the GFCF diet works, and if so, the children who are most likely to improve on such a diet. These studies are evaluating improvements in the child's well-being as well as changes in the core ASD symptoms. Theoretically, if a child's general well-being improves, his learning curve should improve, because he will have greater attention and engagement in the therapeutic process.

Other diets are selected based on the suspected underlying cause of the digestive or dietary issue (for example, milk and milk products will be eliminated if your child is thought to be lactose intolerant or gluten will be eliminated with celiac disease). If your child has hyperactive symptoms, the Feingold diet (eliminates artificial additives) may be considered. If irritable bowel syndrome is thought to be the culprit, the Specific Carbohydrate Diet will be recommended. It is crucial to determine if your child is truly allergic to a specific food, because eating such a food (like peanuts) can be life threatening. A true food allergy requires that your child never eat the particular food, and all caregivers everywhere he goes—school, therapy and after-school programs—need to be made aware of his allergy.

If your child improves on a particular diet, it can be helpful to identify the specific food that was leading to his symptoms. The best approach is to eliminate foods one at a time as you work to discover the particular food that causes your child problems. Restrictive diets can put an undue burden on families. By seeking out the specific food and restricting only that one, there is a better chance that you are increasing the variety of foods that your child can eat, greatly improving mealtime choices and making it easier to prepare meals for the whole family.

Vitamins and Minerals

Your doctor will work with you to be certain your child has the proper intake of vitamins and minerals as determined by the RDA standards based on your child's age. If your child is on a specific elimination diet (such as casein- and gluten-free), supplements are especially important. While it is best to get nutrients from foods, because children with ASD are picky eaters, it may be difficult to ensure that they are getting the appropriate amount of vitamins and minerals in their diets. Vitamin and mineral supplements are found in liquid, tablet or chewable form and you can choose whichever one meets your child's needs. Supplements come in a wide variety of shapes, tastes and colors, allowing you to find the one best suited for your child. While all vitamins are important, there is growing evidence that the majority of children are receiving insufficient amounts of vitamin D. Because vitamin D production is triggered by sun exposure, this issue is compounded in children with ASD who spend much of their day inside for therapy. The minerals zinc and iron are often deficient in children who eat a restricted diet and should be part of any supplementary program. Omega-3 fatty acids are now being recommended for all, but particularly for those with neurobiological disorders.

General Regulatory Patterns

One of the underlying developmental issues for children with ASD is difficulty with regulation—particularly with eating, sleeping and toileting. Each individual develops his own pattern based on the needs of his biological system and the typical regulatory pattern varies widely. These patterns change over time. An infant may sleep from twelve to fourteen hours per day, and teenagers as few as six to eight hours. Toileting is most often delayed in ASD until a child's social-emotional developmental level reaches the three-year-old functional level and until a child's sensory-motor system is able to adequately interpret the urge to "go" in both the urinary and GI systems (see Chapter 17). If your child has difficulties in these areas, he can become more regulated in these areas as therapies progress. If after following a multidisciplinary treatment program, he does not become more regulated, other possible sources of his problems with sleeping or toileting (such as an undiagnosed medical disorder) must be appropriately investigated and treated.

Immunizations

Doctors follow specific American Academy of Pediatrics (AAP) guidelines for childhood immunizations. At the majority of well-child visits, your doctor will either discuss and/or administer the appropriate recommended vaccinations. As previously mentioned, this topic is very divisive among parents of children with ASD. The issue of vaccines requires extra discussion with your doctor. Choosing not to vaccinate your child is a decision that could have very dangerous consequences for your child and your community, and could impact his ability to attend school. (See Chapter 3 for a discussion about immunizations and ASD.)

Dental Care

If your child has difficulty in establishing good oral hygiene routines, it may lead to problems with his oral health. Over time, the neglect of teeth and gums can lead to gum infections, tooth decay and possible tooth loss. Most people do not enjoy going to the dentist. A visit to the dental office, with its bright lights, drills and unfamiliar scents and smells, is very difficult for your child and could easily lead to sensory overload. Along with sensory issues, many children with ASD have oral motor issues. Because of these issues, I would not be surprised if you are reluctant to consider taking your child to the dentist. Yet if a dental routine is not established, he may become more resistant and risk having future problems with his teeth and gums. All children, including those with special needs, should start seeing a dentist by the age of three and then continue routine visits every six months to ensure dental health.

A visit to the dentist will include an oral hygiene examination and checking the health of the gums and teeth, along with a history of your child's food and drink intake. It is an important exam for children with ASD, especially because oral motor delays can prolong bottle-feeding, which is highly associated with increased dental cavities. Your dentist may recommend appropriate fluoride supplementation depending on your community water standards. The dentist will also visually check for cavities and take X-rays if required. He will also check the alignment of your child's teeth, which is especially important once your child's adult teeth emerge. A dental visit usually includes teeth cleaning. With regular visits your child will become comfortable with his dentist and dental hygienist, who will be able to give you tips on ways of teaching and implementing preventive dental care at home.

The Dental Visit

The choice of dentist and office setting can have a huge impact on your child's ability to be comfortable at his dental visit. I suggest the following:

■ Locate a dentist trained in accommodating the special needs of children with ASD by contacting Special Care Dentistry Association (www.scdaonline.org). These dentists understand the underlying concerns in ASD and have modified procedures to accommodate your child's special needs.

■ If possible, visit the dentist several times before actual procedures occur. Most pediatric dental offices have interesting distractions to occupy children during procedures, including video games, movies and so on. Introduce these to your child during the visits. Allow your child to get a visual picture of the room he will be in, the chair he'll be sitting in, the tools that will be used and the office staff to help him gain familiarity with the setting so he can be comfortable in the environment.

■ At the early visits, slowly sensitize your child to the office by introducing him to the toothbrushes and other oral hygiene supplies used. On the first visit most dentists of special needs patients will allow your child to sit in the dental chair, where the dentist can lightly touch his teeth in a fun, interactive manner.

■ Caregivers must always be with the child in the exam room. Use whatever sensory techniques you know to help calm your child in times of high anxiety, especially when there is a lot going on around him. If necessary, bring your own items from your child's sensory rescue kit to help reduce his anxiety.

■ Be creative in meeting his sensory challenges. If your child has extreme light sensitivity, you might consider having him wear sunglasses to the visit, because the dentist will need to have a strong light shining into his mouth. If your child has sound sensitivities, consider earplugs if noisy equipment is required for cleaning or if the office is generally loud.

■ Read developmentally appropriate books with your child about visits to the dentist (see the Resources).

■ If your child has strong visual abilities, I also recommend (if the dentist allows) taking pictures of him in the setting so that you can create his "dental story" to share with him on days you prepare to go to the dentist. Label the photos with the names of the dentist and his staff. On the day of the actual visit you can call ahead, ask who will be present for the visit and pull those pictures out to review with your child in advance. Some idea of what to expect will help to decrease the natural anxiety of an uncomfortable and possibly new situation.

■ If your child is extremely challenged by his sensory issues and needs work beyond a regular cleaning, such as filling a cavity, anesthesia may be required. Your child's primary care doctor and the dentist will help identify the proper anesthetic method for him. If he is going to receive anesthesia, it may be a good time to take a full set of X-rays and clean his teeth, as well.

■ As your child gets older, he may need braces to realign his teeth. The majority of children I see have been able to tolerate braces without difficulty, especially when adequately prepared.

Fortunately, there is a movement at major dentistry schools to train new dentists in working with children with special needs. This should help meet the dental needs of the growing ASD population.

Dental Hygiene Suggestions

■ Encourage brushing. Start at a very young age, using soft or rubber-tipped brushes to massage gums even before teeth erupt.

■ Develop a twice-a-day brushing routine. Consider making teeth brushing a part of your child's bedtime routine. Expect him to be a full partner and make it special for him by allowing him to choose his own toothbrush. Consider using a "spinning brush" to get your child used to the sound and motion of the dental cleaning.

■ If your child has oral motor issues, toothbrushes that vibrate can be very useful to help massage the gums.

■ DIR/Floortime techniques can be used to make brushing as interactive as possible, as well as for oral motor work if needed. At teeth-brushing time you can engage your child by finding out which toothbrush he wants and deciding who's going to turn the brush on if you're using a vibrating brush, who will hold it, who will brush, if he is going to brush up first or down first, who is going to open the toothpaste, who will put the cap back on the toothpaste, who will put it away and where it will go, all of which can be done through circle after circle of interaction. The goal, of course, is to get his teeth brushed. By making it interactive, you can not only help your child learn to properly brush his teeth but also make it a fun experience for him.

Safety

Safety issues are a concern of all parents. Car safety restraints, childproofing the home, stranger safety, gun safety, pool safety and poison prevention are standard pediatric parental concerns. Safety is also a major concern above and beyond the norm for parents of children with ASD. ASD presents a unique set of safety issues that require an even greater proactive approach. Your child, who is growing but not moving as quickly up the developmental ladder, may misjudge situations and that might put him in harm's way.

When Leaving Home

As your child gets older, moving into the teen years, his desire for independence is often not tempered with adequate safety risk assessment. Unaware of potential dangers, he may leave home or school to venture out into the world. As a preventive measure, let people in your community know about your child's situation. Tell neighbors, law enforcement, the fire department and ambulance services. Prepare an information sheet that describes his individual profile (his medical and dietary issues, his favorite attractions and toys, his ability to communicate and how he learns about situations, that is, whether he must have visual contact, use pictures or written words and so on, and the calming techniques that can be helpful in highly charged situations). The information sheet should have a current photo, a physical description of your child and contact numbers for parents and caregivers. (See the Autism Speaks Autism Safety Project at www.autismsafetyproject.org and Autism Risk and Safety Management at www.autismriskmanagement.com for more information.)

Like many parents, you may struggle with telling friends, neighbors and others about your child's situation. However with ASD, as far as safety is concerned, the more those in your community are prepared to help protect your child, the more secure his environment will be. In addition, your child should always have identification on him. You might consider a personal tracking device. Many cell phones now have this capability and may be appropriate for adolescents with ASD.

At Home

Home safety will need to be modified, depending upon your child's interests. Childproof locks on cabinets, gates on stairwells and at doorways and covered electrical outlets, which are usually only necessary for the first few years of childhood, but may need to be maintained longer, until your child understands consequences. Dead-bolt locks and a home security system can help prevent your child from slipping out of the house unnoticed. Fencing can prevent your child from wandering out of the yard or falling into the pool. Your child may have behaviors that can be unsafe, such as throwing utensils or breaking plates and cups, dumping drawers and bins and climbing out of or breaking windows. His natural curiosity might put him in harm's way around the house if he puts items in appliances, flushes things down the sink or toilet, touches burners, turns on hot faucets, chews on wires or crawls into a washer or dryer. Matches, lighters, firearms and so on that are unsecured in the home also pose danger.

A pet may be part of your family. Your animal can be a meaningful member of your child's support team as well as provide him with the potential learning experience of caring for another. Bear in mind that pets in the home introduce new hazards as well as joys. Pets can be unpredictable, and preparing your child for a pet's behaviors is important. Special attention may be needed to isolate your pet's feeding and elimination areas from your child as much as possible.

It may take time to ensure that your home is as safe as it can possibly be—but *it must be a priority*. Start with the areas where your child spends the most time, including his bedroom, his bathroom, leisure areas, the kitchen and the yard. To assess risk, get on the floor and look at the area from his perspective. Look for items that could be enticing but also pose danger. From that vantage point you may see tablecloths that could be pulled, electrical outlets or cords that need to be covered or hidden, heavy items that could be pulled down, items that could be swallowed and sharp corners that could be dangerous for a child with motor-planning difficulties. Move furniture away from shelves so he can't use them to climb. Use locks where appropriate. Keep all medications, hazardous substances and items that are potentially harmful if ingested (detergents, cleaning supplies, insecticides) under secure lock and key. Safeguard your windows. Using visual labels on household items may help your child to understand the function of the items and enable him to use them appropriately. Using visual signs (like a stop sign) on a door that your child should not use may give him appropriate input to aid him in making a good decision. Bathroom safety is important as there are many slippery surfaces, which could be especially dangerous if your child has limited motor control. Use nonslip surfaces in the tub and under bathroom rugs, lock toilet seats if necessary and store bathroom supplies in a locked cupboard. Work with your local fire department so that they know the exits from your home and where your child with ASD sleeps. Teach your child to understand the implications of fire, and using pictures, words or visual schedules, teach him how to respond appropriately.

Pool safety is critical. Drowning is the leading cause of death in individuals with ASD. Extra vigilance when it comes to locks on gates around the pool and exterior doors leading from the home to the pool area is most important. If you visit another home that has a pool, check out the safety features. If you have a pool and you can't find your child, immediately check the pool. Because children with ASD seem to be naturally drawn to the water, be sure your child learns how to swim. He should experience swimming with clothes on as well as in his swimsuit so that should an accident occur, he will be better equipped to self-rescue. Besides the safety issue, swimming is wonderful exercise for kids with ASD. They seem to respond well to being in the water because water provides pressure around the whole body—something many children with ASD crave.

Techniques to help your child learn about safety can be incorporated into your DIR/Floortime routine. As he becomes more adept at pretend play, DIR/Floortime can introduce many imagined situations where safety is involved. Your child can then problem solve the proper behavior and consequences. Creative play and acting out situations with dolls can make more of an impression on him, rather than an adult listing dos and don'ts. Consistent peer and adult modeling about safety is also very important and will decrease his confusion about how to react in particular situations. Reinforce safe and appropriate behavior and employ consistent, appropriate consequences for unsafe or inappropriate behavior. Most safety items can be purchased at a children's store or a local hardware store. A specific website has been created for child autism safety products that emphasizes visual schedules and stories designed for children with ASD (www.mypreciouskid.com).

Parents sometimes develop a "sixth" sense of where their children are and what they are doing. If you haven't already, you will, too! Having a reliable safety-first program in and outside of your home for your child that is especially tailored to his needs will help ease your anxieties and better protect your child during those times when you may be distracted and overloaded by the daily needs of your whole family.

CHAPTER 14

Medical Conditions and ASD

Beyond the childhood wellness and preventative health issues covered in the previous chapter, there are numerous other medical concerns to consider when looking out for your child's health. Your child is susceptible to all childhood illness but these issues are often overlooked because his typical response to feeling unwell may be to increase his ASD behaviors. This is your child's way of telling you something has changed. Unfortunately, the increase in his behaviors is more likely to be seen as just the autism rather than his reaction to discomfort. For these reasons it is important that the whole team be knowledgable of your child's typical behaviors so that you are immediately made aware of any change.

To the best of my knowledge, ASD does not protect against any illness. When your child is not operating at his best, it is important to determine what is getting in his way. While it seems like common sense, it is important to first look for the most obvious cause. If there is an upper respiratory illness making the rounds at home or at school, it is very likely your child may also be suffering. If your child's behaviors change, a thorough evaluation, sometimes by pediatric medical specialists, is recommended.

The process of investigating a possible medical issue begins with a full history documenting any environmental changes that may affect your child's emotional well-being or increase his anxiety. This should cover any possible changes in the family structure, in his home environment (such as remodeling, a change to a new bedroom, illness in the family, parental stress and so on), in the school environment (such as illness or a change of teacher, a change in classroom, a change in his placement within the classroom, a new student, a new school structure and the like) and in the therapeutic environment (such as any change of therapists, any new programs added and more), and should involve checking for any change in medical symptoms. This history is followed by a physical exam and a DIR/Floortime observation taking note of anything new in your child's sensory-motor profile that may be interfering with his ability for sustained interaction and emotional thinking. Particular emphasis is given to whether he has regressed in any of his functional capabilities. If there is a regression, does it affect all areas of your child's functioning or just motor planning or cognition? Determining the extent of a regression will guide further investigation.

Often children develop patterns of reaction to illness and these can serve as "early warning" signs of a possible illness. Common childhood infections, allergies, migraine headaches, constipation, sleep changes or adverse responses to medications are frequent conditions that your child may react to in a similar fashion each time they occur. Your child must be followed over time by his doctor for serious issues such as seizures, comorbid (disorders unrelated to ASD that occur at the same time) psychiatric disorders and autoimmune concerns. A further evaluation, including appropriate laboratory testing, X-rays and EEGs, can be performed as needed. Treatment in these cases depends on the diagnosis and standard pediatric protocols. Sometimes your child may be given a medication to help in clarifying a diagnosis. For example, if he has a suspected migraine, he may be given an anti-inflammatory medication to see if the migraine goes away. Once the issues resolve, your child should be followed closely by his doctor or other specialist. I also find that documenting the illness over time can be very useful, especially if there are repetitive patterns (for example, if your child has increasing autism symptoms every fall, a time when he suffers from seasonal allergies). If your child doesn't improve with treatment or time, it's back to the drawing board to continue to search for the cause of his responses.

Focus on discovering any and all health concerns that could affect your child's well-being regardless of their origin. Whenever we do not feel well, we cannot perform at our best. If your child has sensory processing issues or motor-planning challenges, he may be even more vulnerable to the effects of illness. An illness can often derail his ability to communicate and relate in a significant way. Diagnosing and treating all medical illness will improve his well-being and comfort and get him back on track for learning and relating. When I hear that a child has changing or increasing behaviors, my first thought is that something has occurred to affect his physical well-being. From my point of view, medical illness needs to be ruled out as quickly as possible as a potential cause for the change in behavioral pattern.

It should be noted that in most cases when these illnesses are diagnosed, your child will be treated using standard pediatric approaches. What might be different for your child is how aggressively the illnesses or disorders are treated. Anything that derails your child's ability to communicate and relate can have a detrimental ripple effect in his life as well as that of your family. Allergies, GI disorders, immunological diseases, nutritional issues, seizures and sleep disorders, as well as comorbid psychiatric symptoms, can have a significant impact on a child with ASD. Other medical issues that frequently affect these children include the following:

Infectious Diseases

All children get colds, especially when they are around other children. In some children upper respiratory infections clear up quickly while others may experience complications, such as ear or sinus infections. These complications are more likely to occur if your child has an underlying allergy or issues relating to the function of his ear canal. Ear infections and sinus infections can be extremely detrimental to your child. If he struggles with auditory processing, it will be extremely difficult for him to pay attention and interact with others if his hearing is impaired. If your child is diagnosed with an ear infection, it should be treated aggressively. Follow-up to be sure the infection is gone is important, because if fluid remains in his middle ear cavity, he will be unable to function at his best. If he has chronic ear infections, you may want to discuss ear tubes with his doctor to relieve any remaining ear fluid. You want to do all you can to avoid any problem that could interfere with his learning and movement up the developmental curve. The same approach should be taken with recurrent sinus infections. It's important to diagnose early and treat aggressively and fully.

Dental Discomfort

Regular dental care will prevent cavities and address any before they become a major problem. If your child has mouth sensitivities, oral hygiene can be difficult and you must consider a dental cause for his discomfort. Teething, cavities, dental abscesses or impacted teeth may be present. In addition, dental trauma can always occur, especially in children who have motor-planning difficulties and poor proprioception. (See Chapter 5.)

Endocrine Disorders

Any of the endocrine disorders may affect your child, including diseases of the thyroid (hypo- or hyperthyroid), as well as puberty-related changes, which may affect mood during his teenage years.

Neurological Disorders

In this category, of course, are seizures and seizure-related activity. (See Chapter 16 for a full discussion.) Perhaps one of the more overlooked diagnoses is headaches in children with ASD. I suspect that more severe headaches of the migraine type are frequently unrecognized. A child who starts head banging might be suffering with migraine headaches, which are known to start in childhood—especially in susceptible families. Many times I have been called by a parent who tells me her child has covered his head with a blanket or is hiding underneath couch pillows and banging his head against the furniture. Headaches must be considered as a possible cause for such behavior, particularly if there is a family history of migraines.

Urological Disorders

If your child is experiencing urinary frequency, a urinary tract infection may be the culprit. However, in my experience, children who are constipated often have urinary frequency, because they are misinterpreting signals from their bowels. An illness known as atonic bladder, where the bladder overfills and doesn't empty, causing extreme bladder distention and pain, has been reported in older children with ASD. It should be considered if your child appears to have abdominal pain and bladder or bowel issues. Consultation with a urologist is sometimes required for many bladder-related issues. Children with sensory processing difficulties can become very dysregulated and upset, even aggressive, when bladder function is abnormal. They may not realize the origin of their pain.

Musculoskeletal Disorders

Inflammation of joints, strains and sprains, as well as possible bone fractures, can be missed in children with ASD. If your child is limping or favoring one limb over another, he needs a thorough exam to see if there are any problems.

Medication Side Effects

Dietary supplements, over-the-counter medications and prescription medications all have potential side effects. Many can produce irritability or increased activity that may lead to aggression. A review of all medications and supplements (whether doctor recommended or not) must be made. It is often helpful if you bring a list of all current medications and supplements to your doctor visit, noting any possible changes in the brand of medication used or in the generic supplier. Time and time again I have seen children respond differently to a formulation made by two different manufacturers.

Pain Syndromes

Pediatricians are experts at discovering the source of pain in children, often long before communication is strong. The same skills need to be applied to children with ASD, who may have different ways of expressing pain than you might expect. In fact, pain from any source may elicit your child's typical behavioral symptoms but to a greater degree, including self-injurious behavior. Any clues you might have as to what happened prior to the episode or what might improve or worsen the symptoms may help your doctor as you work together to resolve these issues. It has been said that children with ASD have pain insensitivity, but it has been shown that the opposite is true. Often the children display a greater facial response to pain than typical children.

Chronic pain syndromes are more commonly dealt with in adult patients than children. However, pediatric chronic pain clinics have noted that many of their patients actually have ASD (often undiagnosed). Clearly, these chronic pain issues are overlooked, especially in the ASD population. Individuals with chronic pain syndromes are known to have associated sensory processing issues that may be impacting their interpretation of pain, resulting in their differing behavioral responses. Treatment can be very effective when the sensory issues are addressed.

If your child has increasing behaviors, I suggest first instituting a sensory rescue plan to help him reregulate and then evaluating the cause of his dysregulation. During this time I also suggest that parents and doctors let him know that you are aware something is bothering him and that you will help him feel better. In doing so, you may, in fact, signal to him that you understand he is trying to communicate his distress. Many times in my office I have seen a child's (even a typical child's) anxiety decrease when he is told that we are trying to help him. Four key actions I take to help children feel better and be the best they can be are rescue, communicate, investigate and treat. If your child knows that you are trying to figure things out, it will help him, and taking action can give your family hope and the strength to continue through an often difficult but worthwhile process.

CHAPTER 15

ASD and Double Syndromes

YOU MAY have heard your doctor talking about "rule outs." What this means is that for every group of symptoms that your child might have, your doctor needs to consider or "rule out" those diseases that may cause these symptoms. In addition to searching for missed patterns of illness, investigating signs and symptoms suggesting other underlying medical disorders should be conducted if your child has been diagnosed with ASD. It is not yet known if these medical conditions might be a cause of your child's ASD symptoms. It is possible that the ASD itself, with its myriad of neurological and emotional manifestations, could cause another condition to develop. It could also be merely a coincidence. This investigation is tailored to your child's medical and developmental history and physical exam findings.

Many medical conditions can go hand in hand with ASD. They fall into three main categories:

- Medical disorders that might be related to the cause of your child's ASD (double syndromes, such as Fragile X or Rett syndrome).
- Medical associations that are found in many children with ASD regardless of the underlying cause of the ASD (such as seizures, GI issues, allergic/immunologic diseases, sleep problems). These concerns are so important that I've devoted a chapter to each (see Chapters 16-19).
- Conditions that arise as your child continues to grow. These may be medical or involve increasing target symptoms associated with either ASD core symptoms, new target symptoms or coexisting psychiatric disease (see Chapter 20).

All these issues can affect not only your child's general well-being but also his ASD challenges.

What Is a Double Syndrome?

When your child is diagnosed with ASD, it is important to first determine whether or not his symptoms are actually related to another known disorder.

There are several disorders that coexist with ASD. These disorders are called double syndromes by pioneers in the field of autism treatment and research, Drs. Christopher Gillberg and Mary Coleman. In many cases it is unknown if a double syndrome is due to cause and effect or if it is simply an association.

If another medical disorder coexists with the ASD, additional options for treatment can be pursued. Support and information are available through organizations and groups that are associated with these disorders (such as Fragile X groups). These rare double syndromes are often due to known genetic, metabolic, infectious and toxic causes. In most cases, the basis for the disorder has been discovered; however, it is also known that having the disorder will not necessarily mean that the child will have ASD. Often each syndrome has distinct clinical findings in addition to ASD. The more well-known double syndromes include Fragile X, Neurofibromatosis (NF), Tuberous Sclerosis (TS), Rett syndrome and Williams syndrome. (See Appendix 4 for additional double syndromes.)

It is important that every child be screened for all known double syndromes. This can be done by your doctor or through a consultation with a clinical geneticist and/or other specialists. Your doctor will use both clinical evaluation and laboratory testing to consider whether any of these associations are present. Your child should be examined for certain identifying features of other disorders as they can provide clues to possible double syndromes. For example, your doctor especially needs to watch for skin abnormalities, such as café au lait (large brown spots) or hypopigmentation (large pale spots). If noted, a genetic search for Tuberous Sclerosis or Neurofibromatosis is the next step. If a child has two- to three-toe syndactyly (webbing of the toes), he may have Smith–Lemli–Opitz syndrome (SLOS). In patients with extremely large heads (usually greater than 2.5 standard deviations above the average), doctors should consider PTEN testing for the PTEN Hamartoma Tumor syndrome. Finally, in girls suspected of having ASD with a history of developmental regression, and especially those with progressive motor deterioration, testing must be done for Rett syndrome (MECP2 mutation testing). This is not an exhaustive list of diagnostic characteristics of these disorders but it will give you an idea that there is a possibility that your child's ASD does not exist alone.

Genetic Testing for Your Child

Genetic testing follows the clinical evaluation. This includes blood studies for Fragile X syndrome, the MECP2 genetic test for Rett syndrome (for girls) and an evaluation of your child's genetic makeup with a test known as a karyotype. A karyotype test is an analysis of the type and number of chromosomes that comprise an individual's genetic information. This test needs to be performed with high-resolution techniques for the best results. There are forty-six chromosomes (twenty-three pairs) in a normal karyotype. Half of each pair comes from Mom and half from Dad. Your child's gender comes from one pair of chromosomes, designated as XX if a girl and XY if a boy. Recently, the ASD genetic evaluation became even more powerful with the introduction of advanced techniques, such as DNA microarray technology (CGH microarray). This new genetic evaluation method has revealed even more chromosomal abnormalities associated with ASD. This is the case with the new finding on chromosome 16 (16p 11.2), which has now been linked to ASD. We are just beginning to understand the wide range of genes that may lead to ASD. It is not yet known how these genetic abnormalities might produce ASD. Many hypotheses have been suggested (see Chapter 3). Children with Fragile X who also have ASD symptoms are especially interesting to geneticists since uncovering the Fragile X genetic abnormality might actually provide clues as to the development of ASD. Genetics is an area for exciting research that could eventually lead to refined and improved treatments on an individual level for each child with ASD.

Metabolic Testing for Your Child

In addition to genetic disorders that have ASD symptoms, there also are metabolic diseases and disorders that have been associated with autism. Of course, many of these metabolic diseases and disorders have a genetic basis that has not yet been identified. In most cases children who have these metabolic diseases and disorders are very ill and have difficulty gaining weight, in addition to their developmental issues. Phenylketonuria (PKU), which is now part of the newborn screening, is one of these diseases. In general, the tests that are used to look for these disorders include blood tests for amino acids and urine tests for organic acids. The results of these tests, however, are dependent oftentimes on what your child is eating and drinking. Your child's dietary intake will be combined with the results of the blood and urine testing to see if they fit any known pattern of disease. Metabolic diseases and disorders have very specific treatments, often dietary, and they will vary depending upon your child's diagnosis.

Idiopathic Autism

"Idiopathic autism" is the term used when the cause of the ASD is not yet known. If your child does not have a double syndrome, then he is part of this group of children. In fact, the majority of children with ASD have idiopathic ASD. Researchers generally limit their survey to those diagnosed with idiopathic ASD so that they can investigate potential causes with as similar a study population as possible. These investigations give researchers the opportunity to discover new genetic and metabolic disorders that could also be significant in developing ASD. Once these disorders are defined, new double syndromes emerge, shrinking the true idiopathic group. Such is the case with the recent possible association of mitochondrial disorders and ASD.

Mitochondrial Disorders and ASD

Mitochondria are structures within our cells that play a central role in metabolism and are the cells' energy producers. Mitochondria contain their own DNA, which directs the mitochondria on how to produce that energy. Because the brain places great demands on the body's energy system, dysfunctional mitochondria can result in thinking and movement problems. Public awareness of mitochondrial-related ASD increased in March 2008, when Jon and Terry Poling announced that their daughter had been awarded compensation for an injury possibly caused by a vaccine that aggravated an underlying mitochondrial dysfunction and, in so doing, might have led to her ASD symptoms.

This finding was intriguing to many parents who had wondered if their child with ASD had an underlying mitochondrial disorder. The identification of mitochondrial disorders in children with ASD is particularly challenging due to a lack of specific signs and symptoms. Some symptoms of mitochondrial disorders include very low muscle tone, major difficulties with feeding and developmental delay, which, unfortunately, overlap with symptoms of ASD. Although the Polings were awarded compensation for their daughter, there is still controversy in the medical community not only about mitochondrial disorders and their diagnosis but also about their relationship to ASD. Mitochondrial metabolic markers (including abnormalities of blood lactic acid and pyruvic acid) are found through blood tests. If mitochondrial diseases are suspected, molecular testing for mitochondrial DNA mutations can be done. When I suspect a mitochondrial disorder in a child with ASD, I recommend a consultation with a genetic/metabolic specialist if possible at a center that is familiar with this very complex and changing field of medicine. This will be a hot topic of research in the future and hopefully this research will open avenues of treatment for the select population of children with ASD who have this association.

Drs. Christopher Gillberg and Mary Coleman determined in their research that one-fourth of their caseload had double syndromes. Now, with more awareness and improved diagnostic skills, health professionals are identifying many of these disorders at earlier ages, in which case a child receives the correct treatment plan from the beginning. As a result of early screening, the rate of Fragile X in cases of ASD has dropped from early reports of 16 percent to less than 2 percent. As diagnostic tools become even more sophisticated, it is certain that many children today diagnosed with idiopathic autism will eventually be found to have a double syndrome.

If your child has a double syndrome, there is increased hope as researchers search for the known cause of the syndrome. Once the genetics of a disorder have been identified, the door to treatment, and potential prevention, can be opened wide. This has been the case for Tuberous Sclerosis, Fragile X and Rett syndrome, where clinical trial studies, using products to reverse the genetic effects of these disorders, have been undertaken. The accelerated pace of genetic research in the past decade has moved the ASD field toward potential treatments, and possible cures, only imagined in the past. Each time a treatment is found to help brain functioning in those with double syndromes, there is hope for all with ASD.

CHAPTER 16

Seizure Disorders in ASD

O NE OF the more difficult conversations that I have with parents is about seizures or epilepsy. Although rates of epilepsy in the general population are approximately 0.5 percent, long-term studies have shown that the rate of epilepsy for people with ASD can range anywhere from 4 to 40 percent. The very idea of your child having a seizure can be frightening, but the more you understand about seizures and how they might affect your child, the better prepared you will be to help him if something does happen. The good news is that with proper treatment of their seizures, many children improve significantly.

Your child may never experience a seizure, but if it happens, you need to understand the different types of seizures and how to recognize one in your child. The likelihood that a child with ASD could have a seizure is highest before the age of five and increases again after puberty. Most of us are aware of the "large," or grand mal, seizure. However, there are other types of seizures found frequently in children with ASD. These smaller and less violent seizures may be very brief and may even not be recognized. If these smaller seizures occur frequently, they can greatly impact your child's language, motor planning, sleep, learning and interactions. In some children they may also result in a regressive ASD pattern.

Understanding Seizure Disorders

Seizure disorders, also known as epilepsy, are caused by a malfunction in the brain. During a seizure the electrical impulses that typically govern brain function go awry—it's like having an electrical storm that disrupts normal functioning, especially attention and behavior. An electroencephalogram (EEG) is a test that measures and records the electrical activity of the brain and can help in diagnosing and treating seizures.

A seizure is the actual episode itself and may occur just once or many times over a lifetime. When someone has more than two seizures, they are considered to have epilepsy. Seizures fall into two basic categories—generalized and partial.

Generalized seizures involve large areas of the brain from the beginning of the seizure. This group of seizures includes:

■ **Tonic-clonic (grand mal):** This is the largest and most serious type of seizure. Before a grand mal seizure occurs, your child may experience an aura or unusual feeling. He may then yell or cry out before he loses consciousness, falls to the ground and begins rhythmically jerking his arms, legs and face as his muscles stiffen and relax. Drooling, biting the tongue and loss of bladder control may also occur. The seizure itself can last from a few minutes to twenty minutes. It can be frightening to observe a seizure like this. If your child has a grand mal seizure, it is most important to keep him safe and prevent injury. Afterwards, he will have no memory of the seizure and will often be confused and sleepy.

■ **Absence (petit mal):** During this type of seizure there is usually no aura or warning and a very brief loss of consciousness occurs without major muscle movements. A child may be playing or talking, then may briefly stop moving, stare off into space and after a few seconds continue where he left off, with no memory of the seizure. Occasionally, during an absence seizure, he may have minor repetitive motor movements, such as frequent blinking and/or a mild twitch of the neck, arms or face. Although they are brief and perhaps infrequent, these seizures can happen many times in succession, greatly impacting a child's ability to pay attention and relate.

■ **Status epilepticus:** This is a prolonged (greater than twenty to thirty minutes) generalized, usually grand mal seizure during which the child is unconscious. This is a true medical emergency.

Partial seizures are located in a particular part of the brain and include:

■ **Simple partial seizures:** During these seizures a child does not have a loss of consciousness but may experience weakness, numbness and unusual smells or tastes. Visual changes, dizziness, paralysis or motor movements (such as twitching muscles or limbs, turning the head), may also occur.

■ **Complex partial seizures (temporal lobe seizures):** Complex partial seizures are believed to originate from abnormal electrical discharges in the temporal lobe. During a complex partial seizure a child will have an altered state of consciousness affecting his ability to interact. He may engage in repetitive behaviors, such as smacking his lips, sitting up and sitting down or walking in a circle. This behavior may be accompanied by uncontrolled laughing, fear or visual hallucinations.

DETECTING SUBTLE SEIZURES

Because seizures other than grand mal may be extremely short (a few seconds), they often go unnoticed. There are, however, some specific red flag behaviors indicating your child may possibly be having subtle seizures that require further evaluation. Children with subtle seizures are often described as "unfocused," "spacey," "dreamy," "inattentive, with learning problems" or as having an "autistic stare." If this describes your child, the cause of his behavior may simply be ASD and the way his brain functions—or it is possible that he is having small seizures. When I examine a child in my office, I play with him on the floor, watching for stops or starts in his activity. If he is having a subtle seizure, it is as though a pause button has been hit and he freezes for a second or two before resuming his activity. In one instance a child was playing with a toy elevator by rhythmically moving it up and down when he suddenly stopped, looked to his right, let his hands fall quietly into his lap and ceased all motor activity for a few seconds. Then, just as quickly, he resumed play. Once you become aware of this type of pause, it will become easier for you to recognize similar episodes. Because children with ASD have communication issues, disruptions of speech (as noted in typically developing children who have these seizures) are not reliable indicators of absence or complex partial seizures. Watching for subtle behavioral changes in your child is the key to unearthing problems.

If you suspect that your child may be having subtle seizures, it is important to follow up with your doctor. These episodes need careful observation, monitoring and rigorous evaluation. I suggest videotaping the episode, if possible, to share with your doctor. A visual record of the behavior you have observed will be helpful in determining if further evaluation is required.

The Relationship Between Seizures and ASD

Proposed explanations for the relationship between ASD and seizure disorders include:

- They are separate and independent conditions.
- The same underlying cause results in ASD-like symptoms and epilepsy.
- An epileptic process impairs the early development of the neural networks involved in relating and communicating.
- A localized brain lesion may result in ASD and the potential for epilepsy.
- Epilepsy may result in cognitive dysfunction and ASD symptoms in "vulnerable children."

Further research is needed to determine the connection between seizures and ASD. The key is to determine if your child might be experiencing a seizure episode.

Diagnosing Seizures

If you suspect your child is having seizures, a full medical evaluation is imperative. The first step is for your doctor to take a complete history and perform a thorough physical examination. He may refer your child to a neurologist. To identify underlying seizure/epileptic patterns, the doctor may recommend an EEG. Your child's diagnosis is made using the EEG results together with his medical history and a general observation of his behavior (the doctor's observation, your views and any videotape of your child during a suspected seizure).

The EEG Procedure

To conduct the EEG, electric measurement wires (called leads) are placed gently on a child's scalp and affixed with dissolvable glue. For a period of time ranging from one to forty-eight hours, electrical activity or impulses from all areas of the brain are measured and recorded as a pattern of peaks and valleys. This record is then studied by a neurologist trained to recognize both typical and nontypical patterns of brain wave activity.

EEGs can vary in length. The most common method is to perform the test over a one- to two-hour period after a child has been sleep deprived the night before. The sleep deprivation is done so that he might be drowsy or even sleep during the test. Another way of performing this test is to have prolonged monitoring, up to twenty-four to forty-eight hours in length. This second method captures brain wave activity usually during all stages of sleep, when the brain is the most quiet and abnormalities are more easily detected.

The one- to two-hour EEG can be performed as an outpatient procedure either in a neurologist's office or at an ambulatory center. The prolonged overnight EEG has generally been done in the hospital setting. More recently, ambulatory, in-home overnight EEG monitoring has become available for children.

If you are considering an EEG, you may be very concerned as to whether your child can get through the diagnostic process—particularly if it requires hospitalization. A hospital is not an ideal environment for a child with ASD and may cause him stress. In addition, his reaction to an unfamiliar environment can interfere with the EEG results. However, when the EEG is performed in the hospital, your child may be video recorded through the night in addition to undergoing the EEG monitoring. This allows the doctors to observe for symptoms and any EEG changes at the same time.

A more user-friendly approach is an ambulatory overnight EEG, which allows your child to be tested in his home, while sleeping in his own bed. Many ambulatory centers (with specialists in EEGs done outside of a hospital) have technicians who are knowledgeable about working with children with sensory challenges. The process for the ambulatory EEG is similar to that of a hospital-based EEG. Electrodes are placed on your child's scalp to pick up the electrical impulses that occur in his brain. Once the leads are applied, the technicians wrap pressure bandages around your child's head like a turban to anchor the leads. The other ends of the leads are attached either to a small, lightweight recorder, which is then placed in a special backpack, or later to a unit at his bedside. Your child is then free to go home. The next morning he returns to the clinic, where the leads are removed and the EEG results reviewed by a neurologist. I have yet to have difficulty obtaining an EEG when it is performed in this manner. I suspect the pressure from the head wrap and the comfort of being with his family and sleeping in his own bed eases a child's anxiety.

Before an overnight EEG I suggest that you let your child select a favorite movie so that he can relax before going to bed. Once the leads are on, you will be asked to monitor your child while he is awake for any unusual behavior that may indicate a seizure and to record the exact time it occurs. Your record of your child's behavior will be matched with the EEG to assess whether or not he has had a true seizure. A major drawback of the ambulatory version of the EEG is that many insurance companies will reimburse only for EEGs performed in a hospital. If this type of EEG is not available in your community, consult one of the companies (www.sleepmed.md) that is developing networks across the country to provide this service. They can provide information regarding the nearest centers that may be available to you.

Limitations of EEGs

There are limits to EEG recordings. In fact, many gray areas of interpretation add to the challenge of reaching a definite diagnosis. Not all children who have an obvious seizure have abnormal EEGs, especially when the EEG occurs after the episode, adding to the difficulty of interpretation. Children with no evidence of seizures or impairment can have an EEG showing patterns that are characteristic of epilepsy. These are known as epileptiform abnormalities and occur in 1 to 4 percent of the healthy population. The presence of these abnormalities can suggest a tendency toward epilepsy, but it is not enough in and of itself to make a diagnosis.

It is important to remember that an EEG is merely a snapshot in time. It may not remain the same over time the way a genetic test would. This is why your doctor may suggest repeating an EEG if your child's symptoms change.

Because the EEG represents what is happening in his life at one particular time, it is also not predictive of future seizures.

Another point to emphasize is that EEG recordings are interpreted by neurologists. Although based on scientific information, there is also an art to this reading. Not every neurologist will make the same judgment, especially in cases of nontypical, abnormal patterns, which are often seen in ASD. When there is a question of significance about the EEG findings, I request that the test be read by a second neurologist if possible.

Should Your Child Have an Overnight EEG?

For a child with ASD, research suggests not only an increase in the rate of seizures but also a greater likelihood that abnormalities will be detected on an overnight EEG rather than in a one- to two-hour study, even if he has not had observable seizures. For that reason, I recommend overnight EEGs for all the children I evaluate. If an abnormality is discovered, a door to treatment has been opened.

EEG Findings in Children with ASD Who Do Not Have Seizures

The EEG abnormalities seen in overnight EEGs of children with ASD without seizures are known as subclinical epileptiform discharges (SEDs). They are described as "sharp waves" and "slowing patterns" intermixed with typical electrical activity. It is not known if these are ASD-specific EEG findings, because they may be found in typically developing children, as well. While the presence of these SEDs may go unnoticed in your child's daily life, they may significantly impact his functioning and interfere with his learning and relating.

These SEDs generally occur infrequently yet are more obvious during certain periods of sleep. For this reason they are more likely to be seen in overnight EEGs that include all stages of sleep (50 to 60 percent abnormality) than in routine two-hour studies (14 percent abnormality). These abnormalities are most often seen in the temporal lobes (side) or the frontal lobes of the brain (see Chapter 3). These are the areas where language input, speech output, some sensory processing and motor planning occur. It is quite possible that these abnormal spikes in brain electrical activity indicate dysfunction that is interfering with areas that govern these functions.

In fact, studies have shown that typical (non-ASD) adults who do not have seizures but do have SEDs, as shown on an EEG, may have difficulty with thinking and learning. These individuals are actually experiencing transient cognitive impairment (TCI), a temporary disruption of mental abilities. The occurrence of TCI under these circumstances was described as early as the

1980s. Nearly 50 percent of people studied had a TCI episode that occurred at the same time as the abnormal electrical spikes. Additionally, there was a connection between where in the brain the spike occurred and what mental function was disrupted. For example, discharges on the left-sided language areas of the brain were associated with errors in verbal tasks. A study on the influence of SEDs on complex task performance showed that half of typical adults with SEDs had side-to-side deviation while driving during SED episodes as brief as half a second in length. The impact of this type of episode could be much more significant for a child with ASD who already has major brain pathway vulnerabilities. In fact, it has also been reported that children with ASD who have EEG patterns that show SEDs are more likely to have verbal auditory agnosia (VAA)—a near total loss of receptive language understanding.

What Does an SED Look Like?

The short answer is that you most likely won't notice these episodes when they occur. Some children shown to have SEDs aren't noted to have any difference in their typical behavior until we look back after seeing major improvements following treatment. Others may have very subtle changes noted, as with the other smaller seizures. In my experience with children with ASD it is best to look at a child's behavior as a whole. If he has brief staring spells, major receptive language delays, motor-planning challenges, difficulty sleeping and, most especially, a history of regression, it is possible that he is experiencing SEDs.

EEG Findings in Children with ASD Who Have Had a Regression

Research in the 1990s has helped reveal some possible connections between EEG abnormalities, the presence of epilepsy and ASD—especially as it applies to the regressive form of autism. Regression occurs in about 30 percent of children with ASD. When children regress, they can lose both receptive and expressive language skills, the red flags that often lead to an autism diagnosis. SEDs on EEGs are frequently found in children whose ASD is associated with a regression after eighteen months of age. These children are frequently noted to have difficulty sleeping through the night, waking several times after falling back asleep. Additionally, these children often have major motor-planning challenges.

Information about EEG changes and regression was expanded when research focused on Landau-Kleffner syndrome (LKS), a disorder with characteristics similar to autism as well as unusual EEG patterns. Children with LKS develop normally until they have a major language regression (loss of language, vocabulary, communication), which typically occurs between the ages of three and seven. Their loss of language ability often gives them an autism-like profile. The cause of LKS is unknown, but it is thought that it is due to an acquired autoimmune process that affects brain function. The EEGs of children with this disorder show abnormalities that are unique to LKS. Treatment for LKS includes antiepileptic drugs as well as anti-inflammatory medications, such as steroids and intravenous immunoglobulin (IVIG). In many cases children with LKS appear to respond to these treatments: they regain language and exhibit improved development. As families of children with ASD became aware of LKS (and the apparent improvement when treated), demand increased for an overnight EEG. Although it was rare to find a child with ASD who had a pattern of LKS on the EEG, many exhibited SEDs—especially during sleep. The frequency of these abnormal sleep EEG findings varied between 40 and 60 percent of children with ASD, and was even greater if regression in language skills had occurred.

How Frequently Do SEDs Occur in ASD?

A 2006 study by Dr. Michael Chez and his colleagues investigating overnight EEG patterns in 889 ASD children with no history of seizures found that 60.7 percent of the children (whose average age was four at the time of the study) exhibited these abnormal epileptiform discharges on EEGs versus 1 to 4 percent in the typical population. Similar reports from the National Institute of Mental Health (NIMH) confirm findings of increased EEG abnormalities in children with ASD. This is similar to my own experience: a chart review of my first two hundred patients showed that 48 percent had these patterns on overnight EEGs, although most did not have seizures. Of all the tests I perform the overnight EEG is the one most likely to uncover a potential treatment path.

The Cause of SEDs

Just as there's no clear understanding of the relationship between seizure disorders and ASD, the significance of SEDs is not yet understood. One possibility is that these changes occur when there is an underlying immune reaction in the brain of a child with ASD. In fact, there has been evidence of neurological inflammation in autism in both brain and cerebral spinal fluid (CSF) samples. That also appears to be the case for children with LKS who have shown some language improvement when taking anti-inflammatory steroid medications. Anti-inflammatory medications have been effective in other seizure disorders, such as infantile spasms. An ongoing immune reaction accompanied by an increase in SEDs might then eventually lead to epilepsy and obvious seizures in older children with ASD.

Using anti-inflammatory treatment in these disorders as a model, Dr. Michael Chez studied a group of children with ASD who were first treated with valproic acid and then given anti-inflammatory steroid medication. This study found that EEG patterns normalized and receptive language abilities improved once the steroid was added to the valproic acid treatment. The side effects of steroids, however, are quite significant. Therefore, much clinical research is necessary to further weigh the potential benefits of this treatment.

EEG Controversy in ASD

In the medical community there is not yet a standard approach regarding the use of the EEG in ASD. In the past, ASD evaluation protocols recommended EEG testing if a child had clinical signs that suggested a seizure. So it is not surprising if your child has not been tested. Newer information regarding the findings of overnight EEGs without seizures raises concerns about these recommendations. Controversy, however, remains. The chance of finding an EEG abnormality appears to be significant in children with ASD without seizures. Since the presence of these abnormalities may be greatly impacting their lives, based on the emerging research, as well as my own experience, I recommend this test if possible for all children with ASD.

Treatments for Seizure Disorders

If your child has an observed seizure, in addition to the EEG there is a standard evaluation, including brain scans and laboratory tests, that is completed to look for any underlying brain complications. Based on the evaluation, appropriate treatment will be recommended by your doctor. A consultation with a pediatric neurologist, who can help your family and primary care doctor make an informed decision about appropriate treatment, might also be suggested.

Treatment decisions may not always be based solely on a child's EEG results, but rather on the number and severity of seizures he has, as well as the conditions under which they occur. For example, seizures associated with fevers may be treated by reducing your child's temperature, as this usually prevents further episodes. On the other hand, a child with extremely infrequent episodes (an episode may occur only once or once every several years) and a normal EEG may not be treated at all but should be followed closely for further episodes.

If the decision is made to treat with a medication, the choice will be based on the seizure type, as well as the form of medication that your child will take (liquid, tablets or sprinkles). The specialist can also guide the medication choice based on potential side effects. Appropriate follow-up may include adjusting the dosage, blood tests (for certain medications) monitoring for any changes, including side effects, and determining how long treatment should

last. Follow-up can be performed either directly by the specialist or in consultation with your child's primary care doctor.

The types of medications (see the Antiepileptic medications [AEDs] box)
that can be useful are antiepileptic drugs (AEDs) and anti-inflammatory
medications (such as steroids or intravenous immunoglobulin [IVIG]). The
anti-inflammatory approach has been taken because of how children with
LKS respond to these treatments. If you and your doctor decide to pursue treatment, a treatment strategy should be constructed (see Chapter 20).
Rigorous follow-up during treatment is necessary to evaluate how your
child is improving on the medication and to monitor for side effects (see
Chapter 20).

ANTIEPILEPTIC MEDICATIONS (AEDS)

- Treating seizures with AEDs can reduce the risk of further seizure activity. If
  your child has more than one seizure, he should be considered for treatment.
- Treatment decisions depend on risk factors that predict further seizures,
  including brain lesions, an abnormal EEG pattern and a family history of
  seizure disorders.
- In ASD the rate of seizures increases, especially as your child ages, and is
  therefore a significant factor in making a treatment decision with your doctor.
- Medication choice depends on the type of seizures. Some work well on one
  type of seizure and make other types worse.
- Medications need to be taken on a strict schedule at the same times daily.
- Medication dosages need to be adjusted to achieve maximum effect.
- Medications need to be monitored by your doctor for side effects and blood
  levels.
- A partial list of AEDs includes:
  - Depakote and Depakene (valproic acid)
  - Kepra (levetiracetam)
  - Lamictal (lamotrigene)
  - Neurontin (gabapentin)
  - Tegretol (carbamazepine)
  - Trileptal (oxcarbazepine)
  - Topamax (toperimate)

Treating Subclinical Epileptiform Discharges in ASD

Because there is no consensus on the significance of SEDs in children with
ASD, there is no agreement as to whether they should be treated and, if

so, the best medication to use. Information on possible treatment choices is sparse. Published studies on children with ASD who have SEDs but who do not have seizures focus on treating the children with the medication valproic acid (also known as Depakote or Depakene) alone or in combination with corticosteroids (also known as prednisone or prednisolone). The medication combination was found to be most effective in treating LKS. A study done by Dr. Michael Chez that treated with these medications 173 children who had overnight EEGs with abnormal results found that 69 percent of the children improved on the valproic acid treatment alone. In many cases the EEG showed normal results following treatment. Children who improved increased their receptive language performance, based on doctors' observation and parents' reports.

A 2001 study by Dr. Eric Hollander and colleagues on the effectiveness of valproic acid in treating children with ASD without epilepsy showed that all the children in the study that had abnormal EEGs demonstrated improvement in their repetitive behaviors, social relatedness, aggression and mood changes. Interestingly, some of the children with ASD and normal EEG patterns also improved, but their progress was not as significant as that of the children with abnormal EEG patterns. However, both of these studies did not include an untreated control group for comparison, nor were the parents and doctors blinded to medication choice, thus limiting the ability to provide definitive information on the best course of treatment.

Valproic acid is an AED but it can also improve sleep patterns and be used to stabilize mood, which may also affect a child's ability to function. Other AEDs (Tegretol, Trileptal and so on) have been used to treat children with ASD who have abnormal EEGs but in my experience these medications have not been as effective as valproic acid. However, after reviewing potential side effects of these medications with parents, many doctors may choose to use AEDs (such as Tegretol, Trileptal and Neurontin) rather than valproic acid. Valproic acid may have serious side effects on the liver (rare, potentially fatal chemical hepatitis), bone marrow and pancreas, and it requires frequent blood monitoring. The decision whether or not to use this particular medication is best discussed at length with your doctor. In my practice, I thoroughly discuss all the pros and cons of a particular medication, including potential improvements in a child's ability to relate and communicate, as well as possible side effects and how they will be monitored, with parents before going forward.

If valproic acid is used, blood levels of the medication need to be followed over time because each child's ability to metabolize the medication varies. The most effective blood "trough" levels for children with ASD appear to be between 90 to 120 mg/L. The "trough" is the minimum blood level of medication during the day. If your child is taking valproic acid, his blood can be tested for a "trough" level in the morning, before the first dose of the medication is given. The timing of the next blood tests should be done to enable your doctor to accurately compare levels from one blood test to another and best determine how much medication to prescribe and how often, along with monitoring for side effects. Maintaining a consistent level of valproic acid in your child's blood can be critical to his ability to function. If there has been a decline in his ability to process language or a disruption of his sleep patterns, a blood level should be obtained to see if there is a lowered level of valproic acid, which may be contributing to the problem. On the other hand, if blood levels get too high, your child may develop a hand tremor, irritability or fatigue, also requiring an adjustment in medication dosage.

Some parents in my practice have become so experienced at judging their child's behavior versus medication levels, they can tell with near accuracy their child's blood level of valproic acid based on how their child is functioning. Cameron was a ten-year-old boy who had been treated with Depakote for his underlying seizure disorder. When his blood level was greater than 90 mg/L, his receptive understanding appeared to be at its best. One day I got a call from his mother. "Dr. Ricki, I know something has happened to Cameron's Depakote blood level. He could not follow any of the directions today while in the pool, which he usually just loves and responds to with precision. I was scared because I was worried about his safety."

A blood test confirmed his mom's suspicion. The medication blood level had dropped precipitously to 70 mg/L. When Cameron's mom followed up on his dosage schedule, she found that for the past week the new school nurse had not given Cameron his noon dose of Depakote. This was immediately rectified. On his next blood draw his level was 93 mg/L. "I knew his level was back to where it should be without needing the blood test because he's resumed all of his positive behavior in the pool," his mom reported.

I have followed several hundred children diagnosed at young ages with ASD who are now in adolescence. Approximately half of these children had SEDs on overnight EEGs when they were first evaluated. The majority were treated, most often with valproic acid, with positive results. It is interesting to note that the children in my practice who now have seizures are those who did not take AEDs at a young age. It has recently been discovered that valproic acid can be neuroprotective (protects brain function), possibly preventing future seizures. While there are no clinical studies confirming that valproic acid prevents seizures in ASD, I have often wondered if using this medication in a young child with ASD who has abnormal EEG patterns might prevent future seizures.

Successful Treatment Following an EEG

Jeremy is a four-year-old diagnosed with ASD who had an ambulatory over-night EEG as part of his initial medical evaluation. The EEG revealed that during sleep he had an epileptiform pattern of brain waves in the temporal area of his brain. These spikes in brain activity were not associated with any observed behavior changes but occurred several times during the night. Reviewing the results of the EEG with his parents, I discussed the fact that this was a rather typical pattern that has been seen in children with ASD. Because Jeremy had a history of regression at eighteen months and exhibited very poor understanding and use of language, self-absorption (closely exam-ining his fingers or hand flapping) and motor-planning challenges, as well as a severe sleep issue, waking several times each night, his parents considered the pros and cons of medication and decided to proceed with a medication treatment trial. Prior to my evaluation Jeremy had been receiving therapy with speech, OT, some school services and some DIR/Floortime but had had no documented improvement for over a year. I felt that we had an adequate baseline to determine his progress.

Jeremy's response to medication was incredible. Eight weeks after he began medication, his receptive and expressive abilities had improved remarkably. He had even begun to sleep through the night. He amazed his entire thera-peutic team. He responded more quickly to others. He was engaged in pretend play with toys. He was able to go to Disneyland with his family, participating happily in the complex transitions on the rides, tolerating the waiting and the noise. Most important, he was able to incorporate new language into his conversations so seamlessly that it was hard to remember he'd never used these terms before. Comments such as "Move over," "I want a napkin" or "I am finished" became commonplace. His parents said it was if "his internal light was turned back on." Once his receptive language improved, he was able to start learning and interacting.

At Jeremy's next follow-up visit he was attentive, engaged and creative for the entire hour. This behavior was in stark contrast to my session with him a few months earlier, when his parents and I could make contact with him only through rigorous effort. While Jeremy's positive response to medication therapy was extremely rapid compared to most children I have treated, it has been thrilling to see the change. His family is delighted with his progress. I am hopeful that future studies will help identify the children with ASD who will make progress like Jeremy's, which will help standardize treatment so doctors and families will be better able to make the right choices for the children.

CHAPTER 17

Gastrointestinal (GI) Illness

No one, including your child with ASD, is immune to some form of GI distress (diarrhea, constipation, heartburn, acid reflux). However, beyond typical GI complaints, other GI issues are often present in children with ASD. The existence of GI issues in ASD raises a couple of questions: First, does ASD predispose children to GI symptoms? Second, do GI disorders cause ASD? The short answers are "Possibly" to the first question and "We don't know" to the second. It is possible that your child may be experiencing GI distress and is unable to tell you. Watch for changes in his behavior as that may indicate that he is experiencing some form of gastric distress. Many of the children in my practice have gastrointestinal illnesses. Studies documenting rates of GI symptoms indicate that children with ASD have a higher rate of GI symptoms than either children with typical development or those with other developmental disabilities.

Your child may experience any of the following: heartburn, abdominal pain, bloating, food intolerance and constipation and/or diarrhea. Although all children may have these problems at one time or another, children with ASD are far more likely to have frequent GI upset. Another challenge you may face in helping your child is that symptoms in children with ASD may change over time. Your child may have loose stools when he is a preschooler but have chronic constipation in grade school. An infant who has reflux and persistently spits up may improve, only to experience reflux when he is older. Unfortunately, it's not surprising that children with ASD who have digestive problems are more irritable, show greater levels of anxiety and social withdrawal than typical children and are less likely to respond to treatment.

Children with ASD also have toilet-training delays (particularly with bowel movements) and accidents can occur with regularity. When a child has difficulty with sensory processing, he may not feel the urge to go to the bathroom and is unaware that he needs to. In addition, the process of toilet training can be difficult for him to grasp. An inability to properly sequence all the required steps and coordinate the necessary movements makes toilet training very challenging for most children with ASD. If your child is not toilet trained when you expect him to be, it is not unusual. In my practice, I am not surprised to see children with ASD between the ages of four and five who may not be ready to toilet train. You should be aware that when your child is ready, it may take a little longer than average. However, once your child has advanced to the point that he can understand the process and has made gains in sensory processing and motor planning, there is no reason to believe he cannot successfully toilet train. In my experience most children with ASD eventually toilet train. It can be difficult having a child who is not toilet trained when it is expected. Families in my practice speak of feeling pressure from family and friends, along with the social pressure, to have a child toilet trained on time. If this happens to you, I suggest that you speak to family, friends and caregivers about the challenges this process poses for your child so that they, too, will have a better understanding of these issues.

Common Gastrointestinal Symptoms

Your child may have difficulty in describing his symptoms. If a typically developing child comes to his pediatrician with abdominal pain, the doctor will ask the child where it hurts, how much it hurts, if anything increases or decreases the pain and how long it has been hurting. Communication delays make getting this information difficult. In fact, a child with ASD may not interpret his own body signals accurately enough so that he can identify the source of his pain, making it hard for him to answer the question "Where does it hurt?"

Rather than telling you he is hurting, your child may communicate his pain by an increase in behaviors, such as stimming, withdrawal, tantrums or even aggression. If parents describe increasing behavioral issues in their child, I always consider GI problems as a possible cause. As a parent, it is important that you begin to think of any increase in your child's behaviors as communication from him that something is not right in his body or his world (see Chapter 11). I look beyond the behaviors to determine the root cause of the problem. It goes without saying that if he is in pain from a GI issue that results in overwhelming behaviors, he will not be able to function at his best.

Warning signs for a GI issue that warrant further evaluation include the following:

- Chronic diarrhea or constipation
- Feeding, eating disorders
- Change in sleep patterns
- Food allergies or apparent reactions with eating particular foods

■ Behavior changes, especially self-injurious, aggressive or mouthing behaviors. Mouthing behaviors include drooling, licking and needing to have items (of all kinds) in his mouth, as well as chin pushing.

When any of these symptoms occur, it is important to consider GI problems as the primary source of these changes.

What You Need to Know about GI Problems

If you are concerned that your child might have GI distress needing attention, the information below can give you ideas to discuss with his doctor. There is a wide range of issues that can be affecting any area of his GI tract. However, some appear to be more common in children with ASD. Some of these problems, like constipation, are relatively easy to resolve, while others may require further consultation with a GI specialist.

Gastroesophageal Reflux Disease (GERD)

GERD occurs when food or liquid travels backward from the stomach to the esophagus (the tube from the mouth to the stomach). This can irritate the esophagus, causing the typical heartburn sensation. Symptoms of GERD that your child may have include burping, dyspepsia (the actual taste of the acid) and severe pain (often in the middle chest area). Your child's behavior in reaction to these symptoms can include continuous chin pushing and increased saliva, aggression, self-injury and repetitive motor movements of the arms, shoulders or neck (Sandifer syndrome). Chronic GERD can cause chronic hoarseness, a cough, wheezing, asthma and sinusitis. It also affects the enamel in teeth, resulting in erosions. GERD is a common condition in all children. It is often diagnosed in children with developmental delays and should be considered as a possibility in children with ASD—especially if their behavior suddenly changes. At night some children repetitively fling themselves on their beds in an attempt to relieve the pain. A small study performed by Dr. Timothy Buie of Harvard Medical School found GERD and/or esophagitis in nine children with ASD who showed few GI symptoms but had increasing behaviors. Further study needs to be done to identify how frequently GERD coexists with ASD and under what circumstances. In children with ASD an upper GI endoscopy (visualization of the upper GI tract through a scope during a procedure performed under anesthesia) has shown reflux esophagitis (irritation and inflammation of the esophagus secondary to acid reflux), chronic gastritis (inflammation of the stomach wall lining) and chronic duodenitis (inflammation of the duodenum—the upper small intestine). To determine if your child has GERD, a GI specialist will take a medical history as well as conduct several tests.

These procedures include measuring actual acidity levels with esophageal pH testing and performing an upper GI endoscopy with a biopsy of suspect lesions. Treatment varies and can include behavior changes and/or specific medications. If a child has symptoms that are consistent with GERD, a trial with a medication (for example, a protein pump inhibitor) is used for ten to fourteen days to see if any behavioral improvement occurs before embarking on a more complex, invasive evaluation. If the symptoms continue, however, then testing can be pursued through consultation with a GI specialist (see the What You Can Do if Your Child Has Gastroesophogeal Reflux Disease box).

WHAT YOU CAN DO IF YOUR CHILD HAS GASTROESOPHOGEAL REFLUX DISEASE

Behavior Changes:
- Elevate the head of his bed or crib
- Keep him upright for two hours after eating
- Feed him several small meals a day rather than three large meals
- Eliminate food and drink that seem to bring on symptoms (common culprits include carbonated beverages, citrus, tomatoes, mint, chocolate and fatty or fried foods)
- Encourage exercise

Medications:
- To reduce gas: Mylicon, Gaviscon
- To neutralize or decrease stomach acid: Antacids (Mylanta, Maalox), histamine-2 blockers (Axid, Pepcid, Tagamet, Zantac), protein pump inhibitors (Nexium, Prilosec, Prevacid, AcipHex, Protonix)

Chronic Diarrhea

Although the episodes of diarrhea that we all experience have a variety of causes, including reactions to foods and infections, if your child has chronic diarrhea, your doctor will consider more serious causes, such as bacterial or parasitic infection, overflow from constipation or an inability to absorb certain sugars from food (known as disaccharidase deficiency).

Lactose Intolerance

This is the most common form of disaccharidase deficiency. Without the lactase enzyme required to metabolize and absorb lactose (the sugar contained in milk and milk products) from our diet, excess lactose remains in the GI system, where it can cause gas and explosive diarrhea. Many adults acquire lactose deficiency as they age. One study of carbohydrate digestion in children older than five years of age with ASD found 55 percent of those undergoing an upper GI endoscopy for GI symptoms had lactose deficiency, while 15 percent of those studied had a combined deficiency of several disaccharidase enzymes. Although the frequency of lactose deficiency over the age of five was higher in ASD than in unaffected children, it was still quite high even in the unaffected children with GI disease. It should also be pointed out that this study reviewed patients at a GI specialty clinic who had symptoms requiring invasive evaluative procedures. These rates may not represent the rate of disaccharidase deficiencies in the ASD population as a whole. If your child has a disaccharidase deficiency, such as lactose intolerance, eliminating lactose sugars from the diet is extremely beneficial. Typical foods that have lactose include milk, butter, ice cream, yogurt, cheese and many processed foods. You will need to check labels carefully if your child is affected.

Autistic Enterocolitis

This is a term used for a chronic condition in the lower GI tract of children with ASD. It refers to an inflammation of the ileum (the lower end of the small intestine) and the colon (the large intestine). Autistic enterocolitis is, however, an extremely controversial diagnosis. From 1998 to 2000, Andrew Wakefield proposed that these changes in the digestive system were due to the measles part of the MMR vaccine. He suggested that the vaccine caused increased GI permeability, which allowed certain peptides, known as opioid peptides, to be absorbed into the body. These peptides were thought to be the underlying cause of the neurological symptoms and dysfunction seen in ASD. Most of the authors of this original study later retracted their support of the conclusions, known as the opioid theory, and in 2010 the *Lancet* retracted the entire study, arguing that it did not meet research standards. There is little evidence supporting the idea that the opioid theory is valid or that the MMR vaccine was the cause of these issues.

Constipation

In your child, constipation can occur either alone or along with diarrhea. When they occur together, the diarrhea can be caused by an "overflow" of loose stool escaping around the blockage of severe constipation. Constant stool staining of diapers or underwear without a true bowel movement can also occur with constipation. Abdominal pain, gas and bloating often accompany constipation. In children with ASD, the symptoms may be expressed as repetitive movements that help relieve some of the abdominal pressure and pain, such as rocking, rolling on the floor or constant humping maneuvers. The standard treatment of constipation includes dietary management (eliminate foods that are constipating, such as rice, bananas, cheese), softening the stool (MiraLAX is a gentle preparation that can be used in very young children) and appropriate toilet training (modified for children with ASD to include visual and motor prompts as needed).

Irritable Bowel Syndrome (IBS)

If your child has alternating constipation and diarrhea over a long period of time, it could also be due to irritable bowel syndrome (IBS). IBS is more commonly understood and diagnosed in adults than in children and is most likely caused by a dysfunction of the muscle contractions of the GI tract. Normal gut motility (peristalsis) is an orderly sequence of contractions from the top of the GI tract to the bottom. In IBS, muscular spasms can be painful. Contractions can be rapid (as with diarrhea) or very slow (as with constipation). Children with ASD have major motor issues and it is very possible that they may have difficulties with muscle function in the GI tract. In addition, the connection between the brain and gut function may also be impaired (known as brain-gut dysfunction), causing problems in the way the brain and gut communicate. Given the level of sensory-motor issues in ASD, the presence of these GI symptoms in children with ASD should not be surprising. Children with certain mitochondrial disorders have also been found to have GI issues, possibly related to motility issues. Motility in the GI system (small and large intestine) is regulated, in large part, by the neurons in the walls of the intestinal lining itself. These neurons generally act independently from the brain and activate the contraction and relaxation of the GI tract—known as peristalsis. This system can be overridden by the brain, as we all may have experienced when we've been under stress and needed to run to the bathroom. It is interesting to note that 95 percent of the serotonin in the body is located in the neurons in the GI tract. Serotonin is involved in both phases of motility. Change in the serotonin transmission in both the brain and the GI system may be found to be a link between IBS symptoms in children with ASD. This notion is stimulating research, which could also lead to a new serotonin-based treatment for these sometimes debilitating symptoms.

When I see a child who seems to have IBS, I generally recommend he try the Specific Carbohydrate Diet (www.breakingtheviciouscycle.info), which eliminates complex carbohydrates and significantly decreases the amount of gluten eaten. The gluten-free diet has been seen to help children with gut motility issues (including IBS) who experience both constipation and diarrhea. IBS medications for constipation include fiber supplements (Metamucil, Citrucel) and laxatives (MiraLAX, mineral oil, Dulcolax). IBS medications for diarrhea include Imodium; Pepto-Bismol; antispasmodics to relax smooth muscle contractions, such as bentyl (use with caution as there are serious side effects); and antidepressants. A word of caution: antidepressants are not well studied in children for IBS.

Celiac Disease (Celiac Sprue)

Celiac disease (CD) is an inherited GI disorder that is triggered by gluten intake and prevents the intestines from absorbing nutrients. Gluten is a protein that is found in rye, wheat and barley. It has a toxic effect in the digestive tract, resulting in a malabsorption syndrome that can include severe weight loss, abdominal pain, chronic diarrhea, constipation, vomiting and foul-smelling and fatty stools. It may take years for the full-blown syndrome to actually manifest itself. CD is an immunologic disease that can affect many body systems and may be present with brain dysfunction at any age. It is interesting to note a recent study comparing family history of Celiac disease in one hundred children with ASD showed that 24 percent had family evidence of CD. Because CD is a genetic disorder and is most likely due to an immunologic reaction, children with ASD should be tested for specific CD antibodies (a blood test) before eliminating gluten from the diet. A definitive diagnosis of CD requires a direct biopsy of the bowel performed under anesthesia by a GI specialist. Once the offending gluten is eliminated from the diet, these antibodies disappear. Their absence in a blood test can be an indicator of the individual's improved GI health.

A VEIL SUDDENLY CAME OVER HER

I first met Ava when she was two and a half years old. She had dramatically regressed when she was eighteen months old, losing all her language and social interaction. Her dad said it was as if "a veil suddenly came over her." During the evaluation process her parents made it clear that they were vegetarians, were committed to a holistic point of view and were very much opposed to significant diagnostic or therapeutic interventions. During our DIR/Floortime interaction Ava was withdrawn and often self-absorbed, despite our best efforts to try to improve her attention and engagement. I was especially concerned that she had a significant regression. My recommendations included full laboratory testing. The results of her evaluation, including her overnight EEG, were within normal limits except that she had significant Celiac disease antibodies. It was clear to me that she should try a gluten-free diet. However, foods containing gluten, as it turned out, were the mainstay of the family's diet and there was a deep reluctance on the parents' part to make a change.

Our discussions continued with my encouraging the family to try a gluten-free diet. Finally, because there had been very little change through therapy, they decided to give it a try. Once she was gluten-free, it seemed that almost overnight Ava's "veil was lifted." She immediately began making progress. Within months she had recovered most of the skills she had lost and was quickly catching up with her peers. An evaluation of her mother's entire family uncovered six other individuals, including Mom, who had evidence of Celiac disease. Ava continues to do well as long as she has no gluten. If by chance some sneaks into her diet, as can happen at school or a birthday party, the veil drops again and she becomes detached, self-absorbed and exhibits many ASD-like behaviors. Ava is the one patient that I have seen who has had the most direct connection between gluten and ASD-like symptoms.

Leaky Gut

It has been suggested that some children with ASD have a possible "leaky gut" due to changes in absorption patterns in the GI tract. Although there is no evidence of a true malabsorption syndrome in ASD, like that seen in CD, resulting in a loss of nutrients from the body that could cause poor weight gain and even a failure to thrive, interesting hypotheses regarding changes in the cells in the intestinal wall have opened new areas of research. It is known that there are "doors" between cells, known as "tight junctions," and if these "open," a brief breach is made in the natural barrier of the intestinal wall, causing a leaky gut. A gene, zonulin, located on chromosome 16, a known area of association with ASD, has also been linked to the opening of the tight junctions of the intestinal tract. Once the breach in the barrier has occurred, the wall of the GI tract may become inflamed. This could then produce the GI symptoms of bloating, pain, diarrhea and constipation. This may, in fact, explain why a few children with ASD who have chronic symptoms have been helped by GI treatments that are intended for inflammatory GI disorders. Finding genes that are highly associated with GI function in children with ASD (such as the MET gene) may also further our understanding of the brain–gut connection in autism.

Any GI disease that affects children can also affect your child. The key is not only to watch for symptoms but also to keep an eye on his individual behavior patterns, which may suggest he is experiencing pain or discomfort due to an undiagnosed gastrointestinal illness.

If your child exhibits any symptoms that you feel may be related to his GI tract, alert your doctor. Certain initial steps can be taken to look for common GI illnesses (such as stool cultures for chronic diarrhea) and treat as needed. Once appropriate tests are performed (such as a blood test for CD), dietary changes may be suggested if the test results suggest an abnormality (such as gluten elimination if CD tests positive). Your doctor may prescribe or suggest over-the-counter medications that you can give your child to eliminate either pain or the disorder itself (such as the appropriate dietary and medication treatment for constipation). Chronic GI symptoms may require more extensive testing as recommended by your doctor. See Appendix 5 for further information on evaluating and treating common GI issues in children.

Diet and ASD

As you may already know, much has been written about dietary interventions in ASD. Often these new suggestions come from a few "success" stories in which children with ASD significantly improved on a specific diet. In my experience most children with ASD have at one time or another been placed on a specific dietary plan. The most common diet used in ASD is the gluten-free, casein-free (GFCF) diet. Parents report remarkable improvement once gluten and casein (a protein found in milk and other dairy products) are removed from their child's diet. However, there remains a lack of "blinded" (when both parents and researchers are "blind" to what has been eliminated) studies showing improvement in children who've been placed on these diets. In 2007, a study was done looking at the relationship between dietary intake and symptoms in children with ASD. Data from the diet diaries of sixty-two children three to eight years old with ASD were analyzed by a pediatric dietician and then compared to Recommended Daily Allowance (RDA) standards for the proper amount of total calories, protein, carbohydrates and fat. Dietary intake was correlated with parents' descriptions of stool consistency in each child. Although the reported frequency of GI abnormalities, including abnormal stool consistency (bulky or loose), was 54 percent, no significant relationship between stool consistency and dietary intake was observed. Intake for calories, carbohydrates and protein was adequate and the children did not appear to exhibit excessive carbohydrate intake.

Your child may be a picky eater and you might worry that he's not getting adequate nutrition. Even if he is a picky eater, I encourage you to think of the "big picture" when reviewing his diet. Start with a complete three-day food history of everything he eats. This can then be reviewed with your doctor or nutritionist. As long as his diet contains the essential factors required for growth—protein, carbohydrates and fat, calories and nutrients (vitamins and minerals)—he will be getting what he needs to grow and function.

Food Triggers

When considering food as a trigger for your child's illness, behavior or discomfort, I would first review his eating habits to see if there is an obvious source for a possible allergy or food intolerance. After testing, if a particular food allergy is identified, then that food can be eliminated from your child's diet. If nothing in the testing is abnormal, I often recommend a dietary change to see if eliminating a particular food will help. It is important to be systematic about elimination diets so the clear cause of any GI problems can be identified and subsequently cut from the diet. You don't want to eliminate too many food types at once, or it may not be clear which one is the primary cause of your child's GI distress.

Elimination Diets

Before you remove certain foods from your child's diet, it is important to determine if he has a true allergy to the protein contained in the substance or substances, such as casein or gluten. It is also important to determine if there is a disaccharidase deficiency syndrome (as seen in lactose in milk products) or if there is a toxic effect of the substance on the GI tract itself (as seen from gluten in Celiac disease). A true allergy to gluten can be determined by a blood test that, if positive, will reveal an increase in the blood of specific allergy antibodies of the IgE type (see Chapter 18). If casein (a milk protein) is the culprit, that will be evident from IgE allergy blood tests. Some children on a casein-free diet (no milk or milk products) improve, but they may be lactose intolerant (lactase deficiency) rather than have issues with casein. If a child improves on a gluten-free diet, he may have Celiac disease (see page 242). It is helpful to sort out the underlying cause of your child's gastric distress and work to give him a balanced and nutritious diet, which is essential for growth. If you are not giving your child milk or milk products, it is important that other sources of adequate protein, calcium and vitamin D are made a part of his dietary intake.

If you are like the parents I see in my practice, you will go to the internet for dietary information. Please be cautious—some of the information is valid, but much is not. Such was the story of secretin, a hormone found in the GI tract. Secretin is used in invasive GI procedures to see if the system is working properly. There were a few anecdotal reports that children with ASD improved after an endoscopy where secretin was used. This was followed by a media frenzy, resulting in an explosion of secretin use before any studies could be done to see if it really worked. Once secretin began to be used in a more widespread manner, there were many stories reporting huge improvements in children with ASD treated with the hormone. The fervor for its use was so strong that the NIH funded secretin studies. The studies showed secretin did not perform as advertised and in a few instances placebo performed better than the secretin. The secretin "magic bullet" theory was debunked but not before children suffered side effects of secretin, such as increased irritability and hyperactivity.

Because there is so much information available at your fingertips, having a trusting relationship with your doctor can help you sort through these issues and make educated decisions appropriate for your child. If you read something on the internet or hear it from a friend, bring it to your doctor's attention before trying it on your child. It is always important to keep your child's doctor apprised of any changes you make in your child's diet, medications or other treatments (herbs and the like).

The Relationship Between GI Issues and ASD

There has been much debate about GI issues and ASD. Does one cause the other or are they linked in some way by one root cause? One hypothesis is that a similar gene or genes influence both the neurological and GI function. Interestingly, recent studies have documented the gene encoding the MET receptor tyrosine kinase in children with ASD. This gene was chosen because of its location on the seventh chromosome (a known ASD candidate) and its function. MET signaling is a key component in growth of the cortex and cerebellum, in immune function and in GI repair. A decrease in the activity of MET gene expression was found in a significant number of families in the studies, especially in children from multiplex families (those with more than one child with ASD) and those with GI disorders. This suggests a link to both the behavioral (ASD core symptoms) and medical (GI, immune) abnormalities described. There was no association of the MET gene in those families without children with ASD and GI conditions.

In the previously mentioned study that looked at individuals diagnosed with Celiac disease in families that also had children with ASD, an association was seen between ASD, language regression, a family history of autoimmune disease and GI symptoms. The idea of a possible shared autoimmune process in the development of both the ASD and the GI issues is intriguing and will no doubt stimulate further studies. Hopefully, investigations such as these will lead to advanced treatment protocols designed to meet the individual behavioral and medical profile of each child.

Anxiety, ASD and Gastrointestinal Issues

Children with ASD live in an often threatening, difficult-to-understand world, which can produce an enormous amount of anxiety (see Chapter 20). While anxiety itself can cause GI symptoms, the presence of a GI issue can also lead to anxiety. It becomes a vicious cycle. A recent study evaluated emotional factors related to GI issues in ASD. This study documented that children with ASD and GI problems had significantly higher scores of social withdrawal than children with ASD without GI issues. In addition, the children with ASD and GI problems had significantly higher measures of anxiety than children with ASD without GI problems. Of course, anxiety may cause or exacerbate an existing condition, but if your child has increasing behaviors, especially associated with increased anxiety, I suggest considering the possibility of underlying GI issues. If he has GI discomfort that is not resolved, in my experience his anxiety will remain and there may be little improvement in his behavior. I have seen this downward spiral derail the therapeutic process, interfering with communication and relating. If the GI problems are diagnosed and treated, in most cases the child's anxiety level improves and behaviors return to typical patterns. He remarkably becomes much more socially available and can function much better at home and at school.

Treating GI issues isn't a cure for autism but rather a means of helping your child regulate and feel more comfortable in his own body if he is affected by these symptoms. When he feels better, he will then be able to devote his energy to interacting with you and his treatment team.

CHAPTER 18

Allergies and Immunological Disorders

ALLERGIES (HAY fever, asthma, eczema and food allergies) are extremely common and tend to run in families. If you or your spouse has allergies, 20 to 50 percent of your children will be prone to them, as well. If you both have allergies, this rate goes up to 50 to 75 percent. If there is a family history of allergies, then it is important to watch for symptoms of allergies in your child. Allergy symptoms range from mild to severe but even mild symptoms can cause your child with ASD difficulty concentrating, connecting and learning.

Most allergic disorders are diagnosed by a thorough history and physical exam. Certain allergic reactions may be fairly easy to recognize, such as the sneezing and watering eyes associated with hay fever, the wheezing found in asthma or the itchy, dry rash of eczema. Identifying potential food allergies is not as straightforward. They can be life-threatening (such as a peanut allergy) but may also be the cause of vague symptoms, including GI discomfort, vomiting, diarrhea and abdominal pain.

Allergic reactions occur when the body reacts to specific allergens that enter the body and trigger an immune system response. Common allergens include dust, dust mites, mold, grass, weeds, trees, animals and food. Once allergies are diagnosed, general allergy treatments include managing exposure to allergic triggers and taking medications that target bothersome symptoms. Medications for allergies include antihistamines for a runny nose, bronchodilator inhalers for wheezing and anti-inflammatory medications for asthma and eczema. Allergy shots can be administered in an attempt to bolster the immune system's ability to produce antibodies to an allergy trigger.

Allergies are found in all populations and there is no data to date showing that allergies occur more or less in ASD. It is also unknown if there is a cause-and-effect relationship between ASD and allergies. The important thing to keep in mind is that if your child has allergy symptoms, given his vulnerability, they could further interfere with his communicating and relating. So, if you suspect allergies, it is best to determine if he has them and then seek proper treatment.

Food Intolerance and Food Allergy

We may have an aversion to foods that we think are too spicy or have an odd odor, resulting in our not eating them. There may be other foods, however, that trigger a response that may be toxic or nontoxic. A toxic reaction to a food or other substances can actually cause injury to the GI tract. For example, gluten is toxic for those who have Celiac disease, resulting in intestinal wall damage. A nontoxic reaction can be due to food intolerance or food allergy. Examples of food intolerance include diarrhea caused by the inability to digest lactose sugars in certain foods, as seen in lactose intolerance, or constipation, which can be a side effect of some medications. Given the high rate of GI problems in ASD, parents and physicians often look to food allergies as the cause of a child's gastrointestinal issues. However, when it comes to food allergy, there are some challenges to getting an accurate diagnosis.

Symptoms from allergies develop when allergens stimulate the allergic response in the body. Immunoglobulin E (IgE) is instrumental in the allergic response. When the allergen (what you touch, inhale, ingest) combines with the IgE, a cascade of events follows that will cause the allergic symptoms. If this response occurs in your child's nose, he will get an itchy, runny nose. If it occurs in his lungs, he will wheeze and cough, and if it takes place in his skin, he will get a rash or hives. If this response occurs in the GI tract, abdominal pain and diarrhea will ensue.

Following are some things you should consider when getting an allergy evaluation for your child with ASD:

■ The most common foods that can cause IgE-mediated food allergy include milk, eggs, wheat, soy, peanuts, tree nuts, fish and shellfish.

■ IgE-related food reactions typically occur immediately, within minutes or hours after the food is consumed. They are reproducible; that is, the same reaction will occur the next time the food is eaten. Confirming a specific food allergy will be done through testing by your doctor. If your child has an IgE food allergy, he may already have other allergic symptoms, such as hay fever, asthma or eczema. Occasionally, these allergies are outgrown but they may be lifelong and very serious, as with a peanut allergy.

■ Testing for food allergy is typically done through skin-prick tests or blood IgE testing (known as RAST, short for "radioallergosorbent test"). If allergies are suspected, your child can have either blood tests or a skin-prick test to determine which substance or substances are causing his allergy symptoms. Both the total IgE in the blood and allergen-specific IgE (such as corn, wheat or milk IgE) can be measured. An elevated IgE is expected when there is a specific antigen (a substance that triggers an allergic response) involved. In the skin-prick test done in the allergist's office, a specific antigen is placed on the skin and skin response is recorded. The more allergic you are to a specific antigen, the bigger the redness around the prick area will be.

■ IgG testing is another, more controversial blood test and it is used to measure immunoglobulin G (IgG). Using IgG testing to diagnose allergies is not considered standard or mainstream. IgG antibodies recognize foreign substances in our bodies and respond immunologically to rid the body of bacteria and viruses. IgG antibodies are considered "blocking" antibodies in that they block the allergen from the sites that stimulate the allergy symptoms. Immunotherapy for allergies (allergy shots) is given in the hope that the recipient will develop allergy IgG-blocking antibodies. If you already have IgG food testing results for your child, I suggest you also discuss IgE testing with your doctor to definitively determine whether or not your child has a food allergy.

■ If your child has been diagnosed with a particular food allergy or sensitivity, food elimination is the best way to avoid future problems. Eliminate one suspected food at a time, monitoring your child for behavioral improvement as well as GI symptom resolution, before eliminating another food. If your child does not have a life-threatening allergy and you wish to reintroduce particular foods into his diet, you can do so, while under the care of a physician, again by selecting one food at a time and monitoring him for a reaction.

■ If your child has a life-threatening allergy (such as to peanuts), he must avoid that food for the rest of his life. Talk to your doctor about precautions you can take, including having your child carry an EpiPen (an auto-injector of epinephrine for treating life-threatening allergic reactions) or other medications with him at all times.

■ Gluten (found in wheat products) can contribute to GI distress (see Chapter 17). In some people, gluten can be toxic to the digestive system or it can produce an allergic response. Both gluten-specific IgE tests and tests for Celiac disease will help clarify if gluten is an issue for your child. Gluten can have a general effect on the function of the gut. If you cannot determine the source of your child's GI distress, it may be worth eliminating gluten temporarily to see if there is any improvement. The reintroduction of gluten over time may be possible.

■ Food intolerance may also rarely be non-IgE-related. Non-IgE-mediated food intolerance can result in diarrhea, abdominal distress and, if severe, malabsorption and failure to thrive. The most common foods to cause this reaction are milk, soy and grains. In this situation, symptoms will develop long after the food is ingested. Because the food intolerance is not allergy-based, IgE tests are not positive and the child generally does not have other symptoms of allergic diseases. CD (see Chapter 17) is a form of non-IgE-mediated food intolerance that can have severe symptoms. Although CD is lifelong, other food intolerances can be outgrown early in life. Diagnosing non-IgE food intolerance requires consulting with a GI specialist, who may need to perform diagnostic tests. Treatment will be specific to the test results.

Because little data exist on the relationship between food allergies and ASD, the key to whatever diet you choose is to be certain that your child is receiving all the recommended daily requirements needed for growth and development (see Chapter 13). As always, discuss any changes in diet, medications or supplements with your child's doctor.

Immunological Disorders

Our immune system has two types of blood cells—B cells, which produce antibodies (IgG, A, M) and T cells, which respond to inflammation. When foreign substances enter the body, the antibody immunoglobulin M (the first responder) is quickly followed by immunoglobulin G (the slow, persistent responder). The other white cell responders (T cells) will go to the site of any inflammation to help clean up and heal a wound. When the immune system responds appropriately, your system is able to fight infection and inflammatory tissue heals within an expected time frame. If the immune system is deficient or overwhelmed by an infection, this can lead to serious recurrent, often chronic infectious illnesses that may become life-threatening. If the immune system attacks and destroys healthy body tissue, this is known as an autoimmune response. In the autoimmune response the immune system views its own body tissues as foreign and continues a defensive response after the infection (or other triggers) has passed. When an overreaction occurs in the brain, antibodies to bacteria may mistakenly react with brain tissue, resulting in neurological symptoms (such as tics and obsessive-compulsive symptoms, or PANDAS following a strep infection—see Chapter 21). Although any range of immune responses can occur in ASD, a characteristic pattern has not yet emerged.

Immune Reaction and ASD

There is growing evidence for a link between brain immune reactions and ASD. There appears to be an increased incidence of autoimmune disorders (such as rheumatoid arthritis, thyroid immune disease, Celiac disease and Type 1 diabetes) in families with ASD, suggesting a possible genetic predisposition to ASD along with these autoimmune disorders. A recent study has identified markers of immune activation response (cytokines) both in the brain (in post-mortem specimens) and cerebral spinal fluid (CSF) of children with ASD.

It is not clear if some kind of autoimmune response causes the brain under-connectivity seen in children with ASD or if the autoimmune response is a secondary reaction to the brain changes caused by underconnectivity in the brain. In the meantime, without clarity on the connections between ASD, the immune system and the brain, it can be difficult to get a handle on the best course of action for treatment.

Could Your Child Have an Immune Problem?

I suggest you take a practical approach when trying to determine if your child with ASD might have an underlying immune issue. First, consider whether or not your child is healthy. Children with either immune-deficiency or active autoimmune issues are often quite ill and may have recurrent and difficult-to-treat infections. If your child has a serious immune disorder, he typically could have general complaints that occur on a regular basis, such as unexplained fevers, fatigue, rashes, aches and pain, weight loss and loss of appetite. If an immune issue is suspected, your doctor will obtain some basic blood tests for him, which include:

- **Complete blood count:** This test determines whether your child's bone marrow is producing red blood cells and platelets, as well as the number and characterization of his white cells.
- **Sedimentation rate:** This simple measure detects inflammation in the body. Extremely high sedimentation rates are seen in autoimmune disease; moderate elevation is seen in typical infections.
- **Immunoglobulin electrophoresis:** This test allows all the immunoglobulin types to be quantified, including IgG (and the four IgG subtypes, since only one subtype may be decreased), IgM and IgA. (The immunoglobulin on mucosal surfaces helps protect both the respiratory and GI systems. IgA levels are low in about 10 percent of the population.)
- **T-cell numbers and group characterization:** This test will define the different types of T cells and how many there are in each category. You may have heard of this test since it is the test used to diagnose individuals with HIV/AIDS, where the virus specifically attacks and destroys specific T cells.
- **Tests for specific immunologic diseases:** These tests can be performed as indicated by your child's family medical history and his physical exam.

The tests include a thyroid antibody panel for thyroid dysfunction, an antibody panel for systemic lupus erythemathosus, an RF (rheumatoid factor) test for rheumatoid arthritis, an ASOT (antistreptolysin-O titer) and the Anti-DNase B for post-streptococcal PANDAS (pediatric auto-immune neuropsychiatric disorders associated with streptococcus; see Chapter 21).

These tests can be performed in most labs. If your child has normal ranges, it is very unlikely that immune abnormalities are affecting his entire body. If an immune reaction is localized to a specific area in his brain, much more specialized tests would need to be performed to sort this out. Most of the tools that are presently used in research protocols to identify immune responses, such as increased inflammatory markers in the cerebral spinal fluid (CSF), are only available if your child is a candidate for the research protocol.

One word of caution: determining your child's immune status can be more complicated if your child has frequent common colds. Once children are exposed to other children in groups, it is common for them to have an upper respiratory infection every four to six weeks. Children who have underlying upper respiratory allergies may have them more frequently, as will children who have complicated ear infections or sinus infections. Slight increases in white cell immune responses are expected in these cases. Therefore, the long-term medical history of the child is very important in accurately evaluating lab results.

Treating Allergies and Immune Disorders

Treating unresponsive allergies and/or immune disorders generally requires consulting with a doctor who specializes in allergy and immunology. Further testing, such as scratch or prick tests, can be done to determine more specific allergens that elicit allergic (IgE) responses or to determine your child's ability to respond to infections. The allergist will then recommend specific treatment for your child depending on his diagnosis.

There are two anti-inflammatory treatments that have been considered in treating children with ASD: steroids and IVIG (intravenous immunoglobulin). Both have serious side effects as well as a potential impact on the brain immune processes that might be occurring in ASD. Because of this, making recommendations without adequate research is difficult. IVIG is used for specific immunoglobulin deficiencies or for specific autoimmune diseases. Steroids are used to fight inflammation. For example, steroid nasal sprays can be used for serious hay fever and some use steroid inhalers for asthma. Steroids can also help prevent transplant rejection and in some cases provide one of the mainstays in cancer treatment. Steroids can have serious side effects, so it is important to discuss all the pros and cons with your doctor if they are recommended for your child.

There is continuing interest in identifying the role of the immune system in ASD. Studies of the increased rate of immune disorders in the ASD family, as well as possible links to both GI and seizure disorders in ASD, are becoming clear. Still, we cannot answer the question of whether or not an immunologic treatment should be given to your child if he does not have a specific immunologic disease. However, a large study looking at immune blood markers is being conducted at the University of California, Davis, MIND Institute and it may provide clues as to why children with ASD also have immune changes.

Hopefully, further research into potential immunologic reactions in the development of ASD and appropriate clinical trials using these anti-inflammatory medications, as well as any potential new ones, will also provide both you and your doctor with information to help guide your child's treatments.

CHAPTER 19

Sleep Disorders

W E ALL need a continuous pattern of regular sleep to perform at our best and get the most enjoyment out of life. The more regular the sleep-wake cycle, the better! If your child has difficulty with regulation while awake, it would not be surprising if he has difficulty with sleep regulation, as well. The two can become a vicious cycle: the more dysregulated the sleep, the more dysregulated the day—which then affects sleep and so on. Adequate sleep is important for our general well-being, and this is especially true for children.

Sleep Problems Are Common in Children

You are not alone if your child is having sleep problems. Sleep problems are quite common in typical preschool children, and children with ASD are no exception. A study in the *Journal of Pediatrics* from 2004 reported that preschool children woke during the night between 16 to 25 percent of the time. In addition, 12 percent had snoring or difficulty breathing, 9 percent had difficulty falling asleep and 1 percent of the population studied always seemed to be tired in the morning. In talking to parents of the children in the study, researchers discovered that the children with sleep problems had behavioral issues, such as hyperactive-inattentive behavior, daytime tiredness and sleepiness, as well as emotional and social problems. It is interesting to note that these behaviors are similar to those frequently seen in children with ASD and were found most often in children who snored. The behaviors significantly improved, however, if the children were treated for or outgrew the snoring.

School-aged children with troubled sleep patterns who were studied were found to have similar behavioral issues that interfered with school functioning. Another study in *Pediatrics* followed 829 children between eight and eleven years old to document sleep-disordered breathing (SDB), which includes anything from snoring to obstructive sleep apnea (OSA). This study found that 15 percent of the group snored and 5 percent of these children had obstructive sleep apnea.

Obstructive Sleep Apnea (OSA)

OSA is caused by enlarged tonsils and adenoids, which obstruct the airway when a child is lying down, resulting in decreased oxygen within the bloodstream. Children with OSA have significant increases in behaviors, which include hyperactivity, emotional fluctuations and oppositional and aggressive behaviors.

Because sleep apnea reduces oxygen in the bloodstream, it can kill neurons in the brain. Animal studies have shown that low levels of oxygen in the blood can kill cells in the key memory centers of a rat's brain. These key memory centers are located in the limbic system and hippocampus (the emotional processing center), which is also where underconnectivity has been seen in people with ASD. Lack of oxygen has also been shown to interfere with the process of strengthening the neural connections that are crucial for learning and memory. Finally, improved behavior in children seen following surgery for obstructive sleep apnea is significantly greater than improvements in behavior seen following treatment with stimulant medication (which is often used for attention issues).

Sleep Patterns and ASD

While the sleep disorders in children with ASD could be due in part to the sleep issues seen in the general population, it appears that they are more prevalent in ASD. Children with ASD have unique sensory profiles, such as over-reactivity to light, sound and touch (they can be especially sensitive to sheets, blankets, tags in pajamas and so on), that may disrupt their sleep cycle and interfere with nighttime routines. If your child has difficulty self-calming or transitioning from more stimulating activities to sleep, or if he isn't clear about the expectations and routine of going to bed and falling asleep, it may be difficult to help him to get to bed on time and to fall asleep for the night. Some sensory-sensitive children may experience heightened anxiety at bedtime, further exacerbating their behavior and feeding into their resistance to go to bed. Ensuring that your child gets a good night's sleep is a must to support his daytime activities so he can get the maximum benefit from his therapies.

Studies of parent-recorded sleep patterns show that children with ASD have more frequent sleep problems (53 percent) than children with other developmental disabilities (46 percent) or typically developing children (32 percent). Children with ASD had higher parent reports of insomnia symptoms: difficulty initiating sleep (falling asleep) or maintaining sleep (staying asleep). They had the following symptoms:

- Took a long time to fall asleep
- Had a later bedtime than average
- Slept less and slept inconsistently
- Experienced a higher number of arousals and awakenings during the night
- Woke early in the morning

In addition to insomnia, parents also reported problems during their children's sleep that included snoring or OSA; bruxism (grinding teeth); waking from sleep with confusion and/or wandering; abnormal bed movements, such as rhythmically moving the body and/or legs; as well as daytime sleepiness and decreased attention. Children with ASD who have sleep problems have also been noted to have more changeable mood and impaired social interactions compared to children with ASD without sleep issues.

While ASD can be a prime contributor to sleep issues, a child with ASD might also have a coexisting sleep disorder that can severely impact his sleep patterns over a long period of time. Because of the increased rate of sleep problems in children with ASD, it is possible that the two disorders are related through similar brain pathways. The sleep-wake cycle is regulated by three neurotransmitters: GABA, serotonin and melatonin. These same neurotransmitters have been seen to be altered in ASD and may be a cause of the disturbed sleep patterns so often found in these children.

MELATONIN AND SLEEP

Melatonin is a hormone secreted by the brain's pineal gland to regulate the sleep-wake cycle, thus promoting sleep. Not only has abnormal melatonin production been documented in individuals with ASD but low levels of melatonin have been found in the blood of individuals with ASD, as well as in their unaffected parents. This suggests a genetic origin for this predisposition in a subgroup of children with ASD who have issues with sleep. These findings indicate that this subgroup could benefit from the use of melatonin as a therapeutic supplement.

In addition to the possibility of a common pathway that might lead to developing ASD along with a sleep disorder, medical issues and psychiatric disorders, ranging from epilepsy to GERD to anxiety to mood disorders, may also adversely affect your child's sleep. Unfortunately, some medications used to treat these conditions can also cause sleep problems.

Becoming Aware of Your Child's Sleep Patterns

It is important to be aware of your child's sleep behaviors and patterns. Sleep problems will interfere with his ability to function at his best during the day. Although you may assume that sleep issues are common and not worth discussing, I think it is important for you to bring up any sleep issues (problems or changes in sleep habits) to your doctor. I also think it is important to keep an eye on your child's sleep as he grows.

When trying to understand your child's sleep pattern the following questions, adapted from Autism Speaks Autism Treatment Network Sleep Subcommittee (www.autismspeaks.org), can be very helpful:

- When does your child usually go to bed?
- When does he usually go to sleep?
- Where does he fall asleep? In his own bedroom? Yours? Or another room?
- Does he sleep through the night in this location, or does he move during the night? If he moves, where does he end up?
- Does he sleep alone? Is he afraid?
- If he wakes up during the night, does it have any relationship to weekdays versus weekends?
- Is his wake-sleep cycle different weekdays versus weekends?
- Does he nap? If so, for how long?
- How many hours does he sleep?
- Does he wet the bed at night?
- Does he talk during sleep?
- Is he restless, moving a lot during sleep?
- Does he sleepwalk?
- Does he move to someone else's bed during the night?
- Does he grind his teeth during sleep?
- Does he snore loudly?
- Does he seem to stop breathing during sleep?
- Does he snort or gasp during sleep?
- Does he have trouble sleeping away from home (while visiting relatives, on vacation and so on)?
- Does he awaken during the night screaming, sweating and inconsolable?
- Does he awaken alarmed by a frightening dream?
- If he wakes during the night, how often does it happen?
- In the morning, does he wake up by himself?
- Does he wake up in a negative mood?
- Do adults or siblings wake him up?
- Does he have difficulty getting out of bed in the morning?

- Does he take a long time to become alert in the morning?
- Does he seem tired?
- Does he appear sleepy or fall asleep while watching TV or riding in the car?

When speaking with your child's doctor about your child's sleep, it is important to let him know about your child's bedtime routine. A complete understanding of the bedtime routine can give your doctor clues to the possible issues that may surround your child's sleep. It is also important to review any habits that may be affecting his sleep, such as having caffeine late at night or engaging in stimulating activities before bedtime. Looking at your child's medications and supplements for potential interference with sleep is also important.

If your child has difficulty falling asleep, it may help to make some changes to his room or his bed to accommodate his sensory sensitivities (switch sheets, blankets or pajamas; eliminate light from the room). If his sleep is unchanged by your instituting a calm sleep routine, this may indicate a melatonin synthesis issue. Night wakening also suggests melatonin issues or he may require changes to his sleep environment. It could indicate a primary sleep disorder related to another medical illness, so be sure to mention the issue to your doctor.

Measuring Your Child's Sleep

There are a number of methods of measuring your child's sleep. If sleep is an issue for him, your doctor may recommend a technique called actigraphy, which does not disrupt sleep but measures movement during the night through a small sensor worn in a wristband. It can also measure sleep over progressive nights to identify sleep patterns and help in determining proper treatment. A study using actigraphy measures in ASD showed that the children took a long time falling asleep, confirming what many parents report about their children. The actigraphy also showed delayed or advanced sleep, waking, night waking, inadequate sleep and abnormal activity patterns.

A more extensive measure of sleep is a polysomnography study (PSG). The PSG monitors respiration, heart rate, brain waves and muscle movements during sleeping. If your doctor recommends this type of study, it is generally performed in a specialized sleep study unit, although newer, ambulatory methods may increase its use for children with ASD. To date, very few studies using PSG have been completed in the ASD population. Children and adolescents in the few studies performed had a history of prolonged chronic sleep pattern abnormalities. Not only did these studies confirm the actigraphy data but they also revealed major sleep disorders, including:

- Obstructive sleep apnea (severely disordered breathing due to upper respiratory tissues that block the airway, such as the tonsils and adenoids, resulting in decreased oxygen in the bloodstream)
- Rapid eye movement (REM) behavior disorder (thrashing and moving during the REM or dreaming state of sleep)
- Periodic limb movements of sleep ([PLMS]; also known as restless legs syndrome)
- Epilepsy (or subclinical epileptiform discharges [SEDs])
- Bruxism (grinding teeth)

One of these studies included ten patients from my practice. Each child had a history of serious sleep difficulties over many years. The children underwent PSG and the results showed that each child in the study had at least one of the primary sleep disorders, which allowed us to determine appropriate treatment. Half were diagnosed with two issues. For the three children who had OSA, surgical removal of their tonsils and adenoids led to remarkably improved sleep patterns. Following surgery, each was able to have restful sleep and was much more attentive and engaged during the day. They were also much calmer, as well as interactive, during therapeutic sessions. Once the sleep disorder had been resolved, learning curves accelerated for all three.

Epilepsy was diagnosed in two of the children (one with LKS; see Chapter 16). Both children's sleep patterns and daytime alertness were significantly improved with appropriate therapy. Finally, REM behavior disorder (diagnosed in four of the ten) and PLMS (also diagnosed in four of the ten) were treated, resulting in much improved sleep patterns for these children.

Improving sleep patterns for your child can have a major impact on his quality of life. ASD research indicates that sleep affects not only increased activity, mood and disruptive behavior but especially a child's ability to communicate and relate. Sleep deprivation often engenders increasing repetitive behaviors, further need for strict routines and increased anxiety.

Treating Sleep Problems in ASD

You may need to consult with a sleep specialist to receive a complete evaluation and recommendations for treatment. Beyond medical intervention and treatment there are things you can do to modify sleep routines to help your child develop better sleep habits and get a better night's rest. The following suggestions are based on research and clinical evidence. They have been developed by the sleep specialist members of the Autism Speaks/Autism Treatment Network and modified by my own clinical experience. These sleep strategies appear to be helpful whether the behavior is a learned one or one that is exacerbated by anxiety or the core behaviors of ASD.

Getting a Good Night's Sleep

There are several things you can do to help your child achieve restful sleep. These approaches range from environmental and behavioral changes to medical intervention.

Provide a Comfortable Sleep Environment

Your child needs his own space at night to sleep. He could share a bedroom or have his own room, but he should go to bed in the same place each night. The bedroom should be temperature controlled, quiet and dark. A night-light might be important if your child is anxious in the dark. On the other hand, if your child is sensitive to light, he may require blackout shades on his windows. Strive to keep the room quiet at night, except for possible "white noise" or a low background sound. Your child's individual profile and his sensitivities to particular sounds, smells, touch and light must be considered, and his room and environment modified as needed. If, for example, your child reacts badly to the sound of the vacuum, don't use it during his sleep time. If your child can use only certain types of nightclothes that have been washed in a particular detergent because of his sensitive skin, be prepared and have extra sets for him to change into if accidents occur either before bed (such as pajama sleeves getting wet while washing up or brushing teeth) or during the night. Be aware that if you use something in your child's bedtime routine, such as music or TV while he is falling asleep, he will need to have that same thing wherever he sleeps—at a vacation hotel, a relative's house or at sleepovers. It's best not to count on these extraneous supports to help him to fall asleep.

Establish a Consistent Bedtime Routine

A routine that is relatively short, predictable and consistent night after night, caretaker to caretaker, is important. A routine helps your child learn how to relax and get ready for sleep. A predictable schedule is comforting. Depending on his unique profile, choose activities that will calm him. In general, avoid stimulating activities before bedtime, such as high-energy television programs, videos, computer games or loud music. A routine should begin fifteen to sixty minutes before the set bedtime and should center on the child's bedroom, which should be quiet and ready for sleep. Some parents start their child's bedtime routine with a bath, getting on pajamas, brushing teeth, reading a book, singing a song and tucking into bed. This, of course, is a wonderful time to use your DIR/Floortime skills to have a shared, soothing, yet interactive time with your child (see Chapter 6). A visual schedule of the routine may be helpful for your child to remind him what happens first and what comes next. You can take photos of your child doing each step of the routine and post them on a bulletin board or other surface so he knows what to expect. Using a timer to help your child anticipate the small transitions in his routine can be beneficial.

Maintain a regular schedule. Strive to have a bedtime and wake-time routine that is the same seven days a week. Discuss reasonable bedtimes for your child with your doctor. Some of the parents in my practice are so exhausted from their daily routines that they try to get their child to go to bed much earlier than is appropriate for his age. If he does not need to go to sleep early and is not ready to go to bed, the parents are setting themselves up for failure. You may have noticed yourself that your child gets a second wind in the hour before bedtime and may have difficulty falling asleep if he goes to bed too early. If this has been your experience, consider delaying your child's bedtime by thirty to sixty minutes.

Maintaining a routine is more important for children with ASD than for other children. In fact, they can be thrown off by a weekend routine that is different from their weekday schedule. Your child's sleep will become more consistent if you do not vary his weekend routine more than an hour from his weekday routine—especially while attempting to develop a new or more effective sleep pattern for him. If he is young and has a daytime nap, try to keep these as regular as possible (weekdays and weekends). Have him nap in his bed if you are at home. If he does nap, be certain that he is up by 4:00 p.m. so that the nap does not interfere with nighttime sleeping. Daytime routines, such as meals and snack times, also should be as regular as possible to help with sleep patterns. Exposure to sunlight in the morning and keeping the room dark at night can help maintain regular sleep (circadian) cycles. When your child wakes up, open the window treatments and let natural light into his room.

Help Your Child Fall Asleep Alone

In general, your child should learn to fall asleep without you. This is important because all of us wake up several times during the night, briefly check out what is around us, and then quickly go back to sleep. These wakings are so brief that we aren't aware of them in the morning. However, if your child can't fall back asleep without you, then each time he wakes up, he may need you to be with him in order to fall back asleep. Typically, children with ASD may begin sleeping in their own bed, only to wake up in the middle of the night and crawl into bed with their parents. If your child has a pattern of not sleeping alone, I suggest the following techniques learned in my general pediatric practice. At bedtime sit in a chair next to your child's bed and gradually move the chair farther and farther away from his bed. Eventually, he will become more able to fall asleep without you in the immediate vicinity. If he consistently comes into your room to sleep during the night, buy him a sleeping bag that he chooses. When he comes in to sleep in your bed, have him sleep in his sleeping bag on the floor next to your bed. You can shift the position of his sleeping bag inch by inch from your bedside, gradually moving it farther and farther and eventually back to his room. A benefit of this technique, particularly if your child has difficulty sleeping away from home, is that he can get used to his sleeping bag and can use it when he is away from his own bedroom. Older children who wake up multiple times during the night can be given a "pass" at bedtime. It can be a handwritten card or other token. This pass can be exchanged for something during the night, such as a hug or a glass of water. I suggest giving only one pass each night. If he doesn't use his pass at night, let him redeem it for a "prize," such as a sticker. He can eventually exchange his earned stickers for a special outing or item.

Avoid Naps in the Daytime

In general, a child who sleeps during the day will have a more difficult time falling to sleep at night. Once infant nap times have ended, avoiding sleep during the daytime may help your child develop a sleep-wake cycle that corresponds to night and day.

Consider daytime activities that promote a better sleep-wake schedule. Daytime activities can influence nighttime sleep. Many children with ASD who spend forty hours a week in a therapeutic setting get less exercise than their peers. It is clear that exercise is important for your child's health. Children who exercise tend to sleep better at night but the exercise needs to occur throughout the day and not immediately before bedtime. In fact, exercise right before bedtime can leave your child too alert to fall asleep easily. Also, be sure to avoid giving him caffeinated foods and beverages before bedtime. Chocolate, coffee, tea and colas should not be consumed in the three to five hours before bedtime.

Medical Support for Sleep

If your child is diagnosed with a sleep disorder that does not respond to behavior changes, appropriate treatment with medication may be the next step for helping him to get a good night's sleep. Medications that target insomnia include melatonin, clonidine, trazodone, mirtazapine and occasionally benzodiazepines (see Appendix 6). There are specific medications that are targeted to particular sleep disorders—for example, Requip is used for restless legs syndrome. Medication choices will be made following a thorough discussion of effects/side effects with your doctor. Melatonin is appealing to most parents because it is considered a dietary supplement with few side effects. One study that enrolled 113 children with ASD and treated them with anywhere from 1 mg to 6 mg of melatonin before bedtime reported improved sleep in 89 percent of the children.

Many of the families in my practice long for a good night's sleep for themselves and their children. If your child has a sleep issue, you and the other members of your family may also be in extreme need of sleep. If you are sleep deprived or have sleep problems (insomnia or other issues), then your child's sleeplessness may further compound your problem. I urge you to discuss this with your doctor.

It is clear that ASD and sleep difficulties are interrelated. There are multiple causes of sleep difficulties, many of which are easily treated either by behavioral changes or medication. Further research should help determine the degree to which improving a child's sleep patterns in ASD will positively affect his daytime function and support his ability to communicate, relate and learn.

CHAPTER 20

Understanding Medication and Its Use in ASD

RYAN BOUNDED happily into my office for a visit in the spring of his seventh year, with Diana right behind him. He was wearing an L.A. Lakers jersey, shorts that came down to his ankles and brand-new basketball shoes. He looked great.

"Hi, Dr. Ricki," said Ryan with a shy smile. It was clear that he had made tremendous strides since our visit six months before. The school program we had built was in its third year, and Diana felt that the OT, speech and DIR/Floortime therapists were working together beautifully to keep Ryan progressing.

"Ryan," I said, "I really like your shirt! Do you like basketball?"

"Yes," Ryan replied proudly.

"Wonderful! When is your next game?"

"Saturday."

The fact that Ryan was able to respond to questions, albeit with simple words, was a good sign.

"He's sustaining social interaction for thirty to forty continuous circles," said Diana, "and he's so happy. But there is something that we've all noticed that I'm very concerned about."

Diana told me that even with an intensive sensory-motor program there were times when Ryan was getting overloaded with too much sensory input. He was coping by pacing and scripting (reciting lines from movies, commercials or books), and this was interfering with his ability to interact with his peers. "At first I thought it was a transitional thing, but it's become a pattern for about the last six months and seems to be getting worse. He seems... stuck."

I suggested that we do a complete medical evaluation to make sure nothing was going on. When the evaluation was complete, I called Diana. There was no evidence of either a new or chronic medical issue.

"Well," Diana said apprehensively, "I know that we've talked about the possibility of medication, but I've been resisting. Do you think medication would help?"

"Let's have a talk," I replied.

Medication and ASD

Like Diana, many parents resist using medication for their children. It can be worrisome to think of your child taking medication on an ongoing basis. When I talk about using medications with parents, I am no longer surprised to hear, "No way, no how, will I medicate my child!" Because the medications used for treatment are designed to modulate brain function (the drugs effect neurotransmitters), and because these medications are often the least understood by both doctors and patients, they can inspire resistance, worry and fear. Horror stories of "drugged" children abound and "black box" warnings of possible side effects raise understandable concern in both patients and their doctors.

An Essential Tool—When Properly Managed

What I have learned in my years of practice, however, is that if managed properly, medication can be one of the essential tools in helping a child with an imbalanced or poorly coordinated brain system. As in all of medicine, the proper use of medication is both a science and an art. Treating neurological conditions has improved over the past decade from remarkable advances in science. This includes information on how neurotransmitters and chemicals operate in the brain, the development of more specific, refined medications to increase benefits while reducing unwanted side effects and the development of more palatable or easy-to-take medications for children.

No Magic Pill

There is no magic pill for treating ASD. The goal of these medications is to balance the chemicals in the brain to level the playing field and allow your child to be more mentally available and able to learn. In Ryan's case, in addition to his existing therapies, we used the medication Prozac to decrease his underlying anxiety and pacing behaviors. Diana reported over the next several months that not only was Ryan more comfortable in his own body but he was also interacting more with peers on the playground and teachers in the classroom. By the end of the semester his teacher noted that his reading ability had improved remarkably. Improving his brain function not only affected Ryan's ability to learn but also helped him improve socially and academically.

Because ASD is most likely the result of imbalances in brain chemistry, making the most of a child's learning ability may require using multiple, carefully selected medications to target various symptoms or behaviors—layering, sequencing and balancing medications are all part of the art of treatment. Using multiple medications is a common approach in medicine. For example, effectively controlling asthma may require the use of both a bronchodilator and an anti-inflammatory agent. Treating hypertension typically requires using a beta-blocking drug, a diuretic and an ACE inhibitor.

Because ASD, by definition, exists within a widely varying spectrum of symptoms, there is no one specific treatment. The medications given to a child with ASD are more "symptom specific" than "diagnosis specific." In other words, the medications will treat a symptom (such as anxiety in the case of Ryan) and are not dictated by the diagnosis (ASD). Targeting behavioral symptoms with medications should be considered as part of treatment regimens. In my practice, I treat many facets of ASD, based on the symptoms and behaviors of the child I am treating. Medication management can have a very significant role in helping your child when combined with a carefully designed and executed multidisciplinary treatment plan.

The Art of Choosing the Right Medication

The art of choosing the right medication entails combining scientific information with child-specific observation and experience. It requires listening to the child and his family, both in terms of the nature of the child's issues and how the medication is affecting him. Observation involves communication through the doctor-parent-child partnership with input from other team members. Experience evolves as the doctor—a pediatrician, neurologist or child psychiatrist—builds a base of knowledge collected from the specifics of each individual patient's needs and responses.

If you decide that your child may benefit from this approach, his doctor will seek to:

- Accurately identify and prioritize the symptoms that will be targeted for treatment
- Assess and explain his profile
- Delineate the risks and benefits of various medications
- Initiate a sequenced treatment plan with a careful approach to reach the appropriate beneficial dose while minimizing side effects
- Establish markers of success and/or concern
- Engage you as the "first observers" on the team, to track the efficacy of the medications

Balancing Neurotransmitters

The goal of using medications given to children with ASD is to improve brain function. To understand how the medications work, it is helpful to get a handle on how the brain functions normally. The actual wiring of the brain, as well as other components of the nervous system, exists in the form of cells called neurons—think of them as the tracks that information travels on—which manufacture neuro-electrochemical substances, the neurotransmitters. (See Figure 4.)

Neurotransmitters pair with particular neurons and are extremely important in normal brain function. Synapses (switches) serve as the connections between neurons. Each neuron has many connections through different synapses to many other neurons, which increases the complexity of the system as well as the neurons' ability to communicate with each other. The neurotransmitters carry or transmit specific messages and instructions from the brain to essentially all other areas of the body. Neurotransmitters control memory, mood, sleep, behavior, pain perception and learning. (See Figure 5.)

In ASD not only are there fewer connections between neurons, but there are most likely other abnormalities in synaptic functioning. These abnormalities may result in either too much or too little of a particular neurotransmitter. This in turn can lead to problems with information processing.

For Ryan, his classmates' voices on the playground weren't a call to play; the sounds were painful and increased his anxiety. He began pacing to calm himself down rather than joining in. Ryan's reaction was very common for someone with ASD—he didn't process sensory input as other children did and he didn't react as one might expect. Instead, he experienced an increase in anxiety-driven behaviors. Ryan's behavior made sense to him and was dictated by his underlying brain biology. That his behavior didn't match the situation was an indication to adults and caregivers that something was amiss in his environment and needed to be addressed. In this case medication decreased his anxiety that was spurred on by his noise sensitivity. The change in his brain biology (the Prozac increased the serotonin available for neurotransmission) allowed him to tolerate the noise and return to interactive play. His teachers noticed that Ryan looked much more "comfortable" and "able to participate."

Choosing the Right Medication for the Job

Because the brain is a complex system, resolving an ASD target symptom isn't as simple as finding a medical/chemical replacement for a particular neurotransmitter. Research has shown that neurotransmitters are interconnected and dependent on one another and require these connections in order

Figure 4: Neuron

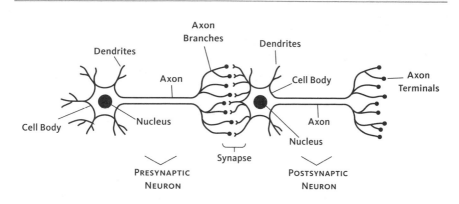

Figure 5: Synapse

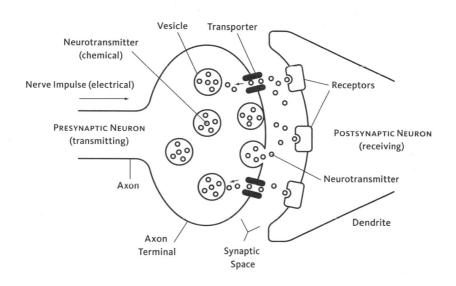

to be produced through connecting synapses. Dopamine, for example, is the most prevalent neurotransmitter throughout the brain and is necessary for the production of other neurotransmitters. Studies have also revealed that certain areas of the brain are concentrated with specific neurons that produce neurotransmitters of one particular type or another. For example, the frontal lobe of the brain is populated by dopamine- and norepinephrine-specified neurons. This area of the brain primarily addresses attention and executive functions. A child with attention deficit disorder (ADD) has insufficient amounts of dopamine and norepinephrine present in that area of his brain for him to be able to sustain attention. Therefore, medications that increase the availability of these two neurotransmitters are most effective in treating his attention issues. On the other hand, many psychotic illnesses are most likely due to the presence of too much dopamine in specific areas of the brain and treatment is geared toward blocking dopamine receptors to calm down the brain's neural transmission.

Specific neurotransmitters have been identified to be associated with various neuropsychiatric disorders. For example, obsessive-compulsive disorder (OCD) is associated with too little serotonin. ASD may have the greatest number of neurotransmitter imbalances, thereby affecting so many areas of brain function. Thus far, over sixty different neurotransmitters have been identified. The neurotransmitters serotonin, norepinephrine, dopamine, GABA, glutamate and acetylcholine are the most likely ones involved in producing ASD symptoms. These neurotransmitters aid in processing sensory input and motor output; play an integral role in memory, attention, sleep-wake cycles, cognition; and are vital to preventing depression, OCD and modulating appetite and mood—all of which are issues in ASD.

Once the neurotransmitter has completed its job in the synapse, it can either reenter the neuron through "reuptake" and go back into the presynaptic neuron or it can be destroyed by enzymes in the synapse. There are many locations where this process can be affected by particular medications, which, in turn, can have an effect on overall neurotransmitter balance. Medications can imitate, stimulate the release of, or change the breakdown of neurotransmitters. Additionally, they can block or bind to receptor sites, thus increasing or decreasing available neurotransmitters. For the most part, the medications prescribed for ASD work by modifying the balance of various neurotransmitters.

The medications that are most often used in ASD are listed in Appendix 6, along with potential side effects. Many of these are used "off label," meaning that they may not have an indication for use in children, or in ASD, in the prescribing information. This is due to the limited number of research studies performed on these uses. However, the information in the appendix is based on physicians' experience using these medications over many years in the situations described.

The Art of Medication Management

Doctors are trained to use diagnostic and evaluative tests to determine what has gone wrong in the body as well as to determine if treatment is working. Unfortunately, to determine success in treating your child for ASD, there is no blood test (as is done in diabetes management), physical measurement (like blood pressure monitoring), physical examination (listening for a clear lung following asthma treatment) or radiology study (a CAT scan or MRI scan used for cancer follow-up) to measure results. We must use clinical observation, which requires careful analysis, blend the science and art of medicine, as well as draw on all the experience and knowledge of the team members who are focused on improving the well-being and learning curve for your child. Your child's course of treatment may have highs and lows, and this requires excellent communication among all team members, as well as a commitment to the long term. Remember, there is no quick fix in autism. Giving your child medication represents only one piece of the treatment program geared to meet his needs. The ultimate goal, of course, is to improve his functional abilities and help him become more available to learning so he can move up the social-emotional-developmental ladder. In my experience, medication management, when used in conjunction with a complete therapeutic program, is an extremely valuable tool to help children with ASD attain this goal.

The Target Symptom Approach

Through my years of experience following children with ASD, I have developed a method to help prioritize decisions about medications based on diagnosing and treating the underlying causes of symptoms, engaging in a risk/benefit analysis of the severity of the symptoms versus potential medication effects and side effects, and observing behavior change in the child as he grows.

The use of medication in ASD requires a very thoughtful process. The first step is to identify the target symptoms that are interfering with your child's progress. Prioritizing which symptom to treat first requires lengthy discussions between your family and the team members to identify and come to a consensus on the issues that need to be addressed first. This list of issues can be reviewed with your doctor.

If your child has a single, identifiable symptom that requires medication, the treatment plan is generally straightforward. However, children with ASD usually have many issues and it takes time to sort through them, decide which to treat, and then prioritize medication treatment plans. Also, target symptoms often change as your child ages and, as a result of therapy, moves up the social-emotional-developmental ladder. As he improves, your child may need a change in the dosage of a medication or he may need to change medications entirely.

Once a target symptom has been identified, the next step is to connect the target symptom to the underlying brain neurotransmitters that could be contributing to the behavior. Based on this, medications that could be helpful can be explored. The pros and cons of a possible treatment must be considered by looking at the desired effect versus the potential side effects of the medications. This risk/benefit analysis often leads to choosing to treat the symptom that is most likely to respond with the least risky and most effective medication.

Once the appropriate medication has been selected, it is administered in a trial format. The drug trial or plan is put into place in order to evaluate the drug's effectiveness for treating a specific symptom. A similar drug trial or plan can be used for any of your child's medications, such as those taken for GI issues or seizures.

If you target a particular symptom to treat in this way, it is easier to monitor progress over time and to watch for side effects. A time frame should be agreed upon to determine whether or not the medication has been effective for helping the identified (targeted) issue. The trial period depends on the length of time it typically takes for a medication to reach a therapeutic level in a child's blood, the symptoms being treated and the time that it may take for improvement. If improved attention is the target and a stimulant medication is chosen, the results can be quick and measurable in a matter of hours. If, on the other hand, Strattera (a longer-acting medication for attention disorders) is the chosen medication, then consensus on whether or not it is working may take several weeks due to the length of time it can take this drug to develop adequate blood levels for results to be evident. If it has been effective, then generally speaking, the medication will be titrated (adjusted) up to its optimal dosage and continued at a steady rate. However, it is important to always be vigilant about side effects throughout the process.

I suggest keeping a medication Treatment Response Chart (see Appendix 7) to document how well a medication is working to alleviate your child's symptoms. Embarking on a medication trial requires a lengthy dialogue, particularly between you and your doctor, not only at the beginning but throughout treatment. As patients in my practice get older and are better able to communicate, I strive to include them in the decision-making process. Many of my teenage patients are very articulate about how they feel on particular medications and whether or not they think the dose they are on is working.

Determining if a medicine is working is challenging, because we know medication results can vary for each child. Because of the variety of benefit and the conflicting information about what works and what doesn't, the right choice of medication for your child can be confusing. The best way to deal with this sparse and contradictory information is to work closely with your doctor to explore possible medications and balance the potential risks and benefits. Always keep in mind that both you and your doctor need to be cautious when choosing treatment options. Because a few positive or negative studies on a general population of children often cannot answer the question about what may be useful for a particular child, the best approach is to tailor the medication to your child's unique profile.

Once symptoms have been targeted, a medication has been chosen and we know what change in symptoms or behavior we are watching for, I suggest starting the medication with as low a dose as possible. This does not necessarily mean the smallest pill available—it may mean using one quarter of a pill or using a liquid or a compounded formula of the medication. When I first started treating children with these medications, I was surprised to see the doses that were being suggested. I suspect these higher doses were one of the reasons why so many side effects occurred. With sensory systems not coordinating well for children with ASD, it is not surprising that too much medication could have untoward effects. If your doctor does not adopt an incremental approach to medication and your child has had side effects from taking a particular medication, speak with your doctor about modifying the dosage. The medication may be ideal for treating your child's symptoms— but at a lower dose.

When you start with the lowest possible dose, it allows you to gently titrate (adjust) the dosage, observing for positive effects and stopping if there is a negative side effect. Too large a dose can overshoot the effective range of the medication for a particular child and only induce a side effect. After determining the optimal dose, continue monitoring the effects and the side effects. Treatment with more than one medication may be beneficial. Each, however, needs to be titrated in a similar fashion.

If all the neurotransmitters are slightly out of balance (as they may be in ASD), then we have to be careful that the medication doesn't create what I call the "teeter-totter" effect—one neurotransmitter too high and another too low. That imbalance is sure to cause side effects. If you are looking to modulate different neurotransmitters, it is important to understand how they relate to one another. Treatment in this case requires balancing two inter-related medications in order to have the best effects of both with the least side effects.

For example, if I am monitoring the effects of dopamine versus serotonin in a child who has both anxiety and attention issues, I may first increase the dopamine levels using a stimulant to boost his attention and decrease impulsivity. If his serotonin levels are too low, his anxiety and repetitive behaviors may increase, and a very slight increase in his selective serotonin reuptake inhibitor (SSRI) dosage may help. For this reason, for some I start the SSRI prior to initiating the stimulants. On the other hand, if his serotonin level is too high, without enough dopamine to balance it out, the teeter-totter tips in the opposite direction. His level of anxiety may improve, but his impulsivity and inattention may increase. This can be prevented by slowly adjusting his medication to get the desired effect on attention. Attaining the proper balance can take time. Remember that it is best to adjust only one medication at a time, while monitoring for any changes.

Finally, it should be noted that in developing a particular medication treatment plan, it is key that all family members agree with the plan and that the goal of using a particular medication for your child is clear to all involved. Clarifying goals and expectations will help your family, extended family, therapists and teachers to better note how well the medication is working, if there are any problems with side effects or if there is an unwanted increase in symptoms.

MEDICATION GUIDELINES WITH ASD

There are a number of issues to keep in mind as you work with medications for your child, including:

- Medications will not cure ASD.
- Medication is used to help ease specific behaviors.
- The aim of medication is to improve your child's functioning to enable him to get the most out of all his treatments and interactions throughout the day.
- Some of these medication trials should be blind. I suggest that a few of your child's therapists or family members residing outside of the household should be unaware that he is on medication. Placebo is thought to work about 25 percent of the time in ASD. (Having people in your child's environment who are unaware that he is on medication avoids the bias of hopeful expectations as well as the negativity of preconceived ideas of what medication can or cannot do. However, with certain medical conditions, such as seizure disorders, the entire team must be informed from the start of treatment, including your child's school, so they may be prepared for any emergency situations.)
- Change only one medication and/or therapy at a time so that changes in your child's behavior can be linked to the medication or therapy that has been altered.
- Use as small a dosage of medication as possible and adjust the dosage depending on your child's needs.
- Treatment Response Charts allow you to follow your child's changes as well as to monitor for side effects (see Appendix 7).
- On a regular basis, reevaluate your child's response with your doctor.
- Make a decision on whether or not medication has made a difference in your child's life. If yes, then continue as long as required. If not, discontinue (often weaning your child off the medication under a doctor's supervision).

Identifying Symptoms to Target for Treatment

My goal is to always work in partnership with families to create the best possible scenario for their child's success. I always develop a plan B (and C if necessary). This partnership is based on an understanding of the most current scientific thought and uses a team approach. It has been proven to be extremely successful through many, many applications. Remember the goal of treatment is to balance the neurotransmitters. By doing so, your child's symptoms are often relieved, improving his ability to function, promoting social interaction and eventually improving his learning curve. However, small improvements are also acceptable as all influencing factors are sorted out.

Although symptoms vary widely from child to child with ASD, the most common symptom clusters I see in the children I treat include:

- Anxiety
- Compulsive-sameness-oriented—repetitive behavior
- Hyperactivity, impulsivity, distractibility (HID)
- Explosive aggression (including self-injurious behavior [SIB])
- Mood changes (including depression and/or manic symptoms)
- Stereotypic motor movements (including tics and Tourette syndrome)
- Motor-planning and motor-sequencing issues
- Delusions, hallucinations and bizarre behavior

Anxiety

Anxiety, worry, fears and irritability are symptoms that can be pervasive in the lives of children, adolescents and adults with ASD. Anxiety can be circumstantial or constant (free-floating anxiety). There is normal expected anxiety (before a test, when giving a presentation or performance, when attending a party or event), which often decreases as a child settles into the situation. There is also serious, debilitating anxiety (general anxiety disorder) driven by fears and worry of all kinds.

Anxiety is common and doctors treat forms of anxiety in patients on a regular basis. Individuals with ASD, due to their unexpected, disconnected sensory-motor processing and function, often perceive the world around them as frightening and painful. It stands to reason that they would live their days and nights with more heightened anxiety levels than those who are not affected with ASD. I have observed children with ASD in myriad situations and have come to believe that anxiety is a primary factor in their untoward behaviors and, therefore, must be evaluated and treated. While it is important to determine the underlying causes of their heightened anxiety, certain medications can reduce the anxiety and better enable interactions with people and situations. In some cases, such as for the extremely overreactive child, medication may be essential, although it must be administered with extreme caution so as not to produce mania (see the discussion of bipolar disorder on page 288).

If your child's behaviors increase in intensity, it may be that he is anxious. His expressive language delays can limit his ability to describe the physical feelings of anxiety that we are all aware of ("butterflies" in the stomach, headache, pounding heart). Instead, he may express these symptoms with increasing behaviors. In extreme cases his anxiety can lead to a tantrum or other outburst. Anxiety can cause your child to become confused, fearful or scared. Determining the underlying causes for his anxiety is essential, but the approach to treating anxiety must be multidisciplinary. (See Behavior as Communication, Chapter 11.) Your child's daily program should include an intense sensory diet (using appropriate sensory-motor exercises to fit his profile) to help calm and regulate him. Always use the techniques that worked best in the past. As he grows older, the same needs must be met, but the techniques will change. Possible strategies include using a hot tub, swimming, massages or body brushing. Swimming is one of the best techniques to get overall body pressure simultaneously (the water is not unlike Temple Grandin's "squeeze machine"). Daily exercise (that raises the heart rate and gets a sweat going to stimulate endorphins) also may be helpful. In addition, environmental changes or sensitivities must be addressed to help comfort your child. Finally, helping your child understand what is happening and what will help him feel better, conveyed in age-appropriate and developmentally matched language and with a calming tone, is a must.

TREATING ANXIETY

When we reflect on how painful it can be for us to experience anxiety, it becomes clear that reducing your child's anxiety levels carefully with medication can be lifesaving. In children with ASD the medications commonly used for relief of anxiety include first the SSRIs, antidepressants, benzodiazepines, followed by BuSpar. There are many options in the SSRI category. Lexapro (escitalopram oxalate) is often one of the better tolerated drugs. It is the most selective of the SSRIs because it is only the L-isomer of the compounds (Celexa is both left and right isomers) and appears to have the most benefit and least side effects of the SSRIs. I suggest starting with a very low dosage of an SSRI (often less than one-tenth of a usual starting dose). In discussing a low dose with your doctor, you can share the following reasons: One, I have seen very low doses be more effective, especially with SSRIs. Two, starting with too high a dose (in other words, the recommended dose in *Physicians' Desk Reference* [PDR]) may result only in side effects—in the case of SSRIs, increased stimulation, increased activity, sleep issues and agitation. Lower doses can be very effective in alleviating symptoms without triggering side effects.

ADMINISTERING SMALL DOSES OF MEDICATION

Because a small dose can't be mixed with a liquid in a drinking glass to deliver the proper amount of medication, it is better given via syringe.

- Use a 1-cc syringe without the needle attached ("TB syringe" in M.D. lingo) to pull up the exact amount.
- Squirt the medicine directly into your child's mouth—aim toward the back of the cheek so you don't activate the gag reflex.
- Follow with a liquid chaser (such as water or juice), thus insuring the whole dose is ingested.

If one SSRI causes an unacceptable side effect, remember to consider trying others. Each compound reacts with different serotonin receptors, resulting in differing benefits and side effects in each individual. Because serotonin receptors are genetically determined, I always ask if the child's parents have used any SSRIs and what they experienced. If a parent has had a positive response to an SSRI, I may start with that same medication for the child. It is possible that SSRIs may improve sensory processing, which in itself could be useful to decrease sensory-based anxiety triggers for a child with ASD.

OVERCOMING ANXIETY

Les is a fourteen-year-old with motor-planning challenges who was using a voice output computer in his middle school classes. He was also seeing a psychologist because of increasing anxiety and overreactivity. Les and I had been communicating for several months about coming to terms with his autism. He was having a very difficult time dealing with the fact that he had no control over his own body. He was more and more reluctant to become a part of the life that his parents, therapists and I knew he was probably capable of handling. While we were doing an evaluation to see if there was a new medical condition that might be driving his anxiety and stress, it became increasingly clear that we needed to consider what else could be done to decrease his anxiety-driven symptoms. His psychologist felt he was just a few steps away from typing independently, but instead of progressing, Les had become resistant, even aggressive. Since he had previous side effects with the SSRIs that had been tried over many years, we decided to address his anxiety by trying the medication BuSpar.

While he was on a very low dose of BuSpar, Les's typing skills began to improve. He no longer "froze" at the keyboard as his stress levels increased. Les described how calm he was feeling. His psychologist later told me that Les was typing more in their sessions than he had in the past six months. Finally, they were able to discuss the real emotional issue underlying Les's anxiety. At our next visit not only was Les calmer but his mother was as well—understandably so. The visit was incredibly fruitful, allowing us to talk about what Les was thinking and feeling and the kinds of issues that were making him unable to function at school. We were able to delve into his deepest concerns: how he appeared to his peers and whether he was overwhelmed by academics or by the teaching style of his teachers and aides. Although those issues weren't resolved at that meeting, getting them out in the open was a first step to determining an appropriate course of action. Les's last comment to me at that session was, "I feel calmer. I have hope. My mother feels calmer." I knew that we were on the right path.

Compulsive-Sameness-Oriented—Repetitive Behavior

This symptom complex is characterized by resistance to change, repetitive thoughts, perseverative talking (the uncontrolled repetition of a response, such as a word or phrase) and compulsive behaviors. Parents often request medication to treat these symptoms. These repetitive, "self-stim" behaviors include carrying objects in odd ways or using the objects, such as sticks, to tap surfaces repeatedly; hand flapping; making odd finger or eye movements; repeatedly lining up objects; and repeating verbal phrases. These stereotyped behaviors constitute one of the "core symptoms" of ASD. These behaviors can be distracting to your child and can become a barrier to his making progress— in learning or interacting with family, friends or classmates. Most children with ASD establish a pattern of repetitive "stims." Over time the pattern may change but their relative intensity stays within a range. Sometimes the intensity increases and gets in the way of learning and interacting with others. If this occurs with your child, you can use this symptom as a clue that something is amiss in his internal or external environment. When this happens with children in my practice, I initiate a comprehensive evaluation. Once all underlying reasons (medical, emotional, environmental) for increased behavior have been ruled out and an intense therapeutic daily regimen of interaction is well established, then the next step is to consider medication.

Repetition can take many forms: a child may repeat actions (repeated tapping), words (echolalia) and thoughts (saying "I want ice cream" over and over). Although the cause is not yet known for certain, there are two possible neurotransmitter-related explanations for a child getting "stuck" and engaging in repetitive behavior. If we assume that neurotransmitters are reduced in ASD, repetitive behaviors may be due to too little serotonin or too little of a neurotransmitter (possibly glutamate) required for modulating motor planning and sequencing. Too little serotonin has been implicated in the psychiatric diagnosis of OCD.

The notion that repetitive behaviors might be related to motor-planning/ sequencing difficulties is very interesting because repetitive behavior is common across the entire ASD spectrum. One can envision a child getting stuck not because he is behaving compulsively but because he is unable to sequence his next movement. Recent treatment trials with Namenda (a medication used in Alzheimer's to modulate glutamate) in adults with OCD indicate that it may relieve symptoms. Namenda modulates the neurotransmitter glutamate, which may, among many mechanisms, improve motor planning and thus help physically move the thought or action along.

When I have asked some patients in my practice what the repetitive behavior does for them, they have often responded, "What behavior are you talking about?" Jacob, who has severe motor-planning challenges but is quite skilled at typing his incredibly advanced thoughts, will repeat some phrases, like "Where's the moose?" or "Let's go home," while he avidly types away on a completely different subject! When I asked him specifically, "What about the moose?" he typed, "Oh, that's what you meant! I guess I didn't even realize that I was doing it, but when I do, it relaxes me so that I can sit and type with you for an hour!" He then went on to say, "And I notice you might be doing the same thing, too, Dr. Ricki, since you always wave your foot up and down while you write!" As I've said before, the kids I know are incredibly tuned in to others! The truth is we all have repetitive behaviors. We engage in them when we are bored, need to concentrate and/or have increased anxiety. Some people curl their hair with their fingers, tap their pencil up and down or jiggle a foot or leg. I am a doodler. I *always* doodle while on the telephone. Without realizing what I have done, I can look down and find an intricate pattern (often the same one) scribbled on an edge of a piece of paper or an envelope. I can't stop doodling (I've tried on many occasions). I suspect repetitive behaviors in ASD are magnifications of the behaviors we all have. Those with ASD may also perform such actions without being aware of them—except that their behaviors are more obvious or appear "odd" to the casual observer. Because we all have some repetitive behaviors, it is always a question as to whether these behaviors then should be completely medicated away for the child. When I asked Jacob if he wanted his behaviors taken away, he said no and I must agree—clearly we all require these outlets for self-relaxing when needed.

However, if repetitive behavior is a symptom of increasing anxiety that may be getting in the way of learning or interacting, then there is less of a debate about whether or not to treat the symptom. Because serotonin is the usual target neurotransmitter for decreasing anxiety or obsession, increasing the amount of serotonin available at the synapse gives the gentle "nudge" needed to pass the obsessive thought, idea and action down the neural pathway. It is not that the thought is eliminated; it still comes up, but it can now be dealt with, instead of becoming repetitive. Another benefit of increased serotonin may be improved sensory processing, which might also ease anxiety. Your child may then become much more regulated, more comfortable in his body on a moment-to-moment basis, less distracted by repetitive thoughts and much more capable of being involved in the world around him.

In contrast to previous studies that have shown SSRIs significantly improve repetitive behavior, a recent study of citalopram (Celexa) in children and adolescents with ASD found no evidence for significant improvement in these behaviors. The outcome measure for this more recent study was clinical evidence of significant change in repetitive behaviors. Studies prior to this one using SSRIs for repetitive behaviors in ASD often found that a child's irritability score improved with treatment. The irritability score is an indication of the physical distress that often occurs with anxiety and depression—especially with OCD-related disorders—which might be a factor in a child's increased repetitive behaviors. The different outcomes of these studies are a reminder of how complex medication management can be for each child. They underscore the necessity for thoughtful decision making, as well as utilizing a systematic approach for choosing the class of medication, dosage and treatment follow-up to get best outcomes.

TREATMENTS FOR REPETITIVE BEHAVIORS

SSRIs are the usual choice for managing compulsive and repetitive behaviors, which are often accompanied by anxiety. If the SSRIs are not satisfactory, next considerations include tricyclic antidepressants (like clomipramine) and/or atypical neuroleptics. These latter categories have a much higher risk of side effects associated with them and need careful monitoring. That said, when used appropriately, these medications can result in positive changes for your child. Medications that may alter glutamate levels are gaining interest in the treatment of repetitive thoughts and behaviors, specifically in OCD. Current treatment trials are ongoing for memantine (Namenda), N-acetylcysteine and riluzole, all of which, if successful, hold promise for this core issue in ASD.

RELIEF FOR REPETITIVE BEHAVIORS

Olivia, an eight-year-old with ASD, had major anxiety, often manifested by increased repetitive behaviors (pacing, repetitive phrases and tapping of objects). She was extremely sensitive to foods, many of which also seemed to increase her anxieties. We decided that she might feel much more comfortable and responsive to her therapies if she had the benefit of a medication to boost her brain serotonin levels. Her parents felt comfortable accepting the risk/benefits of an SSRI. However, even on extremely low doses she became extremely active on several of these medications. Each time a new SSRI compound was available in a liquid form, we tried it to see if she could tolerate the advanced formulation without a side effect. Each time the pattern repeated itself. Finally, when she was eleven years old, we were able to use the newest SSRI at that time (Lexapro), and the results were astounding.

Not only was she able to tolerate this medication without exhibiting any hyperactivity, she was calmer and more interested in her environment, and her pacing behavior markedly decreased. Her therapists, teachers and family were relieved and thrilled. Because these medications have different forms and compounds, each with their own effect and side effect profile, it may take some time and dialogue with your doctor to find the most effective medication for your child.

Hyperactivity, Impulsivity, Distractibility (HID)

HID are the symptoms usually associated with Attention Deficit Disorder and Attention Deficit Hyperactivity Disorder (ADD/ADHD). There is a great degree of overlap in symptoms between ASD and ADD/ADHD. The neurotransmitters involved in producing HID are dopamine and norepinephrine. With decreased levels of these neurotransmitters it is difficult to sustain attention and to control impulses, which leads to extreme distractibility—the child flits from one thing to another, unable to concentrate or focus on the task at hand.

Although these symptoms are often seen in newly diagnosed children with ASD, it isn't clear if they represent true attention disorders and/or serious processing difficulties. While it is important to determine if your child has a true attention or processing disorder, often as a child's ability to sustain an interaction improves, these issues move into the background. Over the years, however, I have noted an increase in the difficulty for children with ASD to sustain attention for long periods and in more complex situations (school or household chores). You may have had the experience of asking your child to go get something in his bedroom and return to you. Although he appears to understand your request, he is usually found some time later doing something completely different in another room entirely. Teachers and therapists consistently describe the difficulty they have keeping a child on task for any length of time, thus limiting his ability to learn consistently. The children themselves also know (as I've said over and over, they are smart kids) that they are not performing the tasks, because they can't remember what was asked of them. Being unable to do what is asked of him may cause an overreactive child to feel increased anxiety as well as increased hyperactivity and distractibility. This may result in a temper tantrum or explosive outburst. Under these circumstances the underreactive child may retreat back into his more self-absorbed world.

SCREENING FOR ATTENTION DISORDERS (ADD/ADHD)

When I know that I have a strong foundation of multidisciplinary therapies for a child and he shows behavior traits similar to the HID cluster, I pursue an evaluation for attention issues. This will include a survey of behaviors at school and at home. If he can use the computer reliably (as the majority of school-aged children with ASD can), then I will use a computer-based test to document his attention at baseline and again after a test dose of medication. The nonmedicated test will assess where he may be having attention issues. The test after medication helps me monitor improvement.

The Conners' Continuous Performance Test (CPT) and the Test of Variable Attention (T.O.V.A.) are two computer-based assessments. The CPT presents a simple visual task that requires sustained attention over a period of time to complete. The test is divided into sections, with the task presented at varying speeds to represent both boring and stimulating experiences, as might exist in a typical school day.

The T.O.V.A. measures attention to auditory and visual information (the CPT is only visual). Each half of the T.O.V.A. test is twenty-two minutes long and has four parts, each presenting the task at a range of speeds from slow to quick. The child's accuracy and response time are then compared to the children of the same sex and age (five to eighteen years old) who do not have attention issues. If a child scores below expected on the test, I will generally give him a one-time test dose of a stimulant such as Ritalin (which works in a short amount of time) and see if his scores improve. It is likely that medication will improve his abilities by helping increase his sustained attention. If the testing improves significantly following this test dose, parents may be more likely to consider ongoing treatment of these concerns for their child.

When I started testing patients with both sections of the T.O.V.A., I expected auditory attention to be more difficult to sustain than visual. I was so wrong! Time and time again the children had sustained auditory attention but were very distractible visually. I hypothesize that although the majority of children with ASD learn visually, they also are very distractible through this sense. It can be challenging to give such a child as much visual input as possible without overwhelming him. These visual distractions may constantly shift his attention from the task at hand.

TREATMENTS FOR HID

The medications of choice for treating your child if he has HID symptoms that interfere with his progress include those that will increase dopamine, norepinephrine or both. Recent double-blind, placebo-controlled studies of stimulants in children with ASD show significant improvement in attention with decreased hyperactivity and distractibility following treatment. Potential medications include stimulants, Strattera, alpha2-adrenergics and tricyclic antidepressants (if the previous medications fail).

I generally begin treatment for these symptoms with either a stimulant, Strattera (especially if anxiety accompanies the inattention) or alpha2-adrenergics. I recommend starting at a very low dose (often one-quarter to one-half of the usual starting dose in ADHD) and titrating up as needed. Although

I use Ritalin during the T.O.V.A. test, I often prescribe one of the longer-acting stimulants for a child's daily use. Given the complex sensory system of children with ASD, I prefer not challenging their systems with a medication that has a four- to six-hour length of action (like Ritalin). Ritalin must be given accurately to avoid the emotional highs and lows that might occur as blood levels of the medication change. Newer, long-acting Ritalin preparations (such as Concerta) can help avoid the ups and downs of shorter-acting Ritalin. My first choice for medicating attention issues often is a formulation that supports dopamine and norepinephrine (like Adderall), as both are most likely decreased in children with ASD. If a side effect occurs that is not eliminated by decreasing the dose, I move on to two other medications—one to boost dopamine (such as Focalin) and, if needed, one for norepinephrine (such as Strattera). Using medications in this fashion allows for accurate adjustments to get each neurotransmitter in the right balance.

One last caveat: If attention and/or distractibility are a significant issue for your child and you decide to use medication, it is highly recommended that it be given every day. There is a common belief that medications are only for "learning in school." In fact, much experience occurs outside of school, especially the opportunity for relating and communicating with family, peers and community. Maintaining his medication on a daily basis throughout the year can help him function at his best at all times.

POTENTIAL SIDE EFFECTS

One of the side effects I most often see in children with ASD being treated with stimulants is increased anxiety. This is not surprising, because the dopamine and serotonin systems are so interrelated and many children with ASD have compromised brain serotonin levels. Other common side effects include decreased appetite and difficulty with falling asleep. These are side effects that can be modulated or overcome. Your child may lose a few pounds before his weight stabilizes. One approach is to give your child a big breakfast before the medication takes effect, serve dinner later and give him a high-protein, high-fat snack at bedtime if his appetite returns at night.

While stimulant medication can interfere with sleep, trouble falling asleep is commonly seen in ASD. Melatonin, a brain hormone that induces sleep, is most likely decreased in ASD. If your child is having difficulty falling asleep, adding melatonin, an over-the-counter dietary supplement, can help. Start with a low dose and then increase it gradually as needed (see Sleep Disorders, Chapter 19).

Side effects that generally require changing to another medication or class of medications include tics, extreme anxiety, aggressiveness and loss of affect (facial expressions or body language). Remember to always return to baseline before attempting new classes of medication. It usually takes a very experienced clinician to design a simultaneous weaning off of one medication and gradual increase of another.

If tics are related to medication, they usually occur as you begin or increase the dosage. I generally reduce the stimulant to eliminate tics. If the tics do not go away at a lower dose and your child is struggling with an attention issue, I suggest considering Strattera or alpha2-adrenergics. In children who do not respond to stimulants or Strattera, TCAs (tricyclic antidepressants) or Risperdal may be considered to enhance attention and decrease impulsivity and distractibility.

Two concerns that frequently arise over stimulant use relate to growth and the possibility of addiction. While there is little risk of "stunting growth" using these medications, if, as in a very rare circumstance, a child's height-growth rate slows down, it will usually pick up to where expected after the medication is discontinued. There is much data on the ADD/ADHD stimulant-treated population that indicate that there is much less substance abuse in treated versus nontreated individuals. Children who have longer sustained attention and less impulsivity and distractibility can make wiser, more thoughtful decisions. Ironically, we often find that if children with ADD/ADHD are not treated, they will resort to self-medication with truly addicting substances—nicotine and street drugs—that also increase brain dopamine and norepinephrine. These substances can improve attention but, unfortunately, can lead to addictive behavior.

EFFECTIVELY MANAGING A SIDE EFFECT

When side effects of stimulant medications arise, a thoughtful evaluation and review by the patient, family and doctor is required. In my experience patients and families will make different choices at this juncture. Some, justifiably so, are leery of attempting further medication. Others are willing to go forward and try another class of medication to treat significant target symptoms.

Adam is a twelve-year-old with Asperger's who was progressing well in many areas, except that his teachers and parents noted his difficulty sustaining attention and controlling his impulsivity. As part of his evaluation a T.O.V.A. test was performed that revealed inattention, distractibility, prolonged response time and variability in responses, which are characteristic of an attention disorder. This evaluation was followed by another T.O.V.A. test, for which Adam received a test dose of the stimulant Ritalin. The results showed improvement in all areas. After much discussion with Adam and his parents the decision was made to begin stimulant therapy. He was started on Adderall and eventually began taking the long-acting form to improve his attention in the evening. His dosage was adjusted over the next several months. Reports from home and school were excellent and showed that he was sustaining attention for much longer periods during class time as well as interacting more fully with his peers. Much to the relief of his parents, homework time was no longer a struggle.

At first, the side effects of the stimulant were minimal. However, several months into the course of treatment his parents called and told me Adam had developed a serious facial tic that over the past week had increased in intensity and had extended from his face to his shoulder. When I evaluated Adam, it was clear that he had a persistent motor tic. My first concern was that the tic was a side effect of the medication rather than the onset of a new tic disorder. We decided to wean him from his medication. His tic resolved within a week of stopping the medication. However, his previous symptoms of inattention, distractibility and impulsivity returned. His medication was switched to Strattera, which proved to be helpful in managing his symptoms and did not result in the tic side effect.

Explosive Aggression, Including Self-Injurious Behavior (SIB)

Aggression (including SIB) is a serious symptom that is one of the most upsetting to children with ASD and their families. Determining the possible triggers for aggression takes much observation and compassion from the therapeutic team. Although there are many possible clinical interventions and approaches to help children with ASD who develop these symptoms, often these behaviors so upset the child and disrupt family life that medication is added to the child's multidisciplinary treatment plan. These behaviors in particular can be the result of many primary triggers, which could involve several neurotransmitter pathways, especially serotonin and dopamine.

Aggression (ballistic movements) can be the result of too much dopamine, which is known to affect impulse control. If your child experiences the slightest change in his environment, it can set off a series of reactions that are out of proportion to the triggering incident. If he becomes agitated, one more incident, such as another child closing a door loudly or someone yelling at him to control himself, may send him over the edge. He could even begin hitting others or himself repeatedly.

If your child has an overreactive sensory profile, he can have an aggressive outburst triggered by increased anxiety, which might come from a decreased understanding of environmental and emotional clues. At these times he may have little control of his behavior and the outbursts can be very confusing for him. His post-episode remorse is often enormous and the outburst may remain upsetting to him for some time. Soothing your child using techniques that you know work and not adding "fuel to the fire" by either shouting or disciplining him will help ease the tense situation.

Although self-injurious behavior is poorly understood, it may be a result of different triggers, including boredom or a need to stimulate or "fire up" the sensory pathway. It may also be part of a continuation of a "chronic pain" pattern (even the smallest stimulus initiates a response). In these cases either a deficiency of serotonin or glutamate or too much dopamine may be the underlying cause.

TREATMENTS FOR AGGRESSION

Once the primary cause has been identified and a full clinical treatment program for aggression/SIB implemented, medication treatment is considered if symptoms remain. When increased dopamine is suspected (as it is in the case of aggressive behavior), mood stabilizers, AEDs and/or atypical neuroleptics are possible choices. It should be noted that the neuroleptics, Risperdal and Abilify are now FDA labeled for treating aggression in ASD. Some of these medications may eventually be used in combination with an SSRI, especially if anxiety is a component of a child's aggression. Other choices include alpha2-adrenergics.

MANAGING AGGRESSION SUCCESSFULLY

Mason, a nine-year-old who is severely challenged with ASD, is nonverbal and overreactive. He had become more aggressive over time. His family was walking on eggshells around him and many of his therapists were apprehensive about working with him. He was getting stronger and the slightest provocation could result in his hitting, biting or scratching. The school district was threatening to move him to a more restrictive environment. His mother was at her wits' end following his most recent outburst, which precipitated her call to my office. Mason had become angry when they were in the car and had kicked out one of the windows. She ended her call by saying, "If something doesn't happen today, I am going to call social services. I fear what's going to happen to my family."

I gently asked if she could come to see me. In the time it took for Mason and his parents to make it to the office, I was able to reflect on how difficult it had been for this family to adjust to having a child with severely challenging ASD, particularly for Mason's mother. She did not believe in medication in general and had resisted discussing using medication to help her son. When they arrived at the office, Mason was unregulated and extremely angry. He began pulling all the toys off of the shelf, gathering them into piles, kicking them and at times hitting and kicking his mother. I dimmed the lights, turned off the music, put the phones on hold and asked everyone in the office to talk in whispers. We instituted a sensory rescue package, which worked to help diffuse the situation. Eventually Mom and Dad and I were able to sit down and discuss what was happening with Mason and develop an appropriate plan to help him. Although I hadn't seen Mason in a long time, it was clear that he was in crisis. It also seemed to me that he would clearly benefit from medications that would address his aggression. In this circumstance I suggested an atypical neuroleptic (such as Risperdal). The risks versus the benefits associated with medication had always been a concern for Mason's family, but after extensive discussion they agreed that the benefits far outweighed the risks and that they would try medication for two weeks.

Within one week of starting on medication, Mason's parents thought that approximately 70 percent of his tantrums and outbursts had stopped. If he had a tantrum, instead of it lasting thirty minutes, it lasted one to two minutes. Mason seemed to better understand the consequences of his actions and he was better able to tolerate frustration. His mother, with a huge smile on her face, told me that life was so much easier now that he was calmer, happier and more able to participate in his therapies and interact with his peers. No longer was social service placement even a consideration.

Once the crisis had passed, we focused on helping Mason better understand what was happening around him and communicate more effectively. Because he was a visual learner, we talked about using visual prompts, putting a plan in place for helping him through transitions and encouraging his parents (together with the team members) to implement appropriate DIR/Floortime interactions. None of this would have been possible unless the immediate situation of his volatility was first addressed. Within a couple of months the change was remarkable. Mason's relationship with his family had improved and they had renewed energy to continue his intensive interactive program.

Mood Changes (Including Depression and/or Manic Symptoms)

Mood can be described as how we "feel" about things. We have all experienced an upbeat or elated mood. Things are totally in balance—we feel good, have high energy, are full of hope and creativity and all things seem possible. On the other hand, we have all experienced a down mood—our energy is zapped, we feel negative, lethargic, and we want to retreat from the world, eat comfort food and sleep. For someone with a mood disorder those feelings of high and low are taken to their extremes—to mania (up) or depression (down)—and either state can be debilitating. Mood extremes require expert treatment that can often be difficult and prolonged. During one of these severe mood changes our brains can either experience an excess of neurotransmitters (excess dopamine in mania) or a severe depletion of neurotransmitters (reduced serotonin in depression).

Mood swings can also be due to bipolar disorder (BPD). However, bipolar disorder is very difficult to diagnose in children because their mood swings can be quite different from the pattern seen in adults with the disorder. Also, it is possible that because some children with ASD are more reactive in general, their highs might be a little higher and their lows a little lower than average. The relationship of mood issues to ASD is complex and not well studied. In my experience, and in that of some of my colleagues, mood concerns complicate the treatment of ASD and need to be addressed. By first handling the mood disorder, we can then have more success in managing the symptoms of ASD.

UNDERSTANDING MOOD DISORDERS

There could be many explanations for an association between mood issues and ASD. People with ASD have been shown to have lower serotonin levels, which could increase their susceptibility to depressed moods. Research has also shown an underconnectivity in neurons plus synaptic changes in ASD. Both of these changes could markedly increase or decrease the available neurotransmitters for effective functioning in various brain locations. In other words, the brain changes seen in ASD can influence mood. Mood issues may also be genetic. When I take a family history of a child with ASD, I sometimes discover a susceptibility to mood changes, including bipolar disorder. BPD tends to run in families and it is important to get a complete family medical history, especially when considering appropriate medication. If you have a family history of BPD, giving your child an SSRI (which increases serotonin) can produce manic-like behavior (although it can also happen to anyone who takes an SSRI).

BIPOLAR DISORDER AND ASD

Although a child with ASD may not fit all the criteria for adult bipolar disorder (BPD), he may fit what is known as the BPD profile. This profile doesn't typically manifest as prolonged periods of melancholy followed by prolonged periods of mania as seen in adult BPD. Rather children with BPD are more often described as exhibiting "rapid cycling," with multiple cycles of highs and lows occurring in one day. Parents may describe their child as suddenly laughing uncontrollably for a prolonged period, then engaging in a period of sustained crying, with tears and deep sobbing, only to revert back to the laughing and then again to the crying—many times during the day. This cycle can be continuous or intermittent, but in either case it interrupts learning, interaction and daily life. A child with ASD who has a BPD profile is best evaluated and managed by an expert, such as a child/adolescent psychiatrist. Medication choices in this situation include atypical neuroleptics, antiepileptic drugs (AEDs), mood stabilizers and lithium. Future study needs to document whether a subgroup of people with ASD have this BPD profile to help improve identification and treatment options.

It is important to note that mood disorders can be extremely debilitating for children with ASD. Their fragile social connections can be disrupted by mood changes, making it difficult for them to function throughout the day. If manic, a child with ASD can be extremely irritable, overly active and aggressive. He may have even more disrupted sleep-awake cycles and markedly escalated perseverative patterns that can't be interrupted using therapeutic techniques that worked previously. He experiences huge internal discomfort, even pain, not completely understanding why he feels the way he does.

Many of my older patients describe the racing thoughts that plague them day and night. "Dr. Ricki, stop the ideas," one teenager said. "I just can't get away from them." If your child is experiencing an elevated mood, it is most important to soothe him as best you can. The key is to stay calm yourself. Don't add "fuel to the fire" by yelling at him, abruptly directing him to do something else or becoming frustrated with his behavior. When your child has an elevated level of dopamine along with the motor-planning issues of ASD, he could reflexively strike out by hitting or kicking. While this may feel purely aggressive, it can be the result of an overloaded system coupled with the inability to regulate movement. I have seen these episodes go down the same path: the child has an elevated mood and is irritable, perseverative, overactive and nonresponsive; the parent, teacher or therapist yells and gets in the child's space with threatening gestures and anger; the child responds with wild movements and tantrums or by yelling; the adult institutes "behavioral action" as punishment; the child is confused and later remorseful for what happened but doesn't understand how or why it happened. When a child is so dysregulated, medication can help correct the underlying neurotransmitter imbalance, stabilizing his mood.

Understanding Depression

Depression may be chronic in nature or may be situational (such as a death in the family, divorce or moving). In ASD, because of difficulty with transitions, depression could be triggered by the loss of a familiar therapist, teacher or friend. I often find, especially as the children move into their teens and become more aware of their surroundings and how they relate to the world around them—particularly socially—that they can become quite sad. Their sadness is often mixed with anger. Some children despise their autism, often blaming it for everything wrong in their lives. Many become more self-absorbed. It is important to acknowledge your child's sadness and his anger and explain to him what is happening. Use direct age-appropriate language. Help him understand what he is experiencing. This is essential in order for him to move on and learn how to problem solve for himself.

Although people with ASD are less able to mobilize serotonin, a neurotransmitter that is needed to prevent depression, diagnosing depression in ASD can be difficult. The onset can be insidious, especially if your child has difficulty with expressive language and has trouble giving voice to his emotions, which make conveying the deep sadness he is feeling next to impossible.

Clues for diagnosing depressive episodes in your child with ASD include excessive crying, irritability, changes in sleeping (often excessive and throughout the day) and emotional retreat. Keeping a close watch on depressive behavior is important because these episodes may be a precursor to catatonia, a now known association in ASD (see Chapter 21). Treating depression requires calm assurance. Let your child know what you think is happening and that the team is there to help him. If your child is able to engage in role playing, you can use doll play or role playing in DIR/Floortime and therapeutic sessions to help him, and you, better understand what is going on. I have found that to successfully treat depression, any behavioral treatment should be accompanied with a medication that impacts serotonin. Medications indicated for treating depression include the SSRIs. If these medications cause unwanted side effects, the second choice group includes tricyclic antidepressants or mood stabilizers, such as atypical neuroleptics.

TREATING MOOD DISORDERS

Categories of medication that can help in these often dire situations include AEDs and/or mood stabilizers, such as atypical neuroleptics, lithium and antidepressants, such as SSRIs, SNRIs and TCAs.

The final "caveat" in mood disorder treatment is that one must be careful using SSRIs in children with ASD who have a BPD profile. In treating general depression, SSRIs can almost be a lifesaver. However, if SSRIs are given to a child with ASD and a BPD profile, they can stimulate a full manic episode that can be very difficult to treat. Therefore, if your doctor chooses to treat your child with an SSRI, the dosage must be adjusted slowly, while monitoring with careful follow-ups every few weeks. If a child gets overstimulated or agitated while taking an SSRI, the medication *must* be tapered off and stopped. When this happens, I usually introduce the use of a mood stabilizer (an AED or atypical neuroleptic). This decision about next steps requires careful consideration by you and your doctor.

MEDICATION AS PART OF A TREATMENT PLAN

Eighteen-year-old Donald was diagnosed by the age of three as being on the autism spectrum. His family implemented the DIR principles from the very beginning and he has a fabulous therapeutic team. His entire program was geared around his individual profile. He consistently showed improvement in all areas. However, at the age of sixteen, Donald became very irritable and dysregulated and demonstrated increasing aggression. He was no longer able to function at home or at school without having an outburst. After a thorough evaluation it was concluded that there was nothing different either in his environment or with his health to account for the changes. The decision was made to try a mood-stabilizing medication (Trileptal) together with an intense sensory diet and DIR/Floortime interactions. Mood stabilizers can often "take the edge off" at a time when one is having difficulty controlling one's impulses. Once Donald's ideal medication level was reached, everyone on his team was very encouraged. One team member remarked, "Donald is doing fabulously. He is so much better regulated, available and focused." After many months at an appropriate level of medication he was also described as "being invested in social discourse, working hard on his schoolwork and trying to do things for himself. His motor planning, organization, self-initiation skills are dramatically improved. It is so exciting."

Three months later Mom reported, "Things have been going so well—he is doing so well across so many domains." She said that his ability to stay in the flow and relate had gone up exponentially. I suspect that the addition of the medication improved Donald's brain chemistry to support learning and allowed his developmental abilities, which he had been working on, to flourish once again. This change allowed Donald and his team to experience great progress: from his making simple connections to working at creative emotional problem solving.

Stereotypic Motor Movements (Including Tics and Tourette Syndrome)

Tic disorders are diagnosed in one out of one hundred boys and, if chronic and associated with attention issues, are termed Tourette syndrome. Tics are spontaneous, uncontrolled movements that can be mild (an eyelid tremor), moderate (a facial/shoulder stutter) or severe (the face and shoulder make a large jerking motion with major arm movement). They can be physical and/or vocal. Given the unusual blend of brain neurotransmitters in ASD, it is not surprising that tics are seen in children with ASD. Studies have yet to explore the prevalence of tics in children with ASD compared to typically developing children. Tics are also known side effects of medication use, especially the stimulants.

TREATING TICS

Studies in Tourette syndrome provide clues to medication treatment for tics. Encouraging results for both reducing tics and improving attention come from the use of atypical neuroleptics, such as Risperdal. However, first line of treatment for tics includes the alpha2-adrenergics and Strattera (especially if treating ADHD and tics). Neuroleptics primarily modulate dopamine; the latter two modulate norepinephrine. Further study will clarify the best choices for tic management in ASD. Of course, if it is determined that the tic is related to another medication, weaning the patient off the offending drug must be considered.

Motor-Planning and Motor-Sequencing Issues

Motor-planning and motor-sequencing issues (coordination and the ability to follow a multiple-step process) affect most children with ASD. This category of symptoms appears directly related to brain underconnectivity. Motor-planning difficulties could actually be the core issue underlying problems children with ASD have with executive function performance (the ability to anticipate outcomes and adapt to changing situations), perseveration (the repetition of behaviors), expressive language (verbal skills) and attention and motor task ability. The last decade has seen an explosion in research in the field of Alzheimer's disease, which also has elements of motor-planning and sequencing difficulties. Targeting the neurotransmitters acetylcholine (AcChol) and glutamate with medications such as Namenda, Aricept and Exelon has proven successful in treating Alzheimer's. In addition, researchers studying Alzheimer's have also looked at brain tissue from the ASD brain bank (Autism Speaks Autism Tissue Program, www.autismspeaks.org/science/programs/atp). Abnormalities in receptors of AcChol were found in this brain tissue. This suggests that adjusting this neurotransmitter may improve symptoms not only for those with Alzheimer's but also for those with ASD. In fact, open-label trials of Aricept and Exelon (both modulate increased AcChol) and Namenda, which modulates glutamate, suggest improvement in ASD. This has also been my experience using these medications. When these medications are successful, the children display improved expressive language, motor planning, sequencing and memory. There has been recent interest in conducting multicenter clinical trials testing using Namenda in children with ASD. Many more medication trials are being conducted with patients with Alzheimer's disease—the results of these studies may be applicable to the ASD population, especially in the much-needed support of their motor-planning systems.

TREATING MOTOR-PLANNING ISSUES

For motor-planning and sequencing issues, Namenda has a very good risk/benefit ratio and is usually my first choice, followed by Aricept or Exelon. In general, I look for changes eight to twelve weeks after the maximum dose is reached but often can be seen earlier. The Alzheimer's treatment experience suggests that Namenda and Aricept may be synergistic (they work together to give an even better than expected outcome). Using both Namenda and Aricept together may be a consideration for your doctor, as well.

When these medications help support motor planning and sequencing, children with ASD are often able to express themselves better both verbally and nonverbally. When this happens, what they are thinking and feeling becomes more clear. Therefore, having more options for treatment for motor planning and sequencing might be crucial for some children.

NAMENDA IN ASD

Christian, who has ASD, was twelve years old when Namenda became available. He has major motor-planning issues. Toileting was a huge issue. Although he could respond to the urge to have a bowel movement, he sometimes would not make it to the bathroom or would get distracted before getting there. He never seemed to follow through with wiping, totally pulling up his pants, washing his hands and so on; that is, with the parts of the toileting process. His mother's comment was, "If I've taught him to toilet once, I've taught him a thousand times, and yet he still can't do it."

Christian's motor-planning issues were so significant that the decision was made to try Namenda. Eight weeks after he began the medication, I got an excited telephone call from his mom. "I just can't believe it, but Christian is not only going to the bathroom by himself and finishing the entire task, but the towel ends up on the towel rack, the water is turned off and he is even locking himself in for privacy!" Christian was also able to express himself somewhat more fluently, but it was his toileting ability that had his family excited. Although my experience with the medication was in its infancy, this encouraged me to think more broadly about Namenda's potential for children with ASD. Namenda (a modulator of the brain glutamate levels) had been used in Alzheimer's to help promote executive functioning and memory, but in Christian's case it was targeting motor memory—and it worked!

In another patient the medication did not have the same results. Jake also has motor-planning challenges, but neither he nor his parents noted any change in his motor sequencing or planning once he was taking the medication. On the other hand, Jake types fluently and is very insightful about how he feels on medications. His comment about his medication was that it was "one of the best he'd ever been on" and while on it he felt his thinking process was the most clear and logical it had ever been.

The experiences of these two boys is a reminder that because one child has responded to a medication in a certain way, it does not necessarily mean your child will have the same response. The corollary is also true: if one child has an untoward reaction toward a medication, it does not mean that your child will have that response.

Delusions, Hallucinations and Bizarre Behavior

Historically, ASD was occasionally described as "childhood schizophrenia." While those days are behind us, unfortunately, on a very rare occasion patients with ASD may slip into psychosis. During these periods the young adult or adult lives in an alternate reality created in his mind. Delusions, hallucinations (visual and/or auditory) and bizarre behavior may all occur. Diagnosing these patterns can be more difficult than usual if the person has expressive challenges. If I suspect psychotic behavior in a patient, I immediately get psychiatric help. This is an emergency situation that requires expert medical evaluation and treatment.

TREATMENTS FOR DELUSIONS, HALLUCINATIONS AND BIZARRE BEHAVIOR

Antipsychotic medications were designed for these situations. They must be used with the utmost care and constant monitoring.

IN AN ALTERNATE REALITY

The following example illustrates comorbidity—the presence of another disorder along with the primary disorder of ASD—and how treatment provided much relief for a young man and his family. Brent, who has ASD, was eighteen years old when he came to my office with his parents. I first spoke with his parents, who told me that their son had been doing extremely well and they had high hopes for him graduating high school. However, over the past year they had noticed deterioration across the board. He no longer seemed as available to interact throughout the day; he was aloof, spending hours in his room on his computer. He was unmotivated and no longer interested in school, homework or outside activities (all of which he had enthusiastically engaged in before). Everyone who knew him was very concerned. I had not seen Brent since he was a young boy and over the next couple of weeks I spent time talking with him individually to try to see if I could get a sense of what was going on. He was extremely high functioning and very articulate. However, it didn't take long to realize that he went off on tangents—talking at great length about what seemed to be his favorite TV shows or computer program websites. Because these shows and sites were unfamiliar to me, I asked his parents about them. They could not recall any shows with plots as he described them.

Eventually it dawned on me that he might be describing an alternative world. As he began to trust me, he finally admitted that he was hearing voices and actually visualizing images of a whole host of friends who he would visit in an alternative world throughout the day. Concerned that he might be on the brink of a psychotic episode, I referred him to a psychiatrist for a second opinion. Indeed, Brent was diagnosed with psychosis and treated. Within a year he had returned to school and, although not back to his previous level of functioning, was once again able to interact with his peers, teachers and his environment.

It is important to alert your doctor to any changes in your child's behaviors. Understanding what was happening to Brent was more difficult because of the nature of his ASD symptoms but eventually we were able to isolate the problem and treat him appropriately.

Tracking Your Child's Progress

Using a Treatment Response Chart (see Appendix 7), the team can monitor your child's progress. If the decision has been made to increase his serotonin in order to decrease his anxiety and perhaps his repetitive behaviors, an SSRI can be used. The ultimate goal is to increase his social interaction and attentiveness. Other potential effects of treatment include improved sensory processing, better eye contact, decreased anxiety, easier transitions and accelerating his learning curve. Possible side effects of the SSRIs include a change in sleep pattern, increased aggressiveness or a change in appetite. These effects and potential side effects in your child can be measured in school, at home and in therapy sessions. By assigning a level of severity to each of these issues, with zero being not present and five being the worst it's ever been, you can document his progress. Once you have established a baseline, you can measure each effect and side effect on a weekly basis along with his medication dosage levels so that the relationship between dosage and behavior can be tracked over time. In general, if there is more than one parent observing, I have each parent fill out a form and send it to me weekly. Because our hope is that improved serotonin levels will help accelerate your child's learning curve, he needs to be on the medication long enough to reach an optimum level. You may find the record keeping intimidating at first but it becomes relatively easy over time. The record then becomes a point of discussion at team meetings, and as mentioned previously, it is especially rewarding when your child can be a part of the discussion about how the medication is working for him.

Follow-up is a crucial part of the trial. Ultimately, a consensus can be reached as to whether the medication was a good choice to safely improve your child's well-being, relating, communication and eventual learning. If a major side effect outweighs the benefit of the medication that was used, then your child will be cautiously weaned off of this medication. The discussion about the next medication to try can begin once he is back to his baseline.

If Your Child Has Several Target Symptoms

Children with ASD often have many of the symptoms of these disorders as well as a variety of other medical symptoms. Clarifying all the concerns is essential but can only be done by understanding your child's individual profile. If you are having difficulty trying to identify all your child's needs, the following step-by-step approach may be helpful. I suggest the following:

1. Identify your child's target symptoms that impede his moving up the developmental ladder and learning.

2. Institute your DIR/Floortime intervention.

3. Look for all family and environmental changes that could be affecting your child.

4. Use a sensory rescue kit as needed.

5. Talk directly to your child (be certain your doctor does as well). Let him know you understand that something has changed for him and that you are going to search and find him help.

6. If any symptoms have increased in intensity, search for a medical cause.

7. If your child is otherwise healthy, determine whether he has a seizure disorder or SEDs (see Chapter 16)—especially if he has regression, poor receptive language, a sleep disorder and motor challenges. If he should have a seizure disorder or SEDs and has been treated appropriately, he may still have other target symptoms that need to be addressed (like anxiety or aggression). If your child does not have a seizure disorder or SEDs, move on to the next step.

8. Prioritize the target symptoms according to your child's needs.

9. Discuss with your doctor what neurotransmitter might be involved in producing a target symptom.

10. Consider medication treatment after a thorough discussion with your doctor.

11. Polytherapy may be needed for multiple symptoms as different medications address different neurotransmitters.

12. Feedback, communication and follow-up with your team and doctor are essential.

13. If your child is more able to relate, learn and communicate, you're on the right track! If not, reevaluate to find what could have been missed.

Coping with Using Medications for Your Child

In my experience even if you understand how medications can change brain biology, you may still have deep concerns about using them. It is important that you let your doctor know your thoughts and feelings on this issue. After talking to parents, I can help support their decisions. If there were any absolutes in the field of the treatment of ASD, it might be easier to make a decision about treating your child with medication. However, research has not yet caught up to clinical experience. I understand how difficult this decision may be. You need time and there are many routes of therapeutic possibilities to try before medications are added to the mix. All valid choices deserve consideration and should be included if needed in your child's multidisciplinary treatment plan. Occasionally medication becomes a first choice. By keeping open lines of communication, respecting each other's viewpoints and keeping in mind that the primary goal is always your child and family, the correct options can be brainstormed, prioritized and implemented.

Finding Expert Help

Throughout this chapter, expert medical advice has been emphasized. Whenever I speak to groups of parents about these issues, I am always asked, "How do I find expert help?" I understand how difficult it can be to find ASD expertise in some communities. As more individuals with ASD seek treatment, doctors will gain more experience. Pediatricians, both general and developmental, child and adolescent psychiatrists and child neurologists are among the experts who might have this type of expertise in your community. In addition, ATN sites across the country and in Canada list doctors who are trained in all aspects of care for individuals with ASD (see the Resources).

A Final Word on Medication

The examples I have presented here are of medications that I have found useful in treating patients in my practice. I have presented this material and the case examples to help you to understand that we are at a new dawn for treating neurobiological disorders. Medications can be extremely helpful for children with ASD when used properly and tailored to the child's individual needs. Having said that, your child's response may be different from any of those presented in this chapter, and the information found here should be considered a starting point for discussion and evaluation with your own doctor.

Long-Term Medical Complications

Medical disorders can have a huge impact on your child's quality of life. They compound the core features of ASD and seriously affect his ability to interact and gain the most from his therapies. A close partnership between you and your child's doctor is required to maintain the vigilance necessary to address medical issues as they arise. Your child may experience any of the previously discussed medical conditions: seizures, GI problems, allergies, sleep issues or mental or emotional problems. The following two conditions, PANDAS and catatonia, can occur in children and adolescents with ASD and cause increasing ASD symptoms, but are frequently overlooked.

Pediatric Autoimmune Neuropsychiatric Disorder (PANDAS)

Pediatric autoimmune neuropsychiatric disorder (PANDAS), associated with streptococcus and with group A beta-hemolytic streptococcal (GABHS) infection, is an immunological disorder that can occur following a strep infection. Strep is a very common upper respiratory infection, particularly affecting school-aged children in winter and spring. Symptoms can be mild to severe and include sore throat, fever, headache and stomachache. Children usually have symptoms when their tonsils and adenoids become infected. The illness is diagnosed by examining a child's throat and pharynx along with doing a throat culture (strep test) for GABHS. The sore throat generally gets better in about five days. While the throat culture is a common way to confirm a GABHS infection, it can also be diagnosed by blood tests that measure GABHS antibodies generated in response to an infection by the bacteria. The two blood tests that check for the antibodies are the antistreptolysin-O test (ASOT) and the antideoxyribonuclease B (anti–DNase B) test.

Unfortunately, in some people, their own GABHS antibodies may cause damage to their organs. In the kidneys this can lead to an inflammatory kidney condition known as glomerulonephritis, which can occur approximately ten days after the throat infection. In the heart, this can cause rheumatic fever, which can occur about eighteen days after the primary infection. In the brain, a syndrome known as Sydenham's chorea can result months after the initial strep infection. Sydenham's chorea is characterized by rapid, uncoordinated jerking movements of the hands, face and feet.

A post-GABHS immunological disorder is diagnosed through a clinical exam and laboratory tests that evaluate the level of GABHS antibodies in the blood. If your child is experiencing a prolonged immunological reaction, these antibody measures will stay extremely high. If your child has neuropsychiatric symptoms following a GABHS infection, he may have PANDAS. The neurological symptoms include a sudden onset of OCD and a tic disorder. The motor symptoms include choreiform movements (persistent, uncontrolled dancelike arm and hand movements) and clumsiness, as well as hyperactivity and tics. The abrupt onset of OCD symptoms in PANDAS differs from the usual course of childhood OCD, which progresses slowly, taking months to years before it is possible to make a definitive diagnosis. It is interesting to note that Sydenham's chorea is also characterized by a sudden onset of OCD about 70 percent of the time. PANDAS is diagnosed by taking a medical history and conducting a physical exam, as well as documenting evidence of a GABHS infection. This is done through a throat culture and measuring strep antibodies in the blood, which can be quite high and persist for months. Typically, as soon as appropriate antibiotics are administered, the OCD behaviors go away. If your child has PANDAS, he may experience remissions and relapses over a long period of time. OCD recurs in approximately 50 percent of patients. However, each episode appears to respond to appropriate antibiotics.

It is thought that PANDAS is a post-GABHS autoimmunity that occurs in a susceptible person. In this case, antibodies to GABHS may react with particular cells in the brain, resulting in the neuropsychiatric symptoms. In fact, there is brain scan data showing inflammation in the basal ganglia area of the brain that has been associated with anti–basal ganglia antibodies found in those with PANDAS.

Although the existence of PANDAS is controversial, a large prospective study in 2002 estimated that most pediatricians would find up to three cases of PANDAS annually if they searched for it. This study noted interesting manifestations of OCD in the children that suggest PANDAS. They included hand washing and a preoccupation with germs, as well as daytime urinary urgency and frequency without symptoms of infection, in over half of the affected children. The urinary symptoms were not present at night. Urine cultures were negative, so there was no underlying infection that might be causing a problem. In addition to the OCD, the patients exhibited emotional fluctuations, separation anxiety, oppositional behavior, age-inappropriate behavior and a new onset of ADHD. If this rate of PANDAS continues to be seen in future studies, PANDAS will prove far more common than other post-GABHS disease, including rheumatic fever and kidney disease.

ASD, GABHS and PANDAS

GABHS illness is often overlooked and undertreated in children with ASD. Because of their sensory issues, especially in the mouth, it is difficult to obtain an adequate throat culture. In fact, I find the reliability of throat culture results to be very poor in children with ASD. False negatives are very common. If this happens to your child, he may not get the treatment he needs. Diagnosing GABHS throat infections most often requires blood testing for GABHS antibodies (using ASOT/anti-DNase B).

It is not known if PANDAS might be more common in individuals with ASD representing an increased susceptibility. There is some suggestion that individuals with autism have a particular immune marker gene (D8/17), which is also hypothesized to be present in individuals who get PANDAS. PANDAS symptoms are very similar to the core features of ASD, so your doctor must have a high index of suspicion in order to diagnose PANDAS accurately. Knowing a baseline of symptoms in a child with ASD makes it easier to be alert to a sudden onset of severe OCD-like behavior, tics, aggression and hyperactivity. It is important that your child's doctor be aware of the existence of PANDAS and its possible relationship to ASD. Diagnosing and treating GABHS throat infections must be vigorously pursued. In my experience the blood test for GABHS antibodies production must be performed in order to diagnose GABHS infection and/or PANDAS.

Treatment for PANDAS can be prolonged. Preventative antibiotics, tonsillectomy and other immunotherapies, such as plasmapheresis (a blood purification procedure), can be considered. Occasionally, neuropharmacological treatment (drugs that work on the nervous system) is needed, especially to help with the intense OCD behaviors that may occur with this disorder.

Lasting Effects of Strep

Kevin, an eight-year-old with ASD, had a sore throat and suddenly began having serious vocal tics that were persistent and repetitive. His pediatrician diagnosed him with a strep infection. No blood work was performed. He was treated with antibiotics and his symptoms, including the tics, resolved. Five months later a follow-up blood test for GABHS antibody titer was performed that was negative. Three years later the vocal tics suddenly returned along with extreme aggression, to the point that Kevin was kicking holes in his bedroom wall. His parents called me, desperate for help, because due to Kevin's behavior, a social worker was pursuing placement in a group home.

After a throat culture proved negative, blood tests showed that Kevin's strep antibodies were markedly increased. His parents were relieved to know that his behavior had a medical basis. Once again, he was treated with antibiotics and the tics and aggression improved. Three months after this second infection his anti-DNase B was still markedly elevated and this lasted for several more months. He had two more similar episodes. Following a near continuous course of preventative antibiotics, Kevin had a tonsillectomy. If his blood tests for GABHS had not been performed, the underlying disease might never have been appropriately treated. Documenting Kevin's pattern of behavior, especially the abrupt onset of vocal tics and aggression, revealed the clues to follow in order to get him the treatment he needed.

Catatonia and ASD

Regression before the age of three is a known marker of ASD. Occasionally, however, regression also occurs in adolescents with ASD. One study cites neurological regression in 12 percent of adolescents with ASD.

If your adolescent has a regression, it is possible that it is due to catatonia. Catatonia is a psychiatric syndrome associated with many other diseases, including schizophrenia, mood disorders, drug withdrawal and liver failure. If your child has catatonia, he will move much more slowly, change his pattern of activities and no longer engage in self-care or practical skills, most of which are dependent on functional motor abilities. Symptoms include immobility; extreme negativity; complete lack of speech (mutism); and odd voluntary movements, often combined with echolalia and bursts of hyperactivity. Catatonia is seen in about 10 percent of acutely ill psychiatric patients and, fortunately, can respond to treatment. There is emerging evidence that catatonia-like features are present in one of seven (12 to 17 percent of) adolescents and adults with ASD. Unfortunately, it is rarely recognized and often not treated appropriately.

Lorna Wing and Amitta Shah published a study in 2000 following 506 adolescents with ASD. Thirty met the criteria for catatonia and another eight had some symptoms of catatonia. The majority of symptoms occurred between fifteen and nineteen years of age. Common features included slowness and difficulty in initiating movements unless prompted. A child with ASD who also has catatonia may be described as having obsessive slowing, an odd gait and odd stiff posture, a tendency to freeze during actions, difficulty crossing lines in the pavement or passing through doorways, incontinence, intermittent excited phases, an inability to complete actions, and a significant decrease in speech or complete mutism, as well as engaging in impulsive acts, bizarre behavior, sleeping during the day and staying awake at night. If you suspect that your child has symptoms of catatonia, a complete medical/neurological evaluation must be performed. Diseases associated with catatonia include infections as well as metabolic, endocrine, neurological and autoimmune disorders. It is also important to note that catatonia has been associated with medical and psychiatric medications (see Appendix 6) and can follow the rapid withdrawal of drugs such as benzodiazepines, gabapentin and dopaminergic medications (like Risperdal).

Symptoms of Catatonia

Symptoms of catatonia are graded as mild, moderate or severe depending on the degree to which your child's functional capabilities are affected. Treatment approaches have been identified for each level of symptoms. Reassessing your child or adolescent from a DIR perspective can provide information on changes in his profile that may be interfering with his interactions and learning. In many cases, response times become painfully slow, requiring changes in the pacing and timing of therapy. The effect of catatonia on the motor system can be profound and often motor prompting can be instrumental in helping your child feel confident about his next step. In the patients I have followed with catatonia, it has been striking to me that each still has the intent to perform an action. I can see this in their eyes as they engage in their slow but purposeful attempts to complete a task. They are profoundly impaired by their motor planning and sequencing, and I can only imagine their frustration and anxiety. Soothing, reassuring feedback for children facing this challenge is essential. Two possible treatments for catatonia are medication (lorazepam/benzodiazepine) and electroconvulsive therapy (ECT) for severely affected individuals.

Catatonia can be life-threatening and requires intensive medical attention. While little is known about the cause of catatonia, recent studies of neurotransmitters in the cerebrospinal fluid (CSF) of patients with catatonia and ASD have revealed very low levels of neurotransmitter precursors, including serotonin and dopamine. Treatment with folinic acid (a coenzyme crucial for the production of brain neurotransmitters) has been used with some success in a few cases.

The connection between catatonia and ASD raises more questions than there are answers. It is important to realize that catatonia is increasingly recognized in ASD and that it may, in fact, occur in the developmental course of autism. If your child or adolescent has a regression or marked obsessive slowing in his movements, these changes may represent the emergence of catatonia. Movement changes can also be relevant if your child has depression or OCD. It's possible that depression or OCD may be more common in the catatonia/ASD group than among others who get catatonia. Increased awareness of catatonia and the ASD connection is essential for effective evaluation and treatment. Research is required to further understand the underlying neurophysiology of catatonia and to define the prognosis. Because similar symptoms are seen in the very young child who regresses and often develops motor challenges and the catatonia-type regression in adolescence, research into this association could help delineate subtypes of ASD. Finally, treatment trials will help doctors best prescribe the proper approach for particular individuals with ASD and catatonia.

Catatonia in a Young Man

I've known Tyler, a handsome young man in his midteens with ASD, for many years. He has a very active, occasionally overresponsive profile. He has many repetitive behaviors, which have varied over time. When visiting my office, Tyler would explore every room, looking for any changes in decor—it became a form of hide-and-seek that he loved. Although he had auditory processing challenges and some anxiety, he was a joy to be around. His big smile reflected his deep affection for those around him. Video clips of Tyler at the age of twelve show him running easily and coordinating his arm and leg movements successfully—sometimes beating his siblings when racing. A video of his thirteenth birthday shows him easily blowing out the candles on his cake, coordinating the cake cutting and handing out pieces to everyone at the party. When he was thirteen and a half, Tyler was prescribed a low dose of Risperdal (.25 mg), which helped him to control some aggression. By fourteen he'd been slowly weaned off this dose. He was also on a low dose of Lexapro (2.5 mg) to control his anxiety and Namenda, which was helping his motor planning. At that time, while in my office, he typed an email to my daughter, whom he'd seen at summer camp. "It was nice to see you at camp. How is college? I go to middle school. I'm in the seventh grade. It's nice to be visiting your mom." It was clear that Tyler not only understood his place in the world but also understood the connections of my family and his relationship to us. In addition, he was able to engage in creative thinking and was making progress academically and socially.

Six months later, I received a distressed call from his parents. While on vacation with the family they realized how much Tyler's engagement had decreased and that all his repetitive behaviors, which had been such a part of Tyler, had disappeared. He was eating less and had lost weight. He attempted to type but could no longer follow through, frequently stopping or repetitively typing the same thing over and over. His parents noted that he couldn't complete physical tasks without a lot of motor prompting. Something as simple as walking into a room would stop him cold. It took him longer to respond to others, he moved with an odd gait and his head was tilted over his shoulder. I was extremely concerned that this change in Tyler might represent a regression. Videos of him at that time revealed that he had extreme difficulty in carrying out a sequence of events. He got stuck while trying to execute a physical task. Previously, he ascended the stairway in his home very quickly, several steps at a time. On the video it took him more than ten minutes to get up the stairs and he could do it only with constant support and encouragement from his parents. He froze at several points, but it was clear to me that he was bound and determined to make it to the top. I viewed another video of Tyler where no motor prompting occurred for more than ten minutes. He was moving from the kitchen to the dining room. It was painful for me to watch the video and see how difficult it was for him to move from one place to another. His head tilted over his shoulder; his arm and neck contorted between steps that froze for seconds at a time. Eventually, he made it to the dining room table, painstakingly lowered himself to the chair and picked up a pen to do his work. He knew what he wanted to do; his body did not respond.

Tyler's language wasn't as fluid as before and clearly his interaction had decreased. However, these changes did not represent a total regression but one affecting his motor system rather than his cognition. His intent remained. His receptive language was intact and he understood what he was being told. His motor system simply wasn't operating effectively. He was not having a pervasive regression.

Tyler had a full medical evaluation, including brain scans and a lumbar puncture, as well as an evaluation of the neurotransmitters in his spinal fluid. His neurotransmitters serotonin and dopamine were extremely decreased and he had a very low folic acid level. He was diagnosed with having moderate symptoms of catatonia. A trial of lorazepam was attempted. Forty-five minutes after the test dose, he was moving much more fluidly. Lorazepam was then prescribed, as well as folinic acid. Tyler gradually began moving with more ease but his movements appeared much more parkinsonian-like—tremors, slow movement, a halting gait. Eventually the decision was made to add a medication that helps in Parkinson's disease (Sinemet), which led to further improvement in his motor planning. Tyler is now back on track at school. Many of the repetitive behaviors seen in his original profile returned (much to his parents' delight). He is even back to riding his bike! I am in debt to Tyler and his family, especially his parents, Liz and Peter, who taught me so much about catatonia and ASD.

If your child has a sudden change in behavior with increasing stereotypic behaviors or an increase and abrupt onset of repetitive behavior, OCD and tics, hyperactivity or increased aggression, a thorough evaluation must be undertaken in order to rule out GABHS and/or PANDAS. Any significant decrease in motor activity should be cause for concern, as it may represent a regression or the onset of catatonia.

PART VI

Creating a Meaningful Life for Your Child

Fostering Independence

"WHAT'S IN his future?" Mary looked worried, reaching for her handkerchief while her six-year-old eagerly grabbed his favorite Thomas the Tank Engine toy from the shelf. "I worry about it all. School, friends, job. Will he get married? Will he live on his own? Will he be happy?" We all worry about these things for our children, but parents of children with ASD have to think about and focus on this issue much earlier and more intensely than others. Although these worries, and sometimes fears, are acute and very real, concentrate on what you can do to help your child be his best. Doing so can refocus your energy and help you to see the opportunities that do exist for him as well as the actions you can take to help him.

What hopes do you have for your child? Usually at the top of the list is that he has a meaningful life. We all want our children to be happy, to develop strong relationships and become productive members of society. We want them to be successful—yet success is defined differently for each child. Although his life may not turn out as you expected at the time of his birth, by using your creativity, you can help your child develop the skills he needs to realize his hopes and dreams.

Every child needs certain critical skills in order to forge a life of his own. Your goal is to help your child gradually experience increased responsibility, encouraging and supporting him along the way. This can be especially challenging when you have a child with special needs. It is understandable if you feel an overriding need to protect him. However, withholding responsibility sends him a subtle message that he can't do the tasks, undermining his ability or desire to try. Baby steps taken throughout his life will teach him the value of assuming responsibility as well as facing the consequences for his actions, making independence (even semi-independence) as an adult possible. Over time, these responsibilities will challenge your child's ideas, initiative, planning and follow-through, preparing him for problem-solving tasks in the real world. Adults with ASD have meaningful lives and this, too, should be expected for your child.

Another way you can prepare for your child's future is by helping him find his particular niche and environment—that place where he can succeed. This requires thinking broadly and thinking of life in the big picture. Help him to discover interests that might lead to a possible career. Provide him with educational opportunities. Foster age-appropriate interests and community experiences. Help him to forge friendships and work through emotional conflicts as he ages. In short help him cope with all the typical trials and tribulations of childhood and adolescence while also dealing with the challenges that accompany ASD. Your child may need extra time and support, as well as modifications, to attain these goals, but he can do it.

The Road to Independence: Raising the Bar of Expectation

In the past the expectations for individuals with ASD were not very high. Often this became a self-fulfilling prophecy, because these children were not expected to be able to accomplish their goals; therefore, they were given limited opportunities to expand their interactions and discover their passions. This attitude of low expectations extended to simple tasks, as well. Life skills, such as self-care or progressive responsibilities, were not considered something that they could accomplish. Caretakers often focused more on their vulnerabilities and acted accordingly by taking over tasks a typically developing child would be expected to do. This behavior (although well-intended) promoted reliance on the caretaker and diminished the child's initiative. After all, if the caretakers didn't expect much of the children, they didn't learn to expect it of themselves. Many years ago I added a component to my treatment protocol entitled "Raising the Bar." I knew that these children could accomplish much if they were given the opportunity and support. Obviously, pushing someone beyond their developmental limits is counterproductive, but I believe that most kids will shine when given a chance!

Raising the Bar at Young Ages

Begin to build self-esteem in your child at a very young age by helping him (typically developing or not) become confident in his abilities. Think of the pride a three-year-old has when he declares he wants to do something by himself—even if he can't quite complete the task or makes a mess while attempting it. If we respond to an incident (a child attempts to pour his own juice and he spills as much as gets into the cup) with anger and discipline, we lose an opportunity to support him in his efforts. If we encourage his effort by telling him what a great job he has done and ask him what he thinks we should do about the spill, we give him an opportunity to problem solve the next steps. By helping him get something to wipe up the spill and allowing him to complete the task, not only will he feel confident about his capabilities, thus increasing his self-esteem, but his problem-solving abilities will also have been supported. The next time something happens, he will think creatively about what to do rather than feeling overwhelmed or letting someone else take care of the problem.

Children with ASD rarely get an opportunity for these simple interactions. In fact, over the years, I have seen many six- to eight-year-old children who are not yet feeding themselves. A vicious circle develops between caretaker and child. If caretakers are always "doing" for the child, the child's confidence in his ability is undermined and then he won't attempt to do things for himself. If we hope children with ASD will become as independent as possible, then we need to approach many of the early self-help skills in the same way as in the example of the child spilling his juice. If a child feels that he might be able to complete a task, what incentive does he have if the adults in his environment are willing and able to do it for him? We would all love to have someone wait on us 24/7 and could easily fall into that pattern unless we were encouraged to start doing for ourselves. I often see what begins as a real need turn into habit, on both the part of the child and the adult.

Each time I see families in the office, I ask specifically about progress on self-help skills and encourage moving the children along by gradually increasing their responsibilities. Parents often ask, "When is my child ready to start doing things?" Attempt to do what's age appropriate in simple tasks, such as choosing clothing, learning to dress, feeding oneself, cleaning up and personal hygiene (brushing teeth, combing hair, taking a bath and so on). Use DIR/Floortime interactive techniques to motivate and encourage your child to complete more and more of each task. Even if he has extremely challenged motor-planning issues, you can facilitate him through sensory-motor input or hand-over-hand activity (guide his hand while brushing his teeth or hair, for example) so he can become part of the process. Breaking down tasks into steps and helping him make choices as to what tool will be used next can be vital in teaching him how to care for himself. Making bath time fun and interactive and having him choose which towel and which washcloth to use, which bath toys and what color soap, help him learn to do it himself. Eventually you can use leading questions to encourage him to become the one to initiate these tasks ("Who's going to get the bath toys today?" or "Who can find the soap first?"). Each time he is engaged in this process, learning occurs, and eventually he may be able to do the entire job on his own! Persistence pays off.

I am often consulted regarding an eight-, nine- or ten-year-old child with autism who is still throwing tantrums, resulting in his being catered to 110 percent by his family and treatment team. In large part this is because nobody has ever insisted that he accomplish even the simplest task. All children need clear limits and boundaries, chores and responsibilities and to know that they are accountable for their own behavior. These skills are critical to developing self-esteem and self-worth and can't be overlooked.

One telling example that illustrates the pattern that might unknowingly be created came to my attention when I saw Henry, an eight-year-old, relatively nonverbal child with ASD, who came in with his nanny when his parents were out of town. It was snack time, so the nanny got out a pudding and started feeding Henry, using a spoon. I was taken by surprise. I fully expected him to be eating on his own. I asked the nanny why she was feeding him, and she replied, "He's not able to feed himself and his parents insist that I feed him, because they do." I immediately looked him in the eye and said, "Wow, Henry. You are so smart. I'm confused. Why aren't you eating by yourself?" I knew he had enough fine motor control to complete the task. "In fact, I'm confident that you can do it, because all eight-year-olds feed themselves, so you can, too." I, of course, said this with a smile on my face and an ounce of challenge in my voice. He grabbed the pudding and the spoon from the nanny and promptly started feeding himself. At first surprised, she then murmured, "What else can he do?" We discussed all the things that Henry might have some control over and should. The next week I addressed this issue directly with his parents, who had returned from their trip to find Henry not only feeding himself but also helping to set the table and clearing his dishes from the table, as well. They realized that they needed to take a more active role in helping Henry move forward. It is easy to fall into patterns and it is probable that your child is developmentally ready for some tasks that you might currently routinely perform for him.

Chores

Having simple chores that get more complex over time is a precursor to learning responsibility, feeling pride in a task well done and maintaining a job while earning both praise and eventual financial gain. Too often your child with ASD may do little to help around the house, while his siblings have long "to do" lists. This imbalance in responsibility can set up conflict between them and subtly gives the message to his brothers and sisters that their sibling with special needs is incapable of doing small tasks or that he is getting preferential treatment. Your child may need some accommodation, so rather than giving him no chores, modify the specific task to his abilities. If he is around five or six years old, consider giving him chores throughout the day to help the family function. Pair him with you or an older sibling or nanny to work as a team. For example, when taking out the garbage, let your child empty the bathroom trash into a larger bag that you hold. Have him help you take the large bag to the trash can. Eventually he will be able to empty all the small household wastepaper baskets into the large bag by himself. When you are doing laundry, he can be responsible for getting his own clothes into a hamper or help sort and pair the family's socks.

Chores can become teaching opportunities. Separating the light and dark laundry or dividing up dry clothes into piles for each family member supports categorization abilities. Toys can be cleaned up in the same fashion. Setting the table is a wonderful chore for most children. If your child has motor-planning issues or difficulty with hand control, he can be responsible for one piece of flatware (putting down spoons at each place) or for passing out napkins. Whatever the task, no matter how small, you will be supporting your child's self-esteem and worth to the family. Allowing him to become an integral part of the family functioning is a vital part of moving along the road to independence. As he gets older and develops more skill-based abilities, tasks can become more complex.

Involve your child in the grocery shopping. Have him create his own shopping list. Initially, it may be very simple—a sheet of paper with a picture (for example, of his favorite cereal). At the grocery store, let him push his own small cart (most stores today have children's carts) and collect his item(s) on his list as you walk through the aisles. Eventually he might put his own item(s) up on the belt at the checkout. When he is ready to think about money, he could use his own to purchase the item(s), collect the receipt and get the change. Let him carry his own bag to the car and be responsible for putting away his item(s) once you get home. Your interactions with him are another way to implement DIR/Floortime throughout the day. A trip to the grocery store might require multiple sessions to prepare for and complete the shopping, especially as he becomes more involved in all the steps. He will have experienced the whole process of grocery shopping many times over long before he has to do it himself. Think of the accomplishment and what this will add to his self-confidence. There is no end to experiences you could devise in this way. Use your creativity to make each one accessible and feasible for your child. Let your ideas flow as you support him by continually "raising the bar" of expectation for him.

Allowance

There are differing philosophies about whether children should receive an allowance for doing chores. Some feel that helping out around the house is part of each family member's job and does not require compensation. Others feel that an allowance is an economic lesson that helps children to understand money as well as what happens later, when jobs pay a salary—sometimes a generous one for a task well done. For children with ASD, structuring chores with an allowance has many advantages. First, it is an academic math lesson. Learning about money teaches and reinforces its use. Money is often a difficult abstract concept to teach, but letting your child earn money for his chores, choose how he wants to spend it, count it out to pay, check his change and manage the receipt make the use of it very real. It takes time and practice to be able to accomplish this. Second, it reinforces responsibility. Third, you will most likely be treating him like his siblings.

INSTITUTING AN ALLOWANCE

Remember that this is an excellent opportunity to use your DIR/Floortime skills, guided by your child's abilities, to help him work out what he would like to be responsible for, how he will get and use his money and what he envisions purchasing.

- Decide with your child what his chores will be. Modify them so he can succeed.
- Create a "chore chart" using pictures and words of daily activities.
- Review the chore chart daily, having him check off each task as he completes it. Each night review what was done.
- Decide on what the allowance will be and how often he will get it.
  - Will he receive money—or stickers or tokens that he can redeem for money?
  - Consider daily pay, such as stickers or a grab bag. For example, if he receives stickers, at the end of the week, let him trade them in for a special toy, outing and so on. Eventually you can have longer periods between reimbursements. Work with him to figure out how much he can earn. One toy per week? One dollar per week?
- Help him to determine how his money will be spent.
  - Have him make a list (words, pictures) of favorite items he wants to save up for.
  - Help him figure out how many days or weeks it will take to earn the item.
- If your child is beginning to do pretend play, set up a "shop" at home. Use play money and let him practice buying and selling at the "store."
- Regularly change the chores he performs to prevent boredom and to teach new skills.

At Play

Tim, an eight-year-old, has been dirt biking with his father since he was two. This is his most anticipated weekend experience with his dad. I recently asked

Tim's dad how much Tim helps him get ready for the weekend—if he helps get the car loaded or is responsible for any of the equipment. "How can he do anything?" his dad responded incredulously. "There is a lot Tim could do," I told him. "His language is emerging. He is helping set the table at home, washing dishes and doing other chores. There is no reason he can't be given some tasks to prepare for going dirt biking." During the visit we worked out some simple chores for Tim, especially being in charge of the equipment used to clean the bikes. Dad decided that Tim could be responsible for keeping this kit clean at home, packing it for the trip, putting it in the car and retrieving it whenever it was needed. Through a series of practice sessions at home, Dad thought he could gradually teach Tim how to use the different tools and later incorporate their use into the weekend. At the follow-up visit, Dad shared his amazement at what Tim could do. "Thank you so much for encouraging me to involve Tim. He loves helping and is so proud of himself. The other bikers have now asked Tim to help them, as well." Suddenly an event where Tim was essentially tagging along became a total immersion experience for him. He was engaged and developing friendships as well as responsibility in a very meaningful way.

Setting Limits

The corollary to responsibility, of course, is putting limits in place. All children do better when they know what is expected of them. Boundaries or limits are set when children are young, often because of potentially dangerous situations such as touching the stove, running into traffic or falling into the swimming pool. As children grow, limits are set because of environmental situations that can create untoward and often dangerous behavior (driving, curfews, alcohol, drugs and so on). Children with ASD can thrive with structure and one of the challenges for parents who adopt a developmental approach such as DIR/Floortime is understanding that they must set age-appropriate and developmentally appropriate limits for their child's behavior. This might be confusing because the emphasis during DIR/Floortime sessions with your child is on discovering what interests him and following his lead, all of which is important for his developmental growth. However, rules and repetition often fit the profiles of children with ASD. Use this to your advantage to help be certain of your child's safety. We all live with structure in our lives. We count on the fact that we will all follow societal rules and regulations. Your child needs to learn not only the broader societal structure in order for him to fit in but also the limitations or boundaries that keep him safe and often will help him stay regulated within his world.

This delicate balance of supporting expectation within a structure is a parental role that requires extra vigilance when you have a child with special needs. Because your child may understand your tone, emotional affect and gestures better than your words, you must match what you say with how you look. Saying no softly with sparkly eyes and a smile may send him the wrong message. Be a stage actor. Convey your ideas with enough visual clarity that the message to your child is clear and consistent. Consistency is important. You, your spouse and caretakers should review the house rules, and once a rule is made—for example, no throwing toys at siblings—then the consequence of breaking it must be enforced by all. Use your DIR/Floortime techniques when he has broken a rule. First, get your child regulated (most children can't respond when they are upset) using the techniques that you know will work. Then engage him at his developmental level, using gestures and words to match the consequence to the behavior (have him put his toys away, spend some quiet time and apologize to his sibling as best he can). Again, you may have to help him or modify how he does this to match his abilities. The idea is that he connects his actions with the consequences and understands the process. Once you set up your "house rules," make a visual chart that fits your child's needs (pictures, words or both) as a reminder to the whole family of your expectations for behavior. Update it as rules change and consider reviewing it periodically in family meetings.

Raising the Bar for the Teenager

One of the hardest phases of a child's growth for all parents is adolescence. This is the time when hormones are influencing the teen's behavior, new connections are made within the brain under this hormonal influence and behaviors emerge that are new and different from those seen during childhood. One of the main goals of the teen years is to learn how to differentiate one's self from one's parents. This is a time when young adults begin pushing away while still being connected to their families. Conflicts are abundant. Think about your own teenage years and the changes you experienced. Healthy growth during this period most likely contributed to your sense of self and independence. While dealing with these issues of increasing independence and still depending on and needing their parents, teenagers also have to deal with their increasing sexuality, as well as fears of growing up. Teenagers with ASD must cope with these issues as well as come to terms with their specific concerns related to autism.

No matter how young your child may be now, eventually he will experience the typical brain and body effects of hormones that take place during puberty. He will experience similar emotional and sexual urges as typically developing teenagers. However, because he may be less experienced emotionally and socially than most teenagers, he may not be able to balance out his thoughts and feelings by discussing them with his peers. Positively interacting with peers, often sharing innermost secrets (that parents never hear about), or learning how to make plans and follow through on them without direct parental support doesn't happen easily for teenagers with ASD. By helping your child experience a full range of emotions (initially during DIR/Floortime and then expanded throughout the day) and by "raising the bar" for him during his childhood, you are setting the stage to allow him to deal with social and emotional issues regardless of his age and challenges. It is imperative that health care professionals lend their support and expertise to you during this time.

I spend many hours supporting parents as they prepare for their child's adolescent years. I have a number of teenage patients whom I've known since the ages of two or three who trust me and are willing to share. When I ask them what it is they want from their parents, the common response is, "I want to be treated like a teenager." Yet when they get angry, they may have a full-blown tantrum. This childish behavior opens the door to discuss, at their level, how they won't automatically be treated like a teenager unless they act like a teenager.

A teenager may be ready to move ahead and yet his parents are not. I understand that parents of a teen with special needs can be more reluctant for this to happen than parents of typical children. Our need to nurture and protect is very strong, and we need to be convinced that it's in our teen's best interest to let him move on. On the other hand, changes during puberty often accelerate addressing this need. It's common to think of a teenage boy as a "bull in a china shop." They are growing so quickly that they have to relearn their body map in order to become comfortable with this new, oversized self. This can be very difficult for a teenage boy with ASD, who already has proprioceptive, motor-planning and sequencing problems. He may have ballistic motions (movements that are not guided and controlled). Combine this with a bigger body and what would be a soft touch from a younger child becomes a push or a shove from an older one. This may be misinterpreted and may feel threatening to others. Added to these body changes are sexual urges that come as a natural consequence of the male hormone. Without an understanding of the context of how to act on these urges, it is not uncommon for a teenage boy with ASD to grab for a breast or cozy up to an unknown female in an inappropriate manner. Teenagers and their parents need to prepare for this inevitable stage of life. Getting ready for adolescence is a process like most stages in life, and fortunately, there is time to plan, adjust and deal with emotional feelings and responses. It is important to be prepared for the ride.

Stan is a fourteen-and-a-half-year-old with ASD who has severe motor-planning issues, including apraxia. He is barely able to approximate simple words. Overreactive, he often bolts from the room at the slightest change in the noise level around him. Even the sound of children and families entering the adjacent waiting room could set him off. A visual learner, he is also extremely visually distractible, flitting from toy to toy during our sessions. He uses two methods to express himself: typing and sign language. I've known Stan since he was three years old. I've always felt he was a smart boy who was locked in an uncooperative body. At his annual visit he now looked like a young adult. He had broad shoulders, long, muscular arms and legs, a stronger jaw and was much taller, having grown nine inches and gained thirty-six pounds in two years. When I commented on his masculine appearance, he was thrilled and gave me a wide but fleeting smile. He immediately picked up his computer to have a conversation with me using supported typing.

"It's great to see you. What do you like to do these days?" I said with a wide smile.

"I like to go with my aide to X Two," he typed, making reference to a video computer gaming place.

"What does it mean to go to X Two?" I asked.

"It makes me feel like a real teenager."

I, of course, was thrilled, because this allowed me to continue the conversation. "If you want to be treated like a teenager, then how should you act?"

I could see his anxiety rising and he appeared ready to bolt from the room but he was able to control himself momentarily. This was a difficult question for him, as I realized that it had never been asked before. Stan's mom also looked a bit frantic at hearing the question. Over the years, I have known Stan to avoid what he doesn't want to face. This day was no exception. He asked if he could go get a snack with his aide. His absence gave me an opportunity to speak alone with his parents to discuss the pressing concerns at home.

After I reviewed the hormonal and physical changes that occur in teenage boys, Mom mentioned that they were having a huge argument about Stan's behavior. This is a typical conflict that I see as kids become teens. Stan wanted to be treated like a teenager yet he was acting out and resorting to much more childlike behaviors, hitting his head against the wall at the slightest upset. Rather than working together to deal with Stan's behavior pattern and developing a plan that would be productive for him, his parents were in conflict. To problem solve this issue, it was important to first determine Stan's parents' individual perspectives on what was happening as well as the goal of their interaction with Stan. The method we used to resolve the conflict, outlined below, of identifying the problem from different points of view and then discussing possible solutions, may be applied to any problem you encounter with your child.

■ **Identify the problem:** When Stan was frustrated because he couldn't do what he wanted to do or was disappointed or anxious, he would go into his room and, using big motor activity, act out by hitting his head or hand against the wall. This behavior would usually last fifteen to twenty minutes and occur many times each day.

■ **Mom's perception:** Mom saw this as downtime for Stan to regulate when he was upset. She felt he ought to be able to go into his room and do this by whatever means possible. She accepted this might involve large repetitive motions because of his challenging sensory-motor issues. As long as he wasn't hurting himself, she thought it was okay, which was why she encouraged him to replace the head banging with feet stomping.

■ **Dad's perception:** Dad didn't feel the head banging was appropriate behavior and insisted that it should be stopped. The foot stomping further aggravated him. He felt Stan needed to learn how to deal with these issues in a more productive manner. He also felt they should be modeling in their home what was appropriate for public settings. Stomping and slamming were not acceptable away from home and no longer acceptable to him when at home. Dad agreed that Stan had sensory needs that required attention but he felt these behaviors would not work in the real world.

■ **Mutual agreement:** We all agreed that Stan should be encouraged to be the best he could be. Both parents agreed his behavior was unacceptable outside of the home. They also agreed that Stan needed to understand and accept responsibility for the consequences of his actions. Without learning better techniques to deal with frustration, he would have great difficulty being accepted by others and developing independence.

■ **Open discussion:** As we discussed both parents' feelings about these issues, Mom realized that she might be enabling Stan's behaviors. She was very concerned about his needs but didn't know what else to do. I asked Dad to share with her what it was like to be a teenage boy. A very rich discussion ensued. It was heartwarming to see Mom understand that she was going to have to change her expectations in order to help Stan. She opened up even more as Dad became more supportive.

■ **Brainstorming ideas and possible solutions:** Finally we talked about ways to support Stan.

▶ Dad would talk with Stan about his own teenage years, emphasizing both his physical changes and emotional feelings. So often teens with ASD feel isolated because they aren't having these kinds of conversations with their family and friends. They feel they're the only one going through this. Stan needed information as well as reassurance that what he was experiencing in puberty was the same for all young men. He needed to know the expectations of manhood, including what is and is not appropriate behavior. Dad could emphasize his own respect for women, including his wife, and how that respect is shown. This is not a one-time talk but part of an ongoing conversation that includes information about sexuality. These conversations will help strengthen the father-son bond and will be important as Stan moves through these uncharted waters.

► Mom has to expect age-appropriate behavior from Stan. I encouraged her to develop a mind-set of what to expect from him. If she kept her eye on the goal of independence, she would realize that this should happen now rather than be postponed. To accomplish this, she needed to do individual emotional work to prepare for letting go of her son.

► The next and very important task was to work with Stan to come up with socially acceptable ways for him to help himself when he's feeling anxious or frustrated. All teenage boys let off steam by running, throwing balls or exercising in a wide range of ways. Stan loved showers and swimming. I encouraged his parents to help Stan realize that instead of banging around the room, he could hop into the shower—a very acceptable means of controlling and regulating himself at home. In addition, for those times when he's frustrated or disappointed and doesn't have a shower available, he needs to learn how to deal with his feelings, always emphasizing that if he wants to be treated like a teenager, he needs to act like one. We also discussed that Stan needed to learn how to express his feelings. Mom said he was unable to do this in the heat of the moment, so I suggested, because he's quickly learning sign language, that perhaps they could teach Stan to sign his emotions. He could signal if he's angry, frustrated, disappointed or if he really needs some sensory help. They could then respond in a supportive way, helping him to regulate. By tying his emotional response to how he calmed himself, he could learn techniques to use as needed on his own. Eventually, using assistive communication, he could consider working with a psychologist to help him deal with his underlying conflicts through traditional interactive therapy.

► The last step was a discussion with Stan. His parents felt they were now prepared to do this on their own once they got home. Clearly none of this would work without his "buy in." Both parents discussed thoughtfully and respectfully how they would bring Stan into the conversation and help problem solve what he could do for himself. I was pleased they were ready to address this with him in the comfort of their own home, where Stan would be more relaxed and have the best chance of becoming an integral member of this discussion. He, too, might have more creative ideas as to things that will help him outside of a clinical setting. A phone call from Mom the following week confirmed that Stan had stepped up to the plate. The shower solution was working. The stomping and head banging had nearly stopped. Most important, Mom and Dad were now prepared to help Stan become even more independent, as they would any teenager.

These are just a few examples of how you might "raise the bar" of expectation for your child. Each time he completes a task, he is developing yet again another neural network that will advance his learning and creative problem solving even further, thus bypassing his severe motor challenges. Feeling like part of the family, especially a necessary and important part of a family, because of what he does to help around the house will be the basis for his independence and future success.

Sexuality in Autism

You might find yourself cringing ever so slightly as you think about your child as a sexual being. This happens to most parents, so you are in good company. Issues related to hygiene, masturbation and appropriate behavior may come up sooner than expected. In addition, sexuality is part of the road to independence, because nowhere do we express our own individuality more than when we understand ourselves as capable of having physical and emotional bonds with others outside of our family. Sexual expression is private and takes place away from the eyes of the family—again, a measure of independence.

There is a wide time frame when your child may go through puberty. In the United States, puberty begins for girls between ages eight and a half and thirteen years. For boys, it begins between nine and fourteen years of age. To the best of our knowledge, children with ASD also follow these patterns, and they are often on the same schedule as their parents. However, early puberty (precocious puberty) does occur more frequently in children with neurologic disorders, so alert your doctor if you notice any signs of body changes in your child earlier than expected. Puberty comes whether you're ready for it or not. Once your child begins to produce hormones, he will experience the same body changes, feelings and behaviors any boy does while morphing into an adult male. You will need to help him be prepared for and deal with these changes. If your child is near or experiencing puberty, you may have many concerns. Parents often worry about teaching about proper hygiene, menstruation and masturbation, as well as about issues they fear, such as inappropriate public displays, pregnancy, sexually transmitted diseases (STDs) and, most important, potential sexual abuse.

To prepare yourself to discuss these concerns with your child, you must also deal with your own feelings about these topics and overcome any hesitancy in talking about them with your children. By understanding that physical, sexual maturity is unrelated to emotional thinking and needs to be addressed, many parents overcome their comfort barrier for this type of discussion. Many seek help from professionals, like a doctor, psychologist, social worker or clergy member. Your doctor can help in a variety of ways. Remember, he is trained and experienced in talking with children and families about changes that happen during puberty. If you have a long-standing relationship, your child may be more comfortable in his office. Rely on this bond of trust to help navigate these waters. Ask about his experience in talking with other families about these issues.

Your child's doctor will approach the discussion without judging or imposing his personal views. Let him know your family values and convictions, including boundaries that are important to you. This will help him frame any discussion with your child. Be certain to discuss your expectations for your child in areas ranging from personal modesty to teen and adult sexuality. Review with him any behaviors that concern you in the context of what is typical for children. For example, masturbation is normal during the toddler period. If an elder child happens to be at the toddler level developmentally, he might engage in self-stimulatory behavior frequently no matter what his chronologic age. If he is older, the issue really becomes not so much the behavior, but what should be done in a public versus private setting.

Your doctor can be a valuable resource for helping educate your child about sexuality, including about pregnancy, sexually transmitted diseases (STDs) and emotional responses to puberty and relationships. In addition, he will also be able to assist in teaching self-care and hygiene. He, of course, will also be concerned about your child's well-being and will continuously monitor changes through puberty that might affect your child's health.

Your doctor can provide information to your daughter regarding menstruation and breast exams. Girls need support through their initial periods, although I've been pleased to see how easily those in my practice have adjusted. Pelvic exams are not necessary before girls are sexually active, but I suggest you have her meet your ob-gyn to begin to familiarize her with the office and the personnel. When a pelvic exam is needed, she will feel safer if you and a familiar doctor are with her. If she experiences irregular periods or mood swings, your doctor will also help evaluate any hormonal imbalances that may be causing them. Sometimes medication is considered to stabilize these hormonal swings. When the decision is made to use treatment, many girls in my practice thrive and are much calmer.

Depending on your family history and values, there may come a time when you want to discuss whether your daughter should use oral contraceptives. Your doctor will review this decision with you and your daughter and, of course, will provide follow-up as necessary. As with any doctor visit, preparation and reassurance that she will be safe are paramount.

Your doctor can help your son understand about erections, ejaculations, wet dreams and masturbation. In addition, he will look for worrisome testicular changes while teaching self-examination. It is important to convey that masturbation is a normal bodily function but cannot be performed in public places. Emphasize when and where his private time will be. Be certain that all family members understand these rules for the sake of each other's privacy. Visual cues may be helpful to indicate when private time is okay. Some describe putting out a favorite toy to indicate it is okay to have private time. When the toy isn't out, private time is not okay.

Topics to Review with Your Child

Educating your child about sexuality begins before puberty and occurs in stages. As your child matures, he will need help understanding the changes occurring in his body. Being informed in the following areas will add to your comfort and prepare you for teaching your child about these matters.

■ Hygiene and grooming begin before puberty as your child learns to care for himself. As you teach him, remember the best ways for him to learn. For example, if he learns best by watching yet has motor-planning challenges, first show him what to do step-by-step (such as wetting the washcloth, washing the genital area and drying off). Initially, you may have to help him, hand over hand, gradually letting him try on his own. Visual pictures or line drawings may also help. Start early and let him learn these steps day by day, week by week, as long as he needs. Eventually he may complete the task as best he can and you can help out where he has difficulty.

■ What is private versus public? Teaching self-care includes not only hygiene and grooming but also how to go into a stall in a public restroom with as much independence as possible. This is especially important when your older child is with you in a public place and is of the opposite sex. Teaching him how to bathe, shower or dress on his own also helps emphasize matters that are private.

■ Sex education includes learning about the human body (what are the parts and what are they used for?). Explanations need to be geared to his developmental level. Be straightforward. Use simple language, gestures and pictures to help describe what you're talking about. You may want to use specialized sex education teaching tools (see the Resources). As your child/young adult matures sexually, this education should include such topics as sexual relationships, intercourse, pregnancy, birth and STDs.

■ The sexual behaviors of their children are often of great concern to parents. Teaching respect for the opposite sex; when to touch and kiss; what is okay and what isn't; and the what and where and how of intercourse, pregnancy and birth all must be covered in due time.

■ Safety. Your child's safety is paramount. Teaching boundaries of sexual behavior is critical. Your child needs to know what he can and can't do. He also needs to know exactly what others can and can't do to him. If someone touches him inappropriately, he needs to know what to do and who to go to for help.

Considerations as You Teach Your Child

You know your child best and can be the best communicator of factual information as well as your family values and expectations. As always, with ASD the message must be made clear and obvious to your child.

■ Make it appropriate to his developmental level and individual differences.

■ Be clear that your child understands what you are teaching. A girl who is menstruating may not even realize what blood is. If she understands where blood comes from, she may think she's going to die. A boy who has a wet dream may think he has urinated in his bed.

■ Use educational teaching tools as needed (such as pictures, written steps, consistent patterns, even rules). Use visual supports to illustrate points. For example, if you are teaching the difference between private and public spaces using pictures of buses, bathrooms, bedrooms, living rooms and the grocery store, you could ask your child which is public and which is private. This can then, of course, be reinforced as he moves from place to place throughout his day.

■ As you talk with your child, speak in an even tone and be careful of your facial expressions and gestures. Reluctance or discomfort on your part will impact on the message.

■ Make it interactive. Use your DIR/Floortime skills to keep your child emotionally connected to the discussion. Learning will go faster, motivation will increase and the memory will last longer.

■ Social stories can often be useful in teaching about sexual behaviors that are okay and those that are not.

■ Expert-facilitated social groups can be helpful. In these groups teens with similar developmental issues discuss facts about puberty changes while emphasizing relationships.

■ Demystify individual issues for your teen that may derail his relationships. If he has sensory dysregulation stimulated by touch, smell, taste, this could interfere with his interactions on a moment-to-moment basis. In addition, your teen may have to directly deal with his frustrations with another. This is especially true when cues are missed between individuals who have similar issues. There can also be cause for concern if your child becomes obsessed with another person, which can be interpreted as stalking, as he might find himself in a troublesome situation. These types of concerns need to be handled as directly as possible, giving the teen solutions on a case-by-case basis.

■ Direct instruction is often required in sex education. Demonstrating how to use a menstrual pad, a tampon or a condom may be necessary.

■ Teach tension-relieving activities. All teenagers require tension-relieving activities of which masturbation is one. Emphasizing the privacy of this activity, you will need to teach tension-relieving techniques for when your child is in public—especially at school, church, the mall or with friends. Relaxation exercises such as deep breathing and systematic muscle tension and relaxation as well as aerobic exercise are all effective techniques.

■ Role playing challenges is especially useful to practice what you are teaching. If, for example, you are emphasizing the concept of touch, who one can and can't touch and where, these distinctions can be drawn through role play (for example, one may hug a family member, but a handshake is appropriate when greeting a stranger).

■ Talk about relationships. As your DIR/Floortime interactions all day long advance with your child, you will want to include information about safety with strangers as well as in relationships. Of course, there are many basic concerns about your child's safety. He must learn that others are not allowed to touch him as well as whom he can and can't touch. If someone touches him inappropriately, he also needs to know what to do and whom to tell. As he matures, counseling will go deeper into what a sexual relationship involves, especially feelings, intimacy and navigating adult life. The responsibilities of parenting and the differences between sexual relationships and emotional intimacy can be emphasized. For example, talking to, caring for someone and thinking about someone comes before sex—and that's okay. Eventually discuss the characteristics of a social partner that he might enjoy. A relationship may happen for your child through mutual interests with another as much as through physical attraction.

Parents are really the best teachers for their children regarding matters of sex and family values. You may be wondering how you can talk about sexuality with your teen, especially if he is challenged in many areas. I review these issues with parents on an ongoing basis. I find that encouragement goes a long way. Dealing with his sexual urges in the context of his understanding will help prepare him for adulthood.

Letting Go but Providing a Soft Landing

All parents go through the process of letting go. Children must be allowed to follow their own path. By leaving the confines of home, they can become even more independent and self-reliant. In today's world this is very difficult for most parents regardless of their child's developmental abilities. The notorious "helicopter parent" who hovers over his child well past when the child can and should be independent is very common. For understandable reasons parents of children with ASD also tend to hover, but they, too, can learn to let go.

As was emphasized in the discussion about "raising the bar," letting go really begins with simple tasks, such as your child becoming responsible for eating, choosing clothes and chores (age and ability dependent), and builds toward eventual independent decision making (problem solving), such as taking the dog for a walk or going into the doctor's office exam room without a parent. As your child takes on increasing responsibilities, you will learn to trust him. Presuming competence not only gives him a boost but it reinforces your belief that he can accomplish the task at hand. If you allow him to make mistakes (as long as it's not dangerous) and give him the leeway to figure out how to solve a problem, you will be giving him the message that you believe in his abilities.

Even a simple task can produce these results. When discussing these steps with seventeen-year-old Tony's mother, she could not believe her son could accomplish a relatively simple task on his own. With encouragement she decided to try. The time seemed right when he needed a birthday card for his brother. Ordinarily Mom would have purchased the card for him and given it to him at home. This time she took Tony to the store. He went in by himself, picked out a card and purchased it without assistance. He returned to the car with a wide grin. When I asked her how it felt, she admitted to being extremely anxious while he was in the store and relieved when she saw his smiling face. We could hardly hold back the tears as she told me the story. Clearly he could accomplish similar tasks. He needed only an opportunity. The next week Mom called to say that Tony had just returned from his doctor visit. For the first time, he requested to see the doctor by himself. He did great and later told his mother that he was always going to see the doctor by himself. Mom was so proud and wanted to tell the world.

Part of letting go means that you and your child also need to let go of using autism as an excuse. While it is easy to let the blame for any problems fall squarely on ASD, resist the urge. No matter what our frailties part of the process of growing up is learning how to deal with them in a positive manner. This may require a mind-set change for you that can then allow you to support your child. Help him understand what he does well and how he can conquer or compensate for his challenges. Do not talk in the third person around your child if this demeans or degrades his ability. (Sentiments like "Johnny can't do this. He's not able to because of his autism" will undermine his confidence if he hears and understands what you are talking about.) If Johnny has difficulty maneuvering a pen, words such as "Johnny can't write with a pen, because of his autism" can be changed in order to reassure to "You have great ideas. I see it's hard for you to use a pen. That's okay. Let's try a different way. Can you show me what you want? Can you tell me? Can you use the keyboard? I can't wait to learn about your great idea!" If he gets negative reinforcement about what he can and can't do, he, too, may adopt his autism as a ready excuse for not taking on things that are more challenging.

"It's my autism" is a frequent response I get from children and especially adolescents with ASD when they act out (such as throwing a tantrum in a ninth-grade inclusive classroom) or don't rise to a difficult task that they can most likely accomplish. Don't let them off the hook. Using autism as a crutch or an excuse tends to reinforce behavior, which can often hinder progress as well as get in the way of his connecting with his peers. Discuss this with your child so that he can see he must take responsibility for his own actions. Acknowledge the autism and that it's a drag. Help him accept who he is and accountability for his behavior. As I've mentioned, when I talk to these kids in an age-appropriate way, much to the surprise of therapists and family, I get an appropriate response. Many of the children who are more verbal or use supported communication take this as an opportunity to talk about how hard it is and how they struggle. Acknowledging you understand the despair of his challenges allows for a deeper discussion. Acceptance is a long road for all of us but it does not mean defeat, especially if emphasis is given to his strengths and the possibilities for the future. It also helps if he knows that you and his team will be there for him to support and nurture him as much as he needs you. I spend a great deal of time with teenagers discussing these issues. It is not easy by any means for them to accomplish this. However, in my experience when parents begin working with their children early to build confidence and acceptance by promoting responsibility and independence, much of the groundwork has been laid to do this hard work.

As your child grows up, expect him to become more self-reliant and move toward increasing independence. Attitude goes a long way and your attitude will definitely be reflected in your child. Remember, you need support while going through the process of "letting go." Friends, family and even professionals can be helpful.

Education

T HE EDUCATIONAL component of your child's program is, of course, one of the most important and yet it is sometimes one of the most difficult gaps to fill. The ideal program would fulfill the expected standard (as determined by your particular state) for children with ASD and at the same time meet your child's individual needs. Start with your child's individual needs and match the educational program to them.

Emotionally connected learning is the most effective way to come to know a subject. Can you remember taking a test in a course that didn't interest you? After taking the final test, you might have said to yourself, *I'm glad I don't have to take another test for that class. I really don't remember much about the subject.* Unless you really cared about the topic, what you memorized to take the test was not important to you and was not retained. On the other hand, if you were asked to take an additional test in your favorite subject, you could probably take it at any time because you connected deeply with the material. Fostering emotional connection with learning material must be emphasized for children with ASD. Under these circumstances, known as emotional or affect-based learning, your child will have a greater chance to retain and build on the information. Model schools using relationship-based educational programs are now in many large communities and include SmartStart in Los Angeles, California; Oak Hill School in Marin County, California; The Lionheart School in Alpharetta, Georgia; The Community School in Decatur, Georgia; Celebrate the Children in Wharton, New Jersey; and the Rebecca School in New York, New York, to name a few. Many schools, especially preschools and early elementary schools, have developmental programs as their foundation for learning and these might be found in your community.

If the ideal school setting is not available for your child, work with what is available (depending on financing) in your community by filling in missing program pieces after school. Given today's educational constraints, most parents are much more involved in their children's education than a generation ago. First, you assess the educational programs in which your child may fit and learn academically, but also emphasize his opportunity to have meaning-ful interactions and form relationships throughout the school day. Then, by finding creative solutions that fill any gaps that the school is unable to fill, you can devise a "wraparound" plan to meet all the needs of your child.

A wraparound program is comprised of home-based, community-based and clinic-based elements that take place outside of the school setting but are designed to complement it. The specific goals of a wraparound program must regularly be revisited (in my practice we do it on a quarterly basis) because the components of the program should be changing as your child grows and as the curriculum changes.

It is important that all the components of the educational program be clear to you. You need to know what your child is expected to learn and how suc-cess will be measured. By being familiar with the school program, you can balance what you must provide for your child. If, for example, he is in a fairly comprehensive academic program with little social downtime, then his after-school program must emphasize social interaction and connection. On the other hand, if he is in a program that emphasizes social activities, academics may need to be the primary component in his wraparound program.

THE INDIVIDUALS WITH DISABILITIES EDUCATION ACT (IDEA)

The Individuals with Disabilities Education Act (IDEA) aims to ensure that all chil-dren receive a free appropriate public education and special services to assist in meeting their educational needs.

- http://idea.ed.gov—contains information on IDEA, which is a law ensuring access to educational services for children with disabilities.
- www.ed.gov—the primary site for the United States Department of Educa-tion; contains information on policies, data, research and issues pertaining to education in the United States of America.

Your Child's Individualized Education Plan (IEP)

Following an assessment, each child with special needs is given an Individual-ized Education Plan (IEP), which outlines the educational goals tailored to his specific abilities and needs. Although recommendations about elemen-tary school educational objectives, approaches and expectations for children with ASD are generally clearly defined for parents by school administrators and teachers, there are predictable challenges making success more difficult. Difficulty with the IEP plan may arise if you feel your child has not been properly evaluated or if you disagree with the means suggested to support his challenges. I often find that parents are concerned about whether or not their child has been correctly assessed.

Clearly your child's assessment needs to be a true reflection of his abilities to maximize his learning in the school environment. Providing your child's teachers with the best possible picture of how he functions in different situations, perhaps even showing videos of his successful DIR/Floortime interactions, may help them understand how well he can do when his needs are supported. It can also be a wonderful illustration of how to effectively support him. Do your best to prepare your child for the assessment. Many of us are anxious in a new situation, especially when we are being tested. Telling your child about the room he'll be in, the person doing the evaluation and whether or not you or another team member will be present will ease the transition. Getting answers to these questions and perhaps visiting the testing area in advance require that you establish good communication with the school district and teachers. The work you do prior to your child being tested can be the beginning of the partnership that you will form with his teaching team. Most teachers want to do their best to support your child and will be grateful for all the information they can get. In the same way that you detailed your child's profile for a doctor visit (see Chapter 13), be certain that your child's profile has been fully outlined for the educational team.

Another obstacle that could derail your child's educational progress is the lack of a good "fit" between your child and his educational staff (teachers, aides, specialty therapists). We have all had the experience of not connecting with another person through no fault of ours or theirs. If things aren't working, it could simply mean that your child's style and that of the staff member are too different from one another. This is not a reflection of the quality of their work as a teacher or as a therapist. To maximize the school environment for your child, keep in mind that the closer the teaching staff matches his profile, the more conducive his learning environment will be. If he is a visual learner with major auditory processing issues, as is often the case, but his aide uses overwhelming language rather than gestures to explain ideas, this may be confusing for him. It is always important to first understand his individual profile, what his functional capabilities really are and under what situations he learns best, and make sure these are addressed during the IEP process. This approach leads to getting the best "fit" possible for him and his teaching staff.

IEP content and implementation may vary by state and school district. Often solutions are suggested that may not be totally appropriate on an individual level. An example of this is a recent trend to no longer provide individualized speech therapy but to give group sessions in a classroom before a child is able to socially understand what is happening. Some schools have occcupational therapists (OTs) for sensory integration, while others do not. This further emphasizes the degree to which parents must involve themselves in their child's educational setting and program.

Another issue that generally needs review in the elementary age group is what happens during nonacademic times, such as recess, snack time or lunchtime. These periods are often when teachers have scheduled breaks and supervision for all the children can be at a minimum. It is crucial to find out how your child is to be monitored, supported and, most important of all, encouraged and facilitated in interactions with peers. How recess and other less supervised times will be handled should be clarified and then documented in the IEP. If there are no clear directives for adult supervision at these times, it could be a missed opportunity for social connection with peers and may expose your child to bullying and potential harm. All too often a visit to a school at times like these will find children with ASD sitting alone or pacing the periphery of the school yard or playground in repetitive patterns. This is not acceptable and the bar must be held high for the adult staff to accommodate your child during these times.

Such was the case for Eli, a seven-year-old first grader attending a developmental elementary school. Staffing schedules changed and Eli's aide took a break during recess, making it difficult to have someone available for him. During these times Eli appeared more anxious than usual and returned to some of his older patterns of behavior, pacing the edge of the school yard and whispering softly to himself. Fortunately, the school team noted this change. A team meeting further clarified that even before the schedule change Eli seemed more anxious throughout the school day. His mother thought this was true at home, as well. Many of his old behaviors, such as pacing and self-absorption, had gradually returned over the last few months and were noted in the outside therapy sessions, as well. Most important, Eli had disconnected from his emerging interactions with a few classmates. A thorough review of potential health-related issues that might be the cause of his behavior change revealed no medical reasons for it. A review of his educational program, however, showed that his academic challenge was increasing and demands on Eli were greater than ever. We concluded that he could benefit from educational support at home that focused on his homework. His teachers agreed to give his mom advance notice of what was to be covered in class so that she could review it with him before and after the lesson. In addition, his aide was scheduled for an earlier lunch, when others could provide support to Eli, so that she would be available for the recess time. We also increased his dose of an SSRI to help with his situational anxiety. Gradually over the next two weeks Eli regained his interest in school and was able to engage with friends. A month later his behaviors were completely gone. As you can see, a team approach is also required to solve problems at school. Each member's input is needed to develop a successful plan. Often multiple solutions will be necessary to resolve an issue.

Options for Elementary School

There are several potential educational options for your child that might be appropriate for him, including public school, private school or homeschooling. Schools may be further characterized by their educational philosophy, ranging from classic, highly structured academic programs to more free-flowing developmentally based programs to programs based on underlying themes (for example, a Great Books curriculum). Many parents choose the more academic programs. These programs often require increased social support to be certain your child truly understands the academics and is not becoming frustrated. Frustration can occur if your child is a visual learner and his program depends too much on auditory input with loose visual support. This can happen as your child grows older and the material studied becomes more complex and reading based.

Public schools, private schools and homeschooling are available for children with ASD at all levels, including preschool, elementary, middle and high school, and college. However, not all options may be found in every community. Keep in mind that the proper educational setting for your child may change depending on his age, developmental growth and particular needs. I have known children who began in public school and then went to private school for middle and high school and vice versa. Make the best effort to match your child's needs with the school environment at every stage of development.

Public School

Different classroom configurations need to be assessed to determine the most appropriate environment for your child. Settings include autism-specific classes that could provide all the services that he needs in one place (academic, OT, speech, social skills) or they may be program specific (for example, the Lindamood-Bell day school program). In some public school districts, special day classes may be held for children with ASD only, or they may have children with differing developmental needs and diagnoses in one class. Inclusion programs can follow a range of configurations—partial inclusion (only one or two classes per day with the mainstream school population) or complete inclusion (in mainstream classes and possibly receiving additional services). The ratios of included children to typically developing children can vary by school district. Another innovative approach is called reverse mainstreaming, where a few typical children attend a classroom of children with developmental disorders.

Private School

Mainstream private schools can be challenging. It is important to determine if the school will allow your child to have an aide in the classroom or permit his therapists to observe in the classroom in order to inform teachers on the best teaching practices for your child (what works and doesn't work in engaging him and moving him into higher-functioning levels).

As mentioned previously, when matching a school to your child's needs, it is important to understand the educational philosophy of the school. This is especially important in selecting a private school. Although there are not always clear distinctions, there are private schools that have a strong academic focus, as opposed to those that are more developmental in nature (such as Montessori or Waldorf-type schools). Developmental schools focus on providing social and emotional support to children. Often these programs emphasize creativity, providing nonverbal outlets for children with ASD, including art and drama. Developmental schools by their nature understand children's learning patterns. All children from preschool until the end of third grade are on different developmental trajectories, gaining skills at different times, and often seeming more unalike than alike in their skills and behaviors. Generally by the end of third grade, children start having more similar abilities. When curriculum goals and objectives are created, children in these types of programs are expected to have continued developmental growth, yet each is allowed to grow in each area at his own speed.

Developmental schools are more conducive to relationship-based approaches, yet they may be hard to find in your community. In addition, there are potential downsides in that these teachers are generally not trained in special education or knowledgeable about ASD and need extra help to understand the needs of a particular child. Often private schools shy away from children with special needs. If the child-to-adult ratio is not appropriate and there is insufficient structure, your child may not get all the support and attention he may need.

PAYING FOR YOUR CHILD'S EDUCATION

Cost is a major factor in determining school placement. Of course, all children are eligible to attend public school. If you feel the public school classroom is not appropriate for your child, then you might pursue private school education. Under certain circumstances the private school you select may have a nonpublic school (NPS) designation, which means that tuition could be provided by your school district. Getting this to happen is not a simple process. Private school funding often depends on the private school having been designated as a nonpublic school. With this designation, private schools generally have contracts for funding from the public school district. Funding also varies state by state, as do requirements and state educational board rules governing qualification for NPS funding. In California it must be shown that a student cannot be taught adequately in a public school setting. It may take several years before it is obvious that a child is not gaining from the public school environment. Unfortunately, parents often have to resort to using advocates and lawyers at an educational fair hearing review presided over by a judge in order to get NPS funding for their child's education. Information on a special education attorney can be found at www.wrightslaw.com.

Homeschooling

Many parents choose to homeschool their special needs child in order to individualize their child's education, allow him to learn in a supportive environment and allow for the greatest amount of flexibility in his program. You can homeschool your child on your own or band together with other parents to homeschool your children together. Regulations on homeschooling vary by state. See www.hslda.org/about/ for further information.

Finding the Right School with the Right Fit

When determining the best school setting for your child, you might want to consider the following:

■ Cast a wide net and look at all the possible schools in your area that you are willing to consider. Take into consideration the travel time from your home and determine if that time will allow you to provide for the needs of your whole family.

■ Know your child's individual profile of strengths and challenges. Think about this when visiting schools. How will your child feel here and how will he fit into the environment? Is the curriculum taught using approaches that are appropriate for him? Will the extracurricular activities be adequately modified for him?

■ Visit potential classrooms if possible. Will the classroom environment work for him? If there are potential barriers to his success, can they be modified? (For example, if there are environmental noises, can your child use earplugs?)

■ While in the classroom, what is your "gut" reaction? Is it warm, inviting, safe and secure? Are there enough adults providing supervision? What are some of the ambient environmental issues that could become sensory problems? Most important, what are the children doing? Are they interacting or are they isolated? What are the adults doing? Are they facilitating the children's play together?

■ Observe children outside the classroom. Does the peer group seem appropriate for your child? What is happening on the playground during lunch? How many adults are out with the children? What kinds of activities are being planned? Are the children having fun and are they interacting with each other? What do you see happening if a child has a meltdown? How would it be handled by the staff?

■ What is the school's policy on observers? Are there two-way windows so that you can unobtrusively observe your own child? Are therapists who know your child allowed to come into the classroom, observe and perhaps give suggestions?

■ Are teachers or administrators excited about enrolling your child? Would you feel welcome? One parent recounted her meeting with the director of a school who told her that the school would accept her son if... She braced herself to hear about anything from a probationary period to some unreachable requirement and was delighted when the director continued, "You promise to keep him here until he graduates so we can watch him grow and develop along with you."

■ What is the school's policy regarding classroom aides? Are they assigned to the class or to individual students? What is their role for the class and for the individual child? Is there one aide or a variety of aides who will work with your child each day? In my experience, children do best when one aide is assigned to them, rather than having to transition to different people throughout the day. Does the school or your team choose the aide? Can you select and provide an aide? If so, will the district pay? Will you be able to communicate directly with your child's aide? How are the aides going to be trained?

■ How are classes arranged? Are they structured year by year or blended, such as a second/third grade mix? Sometimes blended classrooms allow your child more academic and social choices that will better meet his individual needs.

■ How are teachers assigned? Do they change every year, or is there a teaching team over two or more years? The latter can be beneficial if the team is a good fit for your child. Having the same teaching team eliminates the time lost at the beginning of the school year that is usually needed for your child to transition into a new classroom and the teacher to adjust to his learning style.

■ How is communication handled between you and the staff? Are teachers and staff willing to share the curriculum beyond the IEP goals?

■ Can a therapist on your team do a school observation? Appropriate educational programs may be aided by the expertise of multiple team professionals who have backgrounds in educational methods and curriculum choices for children with ASD. In addition, they also may have experience with particular schools in the community, and thus know the schools' administrators and teachers and children with ASD who have thrived (or not) in these settings. Parents may also know particular schools from experiences with older children or knowledge gained from friends and so on. Above all, use common sense while making school decisions. If a setting doesn't feel right for your child, it probably isn't. If it feels good to you as a parent, look deeper to see what the school has to offer your child.

■ If the school is an approved nonpublic school, are you ready for potential funding problems? Are you prepared to self-pay if the school is not an approved nonpublic school, or if your school district won't pay for your choice even if it is an approved school?

■ Once you decide on a particular school for your child, you, along with his team, should develop a transition plan for him. Is your school of choice willing to help?

Additional Considerations Concerning Schools

Within any school setting, there are multiple approaches to accommodating a special needs child. It is important that you investigate the school's particular approach about the following issues. Again, this is all done with an eye toward best matching your child's needs to a program.

Full Inclusion

Theoretically, full inclusion is an attractive option for children with ASD. However, it is imperative that you understand how full inclusion is implemented in a school before choosing this option for your child. If he is fully included in a classroom, staffing must be available to provide the teachers (many of whom do not have special education backgrounds) the necessary training and curriculum modifications that will make full inclusion the most appropriate situation for him. In my experience full-inclusion specialists are few and far between. They often have a huge load within a school district and this may impact the support your child receives in order for him to function and learn. There is more of an impact when one-to-one aides are decreased to a ratio of one to two or one to three, or if the aide is not receiving adequate support. On the other hand, if support systems are intact, full inclusion may be the correct setting, providing him the support, encouragement and interaction with the other students that will greatly enhance his social development.

Many schools provide a combined program with autism-specific and inclusion portions scheduled in the day. This can often be an excellent choice, allowing your child to learn across all settings while also giving him social involvement with peers. If you feel your child is benefiting from inclusion in a particular classroom (often children with ASD do much better in math and science than reading), then he should attend that class. If, on the other hand, you find that he is not grasping the educational material in a class, even with modifications, his time might be better spent in a resource class or autism-specific class where he can receive individual attention and support in the subject. Eventually he may be able to join the inclusion program in this particular subject. In this way you can get the best of both worlds for him.

Aides in Your Child's Classroom

Whether or not your child has an aide in the classroom can be a major discussion between you and the school district personnel. Determining whether or not an aide is necessary is clearly something that should be done on a case-by-case basis, not on a one-size-fits-all basis or by school regulations. There is a tendency to develop autism-specific classes in public school settings in which it is decided that individual aides for the children will not be necessary, because of the increased ratio of experienced teachers. While it may be true that there is additional support, certainly the door should not be closed to discussion if your child needs consistent support throughout the day. In truth, every moment of every day should be filled with as much interaction as possible over long periods of time. An effective aide who knows a particular child can be a vital part of his complete program. This person not only supports your child in the classroom but is also an integral part of the communication system keeping you, your child and teachers linked. His aide will know what's working in the classroom and what isn't. The aide needs to be able to get input from the child's parents and the home team members to help solve any recurrent issues in the classroom. The aide should be able to keep all of you apprised of the school curriculum needs.

Because the aide will be more attuned to your child and his sensory-motor needs, the aide will be better equipped to read him and catch a potential meltdown before it happens. This will allow him to return to the valuable interactive learning sessions as soon as possible—maximizing his school day and avoiding potential embarrassment. Ideally the aide will have the opportunity to work with team members, such as DIR/Floortime specialists and OT and speech therapists, and see other professionals in action with your child. By seeing him in different environments, the aide may gain a deep understanding of how to facilitate interactions, especially with peers in the school setting. An aide may be able to identify potential playdates with classmates and be able to provide excellent feedback during adjustments or changes in medication. An aide's feedback can be valuable to help determine how your child is functioning under specified conditions. Most public schools choose an aide for the child and, unfortunately, limit the communication between aides and family members. Be sure that it is written into your IEP that communication is permitted between you and your child's aide. Additionally, consider asking for a reimbursement of payment for a certain number of hours of a professional supervisor's time for initial and ongoing training for the aide relative to your child's needs.

Curriculum

School programs vary from state to state and can also vary district to district. Contact your local Board of Education to find out specifics in your state, town or district. A school curriculum for your child is developed from his educational objectives through the IEP process. Once this curriculum is agreed upon, you can match his home program to the school-based program. If his class is learning about daily calendars, then it can be helpful to have a similar calendar set up at home. You can support what is happening at school in a fun and interactive manner. For example, each day you might work with him to find the date on the calendar and place a sticker on it to mark the day. The tasks you can take him through could include choosing the sticker; figuring out who will peel off the backing, who will determine where it goes and who will put it on the calendar; and finally, actually placing it on the calendar. You can also emulate certain aspects of your child's school day at home—such as circle time or rug time—so that he will become familiar and comfortable with that structure.

His school curriculum offers opportunities for semi-structured DIR/Floortime at home. If your child is learning about categorizing food at school by sorting pictures of fruits, vegetables and so on, a DIR/Floortime activity based on this aspect of the curriculum could be added to his at-home activities. Plastic fruit, vegetables or other food items could be hidden around the room. He could then be asked to find the items and sort them by category in baskets or on areas of the rug. Not only will you be working on academic subjects, but this activity will stimulate his visual-spatial capacities while also providing a fun way to connect with him. This game could be played by many members of the family. By incorporating his school curriculum into many creative home-based activities, you will have a better understanding of whether or not your child is grasping the intended material.

Peer Groups

It goes without saying that more than academics happens in school. Whether in public or private school, most children experience a full social life at school. Your child needs the same opportunity. Theoretically a full-inclusion class-room is designed to support a child's interaction with peers. By the same token, he should be integrated into extracurricular activities, such as art, music, drama or sports, with modifications as needed. Find out how the school personnel implement these critical elements in your child's daily plan. Many children with ASD tell me that they feel isolated in these settings because they don't share any interests with the typical children. These children often find friend-ships with fellow students in an ASD-specific class or school. Some prefer to be with typical children, with peer counselors or aides to facilitate interactions. Think about your child's social life as an integral component of his day. If the emphasis during the day is more academic with less social interaction, then round out his experiences with community-based opportunities (see below).

Education Beyond Elementary School

Beyond elementary school, educational options can become more confusing. Middle school, high school and beyond often require developing curriculum by thinking outside of the box. Techniques to engage each child and to teach him appropriately may need an entire team (as well as the child) assessing what works best for him. As your child ages, especially beyond middle school, his educational program should provide him with the skills and opportunities necessary to support his interests and abilities. Such a directed school search occurred for Russ, an eleven-year-old with ASD who is skilled at animating movies. His mother was able to find a high school curriculum that included film studies. He is so enthralled with his film classes that he has improved in all his core curriculum work. This is in stark contrast to his educational motivation in a previous school, where film studies was not included in the curriculum. Another patient, Jeb, is wonderful with computers, and early in his schooling we insisted not only that computers be used for conveying his thoughts but also that he learn advanced computer technology skills, which may help in his career development down the line.

Dr. Ricki's Educational Pet Peeves

While not an expert in education or educational curriculum, I have had much experience working with children and their families who have been in a variety of school environments. Over the years, many educational issues have come up again and again. These have become my pet peeves concerning education and children with ASD and can serve as red flags for you as you evaluate particular schools.

Handwriting

Because children with ASD often have major fine motor difficulties, the question of handwriting challenges frequently arises. Holding a pencil and moving it correctly to produce printed letters can be laborious. If this is an issue for your child, find out what the objective of the lesson is. If the teacher is evaluating the quality of your child's handwriting, then yes, he must write by hand. However, if the point is to discover what your child is thinking and feeling, then the answer might not always come through what he can express via handwritten material. This can be especially true if your child has major motor-planning issues. He might be much more fluent on a keyboard—either independently or with supported communication (see Chapter 12). Obviously a person's ideas cannot be solely dependent on his ability to produce handwritten material.

It is very hard for children with ASD to print and it may be easier for your child to learn D'Nealian or cursive writing when he is learning to write. Even minor motor-planning difficulties can lead to problems. When a word is not written continuously, as occurs when printing a word, each break may derail the next step and he will have to start anew. Often specific exercises designed with your child's occupational therapist can be used to develop improved hand control. Some kids like squeezing tennis or Koosh balls; others can improve hand control by drawing, painting or stringing beads. If pencil pressure is a concern for printing exercises, consider using a Magna Doodle, which requires very little pressure to be successful.

Assistive Technology

If a child communicates effectively using assistive technology, he must have it available in the educational setting throughout the day. Far too often children are allowed their devices for only ten minutes a day. No one would require that a deaf child communicate with sign language for only ten minutes out of a school day. Specific details, such as having assistive technology available, should be outlined in the IEP to ensure compliance within the school system. In addition, document the amount of training time his staff requires in order to be efficient communication partners for him, as well as who will do the training.

Failure to Think Outside the Box

A child who is a visual learner may experience difficulty in reading comprehension as he gets older and the textbooks contain fewer pictures. His team may have to work out ways to tap into his existing skills and abilities in order for him to get the most throughout the day from the curriculum.

Curriculum Stalling

The curriculum may stagnate and become too repetitive. This can be devastating for your child, and he could become bored and disconnected from his classmates, teachers or you when this happens. Your team should continually review his school program and keep it challenging as your child is better able to understand the material. The curriculum can also stall if your child hits a comprehension wall.

Gaps in Year-Round School Programming

Learning is a painstaking task for children with ASD. It occurs, and is maintained, when your child can have structure, consistency and daily exposure to both new and old material. Gaps in year-round school programming will often result in academic setbacks for a child with ASD. This especially occurs when the time periods are long, as in a summer break. In today's economy, summer schools are understaffed and operate for brief time periods, if they are in session at all. To maximize year-long retention and foster increased learning of academic material, special consideration should be given to summer academic programming with fully supported staff for children with ASD. If this is not possible, summers are a good time to increase your semi-structured DIR/Floortime sessions at home to support your child's learning.

Not Building Comprehension

Once your child moves beyond early grade levels, he needs to comprehend what he is reading and to be able to put it into the correct context in order to get the most from his academic program. Eventually he needs to problem solve by creating novel ideas based on the core material. If your child is having difficulty with this aspect of the curriculum, much attention must be focused on moving past this "comprehension wall." As discussed (see Chapter 5), there are programs designed to help children with these sensory processing difficulties overcome this barrier (Lindamood-Bell Learning Processes is one such program). If these programs can help the visual and auditory system coordinate appropriately, then your child has a better chance of moving into more advanced educational material. In some cases the curriculum for a particular child can become repetitive due to these difficulties. If this occurs with your child, you might consider an intense period of homeschooling where his particular need can be addressed. This could be done over the summer or during a prolonged holiday break and could continue for many consecutive periods. Rarely, a program of this type may be conducted in place of your child's regular school program. With increased intensity I have seen students improve remarkably in their school setting, allowing advancement in their curriculum.

Navigating High School

Progressing from one grade to another can be a scary transition for children and parents alike. For teenagers with ASD, concerns go beyond the typical issues and can include the size of the school; new safety protections; support moving from classroom to classroom; planning for lunch, PE and any other breaks with decreased supervision typically found in a high school setting; the choice of aide (especially if your child is tall or ballistic in his motions and perhaps needs a male aide); curriculum concerns; finding and keeping friends; and preventing bullying, to name a few. Preparation for high school begins early, often a year before entry, to make it as smooth a transition as possible. Starting early offers an opportunity to think about your teenager's next steps in a more global way, and allows you to look beyond his high school years toward potential directions he may take following high school. Taking a longer perspective may help determine the best curriculum and wraparound program to put in place through his high school years. If, for example, he enjoys cooking and together you envision a career for him in this field, academics could be geared to learning appropriate math skills in order to perform the expected tasks. If he loves computers, expertise in certain computer programs could be critical to his future employment. Thinking in these terms will help you to design what is needed.

Extending the Curriculum

Remember also that learning is lifelong. During his high school years you may have the luxury of extending the academic curriculum beyond the typical four-year high school program. This is another instance where you might decide to give your adolescent the gift of time by extending high school to six years. If your child is in a special education curriculum, he is allowed to remain in the education system until his twenty-second birthday. A six-year plan for high school can relieve some of the academic pressure, which can give a teen more time to devote to social relationships. I have found parents relaxing immensely about high school concerns when they realize that there is extra time for their child to complete expectations. Such was the case for Keith, an eighth grader, and his family. He was a hard worker and had already accomplished so much at his own rate of learning, but it was clear he was learning at about the fourth-grade level. When he was pushed too quickly, his anxiety and subsequent behaviors greatly increased. When he was given an opportunity to continue his academic pursuits for six years of high school, the pressure was relieved. He and his family were able to spend time thinking about how the six years could be best used to accomplish his goals and deepen his relationships with peers.

In my pediatric practice I always discuss with parents and teens their hopes for high school. Parents generally emphasize academics as a major goal. Teens are usually more concerned about their social lives, acknowledging academics more in terms of what their parents might say about their academic performance in subjects! It is their social relationships that usually dictate how happy they are. For teens with ASD the social aspects of high school are also a big concern. By the time they are ready for high school, these kids are beginning to see themselves in relation to their peers and are starting to understand how different their behavior can be from others, as well as how much they might be missing in terms of a social life. Distress over these issues, unresolved anger, even jealousy and worry can derail any of the academic components in a high school program. Children with special needs can have their self-esteem undermined in so many ways that both parents and therapists must always be alerted to a particular child's needs. It is crucial that his interactive school and home program allow him to maintain a growing self-esteem. One advantage of the six-year program could be to reinforce this growth. By feeling good about what he is accomplishing, especially when done in a supportive and calm environment, your teenager can thrive and be better prepared to relate to teachers and especially his peers.

High School Diploma or GED?

Many parents wonder if their child should stay in high school to earn a diploma or pursue a general education diploma (GED). Many children with ASD do not test particularly well on standardized tests, making state exit exams from high school more difficult. Pursuing a GED has its pros and cons. On the plus side there is no need to take state-required high school exit exams; it allows for an individualized program that will meet the teen's specific needs; parental anxiety and pressure can decrease; there is potential to improve the student's well-being, self-esteem and social relationships; opportunities for career paths may open up; and it allows for entrance to community or two-year colleges. On the con side, options for college may be limited, as might job opportunities.

When talking with parents about the goals for their child's high school years, the conversation frequently turns into a discussion, initiated by the parents, about their hopes and ideas concerning all aspects of their child's future. Such was the case with Kenji who was having extreme difficulty on the high school diploma track and was overwhelmed by his homework. He loved music appreciation, could categorize all the great jazz artists and knew their complete playlists, which he shared quite willingly with everyone. He saw himself working in the music field someday. A diploma was not required for him to pursue his interests. After much discussion, Kenji's parents determined that he would enroll in a program that allowed for an equivalency exam at the end of the high school years—if he so wished. Several months after making this decision, his parents were grateful because Kenji was the happiest they had ever known him to be. Without the academic pressure he found part-time work in the music library at a local college. Not only were his academic needs being met in this new setting but he also had friends for the first time where he felt socially accomplished.

Once parents are encouraged to think about their children's strengths and keen interests, I have found them to be very creative in working with their children to orchestrate a plan that expands their child's future options and potential. In this way the high school years can be expanded far beyond mere self-help programs and self-care skill development. I believe all adolescents must be encouraged to identify their interests and talents and be given the opportunity to develop skills that enable them to seek interesting and appropriate careers. Some interests are academic in nature and require education beyond high school. A number of adolescents in my practice have gone on to two- and four-year colleges in order to pursue their goals. There is no ceiling on expectations or opportunities for your adolescent.

Sports, Socializing and Relationships

ALL CHILDREN need exercise. In fact, they need so much exercise that they often exhaust their parents as they run from place to place with their youthful exuberance! Children with ASD need just as much exercise; however, often their motor-planning issues may limit their abilities and the activities that they can participate in. In addition, the long hours they spend in therapy also limit their available free time for play and exercise. They spend long hours sitting face-to-face with adults in the therapeutic environment rather than interacting with other children. Over the years, I've come to realize how critical it is to schedule exercise into children's multidisciplinary programs, because in many ways they have been deprived of the amount of exercise they need. Exercise, as we all know, does many things for us. It improves emotional well-being. It allows us to deal with pent-up energy in a meaningful way, and it supports the growth of bones, muscles, joints and motor coordination. It can become a major social component in each child's life, as well.

For children with ASD, who often have weight issues, exercise, especially aerobic, becomes an even more critical component for maintaining a healthy lifestyle. Not only will exercise help control a child's weight, but it can also establish good habits that will last a lifetime. There are many ways to incorporate exercise into your child's schedule. It's great when an activity can meet his sensory needs, as well. Swimming is an example of this type of exercise. Swimming is not only a total body exercise but it is also similar to a massage, as the pressure from the water can be very calming to the sensory system. Additionally, if a child is successful at swimming, this can become an individual or team sport to pursue. What begins as an exercise program becomes a lifelong community-based experience for many. Look for a pool facility in your community that has a therapy pool. If your child is reluctant to get into cold water, starting out in a much warmer therapeutic pool can be the ticket for success. Some facilities have a family pool area that is kept at a warmer temperature.

As your child becomes an adolescent, the need for exercise often far outweighs the actual amount of time he might have to devote to these activities. If so, make a special effort to build this time into his daily schedule. Adolescence is a perfect time to combine exercise with socialization. A successful approach that has worked for parents I have worked with is to employ exercise "buddies" to work out with their children. Parents hire a young adult (often a college student who is on a career path to become a physical education teacher) to become a companion, or "buddy," for their teenager on a one-on-one basis. These young adults, particularly those who are preparing to become PE teachers, are full of energy, love exercise and are usually incredibly enthusiastic. They fit the bill for what adolescents with ASD need to get them energized, engaged and moving. Many teenagers who have buddies are able to go hiking, ride scooters, bike or roller-skate with them on a daily basis. In general, they love the opportunity. It gives them a chance to have a break from the adults in their environment and "hang out" with more age-appropriate young adults who become peer role models. They have fun together but they also get to go out in the car with them and listen to their music, and they often begin to dress like they do. In most cases, I suggest that these buddies feel free to talk to the adolescent using contemporary language, giving them true experiences in the real world. Exercise and buddy time become some of the most anticipated events for the kids and can be incredibly influential in shaping their behavior and lives. The older buddy has an opportunity to give some peer guidance, perhaps commenting on behavior as he steps up to his position as role model. Your son hearing a buddy tell him that his behavior, such as an inappropriate word or an advance toward the opposite sex, isn't cool and is not what a teenager should do makes much more of an impression than being told the same thing by a teacher or by you. The relationships most teens develop with their buddies go beyond exercise to greater social interactions, such as visiting a buddy's apartment, meeting his roommates, ordering in pizza and watching a movie after several hours of hiking. It should also be noted that buddies can often exercise to a greater degree than parents are able to do, assuring a true aerobic experience for your teen. Buddies have become a mainstay prescription for adolescents in my practice.

Community and Life-Enriching Experiences

Children with ASD are often limited in the variety of their experiences compared to others. Yet they learn much from each situation they are exposed to. Every attempt should be made to allow your child to experience a full menu of what life has to offer. Although you may not get immediate feedback from your child, these opportunities can be significant. Often as children become more verbal (or learn to use supported communication), it is not unusual for them to describe detail by detail experiences that occurred many years before and the meaning they held for them.

If your child is attending family get-togethers; taking part in community-based activities or religious groups or ceremonies; going on vacations, outings to the circus, the beach, the movies or to birthday parties, plan ahead. Choose events that are more appropriate for your child and his sensory profile and provide modifications as needed. With careful attention, these experiences can be successful. Mike was ten years old and had never been able to join his family for their favorite yearly excursion to the circus. Once he learned to use sound-canceling headphones, he was able to tolerate the crowd and noise and join his family. A simple adjustment like Mike's can often expand opportunities for your child.

Community groups are a wonderful opportunity for learning within a social setting. I highly recommend scouting or similar groups. Children can gain much through Cub Scouts, Brownies, Boy Scouts and Girl Scouts. One of the best parts of scouting is the mentoring that is done by the older children in the troop. It is a true social experience that demands interaction and cooperation combined with physical output. I also find that scouting can provide wonderful bonding sessions for a child with ASD and his father or mother. I now have three boys in my practice who have ASD who have become Eagle Scouts. One teenager who has very little verbal output was nonetheless able to provide leadership to his group to improve a hiking path in his community. He received not only the Boy Scout Eagle Award but also a community commendation for his service. This boy was such an integral member of his Boy Scout troop that they insisted he join their swim team, as well. The swim coach was thoroughly supportive and honored him with a letter and jacket at the senior ceremony.

Summer Camp

One of the most worthwhile experiences for children with ASD is summer camp. You may not have considered this an option for your child but parents and children alike tell me it is one of the best times of their lives. First and foremost summer camp is fun. Beyond the fun those attending camp have an opportunity to work cooperatively with others and especially work together with a group in a variety of situations. The camp experience can range from day camp to overnight and may have an inclusive program for all children or be specialized for children with special needs. One overnight camp for those with autism (five to adulthood) is Extreme Sports Camp in

Colorado (www.extremesportscamp.org) but others can be found throughout the United States.

When a child attends summer camp, it is imperative that his aide and/or counselors and staff at the camp help him attend to his sensory-motor needs through activities that will gradually increase his skill level. Stimulating activities, such as hiking and rock climbing, and/or potentially soothing activities, such as swimming and horseback riding, can be included throughout the day. Often children who participate in these experiences become much calmer and slowly build their confidence. Camp counselors report much-improved sensory-motor proprioceptive problem solving. At Extreme Sports Camp, for example, campers river raft, horseback ride, camp out, hike, learn to water-ski (using modified skis) and complete a rope course over a rushing river! Imagine the individual camper's pride and increased belief in what he can accomplish. These types of experiences go a long way to convince a child he has the ability to take on even the most difficult tasks in his life. These kinds of experiences improve a child's self-esteem and motivation. As the children develop even greater regulation, social connections solidify: friendships form, and they become more confident in a group.

For all of this to occur, of course, the understanding and talent of the staff are key factors. Knowing how to get children through the more difficult times and support them in the good times are key to making camp successful.

Friendships

Of course, one of the most meaningful life-enriching experiences is that of friendships, some of which may last a lifetime. As you may know, making and keeping friends can often be very difficult for a child with ASD. A child's struggles with friendships can be very painful for parents of children with ASD. They ache for their children to have friends, to receive phone calls and invitations. They want them to have someone with whom they can share their secrets, laugh and even argue—and then make up! When talking to the children themselves, I find a range of responses to the idea of having a friend. Some want to know when they are going to be able to have a friend as their siblings and classmates do. Others prefer not to have someone close unless there is a specific reason or an interest that they share. In either case parents have to adapt in order to enrich their child's lives. For those who desire friends, the goal is to find venues in which your child can be successful. For those who do not express an interest in making friends, I find great success involving them in groups that tap into their true passions (maybe trains or *Star Wars*). They often find that they delight in being able to talk about or play with their favorite items in the company of others with like interests. While we may not totally understand this type of friendship, it is based on mutual respect (as all friendships are) and can be the beginning of widening and enriching your child's social interactions.

Opportunities exist in special social skills groups for children with ASD, playdates, hobbies, clubs or other organized activities. Remember, it only takes one or two children to develop enduring friendships. Many parents will choose facilitated playdates as a start (see Chapter 8). As your child gets older and more able to sustain longer interactions, he may prefer larger group activities. Some communities have social skills programs either for children with ASD or for children in general who are having difficulty in socializing. General programs focus on teaching essential skills to increase a child's self-confidence in social situations. Challenges are designed so children can experience more success in the classroom, on the playground or in extracurricular activities. They are often small groups (five or six children) of elementary through high school age. Children are given challenge course initiatives that require motor planning, visual-spatial processing and sequencing to complete. By working together, they learn to depend on each other in order to succeed. Children with ASD are often integrated into these groups quite nicely. Because all the children are working on their social skills, those who do not have ASD generally have better language and motor abilities and may assist your child since the goal is for them all to help out as best they can (see www.tomsawyercamps.com/blast). This experiential learning benefits all members. The children in my practice who have attended such a program often say that it is one of the most fun things they do all week. In addition, there are autism-specific social skills groups, often led by expert psychologists and social workers or speech and OT professionals who are more interactive and developmentally based. While many work on social etiquette, look for those that are emphasizing facilitated play in your community.

Pursuing Individual Talents and Interests

Where does your child excel? Does he enjoy drawing, painting or working with clay? What about dance, drama, martial arts or an athletic pursuit? Music? Gardening? Caring for animals? Does he focus on cars, trains or reptiles? Does he live for favorite TV "friends," such as Thomas the Tank Engine or Disney characters? Many of these are common favorites for children with ASD. Whatever your child's interests, each opens the door for community involvement—often throughout his lifetime. Many of these interests can develop into careers. For example, there are train collectors, train magazines, train videos, train clubs and stores devoted to nothing but train paraphernalia.

Some activities, such as music lessons, may actually be therapeutic. This is especially true when the class is focused on rhythm and timing. These lessons can help your child if he has a delayed response time and poor coordination. Some parents have found that their child with ASD has perfect pitch. It's possible that something about the ASD brain underconnectivity allows for a strong local auditory brain connection that results in the child being able to achieve absolute pitch. Children with ASD can be members of musical groups, performing in school and community productions as they gain more experience. *Autism: The Musical,* a recent HBO film (nominated for an Emmy Award), showcased a musical-dramatic production written and performed by a troupe of children and teens who all have ASD. Your child may love playing musical instruments. Clarinets, pianos and drums are favorites of children in my practice, and some are members of their school bands and orchestras.

Other experiential learning opportunities include art and drama. Drama can be especially suited to children with ASD because it focuses on many of the abilities that you work on through DIR/Floortime, such as engaging, gesturing and pretending. Acting can be very movement-based, visual and participatory, allowing your child to join in at whatever level and extent he can perform. Especially significant is the fact that acting allows for the continuous back-and-forth flow that you strive for in all your interactions with your child. Drama is a perfect medium to support creativity, symbolic thinking and logical thought. When children excel at drama, it provides a natural social group of children with like-minded interests. I urge you to continue to explore possibilities for your child.

Defining Success—Let Him Follow His Dream

When children are supported and encouraged to try a variety of activities, they are often more willing and able to pursue their particular interests. Children with ASD need the same encouragement as typically developing children to pursue what they love. Whatever the individual's interest, I suggest to families that they not only support it but also supplement the child's connection with a variety of experiences and adapt those experiences as needed to his special needs. In this way, as long as it is interactive and allows him to engage in problem solving, his interest can be reframed as a success instead of simply as something unusual.

We all have individual strengths and challenges that stay with us our whole lives. In fact, our strengths often shape our preferences, whether we are choosing friends, social situations or our career path. Visual learners are often attracted to visual experiences, including computers and theater, as well as math-based pursuits. Auditory learners might be attracted to writing and reading tasks. A sensory craver who is very verbal may seek out the presence of people and choose a career in sales. A more sensory-reactive individual may choose tasks and activities that are less crowd-based and more one-on-one.

Children with ASD will also follow interests and choose careers that suit their profiles. As your child explores various activities that may lead to a possible career choice, it is important to keep this fact in mind. Matching the activity to his profile makes success more likely, and that success will feed further interests. If you give your child experiences to discover his interests and then support these interests over time, he can find his "place in the sun."

I fully believe that it is possible to find a place where each child can shine. The children that I have worked with are now reaching young adulthood. This group includes musicians, singers, writers, artists, mathematicians and computer specialists who, given the gift of time, will all create a meaningful life. The stories below reflect a few of the wonderful ways in which these adolescents who happen to have ASD are thriving.

Noah is a fifteen-year-old who was diagnosed with ASD at eighteen months. He has extremely strong visual abilities paired with severe auditory processing difficulties. His parents, both connected to the movie industry, provided a lot of visual input for him from a very early age through a variety of media. Although he had very little spoken language, he was extremely artistic. Noah enjoyed creating life-size puppets and has been known to spend months creating his Halloween costumes. Once he became a cell phone for the evening! Noah had great difficulty in school, especially in tasks that required reading comprehension. His parents became accustomed to negative school reports, suggesting that Noah was limited in his opportunities. However, Noah's continued creative expression belied school reports. It became clear that the school did not provide a learning environment that would build on Noah's visual learning ability. So his parents skillfully supported his strengths through extracurricular activities. By the end of elementary school, Noah was active in drama and art (where he exhibited nearly savant artistic ability in form and creativity). In addition, he attended movie openings and children's theater and puppetry shows, eventually learning how to make puppets that would be used in these performances. Although Noah did not seem to be gaining many academic skills, he enjoyed going to school, where he had many strong friendships that he had developed over the years.

When Noah was about twelve years old, his mother discovered a talented teacher who was leading a summer camp helping children with special needs learn through computer animation. Given Noah's skills, this seemed like a perfect match! Within two weeks of the summer camp Noah's special talent was evident. He quickly learned the skill sets required to animate, using a Claymation process to produce a film. Eventually he wrote his own story, drawing each individual animation cel and giving voices to all the characters in his movie. While he was in middle school, his movies were so accomplished that he regularly won international juried film competitions (open to all students). His films were not only beautiful but also poignant and insightful. Watching them, one understands Noah's intelligence, which is far superior to anything he has displayed at school. During this time, Noah's mom told me, "Noah has never been this motivated before. When he gets home, all he wants to do is to write hundreds of storyboards. So I'm trying to build on that skill to work on writing. Because he can sit down and write a script, I'm trying to help him translate that into writing essays and other things."

When it came time to plan for high school, it became imperative to find one that had a program for filmmakers. Noah's response to that idea was, "Great. I can do the film thing and art and drama. These three things are better for me than math and science." Even if an alternative to a strict high school diploma program was required for Noah, the best choice for him was to create a program where he could learn about the academic fields, such as English, history and so on, in a creative way (through animation, art or drama), keeping in mind that animation was probably going to be his career path. By the time he entered a high school program that met these needs, he had already learned the most advanced computer animation techniques, which would most likely guarantee him a job in the animation industry. Using this technique of computer-based learning, which is seamlessly expressed through animation, he has been able to make progress on social-emotional issues, as well as academically, while simultaneously finding his career.

Despite great challenges, observation and creativity can lead each individual with ASD to a meaningful life. Christopher is probably one of the most challenged individuals with ASD that I have met. Diagnosed at age four and essentially nonverbal, at eighteen years of age he learned to communicate by supported communication and alternative communication using a voice output computer. Christopher had such severe sensory processing and motor-planning difficulties that he was unable to function in a school setting. The most secure place for him for many years has been a homeschool environment. During his adolescence his mother discovered that he loved food. He didn't simply enjoy eating. He was most engaged while she was preparing the family meals and she encouraged him to help her whenever possible. With his strong interest in this area she wisely concluded that creating meals might offer him a career path. He enthusiastically embraced the idea of developing a food service business and Christopher's Cuisine was born (www.christopherscuisine.com). Christopher's company delivers lunches twice a week to local businesses. He is involved in all aspects of the business with the support of his daytime companions who facilitate with him. In the days between deliveries Christopher develops his menu, creates his shopping list and goes grocery shopping with a team member. The morning of a delivery, he directs team members to help him cook and put the meals together. Christopher then accompanies a team member to deliver the lunches. During the delivery he has an opportunity to talk with his clients. His work has marked a huge turnaround in his life. He has focus, meaning and interaction with business people in the community, who are quite grateful for his delicious salads and sandwiches. He proudly wears his Christopher's Cuisine apron, both while working in the kitchen and on delivery days. A Christopher's Cuisine cookbook is being planned for internet purchase. When I asked Christopher what the best thing was about having a business, he responded, "Well, the money of course!" (Now, there is a typical teen response!)

After about two years of running his food service, Christopher became increasingly agitated and less willing to follow his parents' instructions around the house. This, of course, was upsetting to his family and team members. It soon became clear that his behavior was a sign of his increasing desire for independence. When I met with his parents, I encouraged them to think of this as a sign of progress and to recognize that Christopher, now in his early twenties, needed to take steps toward semi-independent living. This was a very difficult prospect for his family to face. Christopher had unsuccessfully tried to go out in the world in the past, had had difficulties and had experienced a period of deep regression that took months for him to recover from. However, his parents were able to take the chance, and Christopher now spends his days where Christopher's Cuisine is located. He stepped up to the plate, deciding where all the furniture would go and what he would do there to create his own space. There is hope that eventually he will be able to live independently, supported by his team members 24/7.

Scott is a twenty-four-year-old with Asperger's disorder. Although very verbal, he has had much difficulty with reciprocal conversations, often missing typical social cues. His interests have always been narrow—involving both computers and animals. As a young child he would regularly lecture me about his favorite reptile, animal or dinosaur of the month, including details that only experts might know. He did relatively well in school and was accepted at several colleges. His love of and interest in animals led him to major in zoology. While in college he discovered an affinity for ancient eras, which led him to pursue anthropology—particularly the Mayan period. He secured an internship with a professor who has a grant to study ancient Mayan ruins in Central America. Scott is responsible for characterizing the animals that existed during that time. Before he left on the trip, I asked what it meant to him, and he replied with a fully animated smile, "It is the most spiritual experience I could have." This was the moment of greatest connection I've felt with Scott. I could sense his joy as he talked about his upcoming adventure. I have no doubt that he will excel in this experience. The potential for a career has never been greater for him.

Marcy is a young woman who has high-functioning autism. Because of constant conflict with her parents, she moved out of her home state to live with an aunt and uncle. In her new location, she was aimless and without focus, sleeping half the day and engaging very little with others. She had been unwilling to accept responsibility for her behavior in her own home and now was not helping her aunt and uncle. At her first visit with me she appeared to be "marking time," as if this move to her relatives' house was a punishment. When I asked Marcy what her dreams were, she replied, "Animals." As we explored the topic of animals, it was clear that she wanted to help care for them—especially dogs and cats. She brightened up as we talked, easily engaging about her favorite topic. With a few calls to the local humane society, Marcy was able to secure a volunteer position. A few months later, when she returned to my office, there was a notable difference in her facial expressions and demeanor. She excitedly shared with me what was happening at her job. She loved caring for the animals and clearly had found a niche. She was so successful that she was being considered for a paid position, which she eventually secured. Not only was she working full-time as a veterinary associate but she was also becoming a full participant in home life. Although Marcy had not excelled in school, she was now interested in pursuing the education needed to work with animals. The majority of her original behaviors had dissipated and she was now responsible, respectful and motivated. Tapping into Marcy's interests led the way toward engaging her enthusiasm, which provided the motivation to get her life moving in a positive direction. She now has purpose and meaning built around themes where she can excel. It may take time for your child to discover his talents but it can happen when you support what he loves.

Working with animals is often a favorite career for children with ASD. If you have an animal, you may have noted a special relationship between it and your child. Larger animals have great appeal, as well. Many children with ASD tell me the best part of their week is when they go to therapeutic horseback riding. Their joy goes beyond the usual improved sensory regulation they have after an occupational therapy session. In fact, I have known several who have turned this love of horses into a job. One, a twenty-five-year-old woman with moderately challenging autism, is a stable hand who is responsible for the care and feeding of several horses used in her therapeutic riding program. She is thrilled to be able to help her beloved horses.

Ron is a twenty-two-year-old with moderately challenging ASD. During high school he was in a program in the countryside that allowed him to experience many career opportunities. He gravitated toward tasks that were plant oriented, eventually choosing landscaping as a potential career path. Although he had many processing difficulties that made logical thought more difficult for him, when he was landscaping, he was energized and productive. Efforts are now being made to help him live semi-independently and pursue a career in landscaping.

Helping Your Child Find His Special Interests

Following are some questions you can ask (for your child as well as his team members) to devise an action plan to expand your child's experiences and discover opportunities for him:

- What does he like to do? What are his favorite items to play with? What are his favorite subjects?
- Can any of these be developed into a hobby? For example, can he join a train club, take care of a pet or help plant a garden?
- Are there educational programs that can expand his knowledge? Consider internships or weekend jobs (with support and modification as needed).
- Are there clubs or community resources to provide supportive help at a job? Organizations like 4-H, K-9 Companions and Challenger Sports are all examples. Other options could include helping care for sports equipment or operating as a manager or assisting the coach in some way, if he loves all things sports related.

If your child does not have an obvious interest, don't give up. Remember that many young adults take time to find their way. Continue introducing new experiences geared toward the activities and events that most engage your child. When he is engaged and interested, he will do his best.

Transition to Adulthood

TRANSITIONS ARE a major concern for all parents but especially for parents of children with ASD. Transitions may be small, such as moving to a different table in preschool. They may be much larger and have greater impact, such as switching from middle to high school or high school to college. Whether small or large, each has the potential to cause your child anxiety, discomfort and possibly fear. Transition plans have been discussed throughout this book in order to help you and your child prepare for what's ahead. Remember, the more complex the transition, the more time will be needed to plan and prepare. This is especially true when thinking about the transition from adolescence to adulthood. It may take years to sort through decisions and accomplish all that needs to be done to get him to the next step. In reality, you can't start too early.

Begin transition planning by working with your adolescent to imagine his future. Any avenues you pursue, many of which are detailed in the following sections, follow from this beginning point. Armed with the knowledge of what he finds meaningful, you can begin to consider important questions, such as Where will he live? How will he find employment? How will he access transportation? Will he make friends? Where will his finances come from? Who will be his doctors? Who will provide support services? How do I start this process? You can begin by getting state-specific information about the transition from high school and the law governing your state agencies at www.nichcy.org/pages/home.aspx.

Many of these issues are faced by teens and families in my practice. During this time some parents find it necessary to expand their support teams to include community social services. Your doctor can be extremely helpful during this transition; however, a 2008 survey from the American Academy of Pediatrics (AAP) revealed that less than half of pediatricians routinely offered their patients with special health care needs support in transitioning to adult health care. This likely indicates a gap in understanding or expertise, but if you reach out to your doctor, you may find that he and his office personnel can be of great service. In my practice we begin thinking about these concerns when teens are fifteen or sixteen, often as a part of their six-year high school plan. This leaves plenty of time to find resources, talk to those who have been through the experience, visit programs and evaluate the information you've gathered. Everything you have accomplished to this point that has supported your teen's thinking, relating, independence and interests will help him ease into this next phase of his life.

Remember as you look ahead to always have a backup plan (or two!) just in case the situation changes. As always, your child should be a part of the planning so that he can let you know what he wants and enjoys about the programs you evaluate. Having him be part of the process will aid in his ability to accept change. Once a plan is put in place, he may need a timetable to help him anticipate the changes that will take place in the coming months.

Finding Programs That Are Appropriate for Your Young Adult

There are many options for you to consider. Your doctor can help prioritize your search. The list will depend on what type of program your young adult needs (postsecondary education—college or vocational school—is among the options) and how he learns best (in a classroom, with hands–on training or through real experiences with supports). Within each category the choices also vary. If he is ready to take college courses, he may be able to begin with one or two at your local community college each semester. He could attend full-time yet live at home or in another local setting. He may be prepared to attend college away from home. Patients in my practice have chosen all these options. There is no limit to what you can imagine for your young adult. College students who are relatively nonverbal in my practice use some form of assistive communication in order to do their college work.

Alternative postsecondary choices are usually comprehensive and offer vocational training, a continued life skills curriculum, continuing education, community interaction and, most especially, social, friendship-building components. The emphasis of each program, staff ratios and employment and housing opportunities vary. As always you need to determine which program best fits or matches your young adult's interests and needs.

When you visit potential programs, explore all available options. If possible, observe how the current students in the program are doing. Does the staff "walk the talk"? How do they relate to students? Are they helpful, supportive and nurturing? Do the students seem engaged? If the students are working, do they seem interested in and excited about what they are doing?

Questions to ask include the following:

■ Will the program be individualized for his specific needs?

■ Is the program short-term or does it provide lifelong services? Which is better for your young adult and family?

■ What are student-staff ratios? What are staff qualifications?

■ How does the program build on your child's existing independent skills and achievements to help your young adult become as self-reliant as possible, if he is living on his own (outside the family) with or without extra support? Is there instruction on and assistance for money management, cooking, doing laundry, shopping and hygiene? Is there support to help him learn how to organize his life both on the job and at home, including how to manage time? If he lives in a group home, are there specific skills unique to the home situation, like being a cooperative roommate, sharing responsibility and chores, scheduling bath time and so on, that may need to be practiced and mentored?

■ Do vocational opportunities in the program match his interests? Depending on his interests, this might require specific training through volunteer and/or paid positions. Does the program provide ongoing job support with an aide or a "coach" to help him understand the tasks he needs to perform and ease his social adjustment to the job? If there is a coach, can you get training for him so he can learn the best way to support your child in his new work relationships and responsibilities?

■ You may find programs that include educational opportunities for him, ranging from in-house to a community college to a four-year college. Find out if he can advance as long as he wishes and what academic requirements he must fulfill to participate. This information can be quite helpful as you plan his educational goals for high school.

■ Are there employment placement services?

■ Does the program integrate community experiences and resources for continuing education, recreation, community service, the pursuit of the arts and leisure?

■ What are the support services? Are there job coaches? Do they have counseling and/or classes to help him prepare and organize his life, including goal setting, steps to achieve those goals and monitoring his progress? Who provides these services?

■ Is there continuity from the classroom into the living situation?

■ Will he have continued access to psychological therapy, speech therapy, OT and PT? If this access is not provided by his program, where can he get these needed services and how are they funded?

■ What are the opportunities and support for meeting others and maintaining relationships both within the program and outside?

■ Does the program have built-in services to manage his transportation, medical issues and finances, or will you need another wraparound program?

■ What are the options for different living situations associated with the program? How much support is provided in these settings?

■ How will communication be handled between your young adult, the program and you? Are counseling services available for parents if needed? Does the program work with his physicians to review progress (for example, if he's on medication)?

■ How will his safety and security be assured? (This is especially important for both genders to be certain they are protected from unwanted sexual advances.)

■ How do they handle budding sexual attractions in the program?

■ What is the cost of the program? Are there financial scholarships or public funding?

■ How long do most students stay in the program? For what reasons do they leave?

Transitioning Your Young Adult to Independent Living

As your adolescent transitions into adulthood, his health and well-being must be taken into account and plans should be put in place to meet his individual requirements.

Meeting Your Young Adult's Health Needs

It may be difficult for you to consider changing health care providers. However, it is necessary both to be certain your young adult has the expert care he needs as he gets older and to assure the continuity of his care over the long term. Your doctor can play a critical role in easing the transition by creating an individualized health care plan for your young adult that addresses:

■ Referrals to specific family or internal medicine doctors.
■ Referrals as needed to adult specialist physicians.

- Providing a portable medical summary (www.medicalhomeinfo.org/tools/assess.html).
- Supporting his new doctors as needed about general or specific medical issues related to your young adult. Having your present doctor's insights can be one of the factors in successfully transitioning to new doctors.
- Reviewing health care insurance options after age eighteen.
- Providing medical documentation for program eligibility (such as college, postsecondary programs, vocational programs, Supplemental Security Income [SSI], conservatorship).

Does Your Young Adult Qualify for Financial Assistance Programs?

Once he leaves the educational system, financial support for your young adult will come from different sources. Much of what you anticipate for the cost of his program will most likely require external resources. Fortunately, individuals who qualify can receive public assistance to help provide support. In addition, there are some ways in which private funds can be managed for him throughout his lifetime. These include:

- **Supplemental Security Income (SSI)** is available for anyone older than eighteen years of age who is disabled with limited income (www.ssa.gov/ssi). If your young adult qualifies, the stipend can help support his basic living needs. Your doctor can help you with required medical documentation for eligibility.

- **Medicaid** is a federal program implemented by each state. Medicaid provides a financial safety net for hospitalization and for necessary, often expensive medication—even if his doctors do not accept these payments. Check with local agencies to see if he qualifies for dual coverage through public and private sources.

- **Special Needs Trusts** (also known as supplemental needs trusts) allow disabled beneficiaries to receive gifts, settlements or other monies and yet not lose their eligibility for certain government programs. These trusts are not designed to provide basic support but instead may be used to pay for comforts and other extras not covered by public assistance funds. These trusts typically pay for education, recreation, counseling and medical needs. If a trust has extra funding, it can be used to provide spending money and pay for things that will enhance your child's quality of life, including aides, computers, vacations, movies and so on. There are many ways to set up a special needs trust for your child. If you are interested in a special needs trust, an experienced lawyer can guide you through the process. See www.specialneedsanswers.com/professionals for further information.

Is Your Young Adult Able to Make Decisions on His Own?

This is not only a heart-wrenching question but one that forces you to think about your young adult's future. While making this evaluation, take a practical approach. Can he be responsible for his medical care? Can he be responsible for a loan? What if he signs up (without full understanding) for military service? Once he turns eighteen, he will not need your consent to enter into a contract or take on other responsibilities.

If you feel he is not ready to make decisions about his health, finances and so on, you may want to explore a guardianship and/or conservatorship. Making this decision prior to his eighteenth birthday guarantees that you will be able to remain involved and informed about his medical care. If a guardian or conservator is in place before he turns eighteen, medical providers will be able to release confidential documents concerning his health to you when necessary. You will need expert legal help to navigate either a guardianship or conservatorship. Your doctor will help document any medical need for either of these options.

GUARDIANSHIP AND CONSERVATORSHIP

Guardianship and conservatorship are defined as follows:

- A guardianship is a legal right given to a person to be responsible for the food, health care, housing and other necessities of a person deemed fully or partially incapable of providing these necessities for himself.
- A conservatorship is a legal right given to a person to be responsible for the assets and finances of a person deemed fully or partially incapable of managing these affairs for himself.

What Type of Living Arrangements Would Be Best for Your Young Adult?

If your doctor knows your young adult and family well, he may be able to contribute to this discussion. If not, a social worker should be able to get you started. Where your child lives through adulthood depends on available options, his needs and his wishes as well as yours. Does he want or need to live in a dorm on campus (near or away from your home)? Will he be in a noncollege program that provides community-based housing? Will a home or an apartment be best? Can he live independently, in supported living or in a group home? How much support does he need? Periodic checks or twenty-four-hour support? Will he be in a community-based program or an autism-specific one? Do you anticipate that he'll be in a short-term (less than three years) transition program or one that offers lifetime housing? His needs will change over time, so you may need to think ahead for when he needs a different program or approach.

In order to effectively compare your options, assess what they have to offer and make the best match for your young adult. I suggest that you make a chart listing each facility and what each provides, and then come up with the pros and cons for each. You will need time to evaluate these possibilities—so start your search early.

Are There Resources for Community Involvement and Leisure Activities?

Many times young adults attend day programs, returning home in the early afternoon or at the end of the day. If your young adult has time, continued outside activities can be an important part of his life. Explore with your doctor how he can continue exercise (perhaps at a local Y, at a private gym or in an autism-specific exercise group). He may choose to get involved in a religious community or with art, drama, music or computers or in any specific clubs related to his hobbies and passions. With so many adults who have autism, there may be autism-specific adult groups that interest him. Advocacy groups, including Autism Society of America, are good resources for potential activities. See also www.autism-pdd.net/resources.html.

Supporting Your Young Adult's Social Life and Relationships

As mentioned so often throughout this book, relationship-based approaches can be one of the most effective means to assure your young adult's success. As he transitions to a new team, share with them the insights you have gleaned from your years of experience working with your child and his previous team. A positive, interested response is a clue to how they will approach your young adult. Showing videos of your interactions can help them understand how valuable the relationship-based approach has been to encourage your young adult's communicating and relating. Explain his individual profile. Let them know how to support his interactions—what works and what doesn't. Check in frequently with the new team to see how things are going. When you're with your young adult, ask about friends, who he's meeting, what they do, what he likes and doesn't like about what he is doing. Help him problem solve what he needs to help himself be more successful.

Often young adults with ASD can feel isolated, even alienated, from typical friendships if they have had difficulty sustaining peer relationships. This may lead to sadness, and sometimes depression. If this is the case for your child, the social component of his adult program must be carefully constructed. Look for programs that include the most opportunities for social interaction outside of a job and family. Because learning and development are really lifelong, continue to emphasize the social-emotional growth steps that you have focused on since his childhood. Although he may be at an earlier stage than his peers, he still faces the emotional issues of adulthood. The difference is that he will process these at his own level of understanding. Whether considering separation from his parents, forming a friendship or sexual relationship, or any other adult concern, he may need more support than is typical. It is the relationship with his family and his support team that serves as the "glue" to help him get through these times and move on with his life. Using all the best practices you have learned to support his needs, your new team can be well informed to help. The more often your young adult is able to work out these problems, the more he will be able to expand experiences and overcome even greater challenges to add meaning to his life. Some programs have social skills counselors and psychologists to help him navigate through these issues and others that might be more serious, especially if your child has unresolved issues, such as anger or loneliness.

These types of concerns can be very serious, requiring not only expert understanding but also increased nurturing interactions, which can be informed by his individual needs. If your young adult is living semi-independently (with supervision), be sure to ascertain if staff mentors receive training in how to help residents facilitate their sexual urges and feelings and if they provide ongoing classes in sexuality. If not, where can he receive help? Are there classes or trained professionals available in the community?

Finding Resources in Your Community

Many adults with ASD do not find sufficient options for themselves within their communities. As time goes on, hopefully the younger group of those with ASD will find improved resources when they are needed. The increased numbers of children with ASD have finally been recognized by state legislatures, which are beginning to address their needs as they get older. For example, California now has a statewide initiative to identify housing, education, employment and community resources available for California residents with ASD (California Senate Select Committee on Autism & Related Disorders). Fortunately, resources are expanding.

With approximately one in one hundred individuals affected by ASD, the need for adult services is obvious. Parents of young adults with ASD are developing innovative programs for their grown children. Many envision broad-based living communities where their young adults can live, work and experience full, interactive lives, fully included in all life has to offer. This is, of course, what we all hope for. With recent advocacy efforts, such as Autism Speaks National Town Hall Meeting, much can be done to push these ideas closer to reality.

The journey to adulthood is complex and differs for each one of us, including those who have ASD. It may take extra vigilance to be certain that a path is created for your child. You may find yourself so involved in solving day-to-day problems that it's difficult to take the time to step back and consider the bigger picture. I encourage you to take the time to do this periodically, keeping in mind your overarching goal for your child. By creating a range of opportunities that may have many beginnings and endings, you can help your child create a meaningful and productive life. There is a future for every child with ASD. I can't wait to hear what the future holds for your child!

Handling Your Emotional Responses to Your Young Adult's Transition

Both you and your child are making big adjustments. Your young adult will be letting go of the safest, most secure and loving environment that he's probably known. As one more step in the journey you began years ago, you are continuing the process of letting him go and become as independent as possible. Most parents know when the time is right. But, because the process requires thought and time, I start working on it with families long before they are ready.

I first began this discussion with Trevor and his family when he was nearly sixteen years old. Trevor is an only child with mildly challenging ASD complicated by high anxiety and attention issues. He insisted he would never leave home and that his parents always live in the same home where he grew up. He wanted to always be able to go to his same favorite places to eat, shop and so on, all within a four-block radius of his home. He was so nervous when we started discussing his moving into adulthood that he jumped out of his chair and stomped around the office, declaring, "I will never move. I will always live in my house." Over the next eighteen months, we introduced the notion that most teens eventually leave their parents' home. We gently suggested that because he was doing so well in so many areas, someday he might be able to do that, as well. Although fairly rule-bound, he was beginning to move beyond black-and-white thinking and in small ways that helped the discussion move forward. As we explored these issues, he was able to think about other people that he knew leaving their homes. When asked under what circumstances he might leave his own home, he replied, "Maybe if my parents went with me." I knew that we would be able to work on this over time.

Following my suggestion, Mom and Dad increased Trevor's repertoire of independent living skills, which helped build his self-confidence. By the time he was eighteen, he was doing a good job of caring for himself and helping out with household chores. He still had difficulty with organizational skills. Mom's biggest concern was that he couldn't care for himself if he went away to a program or wasn't living at home, because he always seemed to forget key items that he needed, whether at school or at play. A course of Cogmed Working Memory Training (see Chapter 8) proved helpful with some of his memory issues. Trevor excitedly told me, "Guess what happened today? I was waiting for my mom to pick me up by the sports field. She was late. I put my backpack down. When I saw her, I started walking to the car, but then I stopped! I said to myself, *You better go get your backpack.* So I did. Mom was so surprised." Trevor was bursting at the buttons, he was so proud that he followed through on his own. This was a turning point for Mom, who for the first time could begin to envision her son taking responsibility for himself and his things. Although there were stops and starts in his ability to self-regulate, Trevor was more open to talking about his future. His thinking ability had advanced, so that it was possible to have hypothetical discussions with him. Over time he was able to visualize going away without his family for a few weeks. He agreed to attend a six-week summer program at a residential school for children with ASD. He thrived there, meeting friends and continuing to take responsibility for himself. When he returned, he admitted that he had a great time but that he still wanted to stay at home for another year. Midway through his final year in high school, he was ready to discuss returning to the residential school for the postsecondary program. When I asked him what he thought about going, he replied, "I think I've done about all I can do here. I am ready to go."

Sometimes placement outside of the home becomes necessary before a child or family is ready. The circumstances can vary widely, but if a child is in constant conflict at home and his own safety or that of his siblings is at risk and no other options are viable, then placement outside the home may need to be considered. Depending on the child's residential program structure and demands, he may be able to come home on weekends or take afternoon outings with his parents and family. As hard as this may be to contemplate, I have generally seen this as a beneficial change for the family, because it often gives all involved a much-needed break. The child becomes more independent and families get help understanding better ways to support him. Nonetheless, these are some of the most difficult decisions to make, often requiring intense counseling and emotional support. In the book *Mixed Blessings: TV's "Father Mulcahy" and His Real-Life Family Share Their Story of Raising a Very Special Child,* William and Barbara Christopher share their journey, describing the ups and downs they encountered with their son, including various residential placements for him. You may relate to this poignant story if you find yourself confronting these issues.

Hope for the Journey

All parents of a child with ASD are justifiably concerned about the prognosis for this disorder. As one father asked me, "Does my son have a future here, or should I just not pursue treatment and keep him at home and love him?" He was so confused by the information he had gleaned from many sources and he feared the worst. This particular concern can override others, often blocking parents' ability to develop appropriate connections with their child and then to devise and implement treatment plans.

Previous reports on the prognosis for children with ASD were based on a time period when they were offered very little treatment. In the past they were felt to have limited potential. Programs—if available at all—were not tailored to their needs. Lack of progress was in many ways a self-fulfilling prophecy. Today, given the intense increased awareness of ASD, the more widespread availability of early intervention services and our greater understanding of all the needs of children with ASD, the prognosis and expectations have markedly changed.

In 2008 the first research article to look at and define recovery from ASD was published. In this study, recovery, defined as previously having been diagnosed with ASD by standardized measures but currently no longer meeting criteria for any ASD, was discovered to be in the range of 3 to 25 percent. In addition, the individual defined as recovered could now learn and use skills in such a way that he followed the expected trajectory of typically developing children in most or all areas. Looking at children between eight and eighteen years of age who now met this definition of recovery, they found that they could be at risk for other challenges, including subtle difficulties with anxiety, learning and the use of language. Other outcome studies have shown that the core symptoms of autism tend to improve by adulthood, especially in the area of communication. Several outcome studies have also documented that 10 to 20 percent of adults previously diagnosed with ASD no longer meet the criteria for the disorder.

There are several possibilities as to why this recovery has occurred. The most obvious is that successful treatment has allowed children to gain enough skills to move forward. However, because not all children respond to treatment, there could be something else at play. In one study optimal outcome correlated with a higher identified IQ, receptive language ability, verbal and motor imitation, motor development and early intervention are promising predictors. Clearly the less challenged the child, the more responsive he was to treatment.

Other approaches are needed to address specific challenges for the individual child that might be a barrier to learning. Future studies may show the best outcomes result from modified intervention plans that directly address a child's greatest challenges and are tailored to his individual profile. The programs that have gained widespread use are directed toward early intervention but there is a need to support ongoing therapy throughout the life span. With the growing evidence of brain plasticity and the ability for lifelong learning, this makes sense for those individuals with ASD who are able to learn but on a slower trajectory. Thoughtful approaches that address the needs of the individual may help parents and health care professionals identify the best practices for each person with ASD.

I have great hope for improving the quality of life for children with ASD. In my experience, with appropriate assessment and treatment protocols, all children with ASD can move up the developmental ladder. By emphasizing and supporting the deepening of their relationships, I see children with ASD diagnoses developing spontaneous, creative interactions that are warm and joyful for all. This work supporting the basic skills of social-emotional growth fosters even greater creativity and problem-solving abilities to help your child have a successful and meaningful life.

When teaching a child a task that goes from step A to step Z, the typical child might need instruction on steps A through G and then will take the project to completion from there. Once he learns this task, it becomes his and he can practice it, refine it and come up with new and creative ways of completing the task without parental input. Your child will also learn, but it may be at a slower rate. He may need support at every step and perhaps between steps until Z has been reached. Because this learning is forming connections between neural networks, each time his system is supported, he will further strengthen these networks. However, because of his unique system, he may not retain the ability to perform a task from one day to the next and will need continued support until that task becomes his own.

Remember, his shared emotion with others and the relationships he develops are the "glue" that supports all that he does. I find most children with ASD advance on their own developmental trajectories with this type of approach. I encourage you to discover how your child learns about his world and the best ways to support his individual strengths and challenges to forge strong, regulated relationships. You can then create a program best suited to his needs, evaluating his progress over time. Change course as needed, depending on the clues you get from your child and his behavior. Meet increasing challenge by investigating and turning over every rock until you and your team figure out what the cause may be. Always return to basics. Has his individual profile changed? Are all his sensory-motor needs attended to? Are the therapies providing what he needs and geared to his level? Is there a health concern? Is there a proper "fit" with the setting and people? Has the environment changed? Are there family concerns? Is an emotional need (anxiety or mood) going unattended? This list can go on and on but is always individualized for each situation. Problem solve and adjust your child's program accordingly. Often, when parents hit a bump in the road, their fear of what is happening reignites the worry that nothing can be done. The glimmer of hope for a future for their child briefly dims. Understanding your child's profile, learning that certain patterns of behavior indicate that he is dysregulated and taking corrective action can reassure you that a slip in his progress due to changes in his environment is not a slide back or a loss of cognitive ability. As the cause of his dysregulation is identified and treated, he can and will return to his previous developmental curve.

Autism miracles don't come in a pill or a single therapy. They come in small moments throughout the day. I see these miracles happen every time a parent and child catch that mutual gleam in each other's eyes. These small moments will build as your child becomes warm and related. Some days are not as miraculous as others and you may find extreme challenges on your journey. Believe in your strength, creativity and love. They will help you meet these challenges so you will be ready to help your child be his best. The journey may be long and there will be highs and lows. It takes love, patience, finances and a "village" filled with support—but it is so worth it. Parents and families of children with ASD are among the most dedicated and motivated that I have ever met. I have deep respect and admiration for all who are on this journey, most especially the children, who struggle every day as they strive to be their best. You, too, can do this! You will meet your challenges and strive for miracles, whether large or small, with your child. I know they will come. I promise to continue doing the best I can to create healthy and meaningful lives for all children affected with ASD and their families.

Epilogue

Although spring was beautiful this year, with clear skies and balmy breezes—one of the best parts of living in Southern California—it had been a long and very emotional week at the office. For so many families, IEP time at the school districts had arrived and this year it seemed everyone was facing budget cuts. Somehow we were able to make programs work for each child. I had just sat down at my desk to attack a stack of charts and correspondence when Karen, my nurse of twenty-five years, bounded in with a huge smile on her face. "I have a surprise for you! Someone is visiting and wants to say hi."

In walked a very tall young man, a tousled towhead with a shading of facial hair, sparkling eyes and an outreached hand. "Hi, Dr. Ricki. I just got back from my first year of college. Thought I'd stop by and say hello." He vigorously shook my hand.

My eyes welled up with tears. It was Ryan.

Diagnostic Criteria for 299.00 Autistic Disorder

A. A total of six (or more) items from (1), (2), and (3), with at least two from (1), and one each from (2) and (3):

1. qualitative impairment in social interaction, as manifested by at least two of the following:

    a. marked impairment in the use of multiple nonverbal behaviors such as eye-to-eye gaze, facial expression, body postures, and gestures to regulate social interaction

    b. failure to develop peer relationships appropriate to developmental level

    c. a lack of spontaneous seeking to share enjoyment, interests, or achievements with other people (e.g., by a lack of showing, bringing, or pointing out objects of interest)

    d. lack of social or emotional reciprocity

2. qualitative impairments in communication as manifested by at least one of the following:

    a. delay in, or total lack of, the development of spoken language (not accompanied by an attempt to compensate through alternative modes of communication such as gesture or mime)

    b. in individuals with adequate speech, marked impairment in the ability to initiate or sustain a conversation with others

    c. stereotyped and repetitive use of language or idiosyncratic language

    d. lack of varied, spontaneous make-believe play or social imitative play appropriate to developmental level

3. restricted repetitive and stereotyped patterns of behavior, interests, and activities, as manifested by at least one of the following:

   a. encompassing preoccupation with one or more stereotyped and restricted patterns of interest that is abnormal either in intensity or focus

   b. apparently inflexible adherence to specific, nonfunctional routines or rituals

   c. stereotyped and repetitive motor manners (e.g., hand or finger flapping or twisting, or complex whole-body movements)

   d. persistent preoccupation with parts of objects

B. Delays or abnormal functioning in at least one of the following areas, with onset prior to age 3 years: (1) social interaction, (2) language as used in social communication, or (3) symbolic or imaginative play.

C. The disturbance is not better accounted for by Rett's Disorder or Childhood Disintegrative Disorder.

Source: www.cdc.gov/ncbddd/autism/hcp-dsm.html

The Modified Checklist for Autism in Toddlers (M-CHAT)

Instructions and Permissions for Use of the M-CHAT™

The Modified Checklist for Autism in Toddlers (M-CHAT™; Robins, Fein, & Barton, 1999) is available for free download for clinical, research and educational purposes. There are two authorized websites: the M-CHAT and supplemental materials can be downloaded from www.firstsigns.org or from Dr. Robins's website, at www.mchatscreen.com.

Users should be aware that the M-CHAT continues to be studied, and may be revised in the future. Any revisions will be posted to the two websites noted above. Furthermore, the M-CHAT is a copyrighted instrument, and use of the M-CHAT must follow these guidelines:

(1) Reprints/reproductions of the M-CHAT must include the copyright at the bottom (©1999 Robins, Fein, & Barton). No modifications can be made to items or instructions without permission from the authors.
(2) The M-CHAT must be used in its entirety. There is no evidence that using a subset of items will be valid.
(3) Parties interested in reproducing the M-CHAT in print (e.g., a book or journal article) or electronically (e.g., as part of digital medical records or software packages) must contact Diana Robins to request permission (drobins@gsu.edu).

Instructions for Use

The M-CHAT is validated for screening toddlers between 16 and 30 months of age, to assess risk for autism spectrum disorders (ASD). The M-CHAT can be administered and scored as part of a well-child check-up, and also can be used by specialists or other professionals to assess risk for ASD. The primary goal of the M-CHAT was to maximize sensitivity, meaning to detect as many cases of ASD as possible. Therefore, there is a high false positive rate, meaning that not all children who score at risk for ASD will be diagnosed with ASD. To address this, we have developed a structured follow-up interview for use in conjunction with the M-CHAT; it is available at the two websites listed above. Users should be aware that even with the follow-up questions, a significant number of the children who fail the M-CHAT will not be diagnosed with an ASD; however, these children are at risk for other developmental disorders or delays, and therefore, evaluation is warranted for any child who fails the screening.

The M-CHAT can be scored in less than two minutes. Scoring instructions can be downloaded from www.mchatscreen.com or www.firstsigns. org. We also have developed a scoring template, which is available on these websites; when printed on an overhead transparency and laid over the completed M-CHAT, it facilitates scoring. Please note that minor differences in printers may cause your scoring template not to line up exactly with the printed M-CHAT.

Children who fail 3 or more items total or 2 or more critical items (particularly if these scores remain elevated after the follow-up interview) should be referred for diagnostic evaluation by a specialist trained to evaluate ASD in very young children. In addition, children for whom there are physician, parent, or other professional's concerns about ASD should be referred for evaluation, given that it is unlikely for any screening instrument to have 100% sensitivity.

M-CHAT

Please fill out the following about how your child usually is. Please try to answer every question. If the behavior is rare (e.g., you've seen it once or twice), please answer as if the child does not do it.

1. Does your child enjoy being swung, bounced on your knee, etc.? Yes No
2. Does your child take an interest in other children? Yes No
3. Does your child like climbing on things, such as up stairs? Yes No
4. Does your child enjoy playing peek-a-boo/hide-and-seek? Yes No
5. Does your child ever pretend, for example, to talk on the phone or take care of a doll or pretend other things? Yes No
6. Does your child ever use his/her index finger to point, to ask for something? Yes No
7. Does your child ever use his/her index finger to point, to indicate interest in something? Yes No

8. Can your child play properly with small toys (e.g., cars or blocks) without just mouthing, fiddling or dropping them? Yes No

9. Does your child ever bring objects over to you (parent) to show you something? Yes No

10. Does your child look you in the eye for more than a second or two? Yes No

11. Does your child ever seem oversensitive to noise? (e.g., plugging ears) Yes No

12. Does your child smile in response to your face or your smile? Yes No

13. Does your child imitate you? (e.g., you make a face—will your child imitate it?) Yes No

14. Does your child respond to his/her name when you call? Yes No

15. If you point at a toy across the room, does your child look at it? Yes No

16. Does your child walk? Yes No

17. Does your child look at things you are looking at? Yes No

18. Does your child make unusual finger movements near his/her face? Yes No

19. Does your child try to attract your attention to his/her own activity? Yes No

20. Have you ever wondered if your child is deaf? Yes No

21. Does your child understand what people say? Yes No

22. Does your child sometimes stare at nothing or wander with no purpose? Yes No

23. Does your child look at your face to check your reaction when faced with something unfamiliar? Yes No

Source: © 1999 Diana Robins, Deborah Fein, & Marianne Barton

Laboratory Testing in ASD

THE FOLLOWING describes common laboratory tests your doctor may suggest if your child has been diagnosed with ASD. These provide a basic assessment for many of the medical concerns you and your doctor may have following your child's thorough medical evaluation. If an abnormality is discovered, further testing, consultation as well as treatment may be necessary.

Screen For:	Blood Tests (*urine if specified)	Other Tests
General Health (including nutrition)	Complete blood count Chemistry panel (electrolytes, liver, pancreas, GI, kidney function, uric acid screens) Thyroid panel (T4, TSH, free T4) Iron Ferritin Minerals (calcium, magnesium) Vitamin levels (B6, B12, D) Heavy metals (such as mercury, aluminum, copper, zinc) *Urinalysis	Hearing ■ Audiology or brainstem auditory evoked response (BAER) Vision Extended Sleep EEG (generally overnight) Specific testing as indicated such as: ■ GI testing (see Appendix 5) ■ Imaging (CAT scan, MRI) ■ Polysomnography sleep study
Genetic/ Metabolic	Chromosome karyotyping and/or CGH microarray Fragile X DNA MECP2 (girls) Plasma amino acids *Urine organic acids	
Mitochondrial	Pyruvate Lactate (lactic acid) Carnitine	
Allergy	IgE IgE RAST for specific antigens (food, inhalants, environmental as needed)	
Immunology	Sedimentation rate Immunoglobulin A, M, G (and G subsets) T cell subsets panel	

Double Syndromes Most Commonly Found in Children with ASD

Cause	Associated Syndrome
Genetic/Metabolic	Angelman syndrome
	Duchenne muscular dystrophy
	Fragile X
	Moebius syndrome
	Neurofibromatosis
	Phenylketonuria
	PTEN Hamartoma Tumor syndrome
	Purine autism
	Rett syndrome
	Smith-Lemli-Opitz syndrome
	Tuberous Sclerosis
	Williams syndrome
	15Q duplication
	16P duplication or deletion
Infectious	Congenital rubella
	Cytomegalovirus virus infection
	Herpes simplex encephalitis
Toxic	Fetal alcohol syndrome
Other	Mitochondrial disorders

Evaluating and Treating Common GI Issues in ASD

Disorder	Usual Cause	Typical Evaluation	Potential Treatment
Gastroesophageal Reflux Disease (GERD)	Acid reflux into esophagus	Upper GI X-ray Esophageal PH testing Esophagoscopy with biopsy	Behavior changes Medication
Diarrhea	Infections	Stool exam for blood/white blood cell smear Culture for bacteria/parasites	Specific to diagnosis Probiotic as needed
	Disaccharide malabsorption	Hydrogen breath analysis Biopsy and enzyme analysis	Eliminate lactose (lactose deficient) Specific treatment for other enzyme deficiencies
Constipation	Constipation (+/- over-flow diarrhea)	Exam Abdominal X-ray	Constipation diet Fiber supplement (e.g., MiraLAX)
	Dietary and motility issues	Diet history Exam Abdominal X-ray	
Irritable Bowel Syndrome (IBS)	Motility dysregulation	History Physical exam	Specific Carbohydrate Diet Medication
Celiac Disease	Inflammatory/malabsorption (toxic effect of gluten)	Celiac antibody panel Intestinal biopsy	Gluten-free diet
Inflammatory Bowel Disease (IBD)	Inflammation of the bowel wall	Sedimentation rate Blood tests for malabsorption Colonoscopy and biopsy	Specific to diagnosis
Food Allergy	Reaction to specific dietary protein	IgE specific antibody testing (blood/skin)	Food elimination

Medications Used for Children with ASD

WITH so many medications on the market and new ones continually being introduced, it is no wonder that parents are confused. The following summary of medications that might be useful in treating ASD symptoms is more practical than academic, providing an overview of a range of choices. The categories and medications listed are currently available, but not every available medication is listed here. Note that while new medications are in development that will subsequently be used in ASD, they will most likely fit into one of these existing categories. This is not a complete list of all known effects, side effects or potential drug interactions that might occur. It is meant to guide you in your discussion with your child's doctor. I recommend *Straight Talk about Psychiatric Medications for Kids,* by Timothy Wilens, M.D., for a more thorough review of medications.

Anxiety-Breaking Medications

Benzodiazepines exert their antianxiety effects by regulating the neurotransmitter known as GABA (short for "gamma-aminobutyric acid"). GABA is a calming neurotransmitter, and therefore, the more of it that you have, the calmer you feel. These medications increase the activity of GABA in the brain, instantly reducing anxiety and facilitating sleep. They can be taken safely, as needed on a periodic basis or on a regular basis. The list of these agents is long and includes, among others:

- Librium (chlordiazepoxide)
- Valium (diazepam)
- Serax (oxazepam)
- Ativan (lorazepam)
- Xanax (alprazolam)
- Klonopin (clonazepam)

- Ambien (zolpidem)
- Halcion (triazolam)
- Restoril (temazepam)

When used appropriately, benzodiazepines do not have serious side effects. Sedation and drowsiness often accompany short-term use, which can make them less ideal for children with ASD because engagement and attention are so crucial for their sustained interactions. However, for acute anxiety attacks these medications may give a child or adolescent much needed relief. Occasionally children, especially those with ASD, have an opposite response to these compounds and may get agitated rather than calmed. Therefore, if you choose to try a benzodiazepine, introduce it slowly and monitor its effect carefully, as you would with all these medications.

BuSpar (buspirone), a non-benzodiazepine, can also be effective for treating anxiety, especially in ASD. This particular compound works on serotonin and is sometimes used in conjunction with SSRIs for anxiety. Although side effects are less than with benzodiazepines, they do include sedation and disinhibition, as well as nausea, headaches and dizziness. See Chapter 20 for a discussion of SSRIs and their use for reducing anxiety levels.

Stimulants and Nonstimulants (for Attention Issues)

Stimulant medications have been widely used to treat autism and are likewise typically utilized in the treatment of attention deficit disorder (ADD/ADHD) and depression. These medications primarily increase the levels of norepinephrine and dopamine in selected areas of the brain and work by exerting an effect on the release of neurotransmitters from neurons.

Typically these medications are stimulating, but they may act paradoxically as well: if neurotransmitters are depleted, they have, for many, a calming and focused effect, with feelings of being in control. Stimulants work quickly: on average, they exert their effects within a half hour of being taken. The length of action of these drugs varies by compound, but currently they are rarely effective for more than twelve hours. A 2009 study using Ritalin (methylphenidate) for children with ASD showed significant positive effects on joint attention, self-regulation and mood, in addition to improvement in hyperactivity.

Ritalin (methylphenidate), Adderall (amphetamine), Dexedrine (dextroamphetamine) and a number of other brand-name products from this group are available. Some of these preparations are available in slow-release forms (like Concerta, Focalin and Adderall XR) and are, therefore, longer acting than the typically shorter-acting original versions of these drugs. Tolerance and addiction are real possibilities with these drugs, although in the experience of most doctors who regularly treat ASD and ADD/ADHD, addiction is infrequent when these drugs are prescribed for these disorders. A newer drug, Vyvanse (lisdexamfetamine dimesylate), is an inactive substance until chemically modified by the liver, thus decreasing its habit-forming potential. Side effects of these drugs include hyperexcitability, an increased pulse rate, insomnia, loss of appetite, mania, anxiety and tics.

Strattera (atomoxetine) is a non-stimulant medication for ADHD (especially when accompanied by tics and/or anxiety). It works to improve norepinepherine availability and has very little abuse potential. The onset of action of Strattera is much slower than that of the stimulants. Positive effects might require two to three weeks to become evident. This drug, like the stimulants, appears to bring about a general improvement in functioning. It is also recommended for dyslexia, dyspraxia, clumsiness and depression. Although side effects tend to be minimal, both fatigue and hyperexcitability have been seen with Strattera.

Antidepressants

A huge array of depression-fighting medications are available, any of which might relieve some aspect of ASD. It should be noted that these drugs all present some risk of increasing suicidal behavior, especially in children. Recent data shows that in 2007, following a change in the warnings on SSRI prescriptions of the potential for suicidal behavior, there was a 30 percent decrease in the use of these medications; however, there was also an increase in teenage suicides. I believe the benefits of these medications, especially for children with ASD, far outweigh their risks.

Selective Serotonin Reuptake Inhibitor (SSRI) Antidepressants

Selective serotonin reuptake inhibitor (SSRI) antidepressants include Prozac (fluoxetine), Paxil (paroxetine), Zoloft (sertraline), Luvox (fluvoxamine), Celexa (citalopram) and Lexapro (escitalopram). These popular medications have significant antidepressant effects and typically reduce and prevent anxiety. They work by blocking the reuptake of the neurotransmitter serotonin back into the presynaptic neuron. This blocking increases the availability of the neurotransmitter in the synapse. For ASD, these medications can be effective at improving compulsive behaviors as well as obsessive, repetitive thinking. The downside is that these drugs can cause neurological side effects, such as tremors—although this is a rare occurrence. More common side effects are nausea, weight gain, a feeling of personality numbness, sexual dysfunction, sleep problems and hyperactivity. These drugs can precipitate manic behavior as well and must be used cautiously in families with a history of manic-depressive (bipolar) disorder. If your child uses an SSRI, he must be observed carefully for subtle signs of increased brain activation and irritability, as these can be early signs of possible mania. These signs are decreased attention, decreased engagement, increased activity and irritable mood. If these symptoms occur, he should be weaned from the medication. Consult with your doctor on how best to do this.

The various SSRIs mentioned above differ from each other with regard to the time required for them to reach satisfactory blood levels and have an effect (for example, Prozac might take weeks; Lexapro several days). Likewise, Prozac is a much longer-acting drug than other SSRIs. The length of action, frequency of side effects and degree of serotonin effects vary with these medications and the response to these drugs is very individual. What works for one person might not work well for another. In general, due to the varying responses different people have to SSRIs, more than one of these drugs might have to be tried before determining if this category of medication is effective for controlling the target symptom.

Tricyclic Antidepressants (TCAs)

Tricyclic antidepressants include Tofranil (imipramine), Elavil (amitriptyline), Norpramin (desipramine), Aventyl (nortriptyline) and Vivactil (protriptyline), among others. These older drugs are equally as effective as the SSRIs in relieving anxiety as well as depression in adults (but are not always effective for treating depression in children). They are especially useful with panic and social anxiety. This group of medications, like the SSRIs, block the reuptake of serotonin back into the presynaptic neuron, thus increasing overall serotonin availability for neurotransmission. The downside of these medications, like all families of antidepressants, is that they can cause manic behavior. Additionally, they can cause dryness of the mouth and other mucous membranes, drowsiness, lowered blood pressure with feelings of faintness, weight gain, sexual dysfunction, cardiac rate increases and cardiac rhythm disturbances. It is mandatory to have cardiac EKGs, observing for possible rhythm disturbances and other cardiac electrical disturbances, when taking these medications. For this reason, many doctors avoid this class of medication unless others have been ineffective.

Anafranil (clomipramine) is technically a tricyclic, but it is in a class all by itself. It is the most effective medication developed to date for reducing obsessive-compulsive symptoms, which are prevalent with ASD. It has all the significant side effects noted above with the other tricyclics (which may limit its frequent use) but remains indispensable for many people who are driven by repetitive thoughts and behaviors and who are not responding to an SSRI.

Serotonin Norepinephrine Reuptake Inhibitors (SNRIs)

Serotonin norepinephrine reuptake inhibitors (SNRIs) are likewise reuptake blockers that are used to treat depression. These dual-acting antidepressants increase the synaptic availability of both serotonin and norepinephrine and are used to treat depression and anxiety, as well as obsessive-compulsive issues. The frequently used drugs Effexor (venlafaxine), Pristiq (desvenla-faxine) and Cymbalta (duloxetine) have a similar profile to the SSRIs but, at least theoretically, are more activating and stimulating. The side effects of these agents are similar to those of the SSRIs. These medications are reputedly effective in increasing the spectrum of response. In other words, a greater number of patients might respond favorably to these agents as compared to what you would expect from an SSRI alone. On the other hand, studies of the dual-acting drugs versus the single-acting SSRIs show mixed results. In fact, it is frequently necessary to combine an SSRI with an SNRI. Common side effects of this family of medications are dryness of the mucous membranes, urinary retention and drowsiness.

Norepinephrine and Dopamine Reuptake Inhibitors (NDRIs)

These dual-acting medications are also reuptake blockers that are used to treat depression. The only medication in this family is bupropion (Wellbutrin). Bupropion is FDA approved to help with smoking cessation in adults (it's called Zyban). Bupropion is also helpful for ADHD and depression and can be successfully used in depressed children with mood swings who have experienced behavioral problems while taking another medication, especially an SSRI. On the downside, NDRIs can increase irritability, cause insomnia, decrease appetite and worsen tics and manic behavior. Irritability often signals that the dose of medication needs to be reduced.

Atypical Antidepressants

Trazodone (Desyrel) is an atypical antidepressant: it does not fit any of the above categories. It is a relatively short-acting compound that can be used to treat depression, anxiety and, most especially, sleep problems in children with ASD. Because of its sedating properties, it is not used as frequently as the SSRIs. However, it tends to give very restorative sleep, and because it has about an eight- to twelve-hour length of action, it can be used quite successfully to treat sleep disorders. Common side effects, other than sedation, include dry mouth, constipation and confusion at high doses. In males, however, trazodone has been infrequently noted to cause priapism (painful sustained erections), limiting its usefulness.

Remeron (mirtazapine) is a unique antidepressant with serotonergenic activity. However, it too has sleep-promoting effects and is often used in adolescents with depression and/or difficulty going to sleep. It has also recently been used for treating anxiety in children with ASD. Side effects include excess sedation and upset stomach.

MAO Inhibitors (MAOIs)

MAO inhibitors (MAOIs) are the oldest of the antidepressants. They are among the most effective antidepressants and are useful for controlling social anxiety, agoraphobia and separation anxiety as well as OCD. This family of medications includes Nardil (phenelzine) and Parnate (tranylcypromine). These medications reduce the brain's ability to break down three neurotransmitters, thereby increasing the levels of serotonin, norepinephrine and dopamine available for neurotransmission. MAOIs are the only triple-acting antidepressants. However, the use of these drugs is limited because of their potential to interact unfavorably with other medications, and taking them requires dietary restrictions (especially problematic in children with ASD). Other adverse effects in children include blood pressure swings when changing position, weight gain, drowsiness and dizziness. Most physicians treating ASD will not use an MAO inhibitor as a first choice for treatment due to the significant side effects.

Mood Stabilizers

These medications help stabilize mood swings associated with bipolar disorder (manic depression). In addition, especially in ASD, they may provide help in stabilizing overactivity and aggressiveness, increase frustration tolerance and improve impulse control.

Lithium carbonate, a simple salt compound, is a mainstay in treating bipolar disorder. This drug is in a class all its own. In ASD this natural substance can be used to help reduce behavioral volatility. It appears to work by modulating the inflow and outflow of neurotransmitters in neurons. Using this drug requires blood testing as lithium can have short-term damaging effects on the thyroid gland and, rarely, damaging effects on the kidneys. There is a small variation between therapeutic blood levels and toxicity. I always work closely with a psychiatrist with expertise in managing lithium when it is required for a patient in my practice.

Anticonvulsants

Anticonvulsants, or antiseizure medications, are designed for treating various forms of seizures. They also help stabilize mood by decreasing the amount of abnormal firing of nerve impulses in the emotional centers of the brain. In ASD these medications not only are used to treat seizures but they also are used to decrease volatility of mood, temper, anger and impulsivity. A partial list of these drugs includes Depakote (valproic acid), Tegretol (carbamazepine), Trileptal (oxcarbazepine), Neurontin (gabapentin), Lamictal (lamotrigine), Topamax (topirimate) and Kepra (levetiracetam).

The anticonvulsants vary greatly in their side effects and, depending on the compound used, require close monitoring. Your doctor will review these side effects with you if your child begins treatment with a specific compound. Two of the agents frequently used in my practice are Depakote and Trileptal. Depakote is a primary choice for seizures or subclinical seizures, as well as for controlling mood elevations. However, this medication can have serious effects on the liver and bone marrow, requiring frequent blood monitoring for liver and bone marrow function, as well as medication blood levels. Trileptal is a new formulation of Tegretol, which has a long history of use in seizure disorders. Trileptal is also used to treat bipolar disorder. It rarely affects liver function, but may reduce the number of white blood cells needed to fight infection. Infrequent blood testing is sometimes recommended for medication blood levels, as well as to assess white blood cell count.

Antihypertensives

Antihypertensives were originally developed to treat high blood pressure. They are also effective in children for treating ADD, tics and Tourette syndrome (a tic disorder characterized by physical and vocal tics), as well as many of the aggressive behaviors noted in children with ASD.

Alpha2-Adrenergic Agonists

Alpha2-adrenergic agonists are antihypertensives and include the medications Catapres (clonidine), Tenex (guanfacine) and, the newer long-acting form of guanfacine, Intuniv. They act by altering the release of norepinepherine into the synapse and improving neuron-to-neuron connection. Alpha2 agonists are often used as second-line medications in ADD/ADHD treatment. They increase attention while decreasing hyperactivity and distractibility. They have proven most effective when used either in a primary tic/attention disorder, such as Tourette syndrome, or in a secondary tic disorder, often associated with stimulant use in ADD/ADHD treatment. They are beneficial in controlling symptoms of panic disorder, as well. These medications are calming and effectively facilitate sleep. The most common side effect with these drugs is hypotension (low blood pressure) with faintness and sedation. The latter makes these effective medications for ASD-related sleep disorders.

Beta-Adrenergic

Beta-adrenergic blockers are widely used to treat hypertension, glaucoma and cardiac rhythm disturbances. Inderal (propranolol) and Tenormin (atenolol) are two very commonly used drugs in this family. The beta-blockers are better known by their generic names as they are older medications. Like alpha-blockers, beta-blockers effect norepinephrine or adrenalin neurotransmitter receptor sites. Beta-blockers block the effects that most of us associate with adrenaline and slow the pulse rate, lower blood pressure and generally reduce activity and reactivity. In ASD, beta-blockers have a leveling effect, an antianxiety effect and reduce emotional hyperreactivity. Side effects include hypotension, bradycardia (slow heart rate), lethargy and possible depression. These medications can precipitate an asthma attack and should generally be avoided in patients with a history of asthma. They might be a factor in patients developing Type 2 diabetes.

Antipsychotics

This large group of medications was developed to treat schizophrenia and later became a mainstay in the control of bipolar disorder. They are frequently used to treat ASD. The group can be divided into the "older" and "newer" drugs.

The older medications (antipsychotics) brought about a major change in the twentieth-century treatment of schizophrenia, a severe condition, which is quite set apart from ASD but which includes some behaviors that are seen in ASD. (In fact, "autistic" thinking and functioning represent one of the four hallmark signs of schizophrenia.) The antipsychotic medications include Thorazine (chlorpromazine), Stelazine (trifluoperazine), Mellaril (thioridazine), Navane (thiothixine), Loxitane (loxapine), Haldol (haloperidol) and Prolixin (flufenazine). These drugs appear to work by regulating and typically blocking the action of the neurotransmitter dopamine, decreasing the amount of dopamine available for neurotransmission. Antipsychotic medications can reduce or eliminate delusions and hallucinations, other hallmark signs and symptoms of schizophrenia. When used to treat ASD, this group of medications can help normalize a variety of behaviors, greatly reduce anxiety and typically facilitate sleep. The downside is that these medications frequently cause serious side effects, which include muscle spasms, Parkinson's disease–like symptoms and tremors. These medications may also cause a condition known as tardive dyskinesia, which causes repetitive involuntary movements of the mouth, face and other areas of the body that may be non-reversible in some. Other side effects may include drowsiness, weight gain, drops in blood pressure and sexual dysfunction. Another rare but severe reaction to antipsychotic medications is neuroleptic malignant syndrome (NMS). This life-threatening reaction to the medications includes confusion, sweating and severe muscle tightness along with blood-pressure and pulse instability. If this reaction occurs, seek immediate medical attention.

The newer medications, known as atypicals (short for "atypical neuro-leptics"), are in some ways more effective than the older antipsychotics and generally appear to be much safer. The list includes Risperdal (risperidone), Invega (paliperidone), Zyprexa (olanzapine), Abilify (aripiprazole), Seroquel (quetiapine) and Geodon (ziprasidone). The atypicals are currently being used more frequently than the older medications. They work in a similar way to that of the older antipsychotic medications, although with fewer side effects. These drugs can cause weight gain, drowsiness, an increase in blood sugar, cardiac rhythm disturbances, sexual dysfunction and, rarely, tardive dyskinesia (see above).

Risperdal (risperidone), an atypical neuroleptic, requires special mention as it is the first medication to receive FDA labeling for the treatment of autism. Specific indications for its use include aggression and irritability. Initial studies of risperidone showed reduced repetitive behaviors, aggression, anxiety, irritability and depression in adults with ASD. A large randomized, double-blind, placebo-controlled trial in children with ASD confirmed that treatment with risperidone for eight weeks significantly improved irritability ratings in the treated group. These improved ratings translated into decreased aggression, decreased self-injurious behavior, decreased stereotypical behavior and decreased mania. Documented side effects included initial sedation, which improved as the study continued, and weight gain. No movement disorders (tics) occurred in this study population, although it is a rare but significant possibility. Abilify is one of the newest atypical neuroleptics. It has a complicated mechanism of action, affecting both dopamine and serotonin in differing ways depending on dosage. When effective, it is excellent at mood stabilization and may greatly improve social interaction. In a 2009 study, children and adolescents with ASD who had irritability and were given Abilify showed significant improvement. The medication is safe and well tolerated and has FDA approval for use in ASD. Side effects include possible interactions with other medications, especially the SSRIs, as well as the more typical side effects related to this category of medication.

Other Medications

These medications do not specifically fit into the previous categories. However, they have been useful in treating ASD and some of the associated issues.

Aricept (donepezil), Exelon (rivastigmine) and Reminyl (galantamine) have been shown to have mild to moderate usefulness in treating Alzheimer's disease. This group works by facilitating the neurotransmitter acetylcholine and may also be useful in treating ASD, as it tends to have positive effects on cognitive functioning, concentration and learning. The brain manufactures acetylcholine and likewise breaks down this neurotransmitter through the action of an enzyme known as acetylcholinesterase. By inhibiting acetylcholinesterase, these medications allow for the accumulation of acetylcholine, a neurotransmitter that is crucial to memory function, attention and learning. Side effects tend to be minimal but include occasional gastrointestinal discomfort, diarrhea and increased salivation; at higher dosages, irritability and mania. Aricept use has yet to be studied extensively in children. However, initial reports on children with ASD who were treated with Aricept have shown some improved receptive and expressive language skills as well as improved motor planning.

Namenda (memantine) is another Alzheimer's medication that may prove useful in treating ASD. Open clinical treatment trials have shown positive effects of Namenda on cognition, learning, focus and, surprisingly, motor sequencing. For children with ASD this medication modulates glutamate. Glutamate is a neurotransmitter, which can act like a stimulant, although this drug is not a stimulant per se. Side effects tend to be minimal.

Naltrexone is an opioid receptor antagonist used primarily in the area of addiction medicine. Marketed under the names Revia and Vivitrol, this drug blocks the neuronal receptor sites for narcotics and, therefore, halts the action of narcotics and internally produced endorphins (natural forms of narcotics). In ASD, naltrexone exerts a calming, mood-leveling effect and is used occasionally. Side effects can take the form of GI tract discomfort, drowsiness and, very rarely, liver problems.

L-methylfolate, marketed under the name Deplin, is a prescription dose of the B vitamin folate (better known in its synthetic form as folic acid). The brain requires folate in order to manufacture monoamines, which include the key neurotransmitters dopamine, serotonin and norepinephrine. L-methylfolate has been approved as supportive therapy in treating depression, as this vitamin is critical to the balance and production of enzymes and neurotransmitters, as well as to the process of methylation. While a person's diet might contain plenty of folic acid, there can be problems getting the vital chemical to pass into the brain. Deplin more readily passes into the brain, crossing what is known as the blood–brain barrier and thereby allowing for the increased manufacture of the above-mentioned neurotransmitters. Deplin can bring about an increase in energy levels, can brighten mood and can probably enhance learning. The drug tends to have minimal side effects, including slight irritability.

Treatment Response Chart and Sample Treatment Response Chart

TREATMENT RESPONSE Charts that document your child's progress can be extremely helpful in determining his next steps. They can be utilized for all treatments and are particularly necessary for medication trials. The period length is determined by how long it takes to see results once starting the treatment (such as daily, weekly, depending on expected results).

Treatment Response Chart

Child's Name: _____

Medication: _____ Dose: _____ Frequency: _____

Date Started: _____ Period Length: _____

Target Behavior	Baseline	Period 1	Period 2	Period 3	Period 4	Period 5
_____						
_____						
_____						
_____						
_____						
Side Effect						
_____						
_____						
_____						

In the boxes to the right of target behavior and side effect, score baseline (before treatment started) and each period behavior on a scale of 1 to 5 (1=best/5=worst).

Person Completing Form: _____ Relationship to Child: _____

Locations Observed: _____ School _____ Home _____ Therapy

Overall Assessment of Treatment Trial: _____
_____
_____
_____
_____
_____
_____
_____
_____
_____

This is a sample chart for John Doe's five-week medication trial with Lexapro.

Sample Treatment Response Chart

Child's Name: _John Doe_

Medication: _Lexapro_   **Dose:** _5 mg_   **Frequency:** _Daily_

Date Started: _2-1-2010_   **Period Length:** _1 week_

Target Behavior	Baseline	Period 1	Period 2	Period 3	Period 4	Period 5
Attention	4	4	3	3	3	3
Social Engagement	4	4	3	3	2	2
Transition Difficulty	3	3	3	2	2	2
Perseveration	3	3	3	3	3	2
Anxiety	4	3	2	2	2	2
Side Effect						
Sleep Difficulty	1	1	1	1	1	1
Aggression	1	1	1	1	1	1
Appetite Changes	None	None	None	None	None	None

In the boxes to the right of target behavior and side effect, score baseline (before treatment started) and each period behavior on a scale of 1 to 5 (1=best/5=worst).

Person Completing Form: _Jane Doe_   **Relationship to Child:** _Mom_

Locations Observed: __X__ School __X__ Home __X__ Therapy

Overall Assessment of Treatment Trial: _Excellent response. Johnny had a very good month with increased social engagement. He was much calmer and much more willing to enter into family life. Teachers also commented on his eagerness to participate with his peers in the classroom and on the playground. The whole family is encouraged and looking forward to next steps._

Resources

For Further Reading

Ariel, Cindy N., and Robert A. Naseef, eds. *Voices from the Spectrum: Parents, Grandparents, Siblings, People with Autism, and Professionals Share Their Wisdom.* Philadelphia: Jessica Kingsley Publishers, 2006.

Bailey, Cindy. *Going to the Dentist, A Picture Social Skills Story Book.* New York: DRL Books, 2002.

Baker, Jed. *Social Skills Picture Book for High School and Beyond.* Arlington, TX: Future Horizons, 2006.

Chez, Michael G., M.D., *Autism and Its Medical Management: A Guide for Parents and Professionals.* Philadelphia: Jessica Kingsley Publishers, 2009.

Christopher, William, and Barbara Christopher. *Mixed Blessings: TV's "Father Mulcahy" and His Real-Life Family Share Their Story of Raising a Very Special Child.* New York: Avon Books, 1990.

Donnallan, Anne M., and Martha R. Leary. *Movement Differences and Diversity in Autism/Mental Retardation: Appreciating and Accommodating People with Communication and Behavior Challenges.* Pacific Beach, CA: DRI Press, 1995.

Firestone, Barbara. *Autism Heroes: Portraits of Families Meeting the Challenge.* Philadelphia: Jessica Kingsley Publishers, 2007.

Furth, Hans G., and Harry Wachs. *Thinking Goes to School.* New York: Oxford University Press, 1975.

Grandin, Temple. *Developing Talents: Careers for Individuals with Asperger Syndrome and High-Functioning Autism.* Updated, expanded edition. Overland Park, KS: Autism Asperger Publishing Company, 2008.

Grandin, Temple. *Thinking in Pictures.* New York: Vintage, 2006.

Gray, Carol. *The New Social Story Book: Illustrated Edition.* Arlington, TX: Future Horizons, 2000.

Greenspan, Stanley I., M.D., and J. Salmon. *Playground Politics: Understanding the Emotional Life of Your School-Age Child.* New York: Da Capo Press, 1994.

Greenspan, Stanley I., M.D., and Serena Wieder, Ph.D. *The Child with Special Needs.* New York: Perseus, 1998.

Greenspan, Stanley I., M.D., and Serena Wieder, Ph.D. *Engaging Autism.* New York: Da Capo Press, 2006.

Hall, Elaine, with Elizabeth Kaye. *Now I See The Moon: A Mother, A Son, A Miracle.* New York: HarperStudio, 2010.

Harris, Sandra L. *Siblings of Children with Autism: A Guide for Families.* 2nd ed. Bethesda, MD: Woodbine House, 2003.

Harpur, J., M. Lawlor, and M. Fitzgerald. *Succeeding in College with Asperger Syndrome.* London: Jessica Kingsley Publishers, 2004.

Heighway, S., and S. Webster. *STARS: A Social Skills Training Guide for Teaching Assertiveness, Relationship Skills, and Sexual Awareness.* Arlington, TX: Future Horizons, 2009.

Iverson, Portia. *Strange Son: Two Mothers, Two Sons, and the Quest to Unlock the Hidden World of Autism.* New York: Riverhead, 2006.

Kaufman, Miriam, Corey Silverberg, and Fran Odette. *The Ultimate Guide to Sex and Disability.* San Francisco: Cleis Press, 2007.

Kranowitz, Carol. *The Out of Sync Child.* Rev. ed. New York: Perigee, 2006.

Kranowitz, Carol. *The Out of Sync Child Has Fun.* New York: Perigee, 2003.

Lord, Catherine, and James P. McGee, eds. *Educating Children with Autism.* Washington, D.C.: National Academies Press, 2001.

Miller, Lucy Jane, and Doris A. Fuller. *Sensational Kids: Hope and Help for Children with Sensory Processing Disorder.* New York: Perigee, 2007.

Morrell, Maureen F., and Ann Palmer. *Parenting Across the Autism Spectrum.* London: Jessica Kingsley Publishers, 2006.

Pavlides, Merope. *Animal-Assisted Interventions for Individuals with Autism.* Philadelphia: Jessica Kingsley Publishers, 2008.

Prizan, Barry M., et al. *The SCERTS Model: A Comprehensive Educational Approach for Children with Autism Spectrum Disorders.* Baltimore: Brookes Publishing, 2005.

Siegel, Lawrence M. *The Complete IEP Guide: How to Advocate for Your Special Ed Child.* 5th ed. Berkeley, CA: Nolo Press, 2007.

Shumaker, Laura. *A Regular Guy: Growing Up with Autism.* Landscape Press, 2008.

Sicile-Kira, Chantal. *Adolescents on the Autism Spectrum: A Parent's Guide to the Cognitive, Social, Physical, and Transition Needs of Teenagers with Autism Spectrum Disorders.* New York: Perigee, 2006.

Stacey, Patricia. *The Boy Who Loved Windows: Opening the Heart and Mind of a Child Threatened with Autism.* Philadelphia: Da Capo Press, 2003.

Vitorini, Candace, and Sara Boyer-Quick. *Joey Goes to the Dentist.* Philadelphia: Jessica Kingsley Publishers, 2007.

Wieder, Serena, and Harry Wachs. *Hidden in Plain Sight: Visual-Spatial Challenges in Autism and Learning Difficulties.* Bethesda: ICDL Press, 2011.

Wilens, Timothy, M.D. *Straight Talk about Psychiatric Medications for Kids.* New York: The Guilford Press, 2008.

Williams, Donna. *Nobody Nowhere.* Philadelphia: Jessica Kingsley Publishers, 1998.

Williams, Donna. *Somebody, Somewhere: Breaking Free from the World of Autism.* New York: Three Rivers Press, 1995.

Wiseman, Nancy. *The First Year: Autism Spectrum Disorders: An Essential Guide for the Newly Diagnosed Child.* Philadelphia: Da Capo Press, 2009.

Wolf, L. E., J. T. Brown, and G. R. K. Bork. *Students with Asperger Syndrome: A Guide for College Personnel.* Overland Park, KS: Autism Asperger Publishing Company, 2003.

Sources for Books on ASD, Autism and More

The Autism Society of North Carolina Bookstore
Established in 1988 in response to parent requests for information on autism spectrum disorder (ASD).
www.autismbookstore.com

Special Needs Project (a unique disability bookstore)
Books, videos, DVDs and related items about mental and physical disabilities for parents, professionals, educators, family members and persons with a disability—especially autism.
www.specialneeds.com

The Future Horizons Bookstore
Books, DVDs and conferences on autism and Asperger's syndrome.
www.fhautism.com

Videos, DVDs, Films

Autism Is a World
A short-subject documentary by and about a young woman with autism who uses supported communication.
www.cnn.com/CNN/Programs/presents/index.autism.world.html

Autism: The Musical
Follows five children with autism as they prepare, rehearse and perform in a musical production.
www.autismthemusical.com

Autistic-Like: Graham's Story
Made by Graham's father, this film explores the family's quest for a diagnosis and answers on how to best help their son.
www.autisticlike.com

DIR/Floortime Model
Training DVDs that explain the DIR/Floortime model created by Stanley I. Greenspan, M.D., and Serena Wieder.
www.icdl.com

Organizations

The American Academy of Pediatrics
Information on the health of children. Includes information on autism screening.
www.aap.org

Asperger Syndrome Coalition of the United States/OASIS @ MAAP
Provides articles; educational resources; links to local, national and international support groups; sources of professional help; lists of camps and

schools; conference information; recommended reading; and moderated support message boards.
www.asperger.org

The Autism Society of America
Seeks to improve the lives of all affected by autism by raising public awareness about the day-to-day issues faced by people on the spectrum, advocating for appropriate services for individuals across the life span and providing the latest information regarding treatment, education, research and advocacy.
www.autism-society.org

Autism Speaks
Funds global biomedical research into the causes, prevention, treatment and cure of autism; raises public awareness about autism and its effects on individuals, families and society; and seeks to bring hope to all who deal with the hardships of this disorder. Autism Genetic Resource Exchange (AGRE), Autism Treatment Network (ATN), Clinical Trials Networks (CTN) and Autism Votes are sponsored by Autism Speaks.
www.autismspeaks.org
www.autismspeaks.org/science/programs/atp
www.agre.org
www.autismvotes.org

First Signs
Dedicated to educating parents and professionals about autism and related disorders.
www.firstsigns.org

The Interactive Autism Network
Facilitates scientific research and empowers autism community leaders to advocate for improved services and resources. In addition, anyone impacted by an ASD can become part of IAN's online community to stay informed about autism research.
www.ianproject.org

The Interdisciplinary Council on Developmental and Learning Disorders
Founded by Stanley I. Greenspan and Serena Wieder, the Interdisciplinary Council on Developmental and Learning Disorders (ICDL) has been a pioneer in its work to advance the identification, prevention and treatment of developmental and learning disorders.
www.icdl.com

The International Rett Syndrome Foundation
Provides information, programs and services, as well as funds research for treatment and a cure.
www.rettsyndrome.org

The International Society for Autism Research (INSAR)
Membership-based organization that promotes autism research.
www.autism-insar.org

LifeSPEAKS Poetry Therapy
A poetry workshop for mothers of children with special needs. A member of the National Association for Poetry Therapy (www.poetrytherapy.org).
www.lifespeakspoetrytherapy.com

The National Autism Association
The mission of the National Autism Association is to educate and empower families affected by autism and other neurological disorders, while advocating on behalf of those who cannot fight for their own rights.
www.nationalautismassociation.org

The National Autism Center
Resources for families, practitioners and communities.
www.nationalautismcenter.org/about/

The National Fragile X Foundation
Provides support, education, information on research and advocacy for those with Fragile X.
www.fragilex.org

Patient Advocate Foundation
Provides services to patients to remove obstacles to health care.
www.patientadvocate.org

Research Unit on Pediatric Psychopharmacology (RUPP)
The Ohio State University RUPP at the Nisonger Center in Columbus, Ohio, is a group of professionals engaged in pharmacological, psychiatric, behavioral, nutritional and alternative research on children and adolescents with autism spectrum disorders, ADHD and other childhood disorders.
http://psychmed.osu.edu/

The Sensory Processing Disorder Foundation
Information on services, research, education and more.
www.spdfoundation.net

The Tuberous Sclerosis Alliance
Information for individuals, families, health care professionals and researchers.
www.tsalliance.org

Communication and Learning

Ability Hub
Provides information on adaptive equipment, as well as alternative methods that are available for making computers accessible, for those who have disabilities that make using a computer difficult.
www.abilityhub.com

Assistive Chat
AAC for use on iPad, iPhone and iTouch.
http://itunes.apple.com/us/app/assistive_chat/id379891874?mt=8

Augmentative and Alternative Communication (AAC) Devices
Resources and information on communication devices.
www.dynavoxtech.com
www.prentrom.com

The Center for AAC & Autism
Dedicated to building awareness of the power of AAC to change the lives of children with autism and other developmental disabilities, who are challenged by limited spontaneous communication skills.
www.aacandautism.com

Cogmed
A software-based program designed for improved attention.
www.cogmed.com

Conners' Continuous Performance Test II (CPT II)
This test, taken at a computer, evaluates attention problems and treatment usefulness for participants aged six or older.
www.pearsonassessments.com

Fusion
Fusion offers text to speech, word prediction, a large LCD display with adjustable font sizes, math facts practice and a wide variety of other writing supports, all in an easy-to-use, low-cost platform.
www.writerlearning.com/fusion_overview.php

Hippotherapy
The American Hippotherapy Association has information on hippotherapy and a resource for finding therapists listed by state.
www.americanhippotherapyassociation.org

Institute on Communication and Inclusion at Syracuse University
The Institute on Communication and Inclusion (ICI) is a research and training center that is part of the Inclusion Institutes of the School of Education at Syracuse University. The ICI represents a broadened focus developed over the past twenty years, reflecting lines of research, training and public dissemination that focus on school and community inclusion, narratives of disability and ability, and disability rights, as well as research and training on supported communication. Its initiatives stress the important relationship of communication to inclusion.
http://soe.syr.edu/centers_institutes/institute_communication_inclusion/
    default.aspx

Interactive Metronome (IM)
A neuromotor assessment and treatment tool used in therapy to improve motor planning and sequencing.
www.interactivemetronome.com

Lindamood-Bell Learning Processes
Programs that teach reading, spelling, comprehension and expressive language.
www.lindamoodbell.com

The National Academy of Sciences
Information on science and medicine.
www.nationalacademies.org

Neo (AlphaSmart)
Portable keyboard for AAC.
www.neo-direct.com/NEO/default.aspx

The North American Riding for the Handicapped Association (NARHA)
NARHA fosters safe, professional, ethical and therapeutic equine activities through education, communication, research and standards. The association ensures its standards are met through an accreditation process for centers and a certification process for instructors.
www.narha.org

The P.L.A.Y. Project

The P.L.A.Y. (Play and Language for Autistic Youngsters) Project is a community-based, regional autism training and early intervention program dedicated to empowering parents and professionals to implement intensive developmental interventions for young children with autism in the most effective and efficient way.
www.playproject.org

Proloquo2Go

For use with the iPhone, iPad and iPod touch, this product provides a full-featured communication solution for people who have difficulty speaking. It offers natural-sounding text-to-speech voices, up-to-date symbols, powerful automatic conjugations, a default vocabulary of over seven thousand items, full expandability and extreme ease of use.
www.proloquo2go.com

Pyramid Educational Consultants

Information and products for educators and parents of children (and adults) with autism and other related developmental disabilities. Features information on the Picture Exchange Communication System (PECS).
www.pecs-usa.com

Rapid Prompting Method

RPM uses a "Teach-Ask" paradigm for eliciting responses through intensive verbal, auditory, visual and/or tactile prompts. Student responses evolve from picking up answers to pointing, to typing and writing, which reveals students' comprehension, academic abilities and, eventually, conversational skills.
www.halo-soma.org

Scientific Learning Products

Software products to strengthen brain processing and improve literacy. They include Fast ForWord, Progress Tracker and Reading Assistant.
www.scilearn.com

Speak It!

Text-to-speech application.
http://itunes.apple.com/us/app/speak-it-text-to-speech/id379891874?mt=8

The Test of Variables of Attention (T.O.V.A.)

The T.O.V.A. is a computerized test of attention that assists in the screening, diagnosis and treatment monitoring of attention disorders.
www.tovatest.com

Education

The Council of Parent Attorneys and Advocates, Inc. (COPAA)
An organization whose mission is to be a national voice for special education rights and to promote excellence in advocacy.
www.copaa.org/index.html

The Council for Exceptional Children (CEC)
The largest international professional organization dedicated to improving the educational success of individuals with disabilities and/or gifts and talents.
www.cec.sped.org

Families and Advocates Partnership for Education (FAPE)
FAPE is designed to address the information needs of the six million families throughout the country whose children with disabilities receive special education services.
www.fape.org

The Federation for Children with Special Needs (FCSN)
Provides information, support and assistance to parents of children with disabilities.
http://fcsn.org/index.php

Homeschooling
Information about homeschooling requirements.
www.hslda.org/about/

Insurance Help for Autism
Site specific to California but has information that could be helpful in your state.
www.insurancehelpforautism.com

The Individualized Education Plan (IEP)
Each child with special needs is given an Individualized Education Plan (IEP) following an assessment. The IEP outlines the educational goals tailored to his specific abilities and needs.
www.ed.gov/parents/needs/speced/iepguide/index.html

The Individuals with Disabilities Education Act (IDEA)
Aims to ensure that all children receive a free appropriate public education (FAPE) and special services to assist in meeting their educational needs.
http://idea.ed.gov
www.ed.gov/index.jhtml

The Southwest Autism Research and Resource Center (SARRC)
Autism vocational/life skills training.
www.autismcenter.org/Vocational.aspx

Wrightslaw
Information about special education law, education law and advocacy for
children with disabilities.
www.wrightslaw.com

Safety

Autism Risk Management
Autism training and resources for law enforcement, emergency first
responders, parents, educators, care providers and the autism community.
www.autismriskmanagement.com
www.autismsafetyproject.org

My Precious Kid
Child safety products that specifically address the needs of the child
with autism.
www.mypreciouskid.com/child-autism-safety.html

Health and Wellness

Special Care Dentistry Association
An international organization of oral health professionals and other individuals who are dedicated to promoting oral health and well-being for
people with special needs.
www.scdaonline.org

Extreme Sports Camp
Camp and recreational activities for children on the autism spectrum.
www.extremesportscamp.org

The Feingold Diet
A food elimination diet designed to treat hyperactivity.
www.feingold.org

**LEND (The Leadership Education in Neurodevelopmental and
Related Disabilities Program)**
Funded by the Maternal and Child Health Bureau of the Health
Resources and Services Administration in the Department of Health and

Human Services, LEND provides information on a range of resources, including nutrition.
http://nisonger.osu.edu/LEND/resources/nutrition.htm

The Specific Carbohydrate Diet
Eliminates complex carbohydrates from the diet.
www.breakingtheviciouscycle.info

SleepMed
Sleep and EEG diagnostic services.
www.sleepmed.md

Social Issues
Videos that model appropriate social behavior at home, at school and at play.
www.modelmekids.com

Transition to Adulthood

Guardianships and Conservatorships
Planning for your child with special needs.
www.pueblo.gsa.gov

The National Dissemination Center for Children with Disabilities
State-specific information about the transition from high school and the law governing your state agencies.
www.nichcy.org/Pages/Home.aspx

Person-Centered Planning
Person-Centered Planning is an ongoing problem-solving process used to help people with disabilities plan for transitions, education, employment, lifestyles and the future.
www.pacer.org/tatra/resources/personal.asp

Resources for Adults with Autism/ASD
Information on employment, education, recreation, independent living and more.
www.autism-pdd.net/resources.html

Social Security
Information about Supplemental Security Income (SSI).
www.ssa.gov/ssi

Trusts
If you are interested in a special needs trust, an experienced lawyer can guide you through the process.
www.specialneedsanswers.com/professionals

Support for Family Members

The Sibling Support Project
Dedicated to the lifelong concerns of brothers and sisters of people who
have special health, developmental or mental health concerns.
www.siblingsupport.org

Grandparent Resources

Autism Speaks has a very active group organization that helps not only
with funding but with increasing awareness about autism for all families,
including the extended family members.
www.autismspeaks.com
www.neurodiversity.com/grandparents

Especially for Grandparents of Children with Asperger's Syndrome
www.udel.edu//bkirby/asperger/grandparents.html

Grandparent Support and the Family of a Child with a Disability
http://library.umaine.edu/theses/pdf/coutts-clarkeL2002.pdf

In-Laws and Your Child with ASD
http://autism.about.com

Travel and ASD

Autism Travel
Family travel and autism.
www.autismtravel.org

Autism Speaks
Information on traveling with your child with autism.
www.autismspeaks.org/community/family_services/travel.php

Autism on the Seas
Autism cruises.
www.autismontheseas.com

Society for Accessible Travel and Hospitality
Airport travel safety tips.
www.sath.org/index.php?sec=768&id=2371

References

Chapter Two: What Is Autism?

American Psychiatric Association. 2000. *Diagnostic and Statistical Manual of Mental Disorders.* 4th edition. Text Revision (*DSM* IV-TR). Washington, D.C.: American Psychiatric Association.

Autism Speaks Fact Sheet. 2009. Online at http://www.autismspeaks.org/whatisit/facts.php

Dawson, M., I. Soulieres, M. A. Gernsbacher, and L. Mottron. 2007. The level and nature of autistic intelligence. *Psychological Science* 18(8):657–62.

Edelson, M. G. 2006. Are the majority of children with autism mentally retarded? A systematic evaluation of the data. *Focus on Autism and Other Developmental Disabilities* 21(6):66–83.

Greenspan, S. I., and S. Wieder. 1998. *The Child with Special Needs: Encouraging Intellectual and Emotional Growth.* Addison Wesley Publishing Company.

Greenspan, S. I., and S. Wieder. 2006. *Engaging Autism.* Da Capo Lifelong Books.

Klin, A., D. J. Lin, P. Gorrindo, and W. Jones. 2009. Two-year-olds with autism orient to non-social contingencies rather than biological motion. *Nature* DOI:10.1038/nature07868.

National Institute of Mental Health. *Autism spectrum disorders.* Online at www.nimh.nih.gov/health/topics/autism-spectrum-disorders-pervasive-developmental-disorders/index.shtml

Robins, D. L., D. Fein, and M. L. Barton. 1999. *The modified checklist for autism in toddlers (M-CHAT).* Online at www.firstsigns.org or www2.gsu.edu/~wwwpsy/faculty/robins.htm

Roid, G. H., and L. J. Miller. *Leiter International Performance Scale—Revised (Leiter-R).* Psychological Assessment Resources, Inc.

Werner, E., and G. Dawson. 2005. Validation of the phenomenon of autistic regression using videotapes. *Archives of General Psychiatry* 62(8):889–95.

Zero to Three. 2005. *Diagnostic Classification of Mental Health and Developmental Disorders of Infancy and Early Childhood, Revised (DC: 0-3R).* National Center for Infants, Toddlers and Families. Online at www.zerotothree.org

Chapter Three: What Causes Autism?

Alarcon, M., et al. 2008. Linkage, association and gene-expression analyses identify CNT-NAP2 as an autism-susceptibility gene. *American Journal of Human Genetics* 82(1):150–59.

Amarel, D. G., et al. 2008. Neuroanatomy of autism. *Trends in Neuroscience* 31(1):137–45.

Arking, D. E., et al. 2008. A common genetic variant in the neurexin superfamily member CNTNAP2 increases familial risk of autism. *American Journal of Human Genetics* 82(1):160–64.

Autism Genetic Resource Exchange (AGRE). Online at http://www.agre.org/index.cfm

Autism Speaks. 2007. Annual Report. Online at www.autismspeaks.org/annual_report.php

Baird, G., E. Simonoff, A. Pickles, et al. 2006. Prevalence of disorders of the autism spectrum in a population cohort of children in South Thames: The special needs and autism project (SNAP). *Lancet* 368:210–25.

Bakkaloglu, B., et al. 2008. Molecular cytogenetic analysis and resequencing of contactin associated protein-like 2 in autism spectrum disorders. *American Journal of Human Genetics* 82(1):165–73.

Bauman, M. L., and T. L. Kemper, eds. 1994. *Neurobiology of Autism.* Baltimore: Johns Hopkins University Press.

Braunschweig, D., et al. 2008. Autism: Maternally derived antibodies specific for fetal brain proteins. *Neurotoxicology* 29(2):226–31. Epub 2007 Nov 6.

Centers for Disease Control and Prevention (CDC). CDC statement on autism data. October 5, 2009. www.cdc.gov/ncbddd/autism/data.html

Chugani, D. C. 2002. Role of altered brain serotonin mechanisms in autism. *Molecular Psychiatry* 7, Suppl 2:S16–17.

Courchesne, E., R. Carper, and N. Akshoomoff. 2003. Evidence of brain overgrowth in the first year of life in autism. *JAMA* 290(3):337–44.

Coury, D., et al. 2009. Healthcare for children with autism: The autism treatment network. *Current Opinion in Pediatrics.*

Dales, L., S. J. Hammer, and N. J. Smith. 2001. Time trends in autism and MMR immunization coverage in California. *JAMA* 285:1183–85.

Dalton, P., R. Deacon, A. Blamire, et al. Maternal neuronal antibodies associated with autism and a language disorder. *Annals of Neurology* 53(4):533–37.

Editor. 2002. Time to look beyond MMR in autism research. *Lancet* 359:9307.

Editors. 2010. Retraction—Ileal-lymphoid-nodular hyperplasia, non-specific colitis, and pervasive developmental disorder in children. *Lancet* 375(9713):445.

Etherton, et al. 2009. Mouse neurexin-1alpha deletion causes correlated electrophysiological and behavioral changes consistent with cognitive impairments. *Proceedings of the National Academy of Sciences USA.* 106(42):17998–8003. Epub 2009 Oct 12. [PubMed link: 19822762]

Farrington, C. P., E. Miller, and B. Taylor. 2001. MMR and autism: Further evidence against a causal association. *Vaccine* 19:3632–35.

Fombonne, E., and S. Chakrabarti. 2001. No evidence for a new variant of measles-mumps-rubella vaccine and autistic spectrum disorder. Report from New Challenges in Childhood Immunizations Conference, convened in Oak Brook, IL, June 11–12, 2000. *Pediatrics* 107, E84.

Gao, J. H., L. M. Parsons, J. M. Bower, J. Xiong, J. Li, and P. T. Fox. 1996. Cerebellum implicated in sensory acquisition and discrimination rather than motor control. *Science* 272:545–47.

Glaser, G. What if vitamin D deficiency is a cause of autism? *Scientific American* April 24, 2009.

Glanz, J. M., D. L. McClure, D. J. Magid, et al. 2009. Parental refusal of pertussis vaccination is associated with an increased risk of pertussis infection in children. *Pediatrics* 123(6):1446–51.

Glessner, J. T., et al. 2009. Autism genome-wide copy number variation reveals ubiquitin and neuronal genes. *Nature* 459:569–73.

Gregory, S. G., J. J. Connelly, A. J. Towers, et al. 2009. Genomic and epigenetic evidence for oxytocin receptor deficiency in autism. *BMC Medicine* 7:62. DOI:10.1186/1741-7015-7-62.

Herbert, M. R., D. A. Ziegler, C. K. Deutsch, et al. 2003. Dissociations of cerebral coretex, subcortical and cerebral white matter volumes in autistic boys. *Brain* 126:1182–92.

Herbert, M. R., D. A. Ziegler, C. K. Deutsch, et al. 2005. Brain asymmetries in autism and developmental language disorder: A nested whole-brain analysis. *Brain* 128:213–26.

Hertz-Picciotto, I., P. G. Green, L. Delwiche, et al. 2009. Blood mercury concentrations in CHARGE study children with and without autism. *Environmental Health Perspectives* 118:161–66. DOI:10.1289/ehp.0900736.

Hollander, E., J. Bartz, W. Chaplin, et al. 2007. Oxytocin increases retention of social cognition in autism. *Biological Psychiatry* 61:498–503.

Hornig, M., T. Briese, T. Buie, et al. 2008. Lack of association between measles virus vaccine and autism with enteropathy: A case-control study. *PLoS One* 3(9)e3140. Online at www.plosone.org

Immunization Safety Review Committee, Board on Health Promotion and Disease Prevention, Institute of Medicine. 2004. *Immunization Safety Review: Vaccines and Autism*. Washington, D.C.: National Academies Press.

Just, M. A., V. L. Cherkassky, T. A. Keller, and N. J. Minshew. 2004. Cortical activation and synchronization during sentence comprehension in high-functioning autism: Evidence of underconnectivity. *Brain* 127(8):1811–21.

Just, M. A., V. L. Cherkassky, T. A. Keller, et al. 2007. Functional and anatomical cortical underconnectivity in autism: Evidence from an fMRI study of an executive function task and corpus callosum morphometry. *Cerebral Cortex* 17:951–61.

Kadesjo, B., C. Gillberg, B. Hagberg. 1999. Brief report: Autism and Asperger syndrome in seven-year old children: A total population study. *Journal of Autism and Developmental Disorders* 29:327–31.

Kana, R. K., T. A. Keller, V. L. Cherkassky, N. J. Minshew, and M. A. Just. 2006. Sentence comprehension in autism: Thinking in pictures with decreased functional connectivity. *Brain* 129:2484–93.

Kaye, J. A., M. del Mar Melero-Montes, and H. Jick. 2001. Mumps, measles, and rubella vaccine and the incidence of autism recorded by general practitioners: A time trend analysis. *British Medical Journal* 322:460–63.

Kogan, M. D., S. J. Blumberg, L. A. Schieve, et al. 2009. Prevalence of parent-reported diagnosis of autism spectrum disorder among children in the US, 2007. *Pediatrics* 124(5):1395–1403. DOI:10.1542/peds.2009–152.

Madsen, K. M., H. Anders, M. Vestergaard, et al. 2002. A population-based study of measles, mumps and rubella vaccination and autism. *New England Journal of Medicine* 347:1477–82.

Martin, L. A., P. Ashwood, G. Braunschweig, et al. 2008. Stereotypes and hyperactivity in rhesus monkeys exposed to IgG from mothers of children with autism. *Brain Behavior and Immunity* 22(6):806–16. Epub 2008 Feb 8.

Moretti, P., T. Sahoo, K. Hyland, et al. 2005. Cerebral folate deficiency with developmental delay, autism, and response to folinic acid. *Neurology* 64(6):1088–90.

Morrow, E. M., S. Y. Yoo, S. W. Flavell, et al. 2008. Identifying autism loci and genes by tracing recent shared ancestry. *Science* 321:218–23. DOI:10.1126/science.1157657.

National Network for Immunization Information. Online at www.immunizationinfo.org/thimerosal_mercury_issues.cfm

Pessah, I. N., R. F. Seegal, P. J. Lein, et al. 2008. Immunologic and neurodevelopmental susceptibilities of autism. *Neurotoxicology* 29:532–45.

Roberts, M. 2008. Autism linked to fetal brain cell-maternal antibody interaction. *Neuro–Psychiatry Reviews* 12.

Schechter, R., and J. K. Grether. 2008. Continuing increases in autism reported to California's developmental services system. *Archives of General Psychiatry* 65(1):19–24.

Singer, H. A., et al. 2008. Antibodies against fetal brain in sera of mothers with autistic children. *Journal of Neuroimmunology* 194(1–2):165–72. Epub 2008 Feb 21.

Singh, J., et al. 2009. Trends in U.S. autism research funding. *Journal of Autism and Developmental Disorders* 39(5):788–95.

Sutcliffe, J. S. 2008. Insights into the pathogenesis of autism. *Science* July 11: 321:208–9.

Taylor, B., E. Miller, C. P. Farrington, et al. 1999. Autism and measles, mumps and rubella vaccine: No epidemiological evidence for a causal association. *Lancet* 353:2026–29.

UC Davis MIND Institute Center for Excellence in Developmental Disabilities. 2009. Promising autism treatments, from vitamin B12 to Alzheimer's drug Namenda. Online at www.ucdmc.ucdavis.edu/ddcenter/research_news.html

Wakefield, A. J., A. Anthony, S. H. Murch, et al. 2000. Enterocolitis in children with developmental disorders. *The American Journal of Gastroenterology* 95:2285–95. DOI:10,1111/j.1572–0241.2000.03248x.

Wang, K., et al. 2009. Common genetic variants on 5p14.1 associate with autism spectrum disorders. *Nature* 459:528–33.

Weiss, L. A., Y. Shen, J. M. Korn, et al. 2008. Association between microdeletion and microduplication at 16p11.2 and autism. *New England Journal of Medicine* 358(7):667–75.

Zhao, X., A. Leotta, V. Kustanovich, C. Lajonchere, et al. 2007. A unified genetic theory for sporadic and inherited autism. *Proceedings of the National Academy of Sciences* 103(31):12831–836. Online at www.pnas.org/cgi/doi/10.1073/pnas.0705803104

Chapter Four: Understanding Social and Emotional Development

Greenspan, S. I., and J. Salmon. 1994. *Playground Politics: Understanding the Emotional Life of Your School-Age Child*. Da Capo Press.

Greenspan, S. I., and S. Wieder. 1998. *The Child with Special Needs: Encouraging Intellectual and Emotional Growth*. Addison Wesley Publishing Company.

Greenspan, S. I. 2004. *Social-Emotional Growth Chart*. Harcourt Assessment, Inc., PsychCorp.

Greenspan, S. I., and S. Wieder. 2006. *Engaging Autism: Helping Children Relate, Communicate and Think with the DIR Floortime Approach*. Da Capo Lifelong Books. (Also February 9, 2009.)

Greenspan, S. I., and S. Wieder. *Training DVDs on the DIR Model and Floor Time Techniques*. ICDL Publications Online Bookstore. Online at www.icdl.com

Chapter Five: How Your Child Experiences the World Around Him: The Sensory-Motor System in Action

Ashwin, E., et al. 2009. Eagle-eyed visual acuity: An experimental investigation of enhanced perception in autism. *Biological Psychiatry* 65:17–21. DOI:10.1016/j-biopsych.2008.06.012.

Ayres, Jean, A. 2005. *Sensory Integration and the Child*. Western Psychological Services.

Biel, L., and N. Peske. 2005. *Raising a Sensory Smart Child: The Definitive Handbook for Helping Your Child with Sensory Integration Issues*. Penguin Books.

Blakeslee, S., and M. Blakeslee. 2007. *The Body Has a Mind of Its Own*. Random House.

Brett-Green, B. A., L. J. Miller, W. J. Gavin, and P. L. Davies. 2008. Multisensory integration in children: A preliminary ERP study. *Brain Research* 1242:283–90. DOI:10.1016/j.brainres.2008.03.090.

CNN Presents and State of the Art, Inc. Co-Production. *Autism Is a World*. Documentary film produced and directed by filmmaker Gerry Wurzburg. Online at www.cnn.com/CNN/Programs/presents/index.autism.world.html

Dowell, L. R., E. M. Mahone, S. H. Mostofsky. 2009. Associations of postural knowledge and basic motor skill with dyspraxia in autism: Implication for abnormalities in distributed connectivity and motor learning. *Neuropsychology* 23:563–70.

Dziuk, M. A., G. Larson, et al. 2007. Dyspraxia in autism: Association with motor, social and communicative deficits. *Developmental Medicine and Child Neurology* 49:734–39.

Grandin, T. 1992. Calming effects of deep touch pressure in patients with autistic disorder, college students, and animals. *Journal of Child and Adolescent Psychopharmacology* 2(1):63–72.

Grandin, T. 1995. *Thinking in Pictures: And Other Reports From My Life With Autism.* New York: Doubleday.

Kranowitz, C. S. 2003. *The Out-of-Sync Child Has Fun: Activities for Kids With Sensory Processing Disorder.* Revised Edition. Perigee Books.

Kranowitz, C. S. 2005. *The Out-of-Sync Child: Recognizing and Coping with Sensory Processing Disorder.* Perigee Books.

Lane, A. E., R. L. Young, A. E. Baker, et al. 2010. Sensory processing subtypes in autism: Association with adaptive behavior. *Journal of Autism and Developmental Disorders* 40(1):112–22.

McGonigle, D. 2003. Somatosensory brain maps of pathways to communication. Presentation ICDL 17th International Conference, Nov 8, 2003.

Milne, E., H. Griffiths, D. Buckley, et al. 2009. Vision in children and adolescents with autistic spectrum disorder: Evidence for reduced convergence. *Journal of Autism and Developmental Disorders* 39:965–75. DOI:10.1007/s10803-009-0705-8.

Mostofsky, S. H., P. Dubey, V. K. Jerath, et al. 2006. Developmental dyspraxia is not limited to imitation in children with autism spectrum disorders. *Journal of the International Neuropsychological Society* 12:314–26. DOI:10.10170S1355617706060437.

Oram, C., J. E. Flagg, E. J. Roberts, et al. 2005. Delayed mismatch field for speech and non-speech sounds in children with autism. *Cognitive Neuroscience and Neuropsychology* 16(5):521–25.

Oram, C., J. E. Flagg, E. J. Roberts, et al. 2005. Magnetoencephalography identifies rapid temporal processing deficit in autism and language impairment. *Auditory and Vestibular Systems* 16(4):329–32.

Staples, K. L., and G. Reid. 2010. Fundamental movement skills and autism spectrum disorders. *Journal of Autism and Developmental Disorders* 40:209–17. DOI:10.1007/s10803-009-0854-9.

Tietelbaum, P., et al. 1998. Movement analysis in infancy may be useful for early diagnosis of autism. *Proceedings of the National Academy of Sciences USA* 95(23):13982–87.

Wendling, P. 2009. Auditory delays found in autism. *Pediatric News* 43(1).

Williams, D. 1995. *Somebody Somewhere: Breaking Free From the World of Autism.* New York: Three Rivers Press.

Williams, D. 1998. *Nobody Nowhere: The Remarkable Autobiography of an Autistic Girl.* Philadelphia: Jessica Kingsley Publishers.

Chapter Six: A Comprehensive Evaluation and Treatment Approach—DIR/Floortime

Greenspan, S. I., and S. Wieder. 1997. Developmental patterns and outcomes in infants and children with disorders in relating and communication: A chart review of 200 cases of children with autistic spectrum disorders. *Journal of Developmental and Learning Disorders* 1(1):87–141.

Greenspan, S. I., and S. Wieder. 1998. *The Child with Special Needs: Encouraging Intellectual and Emotional Growth.* Addison Wesley Publishing Company.

Greenspan, S. I., and S. Wieder. 2005. Can children with autism master the core deficits and become empathetic, creative, and reflective? A ten to fifteen year follow-up of a subgroup of children with autism spectrum disorders (ASD) who received a comprehensive developmental, individual-difference, relationship-based (DIR) approach. *Journal of Developmental and Learning Disorders* 9:1–29.

Greenspan, S. I., and S. Wieder. 2006. *Engaging Autism: Helping Children Relate, Communicate and Think with the DIR Floortime Approach.* Da Capo Lifelong Books. (Also February 9, 2009.)

Gulsrud, A. C., L. B. Jahromi, and C. Kasari. 2010. The co-regulation of emotions between mothers and their children with autism. *Journal of Autism and Developmental Disorders* 40:227–37. DOI:10.1007/s10803-009-0861-x.

Chapter Seven: The Evaluation Process

American Academy of Pediatrics. 2007. *Identification and Evaluation of Children with Autism Spectrum Disorders.* Online at www.aap.org

American Academy of Pediatrics. 2008. *Caring for Children with Autism Spectrum Disorders: A Resource Toolkit for Clinicians.* Online at www.aap.org/publiced/autismtoolkit.cfm

Brett-Green, B. A., L. J. Miller, W. J. Gavin, and P. L. Davies. 2008. Multisensory integration in children: A preliminary ERP study. *Brain Research* 1242:283–90. DOI:10.1016/j.brainres. 2008.03.090.

Early Autism Study—What Is Autism? Red Flags. McMaster University. Online at www. earlyautismstudy.org

Gerber, S. 2009. Understanding the development and derailment of comprehension: The impact on engaging, relating, and communicating. Presentation at the International Conference on Development and Learning, November 2009.

Gilliam, James. *Gilliam Autism Rating Scale: Second Edition (GARS).* Western Psychological Services.

Greenspan, S. I., et al. 2001. *Functional Emotional Assessment Scale (FEAS).* Interdisciplinary Council on Development and Learning Disorders.

Le Couteur, A., C. Lord, and M. Rutter. 2003. *Autism Diagnostic Interview-Revised (ADI-R).* Western Psychological Services.

Lord, C., M. Rutter, P. C. DiLavore, and S. Risi. *Autism Diagnostic Observation Schedule (ADOS).* Western Psychological Services.

Luyster, R., K. Gotham, W. Guthrie, et al. 2009. The autism diagnostic observation schedule —toddler module: A new module of a standardized diagnostic measure for autism spectrum disorders. *Journal of Autism and Developmental Disorders* 39:1305–20. DOI:10:1007/s10803-009-0746-z.

Ozonoff, S., et al. 2009. How early do parent concerns predict later autism diagnosis? *Journal of Developmental & Behavioral Pediatrics* 30(5):367–75. DOI:10.1097/DBP.0b013e3181ba0fcf.

Perge Productions. *Autistic-Like: Graham's Story.* Documentary film produced and directed by Erik Linthorst. Online at www.autisticlike.com

Robins, D. L., D. Fein, and M. L. Barton. 1999. *The modified checklist for autism in toddlers (M-CHAT).* Online at www.firstsigns.org or www2.gsu.edu/~wwwpsy/faculty/robins. htm

Schopler, E., R. J. Reichler, and B. R. Renner. *Childhood Autism Rating Scale (CARS).* Western Psychological Services.

Wetherby, A. M., and N. D. Wiseman. 2007. *ASD Video Glossary.* Autism Speaks. Online at www.autismspeaks.org/video/glossary.php

Zero to Three. 2005. *Diagnostic Classification of Mental Health and Developmental Disorders of Infancy and Early Childhood, Revised (DC: 0-3R).* National Center for Infants, Toddlers and Families. Online at www.zerotothree.org

Zwaigenbaum, L., S. Bryston, C. Lord, et al. 2009. Clinical assessment and management of toddlers with suspected autism spectrum disorder: Insights from studies of high-risk infants. *Pediatrics* 123:1383–91.

Chapter Eight: Treatment Plans

Amminger, G. P., G. E. Berger, M. R. Schafer, et al. 2007. Omega-3 fatty acids supplementation in children with autism: A double-blind randomized, placebo-controlled pilot study. *Biological Psychiatry* 61:551–53.

Autism Treatment Center of America. What is the son-rise program? Online at www.autismtreatmentcenter.org/contents/about_son-rise/what_is_the_son-rise_program.php

Bass, Margaret M., et al. 2009. The effect of therapeutic horseback riding on social functioning in children with autism. *Journal of Autism and Developmental Disorders* 39:1261–67. DOI:10:1007/s10803-009-0734-3.

Bratton, S., D. Ray, T. Rhine, and L. Jones. 2005. The efficacy of play therapy with children: A meta-analytic review of treatment outcomes. *Professional Psychology: Research and Practice* 36(4):376–90.

Committee on Educational Interventions for Children with Autism, N.R.C. 2001. *Educating Children with Autism*. Washington, D.C.: National Academies Press.

Connolly, A. M., M. Chez, R. G. Robinson, et al. 2005. Brain-derived neurotrophic factor and autoantibodies to neural antigens in sera of children with autistic spectrum disorders, Landau-Kleffner syndrome, and epilepsy. *Biological Psychiatry* 59(4):354–63.

Cotugno, A. J. 2009. Social competence and social skills training and intervention for children with autism spectrum disorders. *Journal of Autism and Developmental Disorders* 39:1268–77. DOI:10.1007/s10803-009-0741-4.

Dawson, G., et al. 2009. Randomized, controlled trial of an intervention for toddlers with autism: The early start Denver model. *Pediatrics* DOI:10.1542/peds.2009-0958.

Golnik, A. E., and M. Ireland. 2009. Complementary alternative medicine for children with autism: A physician survey. *Journal of Autism and Developmental Disorders* DOI:10.1007/s10803-009-0714-7.

The Gray Center for Social Learning and Understanding. What are social stories? Online at www.thegraycenter.org/store/index.cfm?fuseaction=page.display&page_id=30

Greenspan, S. I., and S. Wieder. 1997a. An integrated developmental approach to interventions for young children with severe difficulties in relating and communicating. Zero to Three: National Center for Infants, Toddlers, and Families 17(5):5–18.

Greenspan, S. I., and S. Wieder. 1997b. Developmental patterns and outcomes in infants and children with disorders in relating and communication: A chart review of 200 cases of children with autistic spectrum disorders. *Journal of Developmental and Learning Disorders* 1(1):87–141.

Greenspan, S. I., and S. Wieder. 1998. *The Child with Special Needs: Encouraging Intellectual and Emotional Growth*. Addison Wesley Publishing Company.

Greenspan, S. I., and S. Wieder. 2006. *Engaging Autism: Helping Children Relate, Communicate and Think With the DIR Floortime Approach*. Da Capo Lifelong Books. (Also February 9, 2009.)

Greenspan, S. I., G. DeGangi, and S. Wieder. 2001. Functional emotional assessment scale: Clinical and research applications. Bethesda, M.D.: Interdisciplinary Council on Developmental and Learning Disorders.

Greenspan, S. I., T. B. Brazelton, R. G. Robinson, et al. 2008. Guidelines to early identification, screening and clinical management of children with autism spectrum disorders. *Pediatrics* 121(4):828–30.

Huemer, S. V., and V. Mann. 2010. A comprehensive profile of decoding and comprehension in autism spectrum disorders. *Journal of Autism and Developmental Disorders* 40:485–93. DOI:10:1007/s10803-009-0892-3.

Hume, K., S. Bellini, and C. Pratt. 2005. The usage and perceived outcomes of early intervention and early childhood programs for young children with autism spectrum disorder. *Topics in Early Childhood Special Education* 25(4):195–207. DOI:10.1177/02711214050250040101.

Ingersoll, B., A. Dvortcsak, C. Whalen, and D. Sikora. 2005. The effects of a developmental, social-pragmatic language intervention on rate of expressive language production in young children with autistic spectrum disorders. *Focus of Autism and Other Developmental Disorders* 20:213–22.

Kasari, C., S. Freeman, and T. Paparella. 2006. Joint attention and symbolic play in young children with autism: A randomized controlled intervention study. *Journal of Child Psychology and Psychiatry* 47(6):611–20.

Kasari, C., T. Paparella, and S. Freeman. 2008. Language outcome in autism: Randomized comparison of joint attention and play interventions. *Journal of Continuing and Clinical Psychology* 76(1):125–37.

Kasari, C., A. C. Gulsrud, C. Wong, et al. 2010. Randomized controlled caregiver mediated joint engagement intervention for toddlers with autism. *Journal of Autism and Developmental Disorders* DOI:10.1007/s10803-010-0955-5.

Lovaas, O. I. 1987. Behavioral treatment and normal educational and intellectual functioning in young autistic children. *Journal of Consulting and Clinical Psychology* 55:3–9.

Mahoney, G., and F. Perales. 2004. Relationship-focused early intervention with children with pervasive developmental disorders and other disabilities: A comparative study. *Journal of Developmental & Behavioral Pediatrics* 26:77–85.

Mackay, T., F. Knott, and A. Dunlop. 2007. Developing social interaction and understanding in individuals with autism spectrum disorder: A groupwork intervention. *Journal of Intellectual & Developmental Disability* 32(4):279–90.

Martin, B., Jr., and E. Carle. 2008. *Brown Bear, Brown Bear, What Do You See?* Henry Holt and Co., BYR Paperbacks.

National Association for Education of Young Children, Position Statement: Developmentally Appropriate Practice in Early Childhood Programs Serving Children from Birth through Age 8. 2009. Online at www.nacyc.org/files/naeyc/file/positions/PSDAP.pdf

National Research Council Committee on Educational Interventions for Children with Autism. 2001. *Educating Children with Autism.* Washington, D.C.: National Academies Press.

"Overview." More than Words: The Hanen Centre. Online at www.hanen.org/web/Home/HanenPrograms/MoreThanWords/Program/tabid/117/Default.aspx

Picture Exchange Communication System (PECS), Pyramid Educational Consultants, Inc. Online at www.pecs.com

Reichow, B., and F. R. Volkmar. 2010. Social skills interventions for individuals with autism: Evaluation for evidence-based practices within a best evidence synthesis framework. *Journal of Autism and Developmental Disorders* 40:149–66. DOI:10.1007/s10803-009-0842-0.

Rogers, S., and D. Delalla. 1991. A comparative study of the effects of a developmentally based instructional model on young children with autism and young children with other disorders of behavior and development. *Topics in Early Childhood Special Education* 11:29–47.

Rogers, S. 1999. Intervention for young children with autism: From research to practice. *Infants and Young Children* 12:116.

SCERTS Model. Online at www.scerts.com

Senel, H. G. 2010. Parents' views and experiences about complementary and alternative medicine treatments for their children with autistic spectrum disorder. *Journal of Autism and Developmental Disorders* 40:494–503. DOI:10.1007/s10803-009-0891-4.

Smith, T., A. D. Groen, and J. W. Wynn. 2000. Randomized trial of intensive early intervention for children with pervasive developmental disorder. *American Journal on Mental Retardation* 105:269–85.

Spreckley, M., and R. Boyd. 2009. Efficacy of applied behavioral intervention in preschool children with autism for improving cognitive, language, and adaptive behavior: A systematic review and meta-analysis. *The Journal of Pediatrics* 154(3):338–44.

Soloman, R., J. Necheles, C. Ferch, and D. Bruckman. 2007. Pilot study of a parent training program for young children with autism: The PLAY project home consultation program. *SAGE Publications and The National Autistic Society* 11(3):205–24.

Wieder, S., and H. Wachs. 2011. *Hidden in Plain Sight: Visual-Spatial Challenges in Autism and Learning Difficulties*. Bethesda, M.D. ICDL Press.

Wong, V. C. N. 2009. Use of complementary and alternative medicine (CAM) in autism spectrum disorder (ASD): Comparison of Chinese and western culture (part A). *Journal of Autism and Developmental Disorders* 39:454–63.

Zigler, E., and S. Bishop-Josef. 2009. *Play Under Seige*. Zero to Three. September 2009:4–11.

Zwaigenbaum, L., S. Bryson, C. Lord, et al. 2009. Clinical assessment and measurement of toddlers with suspected autism spectrum disorder: Insights from studies of high-risk infants. *Pediatrics* 123(5):1383–91.

Chapter Nine: Staying on Track

Greenspan, S. I., and S. Wieder. 1998. *The Child with Special Needs: Encouraging Intellectual and Emotional Growth*. Addison Wesley Publishing Company.

Greenspan, S. I., and S. Wieder. 2006. *Engaging Autism: Helping Children Relate, Communicate and Think with the DIR Floortime Approach*. Da Capo Lifelong Books. (Also February 9, 2009.)

Joosten, A. V., A. C. Bundy, and S. L. Einfeld. 2009. Intrinsic and extrinsic motivation for stereotypic and repetitive behavior. *Journal of Autism and Developmental Disorders* 39:521–31.

Wieder, S., and H. Wachs. 2011. *Hidden in Plain Sight: Visual-Spatial Challenges in Autism and Learning Difficulties*. Bethesda, M.D.: ICDL Press.

Chapter Ten: ASD and the Family

Bayat, M. 2007. Evidence of resilience in families of children with autism. *Journal of Intellectual Disability Research* 51(9):702–14.

Davis, N. O., and A. S. Carter. 2008. Parenting stress in mothers and fathers of toddlers with autism spectrum disorders: Associations with child characteristics. *Journal of Autism and Developmental Disorders* 38:1278–91.

Ganz, Michael L. 2007. The lifetime distribution of the incremental societal costs of autism. *Archives of Pediatric & Adolescent Medicine* 161:343–49.

Kogan, M. D., et al. 2008. A national profile of the health care experiences and family impact of autism spectrum disorder among children in the United States, 2005–2006. *Pediatrics* 122(6):e1149–58.

Neff, J. M. 2009. Respite care: An essential yet unmet need for families with children with special health care needs. *Archives of Pediatric & Adolescent Medicine* 163(1):89–90.

Stone, W. L., C. R. McMahon, P. J. Yoder, et al. 2007. Early social-communicative and cognitive development of younger siblings of children with autism spectrum disorders. *Archives of Pediatric & Adolescent Medicine* 161(4):384–90.

Chapter Eleven: Behavior as Communication

Bellini, S. 2004. Social skill deficits and anxiety in high functioning adolescents with autism spectrum disorders. *Focus on Autism and Other Developmental Disabilities* 19(2):78–86.

Posey, D. J., K. D. Guenin, A. E. Kohn, et al. 2001. A naturalistic open-label study of mirtazapine in autistic and other pervasive developmental disorders. *Journal of Child and Adolescent Psychopharmacology* 11(3):267–77.

Simonoff, E., A. Pickes, T. Charman, S. Chandler, et al. 2008. Psychiatric disorders in children with autism spectrum disorders: Prevalence, comorbidity, and associated factors in a population-derived sample. *Journal of the American Academy of Child and Adolescent Psychiatry* 47(8):921–29.

Sze, K. M., and J. J. Wood. 2007. Cognitive behavioral treatment of comorbid anxiety disorders and social difficulties in children with high-functioning autism: A case report. *Journal of Contemporary Psychotherapy* 37:133–43.

Wood, J. CBT for comorbid anxiety disorders in children with asperger syndrome and PDD-NOS. Cure Autism Now Foundation. Project Period: 6/1/06–5/30/09.

Chapter Twelve: Augmentative and Alternative Communication

Autism Is a World. Documentary. Online at www.cnn.com/CNN/Programs/presents/index.autism.world.html

Bicklen, D. 1990. Communication unbound: Autism and praxis. *Harvard Educational Review* 60:291–314.

Bicklen D., W. M. Morton, D. Gold, C. Berrigan, and S. Swaminathan. 1992. Facilitated communication: Implications for children with autism. *Topics in Language Disorders* 12:1–28.

McGonigle, D. 2003. Somatosensory brain maps of pathways to communication. Presentation ICDL 17th International Conference, Nov. 8, 2003.

Pickett, E., O. Pullara, et al. 2009. Speech acquisition in older nonverbal individuals with autism: A review of features, methods, and prognosis. *Cognitive and Behavioral Neurology* 22(1):1–21.

Rapid Prompting Method. Online at www.halo-soma.org

Chapter Thirteen: Keeping Your Child Healthy

Brachlow, A. E., K. K. Ness, M. L. McPheeters, et al. 2007. Comparison of indicators for a primary care medical home between children with autism or asthma and other special health care needs. *Archives of Pediatric & Adolescent Medicine* 161(4):399–405.

Cermak, S. A., C. Curtin, and L. G. Bandini. 2010. Food selectivity and sensory sensitivity in children with autism spectrum disorders. *Journal of the American Dietetic Association,* 110(2):238–46.

Golnik, A., M. Ireland, and I. W. Borowsky. 2009. Medical homes for children with autism: A physician survey. *Pediatrics* 123:966–71.

Hediger, M. L., L. J. England, C. A. Molloy, et al. 2008. Reduced bone cortical thickness in boys with autism or autism spectrum disorder. *Journal of Autism and Developmental Disorders* 38:848–56.

Herndon, A. C., C. DiGuiseppi, S. L. Johnson, et al. 2009. Does nutritional intake differ between children with autism spectrum disorders and children with typical development? *Journal of Autism and Developmental Disorders* 39:212–22.

Ledford, J., and D. Gast. 2006. Feeding problems in children with autism spectrum disorders—A review. *Focus on Autism and Other Developmental Disabilities* 21:153–66.

Levy, S. E., M. C. Souders, R. F. Ittenbach, et al. 2007. Relationship of dietary intake to gastrointestinal symptoms in children with autism spectrum disorders. *Biological Psychiatry* 62(4):492–97.

Lukens, C. T., and T. R. Linscheid. 2008. Development and validation of an inventory to assess mealtime behavior problems in children with autism. *Journal of Autism and Developmental Disorders* 38:342–52.

Schreck, K. A., K. Williams, and A. F. Smith. 2004. A comparison of eating behaviors between children with and without autism. *Journal of Autism and Developmental Disorders* 34(4):433–38.

Schreck, K. A., and K. Williams. 2006. Food preferences and factors influencing food selectivity for children with autism spectrum disorders. *Research in Developmental Disabilities.* 27:353–63.

Whiteley, P. 2009. Developmental, behavioral and somatic factors in pervasive developmental disorders: Preliminary analysis. *Child: Care, Health and Development* 2004:30(1):5–11 as included in *Pediatric Nutrition Handbook,* 6th ed. AAP (R. E. Kleinman, M.D., ed.).

Yadav, V. K., J. H. Ryu, N. Suda, et al. 2008. Lrp5 controls bone formation by inhibiting serotonin synthesis in the duodenum. *Cell* 135(5):825–37.

Chapter Fourteen: Medical Conditions and ASD

Chen, C. Y., K. H. Chen, C. Y. Liu, et al. 2009. Increased risks of congenital, neurologic, and endocrine disorders associated with autism in preschool children: Cognitive ability differences. *Journal of Pediatrics* 154(3):345–50.

Tordjman, S., G. M. Anderson, M. Botbol, et al. 2009. Pain reactivity and plasma beta-endorphin in children and adolescents with autistic disorder. *PLoS One* 4(8):e5289.

Tordjman, S., C. Antoine, D. J. Cohen, et al. 1999. Study of the relationships between self-injurious behavior and pain reactivity in infantile autism. *Encephale* 25(2):122–34.

Zeltzer, L. 2009. Presentation. Pain in children with autism spectrum disorders. Symposium on Gastrointestinal Conditions in Children with Autism Spectrum Disorders at the North American Society for Pediatric Gastroenterology, Hepatology and Nutrition Annual Meeting, November 15, 2009.

Zeltzer, L. 2001. Sensory and pain thresholds in ASD. International Conference on Development and Learning, 5th International Conference, November 2001.

Chapter Fifteen: ASD and Double Syndromes

Gillberg, C., and M. Coleman. 2000. *The Biology of the Autistic Syndromes.* 3rd ed. London: Mac Keith Press.

Hagerman, R. J., E. Berry-Kravis, W. E. Kaufmann, et al. 2009. Advances in the treatment of fragile X syndrome. *Pediatrics* 123(1):378–90.

Percy, A. K., and D. Glaze. 2008. When developmental milestones are missed: Rett syndrome needs your attention. International Rett Syndrome Foundation. Online at www.rettsyndrome. org/docman/pdf-documents/alan-percy-article/download.html

Poling, J. 2008. Dad in autism vaccine case speaks out. *WebMD Health News* Mar. 6. Online at www.webmd.com/brain/autism/news

Shen, Y., K. A. Dies, I. A. Holm, et al. 2010. Clinical genetic testing for patients with autism spectrum disorders. *Pediatrics* 125(4):e727–35. Epub 2010 Mar 15.

Weiss, L. A., Y. Shen, J. M. Korn, et al. 2008. Association between microdeletion and micro-duplication at 16p11.2 and autism. *New England Journal of Medicine* 358(7):667–75.

Weissman, J. R., R. I. Kelley, M. I. Bauman, et al. 2008. Mitochondrial disease in autism spectrum disorder patients: A cohort analysis. *PLoS One* 3(11):e3815.

Whitehead Institute for Biomedical Research. 2009. Possible treatment for neurological disorder Rett Syndrome—Most common basis of autism in girls. *ScienceDaily.* February 10, 2009. Online at www.sciencedaily.com/releases/2009/02/090209205047.htm

Chapter Sixteen: Seizure Disorders in ASD

Aarts, J., C. Binne, A. Smith, et al. 1984. Selective cognitive impairment during focal and generalized epileptiform EEG activity. *Brain* 107:293–308.

Akshoomoff, N., N. Farid, E. Courchesne, and R. Hans. 2007. Abnormalities on the neurological examination and EEG in young children with pervasive developmental disorders. *Journal of Autism and Developmental Disorders* 37:887–93.

Bardenstein, R., M. G. Chez, B. T. Helfand, et al. 1998. Improvement in EEG and clinical function in pervasive developmental delay (PDD): Effect of valproic acid. *Neurology* 50, Suppl 4, A86 (Abstract).

Chez, M. G., C. Buchanan, M. Loeffel, et al. 1998. Practical treatment with pulse-dose corticosteroids in pervasive developmental disorder or autistic patients with abnormal sleep EEG and language delay. N. M. Perat, ed. *New Developments in Child Neurology* 695–98.

Chez, M. G., C. Buchanan, M. Loeffel, et al. 1998. Treatment of electroencephalographic epileptiform activity on overnight EEG studies in children with pervasive developmental disorder or autism: Defining similarities to the Landau-Kleffner syndrome. *Journal of Developmental Learning Disorders* 2:217–29.

Chez, M. G., M. Chang, V. Krasne, et al. 2006. Frequency of epileptiform EEG abnormalities in a sequential screening of autistic patients with no known clinical epilepsy from 1996 to 2005. *Epilepsy and Behavior* 8(1):267–71.

Chez, M. G., M. Loeffel, C. Buchanan, et al. 1998. Pulse high-dose steroids in combination therapy with valproic acid in epileptic aphasia patients with pervasive developmental delay or autism. *Annals of Neurology* 44:539 (Abstract).

Chez, M. G., M. Chang, V. Krasne, et al. 2006. Frequency of epileptiform (EEG) abnormalities in a sequential screening of autistic patients with no known clinical epilepsy from 1996–2005. *Epilepsy and Behavior* 8:267–71.

Hollander, E., R. Dolgoff-Kaspar, C. Cartwright, et al. 2001. An open trial of divalproex sodium in autistic spectrum disorders. *Journal of Clinical Psychiatry* 62:530–34.

Landau, W. M., and F. Kleffner. 1957. Syndrome of acquired aphasia with convulsive disorder in children. *Neurology* 7:523–30.

Lewine, J. D., R. Andrews, M. Chez, et al. 1999. Magnetoencephalographic patterns of epileptiform activity in children with regressive autism spectrum disorders. *Pediatrics* 104:405–18.

Marescaux, C., E. Hirsch, S. Finch, et al. 1990. Landau-Kleffner syndrome: A pharmacologic study of five cases. *Epilepsia* 31:768–77.

Pardo, C. A., D. L. Vargas, and A. Zimmerman. 2005. Immunity, neuroglia and neuroinflammation in autism. *International Review of Psychiatry* 17(6):485–95.

Plioplys, A. V. 1994. Autism: Electroencephalogram abnormalities and clinical improvement with valproic acid. *Archives of Pediatric and Adolescent Medicine* 148:220–22.

Sarco, D. P., and M. Takeoka. 2009. Epileptic and epileptiform encephalopathies. *eMedicine Neurology*, July 29.

Stefanotos, G. A., W. Grover, and E. Geller. 1995. Case study: Corticosteroid treatment of language regression in pervasive developmental disorder. *Journal of the American Academy of Child and Adolescent Psychiatry* 34(8):1107–11.

Spence, S. J., and M. T. Schneider. 2009. The role of epilepsy and epileptiform EEGs in autism spectrum disorders. Pediatrics and Developmental Neuroscience Branch, National Institute of Mental Health, NIH. Bethesda, M.D.

Steffenburg, S., U. Steffenburg, and C. Gillberg. 2003. Autism spectrum disorders in children with active epilepsy and learning disability: Comorbidity, pre- and perinatal background, and seizure characteristics. *Developmental Medicine & Child Neurology* 45:724–30.

Trauner, D. A., C. Nabangchang, A. Ballantyne, et al. 2002. Developmental aphasia with epileptiform abnormalities on EEG: Clinical features and response to prednisone. *Annals of Neurology* 52(3):566–67 (Abstract).

Tuchman, R. F., and I. Rapin. 1997. Regression in pervasive developmental disorders: Seizures and epileptiform electroencephalogram correlates. *Pediatrics* 99:560–66.

Tuchman, R. 2000. Treatment of seizure disorders and EEG abnormalities in children with autism spectrum disorders. *Journal of Autism and Developmental Disorders* 30:485–89.

Chapter Seventeen: Gastrointestinal (GI) Illness

Bates, B. 2009. Risk of GI disorders increased with autism. Online at www.pediatricnews. com

Buie, T. 2007. Presentation to the Northwest Autism Foundation, Portland, OR. Autism Network for Dietary Intervention. Online at www.autismndi.com/news/display. asp?content=Resources&shownews=20040728195163

Buie, T. 2010. Evaluation, diagnosis, and treatment of gastrointestinal disorders in individuals with ASDs: A consensus report. *Pediatrics* 125(1):S1–S18.

Buie, T. 2010. Recommendations for evaluation and treatment of common gastrointestinal problems in children with ASDs. *Pediatrics* 125(1):S19–S29.

Campbell, D. B., T. M. Buie, H. Winter, M. Bauman, et al. 2009. Distinct genetic risk based on association of MET in families with co-occurring autism and gastrointestinal conditions. *Pediatrics* 123(3):1018–24.

Campbell, D. B., J. S. Sutcliffe, P. J. Ebert, et al. 2006. A genetic variant that disrupts MET transcription is associated with autism. *Proceedings of the National Academy of Sciences USA*. DOI:10.1073/pnas.0605229610.3.

Chez, M. G., C. P. Buchanan, B. T. Bagan, et al. 2000. Secretin and autism: A two-part clinical investigation. *Journal of Autism and Developmental Disorders* 30:87–94.

Chitkara, D. K., S. Nurko, J. M. Shoffner, T. Buie, et al. 2003. Abnormalities in gastrointestinal motility are associated with diseases of oxidative phosphorylation in children. *The American Journal of Gastroenterology* 98:871–77. DOI:10,1111/j-1572-0241.2003.07385x.

Editors. 2010. Retraction—Ileal-lymphoid-nodular hyperplasia, non-specific colitis, and pervasive developmental disorder in children. *Lancet* 375(9713):445–46. DOI:10.1016/S0140-6736(10)60175-4.

Elder, J. H., et al. 2006. The gluten-free, casein-free diet in autism: Results of a preliminary double blind clinical trial. *Journal of Autism and Developmental Disorders* 36:413–20.

Hornig, M., T. Briese, T. Buie, M. L. Bauman, et al. 2008. Lack of association between measles virus vaccine and autism with enteropathy: A case-control study. *PLoS One* 3(9):e3140. DOI:10.1371/journal.pone.0003140.

Horvath, K., and J. A. Perman. 2002. Autism and gastrointestinal symptoms. *Current Gastrointestinal Report* 4:251–58.

Kushak, R. I., H. S. Winter, N. S. Farber, and T. M. Buie. 2005. Gastrointestinal symptoms and intestinal disaccharidase activities in children with autism: 49 (Abstracts: North American Society of Pediatric Gastroenterology, Hepatology and Nutrition Annual Meeting October 20–22, 2005, Salt Lake City, UT: Poster Session I, Thurs., Oct. 20).

Levy, S. E., M. C. Souders, R. F. Ittenbach, et al. 2007. Relationship of dietary intake to gastrointestinal symptoms in children with autism spectrum disorders. *Biological Psychiatry* 62(4):492–97.

Mahikoa, K. 2006. Gastrointestinal illness in autism: An interview with Tim Buie, M.D. *Autism Advocate.* 5th ed.

Nikolov, R., K. Bearss, C. E. Lettinga, et al. 2008. Gastrointestinal symptoms in a sample of children with pervasive developmental disorders. *Journal of Autism and Developmental Disorders* 39:405–13.

Owley, T., W. McMahon, E. H. Cook, et al. 2001. Multisite, double-blind, placebo-controlled trial of porcine secretin in autism. *Journal of the American Academy of Child & Adolescent Psychiatry* 40(11):1293–99.

Sandler, A. D., and J. W. Bodfish. 2000. Placebo effects in autism: Lessons from secretin. *Journal of Developmental and Behavioral Pediatrics* 21:347–50.

Unis, A. S., J. A. Munson, S. J. Rogers, et al. 2002. A randomized, double-blind, placebo-controlled trial of porcine versus synthetic secretin for reducing symptoms of autism. *Journal of the American Academy of Child and Adolescent Psychiatry* 41:1315–21.

Valicenti-McDermott, M., K. McVicar, I. Rapin, et al. 2006. Frequency of gastrointestinal symptoms in children with autistic spectrum disorders and association with family history of autoimmune disease. *Journal of Developmental and Behavioral Pediatrics* 27(2 Suppl):S128–36.

Valicenti-McDermott, M. D., K. McVicar, H. J. Cohen, et al. 2008. Gastrointestinal symptoms in children with an autism spectrum disorder and language regression. *Pediatric Neurology* 39(6):392–98.

Wakefield, A. J., A. Anthony, S. H. Murch, et al. 2000. Entercolitis in children with developmental disorders. *American Journal of Gastroenterology* 95:2285–95. DOI:10,1111/j.1572-0241.2000.03248x.

Chapter Eighteen: Allergies and Immunological Disorders

Atladottir, H. O., et al. 2009. Association of family history of autoimmune diseases and autism spectrum disorders. *Pediatrics* 124(2):687–94.

Atkins, D. 2008. Food allergy diagnosis and management. *Primary Care: Clinics in Office Practice* 35(1):119–40.

Comi, A. M., A. W. Zimmerman, V. H. Frye, et al. 1999. Familial clustering of autoimmune disorders and evaluation of medical risk factors in autism. *Journal of Child Neurology* 14(6):388–94.

Connolly, A. M., M. G. Chez, A. Pestronk, et al. 1999. Serum antibodies to brain in Landau-Kleffner variant, autism, and other neurologic disorders. *Journal of Pediatrics* 134:607–13.

Connolly, A. M., M. Chez, E. M. Streif, R. G. Robinson, et al. 2006. Brain-derived neurotrophic factor and autoantibodies to neural antigens in sera of children with autistic spectrum disorders, Landau-Kleffner syndrome, and epilepsy. *Biological Psychiatry* 59(4):354–63.

Elder, J. H., M. Shankar, J. Shuster, et al. 2006. The gluten-free, casein-free diet in autism: Results of a preliminary double blind clinical trial. *Journal of Autism and Developmental Disorders* 36(3):413–20.

Heuer, L., P. Ashwood, J. Schauer, et al. 2008. Reduced levels of immunoglobulin in children with autism correlates with behavioral symptoms. *Autism Research* 1:275–83.

Hjördís Ó. Atladóttir, B. M., M. G. Pedersen, P. Thorsen, et al. 2009. Association of family history of autoimmune diseases and autism spectrum disorders. *Pediatrics* 124(2):687–94. DOI:10.1542/peds.2008-2445.

Pardo, C. A., D. L. Vargas, and A. Zimmerman. 2005. Immunity, neuroglia and neuroinflammation in autism. *International Review of Psychiatry* 17(6):485–95.

Sweeten, T. L., S. L. Bowyer, D. J. Posey, et al. 2003. Increased prevalence of familial autoimmunity in probands with pervasive developmental disorders. *Pediatrics* 112(5):e420.

Vargas, D. L., C. Nascimbene, C. Krishnan, et al. 2005. Neuroglial activation and neuroinflammation in the brain of patients with autism. *Annals of Neurology* 57:67–81.

Chapter Nineteen: Sleep Disorders

Anderson, I. A., S. C. McGrew, J. Kaczmarska, et al. 2006. Therapeutic use of melatonin in autism spectrum disorder. *Sleep* 29:A297.

Friman, P. C., K. E. Hoff, C. Schnoes, et al. 1999. The bedtime pass: An approach to bedtime crying and leaving the room. *Archives of Pediatric & Adolescent Medicine* 153(10):1027–29.

Gregory, A. M., A. Caspi, T. E. Moffitt, and R. Poulton. 2009. Sleep problems in childhood predict neuropsychological functioning in adolescence. *Pediatrics* 123(4):1171–76.

Harrell, D. B., K. A. Schreck, and A. Richdale. 2008. Sleep in the world of autism: Insight into the sleep problems associated with autism. *Sleep Review* March:18–20.

Honomichl, R. D., B. L. Goodlin-Jones, M. Burnham, et al. 2002. Sleep patterns of children with pervasive developmental disorders. *Journal of Autism and Developmental Disorders* 32:553–61.

Huang, Y. S., H. Y. Guilleminault, C. M. Yang, et al. 2007. Attention-deficit/hyperactivity disorder with obstructive sleep apnea: A treatment outcome study. *Sleep Medicine* 8:18–30.

Krakowiak, P., B. Goodlin-Jones, I. Hertz-Picciotto, L. A. Croen, and R. L. Hansen. 2008. Sleep problems in children with autism spectrum disorders, developmental delays, and typical development: A population-based study. *Journal Sleep Research* 17(2):197–206.

Malow, B. A., M. L. Marzec, S. G. McGrew, et al. 2006. Characterizing sleep in children with autism spectrum disorders: A multidimensional approach. *Sleep* 29(12):1563–71.

Malow, B. A., S. G. McGrew, M. Harvey, et al. 2006. Impact of treating sleep apnea in a child with autism spectrum disorder. *Pediatric Neurology* 34:325–28.

Melke, J., H. G. Botros, P. Chaste, et al., and the PARIS Study. 2007. Abnormal melatonin synthesis in autism spectrum disorders. *Molecular Psychiatry* 1–9:1359–4184.

Paavolen, E. J., T. von Wendt, N. R. Vanhala, and L. von Wendt. 2003. Effectiveness of melatonin in the treatment of sleep disturbances in children with asperger disorder. *Journal of Child and Adolescent Psychopharmacology* 13:83–95.

Richdale, A. L. 1999. Sleep problems in autism: Prevalence, cause and intervention. *Developmental Medicine and Child Neurology* 41:60–66.

Rosen, C. L., A. Storfer-Isser, H. G. Taylor, et al. 2004. Increased behavioral morbidity in school-aged children with sleep-disordered breathing. *Pediatrics* 114(6):1640–48.

Thirumalai, S. S., R. A. Shubin, and R. Robinson. 2002. Rapid eye movement sleep behavior disorder in children with autism. *Journal of Child Neurology* 17(3):173–78.

Urschitz, M. S., S. Eitner, A. Guenther, et al. 2004. Habitual snoring, intermittent hypoxia, and impaired behavior in primary school children. *Pediatrics* 114(4):1041–48.

Wiggs, L., and G. Stores. 2004. Sleep patterns and sleep disorders in children with autistic spectrum disorders: Insights using parent report and actigraphy. *Developmental Medicine and Child Neurology* 46:372–80.

Chapter Twenty: Understanding Medication and Its Use in ASD

Aman, M. G., L. E. Arnold, and S. C. Armstrong. 1999. Review of serotonergic agents and pervasive behaviors in patients with developmental disabilities. *Mental Retardation and Developmental Disability Research Review* 5:279–89.

Autism Speaks Autism Tissue Program. Online at www.autismspeaks.org/science/programs/atp

Bystritsky, A. 2008. Memantine treatment for obsessive-compulsive disorder and generalized anxiety disorder. ClinicalTrials.gov NCT00674219 (unpublished clinical trial).

Campbell, M., L. T. Anderson, A. M. Small, et al. 1993. Naltrexone in autistic children: Behavioral symptoms and attentional learning. *Journal of the American Academy of Child and Adolescent Psychiatry* 32:1283–91.

Chez, M. G., T. Buchanan, M. Becker, et al. 2003. Donepezil hydrochloride: A double-blind study in autistic children. *Journal of Pediatric Neurology* 1:83–88.

Chez, M. G., M. Becker, J. Kessler, et al. 2003. Psychostimulant use in children with autistic spectrum disorder. *Annals of Neurology* 54, Suppl 7:147 (Abstract).

Chez, M. G., S. Memon, and P. C. Hung. 2004. Neurological treatment strategies in autism: An overview of medical intervention strategies. *Seminars in Pediatric Neurology* 11:229–35.

Chez, M. G., Q. Burton, T. Dowling, et al. 2007. Memantine as adjunctive therapy in children diagnosed with autistic spectrum disorders: An observation of initial clinical response and maintenance tolerability. *Journal of Child Neurology* 22(5):574–79.

Chugani, D. C. 2002. Role of altered brain serotonin mechanisms in autism. *Molecular Psychiatry* 7, Suppl 2:S16–17.

Cook, E. H., R. Rowlett, C. Jaselskis, et al. 1992. Fluoxetine treatment of children and adults with autistic disorder and mental retardation. *Journal of the American Academy of Child and Adolescent Psychiatry* 31:739–45.

Delong, G. R., C. R. Ritch, and S. Burch. 2002. Fluoxetine response in children with autistic spectrum disorders: Correlation with familial major affective disorder and intellectual achievement. *Developmental Medicine and Child Neurology* 44:652–59.

Fraser, W. I., S. Ruedrich, M. Kerr, et al. 1998. Beta-adrenergic blockers. In S. Reiss and M. G. Aman (eds.), *Psychiatric Medications and Developmental Disabilities: The International Consensus Handbook* (pp. 271–90). Columbus, OH: Ohio State University, Nissonger Center.

Feldman, H. M., V. C. Kolmen, and A. M. Gonzaga. 1999. Naltrexone and communication skills in young children with autism. *Journal of the American Academy of Child and Adolescent Psychiatry* 38:587–93.

Gagliano, A., E. Germano, G. Pustorino, et al. 2004. Risperidone treatment of children with autistic disorder: Effectiveness, tolerability and pharmacokinetic implications. *Journal of Child and Adolescent Psychopharmacology* 14:39–47.

Gordon, C. T., R. C. State, C. Nelson, et al. 1993. A double-blind comparison of clomipramine, desipramine, and placebo in the treatment of autistic disorder. *Archives of General Psychiatry* 50:441–47.

Grandin, T. 1992. Calming effects of deep touch pressure in patients with autistic disorder, college students, and animals. *Journal of Child and Adolescent Psychopharmacology* 2(1).

Hollander, E. 2001. An open trial of divalproex sodium in autism spectrum disorders. *Journal of Clinical Psychiatry* 62(7):530–34.

Hollander, E., A. Phillips, W. Chaplin, et al. 2005. A placebo controlled crossover trial of liquid fluoxetine on repetitive behaviors in childhood and adolescent autism. *Neuropsychopharmacology* 30:582–89.

Hollander, E., L. Soorya, S. Wasserman, et al. 2006. Divalproex sodium vs. placebo in the treatment of repetitive behaviors in autism spectrum disorder. *International Journal of Neuropsychopharmacology* 9:190–213.

Jahromi, L. B., C. L. Kasari, J. T. McCracken, et al. 2009. Positive effects of methylphenidate on social communication and self-regulation in children with pervasive development disorders and hyperactivity. *Journal of Autism and Developmental Disorders* 39:395–404.

King, B. H., E. Hollander, L. Sikich, et al. 2009. Lack of efficacy of citalopram in children with autism spectrum disorders and high levels of repetitive behavior. *Archives of General Psychiatry* 66(6):583–90.

McDougle, C. J., E. S. Brodkin, S. T. Naylor, et al. 1998. Sertraline in adults with pervasive developmental disorders: A prospective open-label investigation. *Journal of Clinical Psychopharmacology* 18(1):62–66.

McDougle, C. J., K. A. Stigler, and D. J. Posey. 2003. Treatment of aggression in children with autism and conduct disorder. *Journal of Clinical Psychiatry* 64:16–25.

McDougle, C. J., L. E. Kresch, and D. J. Posey. 2000. Repetitive thoughts and behavior in pervasive developmental disorders: Treatment with serotonin reuptake inhibitors. *Journal of Autism and Developmental Disorders* 30:427–35.

Owen, R., L. Sikich, R. N. Marcus, et al. 2009. Aripiprazole in the treatment of irritability in children and adolescents with autistic disorder. *Pediatrics* 124(6):1533–40.

Posey, D., J. Puntney, T. Sasher, et al. 2004. Guanfacine treatment of hyperactivity and inattention in autism: A retrospective analysis of 80 cases. *Journal of Child and Adolescent Psychopharmacology* 14:233–41.

Research Units on Pediatric Psychopharmacology Autism Network. 2002. A double blind, placebo controlled trial of risperidone in children with autistic disorder. *New England Journal of Medicine* 347:314–21.

Research Units on Pediatric Psychopharmacology Autism Network. 2010. Randomized, controlled, crossover trial of methylphenidate in pervasive developmental disorders with hyperactivity. *Archives of General Psychiatry* 62:1266–74.

Stigler, K. A., D. J. Posey, and C. J. McDougle. 2004. Aripiprazole for maladaptive behavior in pervasive developmental disorders. *Journal of Child and Adolescent Psychiatry* 14(3):455–63.

Wilens, T. 2008. *Straight Talk About Psychiatric Medications for Kids*. Third edition. Guilford Press.

Chapter Twenty-One: Long-Term Medical Complications

Chez, M., E. Bell, S. Spence, R. G. Robinson, et al. 2009. Diagnosis and treatment of catatonia in autism: Cerebrospinal fluid neurotransmitter findings and treatment response; role for new therapeutic options. Presentation at International Society for Autism Research, May 7–9, 2009.

Dhossche, D., I. Reti, and L. Wachtel. 2009. Catatonia and autism: A historical review, with implications for electroconvulsive therapy. *Journal of ECT*. DOI:10.1097/YCT. 0b013e3181957363.

Dhossche, D., A. Shah, and L. Wing. 2006. Blueprints for the assessment, treatment, and future study of catatonia in autism spectrum disorders. *International Review of Neurobiology* 72:267–84.

Dhossche, D., L. Wing, and M. Ohta. 2006. *Catatonia in Autism Spectrum Disorders*. Academic Press.

Elia, J., M. L. Dell, D. Friedman, et al. 2005. PANDAS with catatonia: A case report. Therapeutic response to lorazepam and plasmapheresis. *Journal of American Academy of Child & Adolescent Psychiatry* 44(11):1145–50.

Fink, M. 2008. Treating catatonia in autism. *Psychiatric Time* 24(14):17–20.

Hollander, E., G. Delgiudice-Asch, L. Simon, et al. 1997. Repetitive behaviors and D8/17 positivity. *American Journal of Psychiatry* 154:1630.

Hyland, K., S. Spence, and R. G. Robinson. 2008. Neurotransmitter and folate deficiency in autistic patients with catatonia. Child Neurology Society Meeting, Santa Clara, CA, Nov. 5–8, 2008 (Abstract).

Lockyer, M., and L. Rutter. 1970. A five- to fifteen-year follow-up study of infantile psychosis. IV: Patterns of cognitive ability. *British Journal of Clinical Social Psychology* 9:152–63.

Murphy, M. L., and M. E. Pichichero. 2002. Prospective identification and treatment of children with pediatric autoimmune neuropsychiatric disorder associated with group A streptococcal infection (PANDAS). *Archives of Pediatrics and Adolescent Medicine* 156:356–61.

Swedo, S. E., H. L. Leonard, M. Garvey, et al. 1988. Pediatric autoimmune neuropsychiatric disorders associated with streptococcal infections: Clinical description of the first 50 cases. *American Journal of Psychiatry* 155:264–71.

Swedo, S. E., and P. J. Grant. 2005. PANDAS: A model for human autoimmune disease. *Journal of Child Psychology and Psychiatry* 46(3):227–34.

Wing, L., and A. Shah. 2000. Catatonia in autistic spectrum disorders. *British Journal of Psychiatry* 176:357–62.

Wachtel, L. E., A. Hermida, and D. M. Dhossche. 2010. Maintenance electroconvulsive therapy in autistic catatonia: A case series review. *Progress in Neuropsychopharmacology and Biological Psychiatry*, March 16.

Chapter Twenty-Two: Fostering Independence

Greenspan, S. I., and H. Mann. Adolescents and adults with special needs: The developmental, individual, difference, relationship-based (DIR) approach to intervention. *The Interdisciplinary Council on Developmental and Learning Disorders (ICDL) Clinical Practice Guidelines,* Chapter 26, 639–56.

Hume, K., R. Loftin, and J. Lantz. 2009. Increasing independence in autism spectrum disorders: A review of three focused interventions. *Journal of Autism and Developmental Disorders* 39:1329–38. DOI:10.1007/s10803-009-0751-2.

Murphy, N. A., and E. R. Elias. 2006. Sexuality of children and adolescents with developmental disabilities. *Pediatrics* 118(1):398–403. DOI:10.1542/peds 2006-1115.

Chapter Twenty-Three: Education

Commission on Behavioral and Social Sciences and Education. 2001. *Educating Children with Autism.* 1st ed. Washington, D.C., National Academies Press.

Fuentes, C. T., S. H. Mostofsky, and A. J. Bastian. 2009. Children with autism show specific handwriting impairments. *Neurology* 73:1532–37.

National Research Council, Committee on Educational Interventions for Children with Autism. Lord, C., and J. P. McGee, eds. 2001. *Educating Children with Autism.* Washington, D.C.: National Academies Press.

Chapter Twenty-Four: Sports, Socializing and Relationships

Greenspan, S. I., and S. Wieder. 2005. Can children with autism master the core deficits and become empathetic, creative, and reflective? A ten to fifteen year follow-up of a subgroup of children with autism spectrum disorders (ASD) who received a comprehensive developmental, individual-difference, relationship-based (DIR) approach. *Journal of Developmental and Learning Disorder* 9:1–29.

Lasgaard, M., A. Nielsen, M. E. Eriksen, et al. 2010. Loneliness and social support in adolescent boys with autism spectrum disorders. *Journal of Autism and Developmental Disorders* 40:218–26. DOI:10.1007/s10803-009-0851-z.

Laugeson, E. A., F. Frankel, C. Mogil, and A. R. Dillon. 2009. Parent-assisted social skills training to improve friendships in teens with autism spectrum disorders. *Journal of Autism and Developmental Disorders* 39:596–606. DOI:10.1007/s10803-008-0664-5.

Chapter Twenty-Five: Transition to Adulthood

Helt, M., et al. 2008. Can children with autism recover? If so, how? *Neuropsychology Review* 18(4):339–66. Epub 2008 Nov 14.

Index

About the Author

RICKI G. ROBINSON, M.D., M.P.H., is codirector of the Descanso Medical Center for Development and Learning in LaCañada, California, a practice devoted to children and families affected by Autism Spectrum Disorders. She is also a clinical professor of pediatrics at the Keck School of Medicine of the University of Southern California and a senior attending physician at Children's Hospital Los Angeles.

Dr. Robinson is a founding board member of Cure Autism Now and the Interdisciplinary Council on Development and Learning Disorders, and currently serves on the Scientific Review Panel of Autism Speaks, the world's largest autism advocacy organization. As a nationally sought-after expert, Dr. Robinson has devoted endless hours to education, legislation and research efforts on behalf of children with Autism Spectrum Disorders.

Dr. Robinson's website can be found at www.drrickirobinson.com.